DATE DUE

AUG 2 9 2005		
APR 0 4 2007		

Demco, Inc. 38-293

By Charles Reznikoff

VERSE

Rhythms (1918)
Rhythms II (1919)
Poems (1920)
Uriel Accosta: A Play & A Fourth Group of Verse (1921)
Chatterton, the Black Death, and Meriwether Lewis (1922)
Coral and Captive Israel (1923)
Nine Plays (1927)
Five Groups of Verse (1927)
Jerusalem the Golden (1934)
In Memoriam: 1933 (1934)
Separate Way (1936)
Going To and Fro and Walking Up and Down (1941)
Inscriptions: 1944–1956 (1959)
By the Waters of Manhattan: Selected Verse (1962)
Testimony: The United States 1885–1890: Recitative (1965)
Testimony: The United States 1891–1900: Recitative (1968)
By the Well of Living and Seeing and The Fifth Book of the Maccabees (1969)
By the Well of Living and Seeing: New & Selected Poems 1918–1973 (1974)
Holocaust (1975)
The Complete Poems of Charles Reznikoff 1918–1975 (1989)
Selected Letters of Charles Reznikoff 1917–1976 (1997)

PROSE

By the Waters of Manhattan: An Annual (1929)
By the Waters of Manhattan (1930)
Testimony (1934)
Early History of a Sewing Machine Operator (with Nathan Reznikoff) (1936)
The Lionhearted (1944)
(translator) *Stories and Fantasies from the Jewish Past* by Emil Bernard Cohn
    (1951)
(translator) *Three Years in America, 1859–1862* by Israel Joseph Benjamin
    (1956)
(editor) *Louis Marshall: Champion of Liberty: Selected Papers and Addresses* (1957)
Family Chronicle (with Nathan and Sarah Reznikoff) (1963)
The Manner "Music" (1977)

Selected Letters

of

CHARLES REZNIKOFF

1917–1976

edited by
Milton Hindus

Black Sparrow Press   **Santa Rosa**   **1997**

ACKNOWLEDGMENTS

My indebtedness is, first of all, to Marie Syrkin's sister, Zivia Wurtele, and Marie's son, Professor David Bodansky. Also to Camilla Reznikoff Wygan, the niece of Charles Reznikoff who supplied photographs of him, one of which was featured on the cover of the magazine *Sagetrieb* that memorialized the centenary of his birth in 1994 and also gave a preview of some of the letters collected here.

The help of my assistant, Tom Cullen, a graduate student in English at Brandeis University, has been constant and invaluable.

In addition to the libraries in California and Arizona that are mentioned in the Introduction, the library of the Hebrew Union College in Cincinnati should be credited for supplying copies of the correspondence between Reznikoff and *The Menorah Journal* and the Harriet Monroe Poetry Collection at the University of Chicago, which supplied Reznikoff's letters to the editor of *Poetry: A Magazine of Verse*.

I also appreciate the critical reading of the manuscript by Professor Seamus Cooney, and, as always, the interest and encouragement of his publisher, John Martin.

Cover photo by Gerard Malanga.

Black Sparrow Press books are printed on acid-free paper.

LIBRARY OF CONGRESS CATALOGING-IN-PUBLICATION DATA

Reznikoff, Charles, 1894–1976.
    [Correspondence.   Selections]
    Selected letters of Charles Reznikoff, 1917–1976 / edited by Milton Hindus.
       p.   cm.
    ISBN 1-57423-034-4 (pbk. : alk. paper). — ISBN 1-57423-035-2 (cloth trade : alk. paper). — ISBN 1-57423-036-0 (deluxe cloth : alk. paper).
    1. Reznikoff, Charles, 1894–1976—Correspondence. 2. Poets, American—20th century—Correspondence. 3. Poetry—Authorship.
    I. Hindus, Milton. II. Title.
PS3535.E98Z48   1997
811'.52—dc21
[B]
                                       97-25367
                                       CIP

Introduction

LONG BEFORE REZNIKOFF'S DEATH in 1976, the enthusiastic publisher John Martin and his Black Sparrow Press had undertaken to bring all of Reznikoff's writing back into print. Since Reznikoff was in his 82nd year at his death and he had always been a prolific if undervalued writer, this had been an extensive commitment. At his death Reznikoff was correcting the proofs of the second volume of his *Complete Poems*, and soon thereafter, there were half a dozen Reznikoff-related books in print, including my own long essay outlining his life and work.

With this background, it came as a distinct shock to me recently when I learned that one of these books had been declared out of print, and it was perhaps the last title I could have expected, for it was *Holocaust* which seems to have been composed as an answer to my query as to why Reznikoff was one of the few Jewish writers of our time who had not addressed himself to this painful subject. He had answered that his own record of man's inhumanity to man in his volume called *Testimony* and based upon the law records of American courts in every section of the country during the last decades of the nineteenth century and the first decades of the twentieth could be taken as the expression of his attitude on the subject, but upon reflection he evidently felt this was not a sufficient answer, and what resulted was the slim little book *Holocaust* based upon the records of the Nuremberg Trials after World War II and the later Eichmann Trial in Jerusalem. My own copy of the book had been misplaced, and when I tried to obtain it from the Brandeis University Library, I was told that its copy had been stolen, and I ascertained that the Israel Book Shop in Brookline had never heard of the book. That was when I learned from John Martin that he had been compelled to let the title go out of print.

It was hard to account for the disappearance from print of this particular work by Reznikoff except on the supposition that the American public, which also included American Jews among it, had tired of the overexposed subject of the Hitler atrocities, which were painful to read about and not easy to believe or imagine. It was Jewish sociologists who had coined the mocking description "shoah business" (shoah being the Hebrew word for the Holocaust) to suggest that the exploitation of Jewish sentiment and indignation had been made into a profitable enterprise by some scholars. Reznikoff's poetry was, of course, sincere and his manner

5

as usual very restrained and not at all exploitative, so that his poem was to my mind one of the very best that had been produced in its genre, but this did not preserve him from sharing the fate of less scrupulous more melodramatic and sensational writers. In fact, Reznikoff had succeeded with a subject that had been badly worn with use by other hands, in writing what seemed to me a very personal work, which expressed the feelings he had as a reader of the painful material in the court records.

In light of his poetic career, it is appropriate that some of the earliest of the letters printed here should be addressed to Harriet Monroe, the influential editor of Chicago's *Poetry: A Magazine of Verse*, who opened a new chapter in American literary history by her hospitality not only to native voices such as those of Carl Sandburg and Vachel Lindsay but also to expatriates such as Ezra Pound and T. S. Eliot, and even to world figures such as Yeats and the Indian Rabindranath Tagore. Though the changes suggested by Miss Monroe, which these early letters of Reznikoff respond to, kept his work from appearing for some time, she did include samplings of it in her anthologies of *The New Poetry*, and eventually Reznikoff was starred in the 1931 issue of *Poetry* that introduced the so-called Objectivists who were guest-edited by Reznikoff's friend Louis Zukofsky, at the instigation of Ezra Pound.

But the bulk of these letters originate not in Reznikoff's literary life but in his personal one. They are addressed to two important people: his wife Marie Syrkin (1899–1989) and his lifelong friend and sometime employer in Hollywood, Albert Lewin (1894–1967). Lewin, educated at Harvard and encouraged by Professor Kittredge to join the academic profession, chose instead to become a Hollywood writer, director and producer, who served for a time as assistant to the legendary Irving Thalberg. Lewin's film credits include *Mutiny on the Bounty, The Good Earth, The Moon and Sixpence, The Portrait of Dorian Gray, Bel Ami, Pandora and the Flying Dutchman*. What gives a quite special interest, indeed piquancy, to these letters is the revelation contained in a novel found among Reznikoff's papers after his death. It bore a mysterious title, *The Manner MUSIC*, that no one has hitherto undertaken to explain. I have stumbled upon a clue unexpectedly in a stanza of Edmund Spenser's *The Faerie Queene*. It is in Book II, Canto 12, Stanza 70:

> Eftsoones they heard a most melodious sound
> Of all that mote delight a daintie eare,
> Such as atonce might not on living ground
> Save in this Paradise be heard elsewhere:

Right hard it was, for wight, which did it heare
To read what *manner musicke* that mote be:
For all that pleasing is to living eare,
Was there consorted in one harmonie,
Birds, voyces, instruments, windes, waters, all agree.

The *manner music* (which I have italicized) is "right hard to *read*." The title points not only to a difficult composer who is the protagonist of the novel but to the reader of it as well. As for Edmund Spenser, he belongs to a century that was a favorite in Reznikoff's own reading. It is difficult to avoid the impression that the principal characters in this unpublished novel, the composer Jude Dalsimer, his wife and his Hollywood employer Paul Pasha are but thinly disguised versions of the writer himself and the persons closest to him. Of course, they are also separated by the gulf of imagination that separates life from art. But the contribution of reality to art can be gauged only by the readers of these letters.

As I suggested in my review of *The Manner MUSIC* in *The New York Times Book Review* of November 13, 1977, Reznikoff s theme recalls that of Herman Melville in *Bartleby, the Scrivener, A Story of Wall Street*. Melville's concern was for the fate of the stubborn little individualist crushed by the overwhelming American financial reality of the nineteenth century. Reznikoff's testimony is that the situation has not improved appreciably with the passage of another century and the growth of new art forms such as film. In fact, Reznikoff's indictment is even more damning than Melville's. It takes in the whole world of 20th century America, Europe and the plight of the authentic artist in that world. If Oliver Gogarty saw his friend James Joyce as a man talking to himself in his sleep in *Finnegans Wake*, Reznikoff's artist-composer-poet in *The Manner MUSIC* is nothing if not what it means to be a hopelessly isolated individual, a Leibnitzian monad, a Lucretian atom, a solipsistic dreamer cut off in the deepest sense from communication with his fellows in the world that surrounds him. The greater the growth of devices of communicating, the greater paradoxically the sense of each individual's own isolation. In a democracy one may talk glibly of a federal union, and the Marxists have summoned "the workers of the world" to unite, but if each individual is fated to be cooped up in himself, only enthusiastic illusions can seem to bind him temporarily to others as deluded as himself. Keats once wrote in a famous letter: "Above all, they are very shallow people who take everything literal.... A man's life is a continual allegory—and very few eyes can see the Mystery of his life ... a life like the Scripture, figurative." If we may believe his last words, Reznikoff found it a dispiriting allegory indeed.

There is no equality of position between the gifted composer brought out to the film colony on the west coast and his more worldly and successful boss. His name Pasha, in Turkish, connotes the keeper of a harem. Pasha's wife, friends and associates find it impossible to figure out what Dalsimer is supposed to be doing among them. Eventually they write him off as a cipher.

Letters of Reznikoff were acquired by the Library of the University of California at San Diego for its Archive of New Poetry at two different times: in 1976 after the death of Reznikoff and in 1989 after the death of Marie Syrkin. Some of the letters also come from the Film Library of The University of Southern California where the papers of Albert Lewin were deposited after his death. And finally, some of the early letters of Reznikoff have been collected by the Library of the University of Arizona in Tucson. Though the characters of Reznikoff's novel are recognizable as those addressed in these letters, the difference in genre must be borne in mind. The fiction belongs to the genre that Aristotle described as poetry, while the letters clearly are a part of what he called history. Aristotle further differentiates between them when he says that poetry is more generalized and abstract than history, which is a less philosophical genre, since it is tied to the reality of what happened, and often turns out to be stranger than fiction. A historical work, it should be said, is a peculiarly appropriate memorial to Reznikoff, since his own interest in history was so great. Before he took a degree in law and passed the Bar, he had been tempted to take a Ph.D. in history, and his work in his volumes of *Testimony* as well as the detailed account he wrote of the Jews of South Carolina with Uriah Engelman have drawn the attention and approval not only of legal scholars but of professional historians. His own practice of law was minimal, but he made scholarly use of his training when he worked for years on the volumes of *Corpus Juris*, an encyclopaedia of law for lawyers. In addition, he translated the historical account by a German writer of his travels in the United States around the time of the Civil War, and he was commissioned by The Jewish Publication Society of America to edit, in two volumes, the papers of Louis Marshall, an American Jewish lawyer celebrated enough to have been considered a credible candidate for an appointment to the Supreme Court of the United States even before Louis Brandeis was elevated to that position by President Woodrow Wilson. Reznikoff's contributions to the writing of history also include segments of his *Family Chronicle*, much of the material of his *Nine Plays* and *Holocaust*.

The letters to Marie Syrkin, whom Reznikoff married in 1930 and lived with intermittently until his death in 1976, are of particular interest. There are several intermittences in this relationship, extended absences in the 1930s when Charles is working for Lewin in Hollywood while Marie is teaching school in New York, and again in the 1950s and the 1960s when Marie was called upon to teach at Brandeis University while Charles was editing *The Jewish Frontier* in New York. But Marie returned from Cambridge to New York at least once every month and, after her retirement from Brandeis, she moved back to New York to live with Charles and assumed the editorship of the Herzl Press as well as *The Jewish Frontier*. While Marie was Charles's first and only wife, he was Marie's third husband. These letters clearly reveal a man very much in love, who feels himself fortunate to have obtained Marie's hand. Her feelings for him, clearly delineated in the memoir of their marriage which she wrote at my urging for my 1984 volume *Charles Reznikoff, Man and Poet*, were strong but much more problematical. Never could he have been described as an adequate "provider," and Marie not only earned more but, until called to assume a university post, felt bitter and enslaved to her teaching job in a New York city high school, for which she was overqualified.

Her marital history had been checkered and unhappy before she met Charles. Her first choice had been the prolific writer and well-known Zionist publicist Maurice Samuel, whom she had married impulsively while he was still unknown and penniless, and she was in her teens and below the age of consent. When her father, Nachman Syrkin, founder of Labor Zionism, was confronted with this situation his reaction was not at all that of the revolutionary idealist she had taken him to be, but the injured parent who turned for redress to the American courts which intervened at his request and annulled the marriage. It was a decision, however justified at the time, that would haunt his daughter for the rest of her life, despite the almost worshipful attitude she had towards her great father, whose literary remains she edited after his early death, for which she must have harbored feelings of guilt. Her resentment was no doubt exacerbated by the fact that her young lover soon attained celebrity as a writer not only in the Jewish circles frequented by her father and his comrades but in the larger arena of American literature. His publisher Alfred Knopf issued over twenty successful books by him, and in the course of time he became a busy lecturer and a radio personality whose program with Mark Van Doren, *The Eternal Light*, was featured weekly by The Jewish Theological Seminary for a whole generation.

The letters are not only revealing of an intense domestic drama, they shed light upon the atmosphere of the American scene in both New York and Hollywood during some of their most interesting decades, the 1920s, 1930s, and 1940s. They speak of many signal literary and dramatic events of that period, observed from the angles of the print-culture of New York, the legitimate theater on Broadway, and the new art-form developing on the west coast by mostly transplanted New Yorkers. Both Lewin and the movie business, we must remember, started out from New York.

From the beginning, Lewin tantalizes his friend with the temptation to follow his lead in abandoning the security of a recognized career and take his chances by "going west." It was the same old American temptation held out before the youth of America by the nineteenth-century editor Horace Greeley. But even as Reznikoff eventually succumbs and uproots himself from his native grounds, he does not bring Lewin's determination and ambition with him. He never for a moment surrenders his sense of privacy and individuality that are the hallmarks for him of a writer's authenticity. He is completely incapable of becoming an organization-man for whom the achievements of his "team" are capable of filling the void of his personal creativity. There is a contrary spiritual movement as well, of course, since Lewin, even at the height of his worldly prosperity, is drawn to the east as his real home, because that is where his family still lives and where he himself will return after his retirement. He cannot resist the feeling that Reznikoff's is the right choice after all, that it is better to follow one's boyhood poetic dream even if one fails, than be caught up in someone else's dream of the meaning of success. He never loses his great respect for Reznikoff's skill as a poet and is positively thrilled by Reznikoff's dedication to him of his self-published little book *Five Groups of Verse*. This date, 1927, marks the seal of their lasting friendship. In his letter of appreciation for this honor (not printed here), Lewin cleverly mimics the prophetic style of his friend, especially as it is embodied in the last poem of that book in which Reznikoff assumed the persona of the Biblical prophet Samuel. Lewin never wavered from the faith in Reznikoff he had once expressed in a letter to his brother in 1922, when they were both twenty-eight years old: "Charlie Reznikoff has recently printed three plays which I read some time ago in manuscript. The last two of them— The Black Death and Merryweather Lewis—are good, but the first, Chatterton, is magnificent. There has not been such a note in the English drama since John Webster. If Charlie has not sent you a copy of the booklet, write him for one or buy one at the Sunwise Turn. I believe that Charlie is the greatest living English poet, and some day the blind world will wake up and agree with me."

10

There is a passing hint in these letters that the memory of the fiasco of Marie's first marriage survived long enough to provoke Charles's jealous unease. Her second marriage, some years later, had taken place while she was a student at Cornell, to an instructor in Biology, Aaron Bodansky, who was the author of a standard textbook in his field. Marie, who took her Bachelor's and Master's degrees at Cornell, majored in English literature, and her best friend there was Laura Reichenthal, better known to the world as Laura Riding and still later as the muse and inspiration of Robert Graves's *The White Goddess*. While married at Cornell, Marie became the mother of two boys, one of whom died in infancy, while the other survived to become a scientist like his father, though his field was physics rather than biology. It is this son of Marie's who is mentioned in Charles's letters along with her half-sister Sylvia (after the early death of Marie's mother, her father remarried).

It is clear that Marie's marriage to Charles was a natural development but also that it was an unequal match. Her first marriage had been suddenly brought to an end and her second was unhappy. If she had thought of divorce (exceptional in those days among immigrants) the obstacles she faced in obtaining it were formidable. In New York and virtually every other state of the union except Nevada, divorce involved a difficult, degrading and expensive legal process. The Syrkins, despite the father's renown in Zionist circles, were far from being affluent, and Dr. Bodansky, the husband, was reluctant to consent to a divorce. He had no desire to part permanently from the mother of his children, though he could not help recognizing that their temperaments and interests were far apart. It was not uncommon for such ill-assorted unions to survive "for the sake of the children." The courtship of Charles lasted for several years and did not come to a head until 1930 when they reached an understanding that Marie would travel to Reno, stay long enough to fulfill the residence requirements and obtain a divorce that would free her to marry Charles.

Though it is amply evident that the marriage was far from being purely romantic and uncalculated (at least on her part) it was also far from being the tragic mismatch depicted in the posthumously published *The Manner MUSIC*. What bound them together most was the love they shared for literature, and it is this love that must be credited for her consent to John Martin's proposal to publish the book which she found surprising and painful to read. But she could recognize that it was authentic and that it ought to be shared with the world. She had never failed to sympathize with his creative élan or to respect what may have seemed to others extravagant ambitions. She shared the feelings, in other words, of his

11

friend Lewin. What she savored most were the brief imagist lyrics of his early work. She singled out what seemed to her an incomparably beautiful and moving line, "And the day's brightness dwindles into stars" and had the words incised on his tombstone which identified him "a maker," the old English term for poet.

Marie was thirty-one and Charles thirty-six when they married, so they could have had children of their own; they never did so, because, though he loved her very much, he hesitated to undertake the support of a family. The letters indicate that they entered the relationship with the understanding that Marie would continue to teach in order to support herself and her son, while Charles contributed his fair share to the household expenses. His income was derived from part-time employment, occasional publisher's commissions, and for a time being a salesman representing his parents' millinery business. As he conceived of it, being a poet was itself a full-time job, and Marie agreed with him. It was she who, from the start, always contributed the greater share to their expenses, even though a sense of *noblesse oblige* as the daughter of her eminent father impelled her to reject any compensation for her heavy editorial and literary labors on *The Jewish Frontier*. She was always too keenly aware of the shortage of funds in her party's treasury. Her salary as a teacher loomed large in her eyes during the great Depression. Modest as it was, his earnings were still less, even when he was employed as a factotum by Lewin in Hollywood. Lewin's own salary, of course, entirely dwarfed those of Marie and Charles combined. Hence the frequency of the artistic gifts to them from the Lewins, which, though appreciated no doubt as tokens of esteem and affection, could not but remind them of their very different status in the social world.

For the reader of Reznikoff's other works, the letters contain some surprises. It is hard to envisage him as a young man, employed in his father's business and with virtually no cash to spare, writing during the 1920s of visits to his stockbroker, or taking it upon himself to offer encouragement and advice to his affluent friend Lewin with regard to investments in Los Angeles real estate. We have to remind ourselves that to Reznikoff, as a young man in the optimistic 1920s, his prospects would have seemed very different from what they proved in retrospect from the vantage point of the 1970s. The Twenties were a period in which he was invited to become a contributor to the new *Reader's Digest* in 1925, in the company of some of the most notable and successful writers of his time not only in this country but in England as well. Charles Reznikoff, in his twenties, bore little resemblance to the fictitious Jude Dalsimer in the novel he would leave behind him half a century later. He was a hard-working, well-educated, sanguine young fellow with a world of opportunities open before him, confident of his own ability to bend that larger world to his will. One of his problems in those early years was keeping his weight down so that he might cut a more attractive figure in the eyes of his beloved. That is hard to imagine until one remembers that the very quintessence of romanticism, Lord Byron, suffered from being over-weight. That is not incompatible apparently with the ability to write sensitive verse.

Reznikoff's feelings for Marie transpire through many of the letters but nowhere more clearly than in that of April 14, 1930:

> Dearest, I have a great faith in the power of emotions: at one time hate enabled me to do what I would otherwise have found impossible. Likewise, love for you at one time helped me over some stumbling blocks. My love for you has grown so great that I feel strong enough to climb—and carry you—anywhere. Darling, our love should make us unafraid and joyful in the face of anything. Darling, how I wish that I were in pain instead of you—at least I am home among friends. Dearest, when you come home and we marry, we shall never be parted again! I kiss you, and writing this, my heart beats faster. Hand in hand through everything!

He is writing to her while she is ill in Reno, preparing to get her divorce. She is also thinking of a trip to Los Angeles before returning to New York, and Charles has some advice for her with regard to his friends, the Lewins: "As soon as you arrive in Los Angeles, call up the Lewins. Now they may invite you to stay at their house; again, they may not. Expect absolutely nothing. Our relation, I am afraid, has long ago become mere phrases. If I were in a position to do anything for them, they would give you a wonderful time. As it is, I don't know what time you will have. However, be your own dear self and expect nothing." He confesses on April 30 that he has two loves: Marie and his own writing; his imagination can go no further: "I expect, of course, to provide for myself, for you, too, if necessary; for you, necessary or not, soon; I love you and I love my work, neither, as I see it, interferes with each other; on the contrary, I expect my love for you to feed my work—and my love for my work to feed you."

A year later, in April 1931, he is writing her from the road on which he is traveling by bus to sell his father's merchandise: "Dearest, I think I have learnt to make these trips most enjoyable. If only you could be with me, darling. I think of you a thousand times a day. We could have such good times together. I hope this separation will be the last and after this we will see everything together and have twice as good a time."

On his first trip to the west coast in May 1931, he is not enthusiastic about Los Angeles but recovers some of his old feelings about his friend Al Lewin: "In other words, in another week I should have had enough of Los Angeles, and I would leave today were it not for my friendship for Al Lewin and the feeling that to leave almost as soon as he returns would be unfriendly. We have talked a good deal together, in fact we spent all of the day yesterday talking until Pilniak, Freeman, and River came, and I feel more than ever that he has a lovely mind."

A few days later, the same theme is resumed. "In the evening Al and I went to another preview. He is anxious that I stay on all summer in his house, but I feel that I should not. We have now resumed our ancient harmony of mind, but it is not easy for me to work here—during the day it is so hot and at night, there is almost a constant round of entertainment—and the only way I'll ever make money is through the sale of my books—if and when."

An interesting reflection on his own method of composition occurs in March 1932: "As for my own work, at present it is this: I divide it into work horizontal and vertical. The 'vertical' is the moment, the as/is; if possible from the top of the sky to the bottom of the earth. For that my instrument is the poem,—and, of course, I rarely succeed.... That brings me to the 'horizontal'—the succession of events, the story, the years. As for that I work at the 'novel'—in prose."

When he compares himself, rarely, to other poets his gaze is directed upward rather than downward: "Other than Pound, I know no one except T. S. Eliot who is genuine.... I had been working at a novel for about a year and still a great deal of work to do on it, but have grown tired of the people and their small talk. Verse, however, I still find exciting and there is much to be done, for both Eliot and Pound are in high-grade furnished rooms in good neighborhoods, but I think myself on the highway—with little done and very far to go."

His second visit to Hollywood in 1938–39 provokes an interesting bit of self-criticism; "I am afraid that this [the leisure to write] is to be obtained, by those not born to it, only by the surrender of comfort or face. The leisure I have had to quite an extent this past year has been at the expense of face. I think it was worth it for it enabled me to clarify many thoughts I have had about my writing." There are fleeting mentions, during this time of projects, the fruition of which may be recognized in his

14

medieval novel *The Lionhearted* and his autobiographical *Family Chronicle* and possibly a suggestion of *The Manner MUSIC*: "As for the other books, the historical one, the one based on current life, they must wait the completion of this which is becoming all engrossing. I will try to keep the diary going, however, but I will not spend any real time on it ..." and, again, three days later: "I go upstairs and go to bed, my mind busy with calculation: if I have a hundred and forty pages of my autobiography to revise and I do it at the rate of a page a day, slowly, carefully, filling in all the chinks and crannies, and if in the meantime I manage to do my research for my historical novel, slowly, carefully, soaking myself in the time and place, and meanwhile, too, jot down these notes for a novel of the life swirling about me—and so fall asleep."

Toward the end of 1939, he notes: "I have another, a better novel if not a better book, on my chest and think I shall write prose, from now on, steadily, as I hope to write verse."

The letters continue after he leaves Hollywood, as he writes Lewin about the new projects the latter is undertaking. One of the most important of these was Lewin's adaptation of Somerset Maugham's novel *The Moon and Sixpence* (a fictionalization of the life of the painter Gauguin). Lewin sent his script, which had won the enthusiastic approval of Maugham himself, to Reznikoff for his criticism. In commenting on it, Charles makes one of his most significant and far-reaching observations on the relation of art and ethics: "I now come to a more important matter. I am not at all convinced of Strickland's regeneration at the end. I almost shuddered when he said, "Love." I see Strickland as a gangster—without a gang; callousness for art's sake. He is not regenerated by his art—to show you how mean he is he burns his best work. If that's not pure cussedness, it's insanity."

It is clear moreover that the strict measure of justice he metes out to others is the same as that by which he himself is prepared to be judged. The composer Jude Dalsimer in *The Manner MUSIC* also makes a bonfire of his own unwanted manuscripts, but the reader is left in no doubt that, in doing so, he is both pathetic and insane. As for Jude Dalsimer's creator, Reznikoff himself, he husbanded carefully every product of his genius, prepared to leave to others more sympathetic in another time the decision as to whether they are worth preserving.

Reaching the terminal point of a task inspired equally, I think, by a detached assessment of objective value and the piety of an old friendship always recalled with pleasure, I am reminded, *mutatis mutandis*, of some lines written by Tennyson about his dear dead friend Arthur Hallam in the poetic sequence he called *In Memoriam*:

>So word by word, and line by line,
>>The dead man touched me from the past,
>>And all at once it seemed at last
>The living soul was flash'd on mine,
>
>And mine in his was wound, and whirl'd....

Milton Hindus
Newton Centre, Massachusetts
June 9, 1996

Selected Letters of Charles Reznikoff
1917–1976

Abbreviations in the Footnotes

BDF   Thomson, David. *A Biographical Dictionary of Film*. 3rd. Ed. NY: Knopf, 1994.

Britannica   *The New Encyclopaedia Britannica*. 15th ed. 12 vols. Chicago: Encyclopaedia Britannica Inc., 1995.

CGLE   Ousby, Ian. *The Cambridge Guide to Literature in English*. Cambridge: Cambridge UP, 1993.

CBD   Thorne, J. O. ed. *Chambers Biographical Dictionary*. NY: St. Martin's Press, 1962.

DAB   *Dictionary of American Biography*. NY: Scribners, 1928–95.

DO   Osborne, Charles. *The Dictionary of the Opera*. NY: Simon & Schuster, 1983.

Felleman   Felleman, Susan. *On the Boundaries of the Hollywood Cinema: Art and the Films of Albert Lewin*. Ann Arbor, MI: UMI, 1994.

HFG   Walker, John ed. *Halliwell's Film Guide*. 8th Ed. NY: HarperCollins, 1991.

IDFF   Thomas, Nicholas ed. *International Dictionary of Films and Filmmakers*. 4 vols. Detroit: St. James P, 1992.

Katz   Katz, Ephraim. *The Film Encyclopedia*. 2nd ed. NY: HarperPerennial, 1994.

MPG   Nash, J. R. and S. R. Ross eds. *The Motion Picture Guide*. 10 vols. Chicago: Cinebook, 1985.

A selection of photographs follow page 176.

To Harriet Monroe, October 27, 1917

1752 Union St., Brooklyn, NY

Dear Miss Monroe,[1]

In this group are three sent you before and resumed, but which I have re-rhythmed.

There is also one whose lines, "Her whiteness glowed in a powder-box," are taken from a couplet I wrote and had printed with a number of others in a college annual six years ago. The original ran:

> "in what powder-box, anon!
> gleamed the whiteness of that brow."

May I ask you to read one of those sent you last month and which you still have, as follows, leaving out the second stanza:

> I met in a merchant's place,
> Diana,
> Lithe body and flowerlike face.
> Through the woods I had looked for her
> And beside the waves.[2]

Very truly yours
Charles Reznikoff

To Harriet Monroe, March 12th 1918

1752 Union Street, Brooklyn, New York,

My dear Miss Monroe,

I am not sorry that you did not print as yet the two poems I sent you a year ago because reading them over now I have changed them as the within show. The changes are all omissions: in the *Futility* an omission 1. of a needless repetition and a forced rime, 2. of two trite figures, 3. of empty phrases at the end; the effect of all the omissions is to make the rhythm

---

[1] Harriet Monroe (1860–1936), Chicago born poet and critic, founded the magazine *Poetry* in 1912 (CBD).

[2] This stanza reappeared as section 8 of Reznikoff's volume *Rhythms* (1918).

much better, I think. In *The Dead* I left out from the next to the last line the word small and its belittling notion whereas I want just the opposite. By putting the two stresses on *brown* and *hill* together I gain in rhythm the sense of weight which I want.

If you care for these changes and will print the poems as changed, I shall be glad to have you do so. I would not care to have them printed unchanged. Do you mind letting me know and also when they will appear? If you do care for them don't bother sending me that $15 since *Poetry* needs it.

Very truly yours,
Charles Reznikoff

To Harriet Monroe, April 13, 1918

Dear Miss Monroe,

I don't know what to do about *Futility*. I do not care for the ending you suggest though I gave it the consideration any suggestion of yours merits. I like my last version best, but if you still care for the original *Futility* use it. Perhaps I am mistaken.

Very truly yours
Charles Reznikoff

To Albert Lewin, [early 1918]

1752 Union St, Brooklyn

Dear Lewin,[1]

I have been called for an examination in the local draft board, sent to the medical advisory board to have my eyes re-examined. I expect under

---

[1] Albert Lewin (1894–1968), film producer, writer and director was a lifelong friend of Charles Reznikoff. The two met in New York in 1916 after Lewin had earned a Master's Degree in English Literature from Harvard University. Lewin worked briefly as a teacher—he was teaching verse writing at the University of Missouri in 1917—before moving to Hollywood and beginning a long and successful career in the movie industry. Lewin married his maternal first cousin, Millie, in 1918, then

the new regulations to be drafted for military, or in any event clerical duties. I would like to get out a little book before I am set to these. So I am sending you what I care for and hope for your criticism as soon as possible; most of these you have already read and you will note that in some instances I have been mindful of what you have said. You may scribble anything you wish in the margins, and above all mark those which you think I ought to include.

In getting out this booklet I wish to set up a precedent for myself. I would like to get out one every year. I do not care for the magazines as an outlet, and do not suppose I can get a publisher for some time. Of the group I am sending, nos. 1 and 2 have been accepted by *Poetry*, as you know. Miss Monroe added no. 24 in October or November, but as you know she has printed nothing as yet and I don't know when she will. When I think of what I have read in *Poetry* I am inclined not to care if she never

worked as a film reviewer for *The Jewish Tribune* before getting a job working in New York as a reader for Sam Goldwyn. He moved to California in 1923, and when Metro-Goldwyn-Mayer (MGM) was founded in 1924, Lewin was writing screenplays and scenarios for the new studio. In 1927, he became head of the MGM story department, and in 1928, he became the personal assistant to MGM's "boy wonder" Irving Thalberg. By 1929, Lewin was a producer, and in that capacity oversaw the production of some of MGM's finest films including: Greta Garbo's last silent picture, *The Kiss* (1929), Lunt and Fontanne's only sound film, *The Guardsman* (1932), and two Academy Award winning best pictures, *Mutiny on the Bounty* (1935) and *The Good Earth* (1937). Lewin quit MGM following production of *The Good Earth* and the death of Thalberg in 1936.

Between 1937 and 1939, Lewin produced three films for Paramount: *True Confession* (1937), *Spawn of the North* (1938) and George Cukor's *Zaza* (1939). It was during this period that Lewin brought Reznikoff to Hollywood to work for him as a researcher and reader. Reznikoff's letters to his wife Marie Syrkin detail his experiences in Hollywood which would later serve as the inspiration and source of Reznikoff's posthumously published novel, *The Manner MUSIC* (1977). Frustrated working at Paramount, Lewin quit in 1940 to found Loew-Lewin productions with David Loew, a former fraternity brother of Lewin's at New York University and founder of the Loew's theater chain. It was then that Lewin got the opportunity to write and direct his first feature film, *The Moon and Sixpence* (Loew-Lewin, 1942). Lewin followed this with five other directorial efforts: *The Picture of Dorian Gray* (MGM, 1945), *The Private Affairs of Bel Ami* (Loew-Lewin, 1947), *Pandora and the Flying Dutchman* (Dorkay Productions, 1951), *Saadia* (MGM, 1954) and *The Living Idol* (MGM, 1957). In 1959, Lewin suffered a heart attack and retired from the film industry.

In his final years, Lewin traveled with his wife Millie, who died in 1965, and published his first novel, *The Unaltered Cat*, in 1967. Albert Lewin died of pneumonia on May 9, 1968; Charles Reznikoff delivered his funeral eulogy (Felleman 253–73).

will. Nos. 6 and 8 have been accepted by *The Midland* of Iowa City a month or two ago. *Poetry Journal* of Boston to whom I sent about seventeen bits of verse at that time, has written me through Edmund Brown that he would like to make a selection and, of course, I am willing. But when I consider what all magazines publish I feel it no honor to appear in them. I think little enough of my own stuff, but rejection or acceptance by these means nothing to me. I would like then once a year to get out a book, of four pages if it so happens in this case, or of forty if I have had the luck, and to keep on doing so until I find a decent book-publisher.

When I am examined on this Wednesday and hear the result, if it is military or clerical service as most likely, I will at once write *Poetry, The Midland & Poetry Journal* asking them to allow me to print because of the peculiar circumstances, draft etc. Of course this will mean that they can not, or at least would not care to print what they had previously accepted, after me, but you already know how great *that* loss is. Surely I can not wait a half year or a year before they print and then to get out my booklet, when I may be in France, hell or heaven.

I wonder whether I ought to trouble you, drowned in themes as you now are, with this letter and these poems. However here they are. Write me, if you can and care to, how you are affected by the draft and anything else about yourself.

My regards to the columns on the campus.

Yours
Charles Reznikoff

Just a cursory criticism will do. I would like to hear from you by this Saturday. There may be so little time.

To Harriet Monroe, [c. April 1918]

1752 Union Street, Brooklyn, New York

Dear Miss Monroe,

As to *Futility* I too do not like the "lopped-off" ending, nor the original with its trite harp and sword images, its abstract *all I fight for* used with its concrete *be blown by the wind away*. I have rewritten *Futility* again and finally. In this last version I think I am nearer perfect expression, but I leave you free to choose which of the three variations you like best.

Answering the military information card, I have just been informed by the local draft board that as a result of physical examination I have been qualified for special and limited military service as a clerk. Bad eyesight.

> Very truly yours,
> Charles Reznikoff

To Harriet Monroe, May 4th 1918

1752 Union Street, Brooklyn, New York

Dear Miss Monroe,

I expect to be drafted very shortly into service as a clerk. I would like to print this month a booklet of verse including the three poems you have accepted. Will you allow me to use these three? I suppose this means that you could not use them in *Poetry* afterwards. I am sorry, then, that I have given you so much, for you, fruitless trouble. I shall remember the kindness of your criticisms and of your acceptance. I do not want to put you to the additional bother of replying, if I do not hear from you in a week's time I will take it you consent.

> Very truly yours
> Charles Reznikoff

To Albert Lewin, May 4, 1918

Dear Al,

I was just about to write you a long letter about a lot of things, but what's the use when I shall probably see you in a month. Thank you for your criticisms. I am almost tempted to quote Helen Hoyt's poem to a tree beginning, *How can you be so patient?*

> Yours
> Charles

To Albert and Mildred Lewin, [August 1918]

> 1752 Union St, Brooklyn, N.Y.,

Dear Mr and Mrs Lewin,

I have your card and am impressed by the engraving and your middle names.[1] When we were dining together a week or so ago, Al refused the *pate de foie gras*. Remembering how before he had eagerly eaten everything, I knew at once a great wholesome influence had entered into his life.

> With best wishes
> Charles Reznikoff (who ate
> the *pate de foie gras* and became
> ill).

To Albert Lewin, May 9, 1922

> 1752 Union Street, Brooklyn, New York

Dear Al,

Michael Carr told me of your letter.

Do you remember when I was planning to become a printer and we asked how long the apprenticeship lasted? Wasn't it four years?

I have my manuscript *Chatterton* back from *The Dial* with a supercilious note from Seldes.[2] I haven't sold a hat for months. Covered the Yiddish theatre at Bergman's request. Two vile plays. One criticism he didn't use, the other cut. (I told him he could. The other play quit in a few days.)

Has *Helen's Babies*, a best seller of '73, been done in the movies? It's funny. Began *World's Illusion* and *Moby Dick*. Just read fifty pages of the

---

[1] Albert [Mindlin?] Lewin married Mildred Mindlin-Jacobs on 17 August 1918 (Felleman 256).

[2] Gilbert Vivian Seldes (1893–1970), journalist and critic, was managing editor (1919–23) and regular dramatic critic (1923-29) of *Dial* magazine (DAB). Reznikoff published his verse play Chatterton along with two other plays in a volume entitled *Chatterton, the Black Death, and Meriwether Lewis* (1922).

former. Looks to me much more important than *Growth of the Soil*.[1]

Met Milly some time ago in a restaurant with Rose Heller. Milly is looking better than I have ever seen her, the strain of house-keeping off. Also met your room-mate Mayer.[2] Had a friendly chat.

C.R.

To Albert Lewin, July 23, 1922

Brooklyn, N. Y.

Dear Al,

I have not been able to write before this. I was already revising *Chatterton* etc. and at the same time trying to get hat business. I was daily exhausted.

I revised under pressure and in a hurry because Roth wanted the plays this week.[3] Roth is contemplating a quarterly. Arthur Symons, Ford Madox Ford and others have consented to be contributing editors.[4] For his first number he has an essay by H.D., who has also promised him her novel, a translation from the French by Arthur Symons, my plays and a novel. Originally he planned to reprint *Ulysses*. I advised him not to, and since he has been reading *Ulysses* he has become doubtful. A jail sentence is almost certain. Roth bought a copy for $40—but I have not seen it as yet. He promises to lend it to me. If he should publish *Ulysses*, he would make

---

[1] John Habberton (1842-1921), *Helen's Babies* (c.1876). Jakob Wassermann (1873-1934), *World's Illusion* (trans. by Ludwig Lewisohn; 1930). Knut Hamsun (1859-1952) *Growth of the Soil* (trans. by W. W. Worster; 1921). Herman Melville (1819-1891), *Moby-Dick* (1851).

[2] Edwin Justus Mayer (1896-1960), screenwriter and playwright whose plays included *Children of Darkness* (1930).

[3] Sam Roth (1894-1974), a publisher convicted six times for violating anti-obscenity laws, illegally published James Joyce's *Ulysses* among other banned works. Roth published Reznikoff's *Poems* (1920).

[4] Ford Madox Ford [Hueffer] (1873-1939), English poet and novelist, was the author of approximately forty books including *The Fifth Queen* (1906) and *The Good Soldier* (1915). Arthur Symons (1865-1945), Welsh poet and literary critic whose books included *The Symbolist Movement in Literature* (1899) (CGLE). H.D. (Hilda Doolittle) (1886-1961), American-born poet, was a leading poet of the Imagist movement.

enough to float the magazine, but now——. If he does not publish in two months, I'll print as before. I am enclosing copy of *Chatterton, Black Death* and *Lewis*.[1] Please return these, because I have only one other set. Roth has the originals. There is no hurry about returning though.

I saw *From Morn till Midnight*, also Estelle Winwood in the dramatization of Dostoievsky's *Idiot*.[2] By the way, if you read *World's Illusion*, read *The Idiot*. (A Roth suggestion). There is much that I wanted to talk to you about, but I am too tired, or too indolent to write, except this——

I suggest as a refuge from the irritation of your daily work, that you begin a novel or play. Begin something large enough to lure yourself in. You are probably too tired at night to do much, but perhaps you can accustom yourself to work an hour or two, before work. Two hours daily work will probably exhaust all you have to say that day, and then you can turn to your bread-and-butter work with relief, as relaxation. A little work *each day* at the end of the year—see the bulletins the savings-banks issue.

Charles

To Albert Lewin, 9/16/22

1752 Union St., B'klyn, N.Y.

Dear Al,

I would like to put off this letter until I feel fresh and have lots of time—but that may be too far off.

Thanks for returning my *Chatterbox* etc. and your card and letter, sugar

---

[1] Reznikoff published his volume of three plays, *Chatterton, the Black Death, and Meriwether Lewis*, in 1922.

[2] *From Morn till Midnight* (*Von Morgens bis Mitternachts*) by Georg Kaiser (1878–1945) with English translation by Ashley Dukes was produced by the Theatre Guild at the Garrick Theatre. The play, which tells the story of a bank cashier who embezzles 60,000 marks in order to win a woman and who goes insane when his advances are rebuffed, was described by a reviewer for *The New York Times* as "a curiously arranged thing, [in which] the first act gave promise [but] the second seemed more like vaudeville" (22 May 1922): 17. Estelle Winwood starred along with Margaret Mower, Beatrice Wood, and Thurston Hall in the dramatization of *The Idiot* written by John Cowper Powys and Reginald Pole in a benefit performance for the Babies' Welfare Association at the Republic Theatre on 7 April 1922. The performance was repeated on 9 April 1922 at the Little Theatre (*New York Times*. 8 April 1922: 18).

and all,—but I'm on diet.[1] This is what I intend to do with them—that is the plays. I'm through with Roth. It happened this way. He was planning to print his own novel anon. in *Two Worlds* instead of *Ulysses*. That was all right, but in discussing possibilities of sale—which I considered doubtful, he said he was sure of a sale. Why? I asked. Then for the first time he told me of a plan to print *Sonnets to the Lady Jones* or maybe *Songs* in the number. This Jones is a woman with whom he lived in London, a cheap 14th St. face. I had seen her photograph. His songs, which he had let me read when he came from London, are cheaply smart, attempts to be naughty, but badly bad. I turned up my nose, I suppose; but he flared up and said, "*The Songs to Lady Jones* are going to be printed, are better than anything you can write in ten years for grace, if you don't care to appear in the same issue with them, you can have your plays back at once." "Very well," I said, got them back, and after a while left the Rothian atmosphere joyfully. I had, then, this experience with Bergman who was very nice, but, poor fellow, can't help himself. He suggested that he might be able to use a play for the New Year issue, to be specified on. Doubtfully I said I'd let him read *Black Death*.[2] He read it, and accepted it, but then hesitated because some of it seems anti-zionistic and the special issue is to be very zionistic. I suggested that he avoid responsibility by showing it to his new chief who is very much interested in literature. Bergman did so, and I saw their comments, the new chief did not care for verse and certainly wanted something cheerful for this issue; Mosessohn, the Rabbi, did not care for it for any issue. Bergman wanted to print it in a subsequent issue, but I didn't want him to get into trouble because of me, publication in *The Jewish Tribune* was certainly not worth it; besides, he told me afterwards that his plan was to submit *Black Death* to Louis Untermeyer and others and show their opinions, which he was sure would be laudatory, to his chiefs.[3] But of all this I was not at all sure, and in no spirit of impatience I think, I escaped joyfully. Now I'm back at my old stand, private publication; but I'm going to have the books for sale some place. Mrs. Mowbry Clark of The Sunwise Turn, 44th St., may handle them; but I'm to see her

---

[1] Reznikoff's *Chatterton, the Black Death, and Meriwether Lewis* (1922).

[2] Reznikoff's "The Black Death" was eventually published in *The Menorah Journal* 10:4 (August–September 1924): 381–385 as well as in *Chatterton, the Black Death and Meriwether Lewis* (1922).

[3] Louis Untermeyer (1885–1977), anthologist, editor, and poet, wrote the introduction to the first edition of Reznikoff's novel *By the Waters of Manhattan* (1930).

tomorrow again about the printing. I'll send you a copy, of course, as soon as I get them. At present, I intend to keep on printing privately and not look for publishers or producers, beyond mailing 3 or 4 of the latter (Theatre Guild etc) printed copy. But I can set no hopes in any of this, and must train myself to be indifferent. Next year I am planning an altogether different play, but it may not materialize.

Your plan of going to Los Angeles wouldn't do. The millinery situation is about like this: I can't sell what we can make and what I can sell we can not get goods *for*, raw material, I mean. I don't think I'll earn $500— this year. And I intend to quit my cousin, but why go into that vexation.

I have not been reading much recently. I started the dictionary again, 3 pages a day, and am now on p. 120 or so. It will take me a year to finish it, by which time I'll know that cantaloupe is correctly pronounced cantal*oop*, that caterpillar probably comes from an old French word meaning *hairy cat*. I don't think I'll even know that, because I notice that my extracts all begin with *ca*, so I suppose I've forgotten all the words beginning with *a* or *b*.

I don't suppose you'll miss much in plays. Nothing of importance has appeared so far. Brock Pemberton produced a translation of an Italian comedy, reset in U.S.A; but everybody agrees that it is tedious, and the outline of the plot given is silly.[1] The Russian Art Theatre is coming after Jan 1st but since they represent the conservative realistic theatre in Russia, perhaps there won't be anything dazzling.[2]

Mrs. Luton—I dropped in one day—told me about Block leaving. Perhaps you had best write her, if you have not done so; because she is very friendly toward you and appreciates the attention of a letter. Michael Carr was away all summer and is expected back after Oct 1st.

I'll write again some day.

C.R.

Remember me to Milly. I hope she likes it out there. The climate ought to be good for her.

---

[1] Brock Pemberton (1885–1950), Broadway producer whose productions included Luigi Pirandello's *Six Characters in Search of an Author* (1922), as well as *Strictly Dishonourable* (1929) and *Harvey* (1944).

[2] Konstantin Stanislavsky (1863–1950) founded the Moscow Art Theatre in 1898 and the Theatre had its first great success with Anton Chekhov's 1896 play *The Seagull* in the same year. Chekhov would go on to write two other plays for the Theatre: *The Three Sisters* (1901) and *The Cherry Orchard* (1903) (Britannica).

To Albert and Mildred Lewin, Oct 29th [1922]

Dear Al & Milly,

Millinery is easing up, I'm drafting a new play—which is so much easier than publishing—I've more time and can write you oftener, but I'm just going to scrawl in pencil because that's easier—And you're not to consider yourself under any obligation to answer at once or at all.

I slipped your letter under Carr's door, he was out but I'm to run in and see him next week. I was in there a week or so ago, and he showed me some of his work. It was the first of his work (except the spring or was it autumn? woods on your dining room wall) to move me as pictures and not essentially as ideas. One picture showed a lot of roofs of cottages and factories in the background beside a river. The river colorless, the sky colorless, the roofs under a heavy fall of snow (seemingly, though M. C. had seen sunlight—but this does not matter, the white color or rather absence of color was there). The walls were a violet blue. There were only two colors in the picture if white is a color, white and that blue. It is sad to the point of tears. It is a factory town at dawn or in winter, dreary, colorless and the other adjectives. Then M. C. showed me how he came to do it. First he had made a real drawing, a sort of photograph in color of that city. There was green in the back yards, blue in the river, in the sky, yellow patches of earth, bits of red, brown in the walls of the houses Then he subtracted every color, but the color that left that mood. He had another picture of a yard in a factory, with huge bottleshaped tanks, close to at hand, slightly tilted as if about to fall on you, all blacks and violets and a faint glow of red from a distant furnace, a narrow sky shut in by the buildings. Then there were other pictures not so successful in which tanks were tilted too much and not so effective, factory chimneys lost in utter dusk—writing at this point I am interrupted by a cousin who came in for legal advice. And then a matter of my father's came up and it's almost a week since I stopped in the middle of a word. I received your clipping and am glad to see you in *The Los Angeles Times*. Went to see *R U R* yesterday afternoon and did not like it much, but *Six Characters in Search of an Author* (Brock Pemberton) is delightful.[1] Saw that at night. The house half empty,

---

[1] *Six Characters in Search of An Author* by Luigi Pirandello (trans. by Edward Storer) was reviewed in *The New York Times* on 31 December 1922. *R U R* by Czech playwright Karel Capek was described in *The New York Times* as "a parable" in which robots stand in for "the mechanical workers of our mechanized civilization—human cogs and levers" (10 October 1922): 16.

but *R U R* is jammed. Write you more about these two plays another time. Haven't had a chance to see Carr since leaving him your letter. So long. By the way, see Elie Faure's second volume, *Mediaeval Art.*[1]

C.

To Albert Lewin, Nov 18th [1922]

Dear Al,

If I don't scribble this note now, I suppose I'll not get a chance to write for a week or two. I'm about to start revising the play I'm working on. It won't be finished for months, but I want to begin organizing. It's about Lincoln, partly, inspired by dislike for Drinkwater's.[2]

I wrote a note to the School of Journalism to Cecilia Rubinstine. Never a word in answer. Maybe I am in the bad graces of Aunty Anzia.[3] I have had no "reactions" from *Chatterton*, as yet. I sent a copy to Theatre Guild, for whom Lewisohn is a reader.[4] I will not send him a copy personally; nor Van Doren.[5] To do that would be to admit that they are people whose opinions are important. Such admission would get me nothing, it never has; just vexation at humiliating myself. Mark and Carl van Doren, for instance, had the booklet Roth printed. Afterwards, M.V.D. reviewed about forty books of verse printed that season. He never mentioned mine.

---

[1] *Mediaeval Art* was the second volume of Elie Faure's 5-volume *History of Art* (trans. by Walter Pack; 1921–1930).

[2] *Coral*, published in *Coral and Captive Israel* (1923). John Drinkwater (1882–1937) published his play *Abraham Lincoln* in 1919.

[3] Anzia Yezierska (1885–1970), Polish born American novelist, author of several books dealing with Jewish immigrant life in the lower east side of New York City including *Hungry Hearts* (1920) and *Bread Givers* (1925).

[4] Ludwig Lewisohn (1882–1955), teacher, literary critic, novelist, editor and Zionist who wrote more than thirty books (DAB).

[5] Carl Van Doren (1884–1950), literary critic and Pulitzer Prize-winning biographer, was the literary editor of *The Nation* from 1919 to 1922 and *Century* magazine from 1922 to 1925 (DAB). His younger brother Mark (1894–1972), an accomplished poet and literary critic, became a book reviewer for *The Nation* in 1920 and served as its literary editor from 1924 to 1928. Both brothers taught at Columbia University. Mark Van Doren's final book, *In the Beginning, Love: Dialogues on the Bible*, published posthumously in 1973, was written with Maurice Samuel, the first husband of Reznikoff's wife Marie Syrkin (DAB).

I don't care much about the mention and I don't want to cheapen myself seeking it, or seeming to.

I am sorry that you have such annoyance at your work. I suppose you must expect that and a good deal more. It takes about ten years to get anywhere in a profession, and you're only been two years at yours. I've said that before, but it won't hurt repeating. If I can get a line that will sell well enough, I may go to the coast in January or February and I'll tell it to you again personally.

I've seen *Torch-bearers* and *Hospitality*, the last twice.[1] An Equity Players Production. Last night, Friday, only part of 2 rooms in the 2nd balcony was filled. I suppose it's a failure financially. It's the best realistic play I have ever seen. Perhaps, it's foolish to say the best, but its in a class with *S. S. Tenacity*.[2] More vigorous. Far better than St. John Ervine's. The audience, what there was of it, was much moved. The write-ups were so bad that a suspicious hand like myself was taken in. I only went because the seats were 25¢ in the second balcony. The acting is beautiful. Louise Hale, Tom Powers, the play is rich, pathetic touches, fun, lots of it, and a good theme—oh well, if one is to stop being vexed by such things—Regards to Milly.

C.R.

This is a Goldwyn year

---

[1] *The Torch Bearers* by George Kelly was described as a "hilarious comedy [which] deals roughly—very roughly, in fact—with the rehearsals, the performance and the subsequent recriminations attendant on the presentation of a one-act play" in *The New York Times* (30 August 1922): 10. In contrast, Leon Cunningham's *Hospitality* was described by the *Times* as "a serious play, with lighter moments, a passionate play with the passion rigidly suppressed except fitfully" which takes place in a boarding house and "proceeds to a climax carefully calculated to shock" (14 November 1922): 16. The reviewer for the *Times* also praised the performances of Louise Closser Hale as the boarding-house keeper and Tom Powers as her college student son.

[2] Sidney Howard's *S. S. Tenacity* based on Charles Vildrac's *Le Paquebot Tenacity* premiered at the Belmont Theatre on 2 January 1922. *The New York Times* described the play as a "little muddled in performance and more than a little deranged by the hocus-pocus effort to pass itself off as a full evening's entertainment" (3 January 1922): 20.

To Albert Lewin, Dec 6 [1922]

Dear Al,

Will write you a letter soon. Many thanks for your letters to Will and *The Tribune* man. Glad to hear that your lane has turned. Can't take on Will's affair. Can't write coherently just now—am on a food drunk. Have had a cauliflower omelet and egg salad at William's Cafeteria; tea and chocolate cake at Alice Foot MacDongal's Coffee Shop, griddle cakes, cocoa and squash pie, at a place I forget the name of (very bad), mashed turnips, red cabbage, broganza (?) beans, sliced oranges, fruit salad (2 helpings) at Fischer's on 42nd Street & 8th Ave—a new place—all the stage-hands eat there. Am now going out for some more.

Remember me to Milly.

C.

To Albert Lewin, 12/18/22

Dear Al,

I have thought, at times, of what I should like to say to you and I hope you heard me then, because, not written down at once, what I had to say is forgotten, because really not important, or if not forgotten, I no longer have the wish. Above all, I am anxious to advise you and to get your advice; but what spare time I have is now spent in revising the play I'm working on. I want to make it as sad as a rainy day in winter here in New York. And when I get through with the day's work, I don't feel like writing anything else, not even a note, so I may not write you after this, for a while, say a month or two. I have been thinking of going back to law, afterwards, and of other things; but I am far from taking any steps. I expect to see the new German play that the Selwyns are producing with Ben Ami, commencing Saturday.[1] If exciting, I'll write you about that. Otherwise, accept now my best wishes

---

[1] *Johannes Kreisler* by Carl Meinhard and Rudolf Bernauer (adapted by Louis N. Parker) premiered at the Apollo Theater on 23 December 1922 starring Jacob Ben-Ami in the title role. *The New York Times* described it as "a scenic tour de force" to be admired for the "novelty" of its stagecraft in presenting "no less than forty-one changes of scene" but criticized for its "fair-to-middling story" (25 December 1922): 20. See Reznikoff's letter dated February 1923 for his reaction to the play and his description of its story.

for the New Year and give mine to Milly and consider how fortunate you are—may I snatch at your skill?—how fortunate you are in being a Millyionaire.

Yours,
Charles Reznikoff

To Albert Lewin, [End of 1922]

1752 Union Street, Brooklyn, N.Y.
Sunday,

Dear Al,

I've been to see two plays, both of them poor. The Equity Players, Augustin Duncan, Rollo Peters etc., produced *Malvaloca*, from the Spanish, Jane Cowl, the heroine.[1] She was good in the funny bits, but when she got to crying about her past, and Rollo Peters in a hoarse, passionate, and monotonous voice declaimed about marrying her despite her past (thereby clutching her) and about the agony of marrying because of her past (thereby clutching himself) it became a very tiresome piece. They used solid sets, that is the same set for the three acts, with slight variations. I am told that this is effective if the lighting is skillful. But when you see the magnificent arches and corridors that the audience applauded when a convent, appear as part of a foundry, and reappear as a room in a private house, it becomes a little monotonous. However, the seat cost only fifty cents. They are promising their next to be a great American play. The other play, *Thin Ice*, makes me sore at Heywood Broun. My impression was that he got quite enthusiastic about it, and so did the *Post*, *Times*,etc.[2] The plot was admittedly stale, about a butler who had been superior officer of the master in the army, setting the house to rights and marrying the wealthy sister-in-law, though the butler

---

[1] *Malvaloca* translated by Jacob S. Fassett from the Spanish of Serafin and Joaquin A. Quintero starring Jane Cowl as Malvaloca and Rollo Peters as Leonardo was described in *The New York Times* as a "tolerably interesting, old-fashioned, tear-drenched, heavily sentimental romance." The *Times*'s reviewer praised Cowl for her "finely tempered and genuinely touching performance" and Peters for evoking "just the right romantic accent and glamour" (3 October 1922):22.

[2] Percival Knight's *Thin Ice* was described as "an odd, bright and incorrigibly likable little comedy [with a] preposterous plot" by *The New York Times* (2 October 1922):20.

himself it turns out inherits a fortune and a baronetcy, all this was admittedly not new or true, but the dialogue and the situations! I spent a dollar to get these. It was very mildly funny. The audience came to laugh and did. Everybody found it very funny when the butler ordered the valet, who was assisting, to execute the orders given to him [illegible]. The audience either had servants or were servants to take this situation, repeated again and again, so hilariously. By the way, I have been reading Congreve's *The Way of the World,* and hope to read all the others.[1] I was wearied at first, but ended up very humble and impressed. His plot and people are ridiculous, unimportant puppets (and therefore he is not one of the great writers, I mean to rank with Aristophanes): but the outpour of speech, the wit (though unimportant), the glorying in language for itself, for the sound of words, the throng of ideas; I invite you to this feast, if you have not already partaken. I read Shaw's *Caesar and Cleopatra,* and this is so thin by comparison.[2] So much for offhand criticism.

I saw Michael Carr the other day. He is back from four months in the country. I had little time to talk to him, because he was in his room which was all messed up and was about to commence a clean-up. The Sunwise Turn is printing my booklet, as printers not publishers.[3] They seem to be very decent people and humorous. I used to carry my proofs in the bottom of my millinery box—have you ever seen one of those large white paper boxes? "You have such a queer brief-case," one of them told me. I expect, as usual, to get out of the millinery. And I will, though I have at present nothing good or sure. I have made this year to date about $800, I need more than that to get on now, if I am to dress and eat the part of salesman. At this point I feel I must stop. Good night. Will send you three copies of the booklet.

With kindest regards to Millie and grateful memories of her Saturday night dinner,

Charles

---

[1] William Congreve (1670–1729), *The Way of the World* (1700).

[2] Bernard Shaw (1856–1950), *Caesar and Cleopatra* (1898).

[3] *Coral and Captive Israel: Two Plays* (1923).

To Albert Lewin, [February 1923]

752 Union Street, Brooklyn, N.Y.
Friday. & Sunday

Dear Al,

I have just finished a revision of the play I am doing, and it seems a tedious affair. I am putting it aside for a few months.

Please try to get hold of Schnitzler's *Gallant Cassian*.[1] I saw it performed by marionettes and liked it immensely. I am reading Swift's *Tale of a Tub*.[2] It has a ponderous humor, a tale that must bear the accumulations of young Swift's note-books. You might read it, it is not too long. But I don't know why I assume that you have not. Leo Shestov's *All Things Are Possible* are philosophical and literary comments, often very amusing.[3] I think you would like them. I intend to translate for you two playlets of the Polish Jew, Peretz, from the translation in German by Eliasberg. Peretz is ranked highly by the Jews, and these playlets show a power and horror somewhat different. I think I'll send them to you in my next letter, but I will not polish them; just to give you an idea what's he like. An ex-pupil of Kittredge might like Frank Mathew's *Shakespeare's Image*, a new book.[4] I just skimmed it. He has an interesting idea that Shakespeare rewrote his plays and points out contradictions and early and late Shakespearean rhythms in the same play.

I saw about a dozen plays, of which only one is important, Claudel's *Tidings Brought to Mary*.[5] Staged like stained-glass windows animated. Has the most dramatic shock I've seen in years. One of the Theatre Guild's financial failures. *Johan Kreisler* is not much.[6] Very clumsily staged, I heard

---

[1] Arthur Schnitzler (1862–1931), *Der tapfere Kassian* (trans. by Adam L. Gowans; 1914).

[2] Jonathan Swift (1667–1745), *Tale of a Tub* (1704).

[3] Leo Shestov (1866–1938), *All Things Are Possible*. (trans. by S. S. Koteliansky; 1920).

[4] Isaac Leib Peretz (1851 or 2–1915). Frank James Mathew (1865–1924), *An Image of Shakespeare* (1922). George Lyman Kittredge (1860–1941), Shakespearean and Chaucerian scholar.

[5] Paul Claudel's *The Tidings Brought to Mary* was described in *The New York Times* as a mediaeval mystery, a curiously undramatic composition, in which one hears much of the crusades and of cathedral building, husbandry and the laying of new roads, while slowly and almost inarticulately a story unfolds of love and leprosy, of dark human passions and divinity in a woman's heart" (25 December 1922): 20.

[6] See the note to Reznikoff's letter to Lewin dated 18 December 1922.

a woman call the scenes *postage-stamp effects*. They shift the lights to different corners. A dull play except for a nightmare bit and the scene that follows. Kreisler is a musician at a court. He is trying to have his opera produced. He has a number of professional enemies and one rival in his love for Princess Aurelia. This rival is the Minister of Art. The Minister insists that Kreisler insert into the production of his opera, a silly ballet written by one of his rivals in music. Kreisler refuses, but his love, Princess Aurelia, persuades him to consent in order that the opera might be produced and Kreisler's position at court maintained. Going over the music at night in his room, Kreisler sees his three rivals in music approach. Their feet dangle as if they were hanged, and they are laughing at him, a shrill squeaky laughter. Kreisler springs up from his chair, still holding the baton, with which he had been beating time to the music, and advancing, denounces each one of the three, lauds himself, proclaims the eternal value of his work. They keep on laughing, until he strikes each head off with a gesture of his baton. At the gesture, each head in turn seems to float off and the three retire. Kreisler turns in triumph and sees seated in his chair the Minister of Art with a Cheshire grin on his face. Kreisler denounces him and then tries to gesture his head off with a stroke of the baton, but the Minister's image bursts out in a hearty laugh. This bit was effective.

I also saw the Russian Art Theatre. Well-trained acting, and in one bit more than that; but without Russian I could not get very much. This is the best, probably, of a theatre that is crystallizing and ceasing to exist. *The World We Live In* is a Brisbane editorial by those journalists, the Capeks.[1] The foundry scene was somewhat impressive, a lot of chimneys etc.

Well, Al, I have been interrupted at this short letter half a dozen times. And now I must go to the funeral of an aunt of mine who leaves five little children. It is snowing outside. Write me what you are doing and remember me to Milly.

Yours,
Charles

---

[1] *The World We Live In* by Josef and Karel Capek (adapted by Owen Davis) was sarcastically described in *The New York Times* as "a libel on the insects" which are characters used to present "a bug-eyed view of the human race" (1 November 1922):16.

To Albert Lewin, [March 1923]

Tuesday—Next Week.

Al, I must put off a long letter to you until I am through revising the play. I'll mail you a copy then. I have about 25 closely written pages. It will be a third of that.

I had a singular experience a few weeks ago, which consisted simply of looking at the snow-covered garage in back of the house in the moonlight. I had been working very hard at hats, sweaters, trade press, dictionary, Hebrew, play and teaching English to Russian artists (of which some other time). When I got home that night and got into bed, I felt my nerves gone. I wanted to go somewhere, anywhere, though I wasn't physically tired. I tried every possible thought and system of thinking I could snatch at then to cure myself. Nothing worked. I happened to look out of the window and saw the aforesaid snow etc. I forgot myself for an instant. That was enough. I looked out of the window until I fell asleep and woke up fit. From all this I refreshed a dramatic theory: all cheap philosophy in which I include all my philosophizing, banned, emotional objects only. I'll go into this some other time. Here's the stenographer.

I have just time to add: did not have time to read story you enclosed; did read Von Hoffmansthal's article in March *Dial* which is the best dramatic criticism I have read for a long time.[1] Hits O'Neill's *Hairy Ape* where I have lunged at in talk, but always missed the essential. Also read "The Woman Kneels"[2] in the same issue and admired it much. Also Gobineau's *Renaissance*.[3] As a result, read half Benvenuto Cellini, and part of Machiavelli.[4] Will write you more of the *Renaissance*. Gosh, if I only had time to breathe. I suppose you feel the same.

Regards to Milly

---

[1] Hugo von Hofmannsthal. "Vienna Letter: February, 1923." Trans. Florence Nelson Llona. *The Dial.* (March 1923): 281–288. Eugene O'Neill's (1888–1953) *Hairy Ape* was described by *The New York Times* as "a bitter, brutal, wildly fantastic play of nightmare distortion ... a monstrously uneven piece, now flamingly eloquent, now choked and thwarted and inarticulate" (10 March 1922): 18.

[2] The actual title of the story is "The Kneeling Woman" by Paul Morand which appeared in the March 1923 issue of *The Dial*.

[3] Joseph Arthur Gobineau (1816–1882), *The Renaissance* (English edition; 1913).

[4] Benvenuto Cellini (1500–1571), Florentine sculptor, goldsmith and writer. Niccolò Machiavelli (1469–1527), Italian writer, statesman and political theorist.

There's about 10 thousand things to do in this office and no money to speak of in sight yet. But if I manage to get things systematized—in my next letter will write plans etc. You know how glad I am to hear that you have changed for the better.

To Albert Lewin, May 7, 1923

280 Broadway

Dear Al,

Little Theatre Films Inc. sounds profitable and glorious. Of course you may run into snags. Remember the first starved production of The Theatre Guild. And I remember that wretched picture of Victor Seastrom's on a poem by Ibsen.[1] But ride on.

Your reference to *Chatterton* is interesting. I must read it one of these days and see what it's all about. I plan another booklet this autumn. I have put the finished play aside and want to read it again in a few months before making carbons. Then I'll send you one.

American Trade Press brought me $100 last month. I have it down so that I have some time on my hands now and have commenced the study of Hebrew. English is towns, fields, rivers, lakes, woods, and perhaps the sea, not too stormy; but Hebrew, rocks, sand, and glaring sun. You ought to get someone to read you some Hebrew out of Genesis and compare it with the tame English of King James. I'm going into the desert. Regards to Milly and good luck to the Inc.

Charles

---

[1] Victor Sjöström (Seastrom) (1879–1960), "the father figure of Swedish cinema." His silent film, *A Man There Was* (1920), was based on a poem by Ibsen. Sjöström eventually gave up directing for acting, appearing in Ingmar Bergman's 1957 classic, *Wild Strawberries* (BDF). In 1923, Al Lewin worked as a script clerk to Seastrom while at Goldwyn (Felleman 257).

To Albert and Mildred Lewin, [early 1923]

Sunday

Dear Al and Milly,

Just a note to remind you that you are gone but not forgotten. I'm too tired to write you that letter to-night. I have a new job—trying to get ads for *The Menorah*. Ugh. Also trying to write musical criticism for *Jewish Tribune*. More about this in my letter—*letter follows*.

C.

To Albert Lewin, [early 1923]

American Trade Press, New York City
Wednesday

Dear Al,

I don't know how long this letter is going to be, but I'm going to write until the stenographer comes back from lunch.

As you see by the above letterhead, here I am. Will's book business seemed to me to turn mostly on selling books by telephone and I hate talking books to everybody. Even selling books by mail is unpleasant if most of the books are detestable. However, I am much obliged to you and Will for your interest and kindness in this matter.

I am through selling hats. To use the technical phrase, we parted by mutual consent. I had and still have, I suppose, an opportunity, to use another technical word, to get into the sweater business. However, I'm experimenting with the above at present. It is Louis Resnick's business and I'm general manager. Louis Resnick is an old friend of mine, a publicity man who came in from Chicago some time ago. He is doing publicity for a number of public welfare organizations and public utility corporations. The above is a side line. We sell foreign trade news to American trade papers. I don't have to write any. I don't think much of the prospects, particularly the prospects of my doing as much work at my plays as I'd like to. As general manager, I manage mostly myself and part of the time a stenographer.

To Albert Lewin, [early 1923]

Dear Al,

I have been too bothered by my jobs to write you a letter, though I was about to—often. (I have just been fired as advertising solicitor for *The Menorah Journal* and am to start with Nicholas Brown.)

I can't send you copies of "Coral" and "Captive Israel" just yet (though I have them printed). I promised not to publish before "Cap. Is." appears in *The Menorah Journal* for December.[1]

I have your story and am glad you are doing work of your own.[2] I read it at once, of course.

To Albert Lewin, [early 1923]

Saturday afternoon

Dear Al,

Unless I write this now in this post office, using this damnable pen, paper, and ink, your article, letter, and Christmas card will go unanswered for another week. Thank you for them.

I am sorry that in the midst of all your work you have had the trouble of writing so lengthy a notice of me, but I should like to revise what I have written and gather them all up into a balanced and finished book. Perhaps in four years. Then I may be ready for your articles and praise, but not now.

I should have liked to have met Lapworth but did not.

I have been thinking of your Botticelli story at times; it is undoubtedly clever, but—but, perhaps, that is enough. I am glad to see that you are doing work of this kind, and you know, of course, how many failures are behind a success—not that I consider the Botticelli story either as yet. In a few days I expect to send you *Coral and Captive Israel* and I should be much

---

[1] Reznikoff printed *Coral and Captive Israel* in 1923. "Captive Israel" later appeared in *The Menorah Journal* 10:1 (February 1924): 38–45 and along with *Coral* reappeared in his self-published *Nine Plays* (1927).

[2] Lewin's story, "Botticelli in Hollywood," was published by his college fraternity's (*Pi Lambda Phi*) magazine, *The Frater*, Vol. 5, no. I (March 1925), pp. 3–6. (Felleman 46n).

obliged for adverse criticism. Paul has come in from Boston and tells me of *A Man's Woman* by Frank Norris.[1] The first two chapters about a party lost on an ice floe. A good movie? I picked up *The Autobiography of Mark Rutherford.*[2] See the *Encyclopedia Brittanica*. Rather good. I am sorry that I am not more talkative this afternoon. Good bye and a happy new year, Al and Milly.

C.R.

To Albert Lewin, [April 3, 1924]

Thursday

Dear Al,

I know that you do not misunderstand my not writing you or my writing briefly. I have been and am bothered by the business I am in, and the spare time I have I spend working at some plays. As always, I have crumbled these and am now working them into bread crumbs. Perhaps, if I had pleasant news, I'd write a letter.

C.

To Albert and Mildred Lewin, [April 12, 1924]

Saturday

Dear Milly and Al,

Thank you for your note. You have undoubtedly received mine of the 4th.

I am working hard at N. L. Brown's, earning little, and learning less. (He owes me $150—back pay—this is a secret, please!) I have a lot of quiet satisfaction in thinking that you are getting ahead, that my sister is (notice

---

[1] Frank Norris's (1870–1902), *A Man's Woman* (1900).

[2] Mark Rutherford was the pseudonym of William Hale White (1831–1913), *The Autobiography of Mark Rutherford* (1916).

the letterhead), [This material has been lost.] and Paul has an appointment at Cornell to begin in September.[1] He is going to read a paper before a doctor's convention in Chicago for his department at Harvard. I hope that you won't think that I am dissatisfied. I have never felt so much at ease, but curiously enough when I begin to talk or write about myself, I talk my troubles—and I have never had less—or minded them less.

I wish we knew enough Hebrew for me to write you a nice blessing.

C.

To Albert Lewin, [November 23, 1924]

Dear Al,

This is a postscript to my last letter. I went by the Cherry Lane Playhouse last night and saw Congreve's *The Way of the World* and got dead drunk on the wit and English of it.[2] I have never had so glorious a time since Synge's *Playboy*. These old plays act, and on the stage the plot itself which the books invariable sneer at, takes on a surprising life. I am bubbling over with it, and though I have a lot of work to do this morning, I have to get it out of my system somehow, so I am writing this to you. I took Lily to it and we sat in the front row. Many seats were vacant and I give the play only a week or two more, and with enough wit to stock all the plays in town for a decade. Excellently acted. Oh, what a play is there, my countryman. I am completely reconciled to English, only now I must use it timidly *con vergognosa fronte* (line 81—Canto 1—Dante's *Inferno*). Since you have been in California, I have never seen anything that I thought you missed except this, and here's wishing that you see the Stage Society do it in London. Oh, Ally, I am all exclamation marks, like Jeff in the last picture in the comic strip.

I also found my Martial's translations, and here are a few—some other time, Al. I've got to get to work. How are you getting on with your work. From the brevity of your last letter, I suppose you're hard at it.

C.

---

[1] Dr. Paul Reznikoff, Charles's brother.

[2] William Congreve (1670-1729), *The Way of the World* (1700). John Millington Synge (1871-1909), *The Playboy of the Western World* (1907).

To Albert Lewin, [January 1925]

1379 Union Street, Brooklyn, N.Y.
Thursday

Dear Al and Milly,

I sent four *Chattertons* under separate cover, Tuesday, I think. Behn is welcome to either *Chatterton* or *Coral* or *Captive Israel*. Should he want *Chatterton*, I have a few changes to make. Many thanks for your part in this. Should nothing come of this, as you intimate, nothing has come out of so much, that I am quite used to it and take it as a matter of course.

Al, I am glad that you told Miss Shearer whatever I wrote—I am trying to remember just what—and am somewhat astonished that you have proved to be—in addition to your other capacities—Mercury.[1] Had I known that the service was so good, I would have taken some pains with my message.

I send you a clipping that you may have seen and no doubt you will be as anxious to see *Weary Death* and *The Street* as I am.[2] Have you heard of them? Whenever you write me again, if it is not too much trouble, will you return the clipping? I want to keep it until I see these films.

I have not seen *They Knew What They Wanted* because I judged from the notices that is not worth while.[3] Should it move away from the Garrick to a theatre where one can hear in the cheap seat I may go to it. I am reading Waley's book on Chinese painting.[4] I have read Ring Lardner's *How to Write Short Stories*.[5] He has some wise cracks, but if it were not for "The Golden Honeymoon" not worth bothering about.

I have seen *Greed*.[6] Von Stroheim has not done anything wonderful to

---

[1] Norma Shearer (1900–1983), Academy Award winning best actress in 1930 for *The Divorcee*, was the wife of Irving Thalberg (IDFF).

[2] *The Weary Death* (also known as *Destiny*) was a 1921 German film directed by Fritz Lang and featuring Bernard Goetzke, Lil Dugover, Walther Janssen, and Rudolph Klein-Rogge. *The Street*, another German film, was directed by Karl Grune and starred Eugen Klopfer, And Edege-Nissen, Leonhard Haskel, and Lucie Hoflich (MPG).

[3] *They Knew What They Wanted*, the winner of the 1925 Pulitzer Prize, by Sidney Howard, premiered in New York on 24 November 1924. The romantic comedy, starring Pauline Lord and Glen Anders, was described as a "gentle piece," and the cast was praised for their "admirable" performances in *The New York Times* (25 November 1924): 27.

[4] Arthur Waley, *Introduction to the Study of Chinese Painting* (1923).

[5] Ring Lardner (1885–1933), *How to Write Short Stories* (1924).

[6] *Greed*, directed by Erich Von Stroheim, was a 1925 release from Metro-Goldwyn based on Frank Norris's 1899 novel *McTeague* starring Gibson Gowland as McTeague and ZaSu Pitts as Trina.

the book to justify any such word as "genius"; he is an intelligent, clear thinking man of good taste, who has studied and assimilated those foreign pictures we caught a glimpse of in *Shattered*.[1] His *Greed* is logical and admirable, but not thrilling. He is not as good as Norris in Tina. If I remember Norris's Tina, he explains her cupidity by her German peasant blood and her early and rigid training, which has its origin in a rational fear. But Von Stroheim's Tina is a "nut," her cupidity arises directly out of her timidity, there is an irrational fear in her eyes and it is not effective. All in all, I found *Greed* cheerful. The symbolism of the bird, trite enough, pleased me immensely. But that's Norris. And the hard, ugly faces in clear outline, like the paintings of the Flemish, were fine. Farnham made an excellent job. How good, of course, I can only guess at; but I remember what you told me about the whiskey bottles, and found all references to McTeague's father cut out except a title.[2] Farnham was right, it is not necessary to build all that up as an introduction to McTeague himself. These, or similar things, are latent in everybody.

As for Sir Robert Ayton—one or two of his songs are in every anthology of Elizabethans.[3] I imagined that the collected works would be stunning, but since writing you, I glanced at them and found little more than the anthologists did.

I have just discovered strudel and cheese, but am recovering.

C.R.

---

[1] *Shattered* (1921), directed by Lupu Pick from a script by Carl Mayer, was notable for its lack of subtitles.

[2] As an assistant editor at Goldwyn in 1923 Al Lewin had "the unique opportunity to view the original, uncut version of Erich von Stroheim's *Greed*" (Felleman 257).

[3] Sir Robert Ayton (1570–1638), Scottish poet.

To Albert Lewin, [February 14, 1925]

1379 Union Street, Brooklyn N.Y.
Saturday.

Dear Al,

Just a line to let you know that I think of Los Angeles often and chocolate mousses with preserved fruit.

I am about to finish the novel or novelette I was telling you about and now I am about to start the picnic of revising it and getting some sort of prose style. I think that will take me about two months, and unless something important comes up, I probably won't write you until then. Then you can see what my prose has become.

I don't remember *Between Worlds* at all. Waley's *Chinese Painting* is too expensive to buy—$20, but if you can borrow a copy, you should. I am not quite through with it myself. Someday when I'm flush, I'll get a photostat made of one of the prints in the back, and send it to you.

Thinking of you yesterday and that I ought to answer your letter, I went into Gertner's for some butter-cake. I wish to goodness I could associate you with something less fattening.

I have finished the first Biblical play in a series that may take me from four to forty years—forty years in the wilderness—but, I forget, you don't know the Bible. The *Menorah Journal* will print *Uriel Acosta* revised version—1924 model—in a week or two and I'll have them send you a copy.[1] By the way, if you care to do anything at all in a Jewish theme—poem, essay, or story—you can be as sarcastic as you like—*The Menorah* will probably take it and if they take it, will pay for it. Should you send something, let me know about it.

C.

Do you think *Jews and Jewness of Hollywood* would be worth doing?

---

[1] "Uriel Acosta" appeared in *The Menorah Journal* 11:1 (February 1925): 35–42.

To Albert and Mildred Lewin, [June 1925]

Wednesday,
1379 Union Street, Brooklyn, N.Y.

Dear Al and Milly,

As soon as I come across a story "sentimental, humorous and pathetic, simple, concerned primarily with the trials of a young woman," I may even wire you.

The Menorah has been told about Jim Tully[1] and the suggestion made that they write you. There is still almost a month's revision before me on the novel—or novelette—for it will run only about 25, 000 words.

A friend of mine, Harry I. Luber, will be in Hollywood soon.[2] You met him, I believe, at Belmar. He is in the business of financing motion pictures and his company is, I understand, the largest in business. I have often spoken to him of you and he intends to get in touch with you.

I read some stories by Aldous Huxley and thought him clever, but not very clever, and only remember dimly what they were all about.[3] I read *Prancing Nigger*, which is hardly more than a short story, and remember it as well-written, intelligent, and musical comedy.[4] I only began *South Wind* and have had no time to go back to it, and not much desire, but it seems to have more to it than *Prancing Nigger*.

I was much moved by *My Life, the Story of the Peasant Woman Annissia*, edited by Count Tolstoy, published a year or so ago by Duffield.[5] Waldo Frank in the new issue of *The Menorah Journal* has a review of *Celestina*, recently included by Dutton's in their Broadway Translations ($5).[6] This is

---

[1] Jim Tully (1891–1947).

[2] Harry Israel Luber (1883–1963) "a stockbroker, [was] a member of the New York Stock Exchange since 1928, when he paid $295,000 for a seat [and] a partner of Luber & Co." (*New York Times* [28 July 1963]: 64).

[3] Aldous Huxley (1894–1964), English novelist and essayist, author of *Brave New World* (1932) and five collections of short stories, including *Limbo* (1920), *Mortal Coils* (1922), and *Little Mexican* (1924) (CGLE).

[4] Ronald Firbank (1886–1926), *Prancing Nigger* (c. 1924). Norman Douglass (1868–1952), *South Wind* (1924).

[5] Count Leo Tolstoy (1828–1910), *My Life, as told by the Peasant Anissia, to T. A. Kouzminskaya*, revised and corrected by Leo Tolstoy (Trans. by Charles Salomon; 1924).

[6] Novelist and journalist Waldo Frank's (1889–1967) review of Fernando de Rojas's *La Celestina*, "The Father of Spanish Prose," appeared in *The Menorah Journal*. 11:2 (April 1925): 152–158.

an important book, supposed to be the first important novel or play—it is a cross between the two—in Spanish and you should read it. The speeches of the hero and heroine are a little dull at the beginning, but the speeches of the servants, the bawd, the whores, and the ruffians are stunning—not shocking.

I was shocked at the performance of Congreve's *Love for Love*.[1] I expected much after *The Way of the World*. But it was annoying to find that magnificent speeches, "the salt of the play," had been completely left out. They left in, however, to be true to the author, I suppose, all the dirty jokes, and these were not tossed off as at the Cherry Lane Performance, but drawn out and stressed for all the giggling stenographers in the audience. Helen Freeman played the heroine heavily, as if she were a loose woman well on in the thirties; and that isn't the way it should be played at all, but briskly, lightly, girlishly, Irish. Enough of that.

Of course you've seen *Grass*.[2] Somewhat dull, except for those with a historical background. I thought of *Nanook of the North*. First the hunter, now the herdsman. Who is Monta Bell? *Lady of the Night* was an interesting example of the algebraic equation in the movies, door for door, dream for dream.[3]

C.R.

---

[1] *The New York Times* described William Congreve (1670–1729) as "the finest wit and stylist in the English prose theatre" (1 April 1925): 21. The *Times* noted that in the production by the Provincetown Playhouse at the Greenwich Village Theatre the "play was heavily cut" and described the resulting presentation as "a little too casual and lyric, perhaps not so brittle and brilliant and downright as Congreve demands, but full of ginger and felicity."

[2] *Grass* was a 1925 Famous Players–Lasky production written, directed and photographed by Merian C. Cooper and Ernest Schoedsack was a documentary about Nomadic Iranian tribes. *Nanook of the North* was a 1921 documentary about an Eskimo directed by Robert Flaherty whom Lewin was to meet and become friends with in 1927 while both were working at MGM (Felleman 258).

[3] Monta Bell was the director of the 1925 MGM silent film *Lady of the Night* starring Norma Shearer and Malcolm McGregor (MPG).

To Albert Lewin, [July 1925]

1379 Union Street, Brooklyn, N.Y.
Saturday Night

Dear Al,

I haven't heard from you for some time—is everything all right?

The Mr. Luber I wrote to you about tells me now he is not going to the coast until Autumn. Paul went to see your cousin in East Orange a month ago and he heard there that you were coming to New York in August.

I haven't done much this year. It took me a long time to be able to make use of a whole day. I finished two plays in verse which I would have done anyway and half a novel. The plays are part of a long series. I hope to finish the novel in three or four months and expect lots from doing it.

I hope to see you in August—and that's only two weeks off.

C.

Remember me to Milly.

To Albert and Mildred Lewin, [September 13, 1925]

1379 Union Street, Brooklyn, N.Y.,
Sunday

Dear Al and Milly,

I borrowed this machine from Louis Resnick and so ought not to complain about it, but look at those spaces.[1]

I see Milly's letter was mailed July 21st. Almost two months. I have been working at what I am pleased to call my novel, in addition to the usual stuff, and writing anything else—well, I just keep putting it off. When I first got Milly's letter, I had a bright idea. I was going to get a lot of postals with the poems about a new house printed on them, wishing you lots of luck etc. but silly ones, you know, and mail you one every day for a month or so. Well, those I found in this neighborhood seemed too sensible, all except one. That was a dandy, but the man was sold out of it.

---

[1] The typescript is strewn with unintended spaces between letters, which we have not attempted to reproduce here.

Then I thought I'd send you something for a new house, but out of my weekly allowance of five dollars, I've just paid Paul two dollars I owe him, and I have to take a girl I don't care about to see a picture (*Siegfried*) on Friday night.[1] I've already seen *Siegfried* twice. It has some fine bits, but I don't want to go again. What a terrible machine this is. Resnick told me it was in excellent condition and I suppose when he gets it back like this, he'll think I did it. I saw *Outside Looking In*, based on Jim Tully's book. I'll tell you about it when I see you.[2] I'm too tired to tell you about it now, except that it's like *What Price Glory*,[3] stupid plot, some rich talk, but it doesn't stir you as much because the war came home much closer. And these bums are essentially not interesting, the loud mouthed, the silent, they're all alike, bums . This is a terrible machine. I suppose Milly thinks I'm putting in all these spaces to fill up the letter, but honestly, they just happen. There's a wonderful restaurant near Grand Central. Viennese. What pastry. What pastry. What—oh, oh, oh, oh. Gosh. Permit me to wish you much happiness in your new home, and myself a wife to write my letters. I have found the things I copied from Martial's epigrams and I—. No, I can't write them now . Dinner is ready. Besides I wouldn't type them on a machine like this; but the very next letter you get from me, may be nothing but a lot of his epigrams. Good luck. Don't bother writing. I know what it is to write a letter.

C.R.

---

[1] *Siegfried* (also known as *Siegfrieds Tod* and *Siegfried's Death*) was a 1924 German film directed by Fritz Lang and starred Paul Richter and Margarethe Schlon (MPG).

[2] *Outside Looking In*, a comedy by Maxwell Anderson, was a dramatization of Jim Tully's "hobo autobiography" *Beggars of Life* (*New York Times* [8 September 1925]: 28). The *Times* reviewer praised this "picaresque drama" for its "sardonic humor." Reznikoff was to meet Tully in Hollywood (see below, letter 7, May 3rd 1931).

[3] *What Price Glory*, a play by Laurence Stallings and Maxwell Anderson, was later made into a silent film directed by Raoul Walsh and starring Victor McLaglen, Edmund Lowe and Dolores Del Rio in 1926 (MPG).

To Albert Lewin, September 25, 1925

1379 Union Street, Brooklyn, N.Y.

Dear Al,

Here are some of the promised Martial's epigrams. The translation is by M. S. Buck.[1] Book One, Epigram 16: Here you may read some good things, some indifferent, but more bad.

Not otherwise, Avitus, is a book formed.

Book One, Epigram 17: Titus presses me to become an advocate and often says, "There is great profit." But the great profit of a farm, Titus, comes from the work of a farmer.

Book One, Epigram 41: What are you then? ... like the unhappy wanderer beyond the Tiber, who exchanges sulphur matches for broken glass, like him who sells pea soup to the idle crowd, like the owner and keeper of vipers, like the vile boys of the salt sellers, like the hoarse cook who carries sausages in his warm pans ...

Book One, Epigram 83: Your little dog licks your face, Maneia; it is not surprising that a dog likes turd.

Book One, Epigram 100: Afra has "mammas" and "papas"; but of any of these she could be called the grandma.

Book Two, Epigram 5: Two miles separate us and these become four when I have to return. You are often "not at home." I do not mind going two miles to see you, but I mind going four not to see you.

Book Two, Epigram 13: The judge claims his fee and your advocate his. I advise you, Sextus, to pay your creditor.

Book Two, Epigram 87: You say that beautiful girls are ardent with love for you, Sextus, you who have the face of a man under water.

Book Three, Epigram 18: At the beginning you complain of hoarseness. Since you have excused yourself, why recite?

Book Three, Epigram 19: ... among the figures of wild beasts is seen a bear. While playing, Hylas, sounding its yawning mouth, thrust his young hand into its throat. But a viper, more deadly than the beast had been if alive, lay hidden in the bronze depths. The boy saw no snare, until he felt the sting and died. O pitiful! that the beast was unreal.

Book Eight, Epigram 40: It is not a garden or a vineyard that you are to guard, Priapus, but a thin wood from which you were born and can be born again. I warn you keep away all thievish hands and preserve this

---

[1] *Martial Epigrams*, translated by Mitchell S. Buck, privately printed, New York 1921.

wood for my master's hearth. If the wood fails, you yourself are wood.

The United States Postal authorities worship other gods. I am prevented, therefore, from sending you Epigram 68, Book Three, and another epigram in the same book whose number I have lost. But that is all.

I have read Keyserling's *Travel Diary of a Philosopher*, and think it a rich book; but I am assured by someone who has specialized in philosophy that it isn't much.[1] I'd read it if I were you, particularly the first volume. I am told by the same specialist that there are much better books about Hindu philosophy: should I read any, I'll write you.

I don't like to send you any of my work when you are so busy, because a manuscript always suggests a careful reading. The novel I am working on now is not much; but I have a theme on my chest that is better. The series of plays I am working on is also not much; but I shall have to spend at least two more years at it.

I guessed that something was wrong with Engel when I saw Laura Jean Libbey advertised by someone else.[2] The chance to direct certainly looks good; nothing could be more delightful than to offer suggestions, such as an outsider's would be. I suppose I could get a line of hats and sell my way across the coast; of course, that would take a lot of time from my own work. However, I have put off thinking about anything like that until I finish the novel, and that's a month or two off.

I am sorry I wrote such a silly letter to answer Milly's, but after writing and reading most of the day, I find myself stupid. I wonder if that is how Goldsmith got his reputation for being a "gooseberry fool."[3]

Yours,
Charles

Best wishes for a happy New Year, Al and Milly.

---

[1] Hermann Alexander Graf von Keyserling (1880–1946), *The Travel Diary of a Philosopher* (trans. by J. Holroyd Reece; c. 1925). Interestingly, Maurice Samuel (1895–1972), ex-husband of Reznikoff's wife Marie Syrkin, translated Keyserling's 1928 book, *The World in the Making* for Harcourt, Brace & Co. of New York in 1927.

[2] Laura Jean Libbey (1862–1924), prolific romance author.

[3] Oliver Goldsmith (1728–1774), essayist, novelist and playwright.

To Albert and Mildred Lewin, January 24, 1926

1379 Union St., Brooklyn, N.Y.

Dear Al and Milly,

I meant to write you long before this and a letter at that instead of a note; but after writing all day I am afraid that even a letter will break my back.

Thank you for your Christmas card and I gave Luber his. I called up Michael Carr a week or two ago and he told me he had just written you a long letter. I have made up my mind that I am not going to leave home until I have my novel placed and that may take a long time. The plays I am writing on call for a lot of reading and that, too, makes me reluctant to leave 42nd St. However, should my novel be accepted, I'd like to go to California—best of all, on foot. However and however—

I wish you would do this, Al—though this is harping on an old theme. Play at writing a novel, write only two or three hundred words a day, if you have no strength for more, and I am sure you will soon find live people under your hand. Two hundred words a day will mean seventy thousand at the end of the year—quite a novel. Don't write for the movies or for anybody but yourself—and Milly, and I think you'll have a witty and rich book. If not your first-born, the next. (Why not a novel *about*—not *for* the movies?)

And now, good-bye. Today is Sunday and I won't write another word.

C.R.

To Albert and Mildred Lewin, April 12, 1926

1379 Union Street, Brooklyn, New York

Dear Al,

I am almost excited at your salary.[1] You have undoubtedly resolved to save most of it. Please do. I am glad that Milly is an economist.[2]

---

[1] Lewin was working for MGM writing continuity and scenarios for silent films (Felleman 258).

[2] Millie Lewin earned a Master's Degree in economics from Columbia University in 1921 (Felleman 257).

I bought a locker at Manhattan Beach for the season. Last summer I did a good deal of writing at Brighton Beach—almost deserted in the morning—and played handball and bathed in the afternoon. I planned to do the same this summer—to begin May First. Should I go to California at all, perhaps it would be best to go in October. I do not suppose the rainy season begins until November. I am anxious to be with you, but I must spend my money carefully to get the most sunshine for it.

Some time ago I wrote you that I did not want to send you anything in manuscript because that always implies a careful and troublesome reading—you are too busy for that. If you were not doing anything, I would show you everything. Again, now that some of my things are almost finished, I am tempted to wait until they are before showing them to you.

I have neither read nor seen nor heard anything "stunning," except some of Gieseking's piano playing—especially a composition by Hindemith (a new German composer).[1] As for plays I have only seen John Ford's *Tis Pity She's a Whore* and came away humble. I would have seen "Bocksgesang" though I read the play in German two or three years ago, and I would see Evreinov's play now at the Theatre Guild's Theatre—you probably saw this in Los Angeles—and I certainly would see O'Casey's *Juno and the Paycock*, but I do not think I can spare the money. The cheapest seat for the O'Casey play is $2.65. I contented myself with reading it and you might. Macmillan published it. I have seen two motion pictures advertised

---

[1] *The New York Times* praised Walter Gieseking's "broad and commanding effects" and described Paul Hindemith's (1895–1963) "Klaviermusik" as "most interesting ... music completely of the present age, or the more superficial side of it; music of intensely nervous quality, ironic, and of a driving energy. Music that arrests the attention and gains its ends, and yet is barren of results" (3 March 1926): 27. *The New York Times* described the Lenox Hills Players's production of John Ford's 1633 blank verse play, *'Tis Pity She's a Whore* as "a long poetic tragedy, reserved, austere, with no smudge of baseness or bawdy jesting ... acted as seriously and earnestly as Ford composed it" (24 January 1926): 7:1. The *Times* praised the Theatre Guild's production of Franz Werfel's (1890–1945) *Goat Song* (*Bocksgesang*) for its "excellent exhibitions of acting" but nonetheless concluded that the play "leaves no single, purposeful impression on the audience" (26 January 1926): 18. The Theatre Guild's production of Nikolai Nikolaevich Evreinov's (1879–1953) 1919 play *The Chief Thing* was deprecated by the *Times* for being "colorful but seldom crisp" (23 March 1926): 18. Sean O'Casey's *Juno and the Paycock*, "[a] tragedy (which might be a comedy quite as logically)," was lauded in The *New York Times* for O'Casey's "skill of construction," however the 1926 production at New York's Mayfair Theatre was panned for its lackluster performances and "ineffectual direction" (21 March 1926): 8:1.

as greater than *Caligari*.[1] They are not. You have probably seen *The Three Wax Works*, too.[2] It is a sort of a stew into which some good ideas—leftovers—are thrown. *The New Enchantement* (a French picture) has some interesting faces and sets, but the feeblest of stories.[3] Among the books I read, *The Life of Henri Brulard* by Stendhal and *An Anthology of the Works of W. H. Hudson* by Garnett are earnestly recommended.[4] I suspect that all of Stendhal is decidedly worth reading. Did I write you of *Calisto and Melibea* also known as *La Celestina* (under this title among E. P. Dutton's Broadway Translations) by Fernando de Rojas?[5]

Charles

To Albert Lewin, [late 1926]

1379 Union Street, Brooklyn, N.Y.
Sunday

Dear Al,

It is very good of you and Milly to want me to be your guest and unless something unforeseen turns up, I'll go to California in the fall. I have the fare. Thank you for offering it—but, Al, please don't be reckless with your money. Mr. Luber told me of your real estate investment and what he said to you about it. Now as to that—don't mind him. It's his nature to be gloomy about real estate investments—I have never known him otherwise—and I do know he has never made money at them. Real estate in Los

---

[1] *The Cabinet of Dr. Caligari* (*Das Cabinett des Dr. Caligari*) directed by Robert Wiene was a classic 1921 German expressionist film starring Werner Krauss and Conrad Veidt (MPC).

[2] *Waxworks* (*Das Wachsfigurenkabinett*, a.k.a. *The Three Wax Works*), a 1924 German silent film,was directed by Paul Leni and starred Conrad Veidt, Werner Krauss, and Wilhelm Dieterle (MPG).

[3] *The New Enchantment*, directed by Marcel L'Herbler and starring Georgette Le Blanc-Maeterlinck and Jacques Catelain was described in *The New York Times* as "intensely original with weird settings and queer ideas which are often mentally stimulating" (15 March 1926): 18.

[4] Stendhal (1783–1842), *Vie de Henry Brulard* (1890). William Henry Hudson (1841–1922) *A Hudson Anthology* (ed. by Edward Garnett, 1924).

[5] See Reznikoff's letter of April 1925.

Angeles is bound to prove a good investment—if you can hold on: you may have to wait through a cycle of depression.

I will watch *Blarney* and write you in detail about it: please keep me posted as to when it will appear.[1]

C.R.

To Albert Lewin, January 3rd, 1927

1379 Union Street, Brooklyn, New York

Dear Al,

It was good of you to write without saying anything about my not having written for such a long time, but, as you understood, I have no news. I have revised my novel to the point of receiving blunt rejections, and am now thinking of turning it into verse. I should like to do the same to a novelette I have written. This will mean that a somewhat protracted experiment in prose has failed; and if so, I am not too sorry about it, because I have never been able to think of prose without a slight feeling of depression; the prospect of doing verse, on the other hand, always exhilarates me somewhat—like a glass of wine, or when I think of verse as a steady diet, pleasant as it is, I must think of making a living—if I am to continue to feed on verse. I have decided to go into the publishing business. This is to be hardly the seed, but rather the spore of a business. At first I shall publish—I hope—my mother's autobiography, then my verse.[2] None of this will sell, of course, but I hope to learn a little more about typesetting—for I expect to set my own type, and eventually do my own presswork. Then, I may get out something that will be worth while and will sell—not mine. I have two books in mind. All this may prove to be a dream; however, I am going to put it to the test of reality this month.

I have not been to see any pictures, to speak of. I'll look for yours. I saw

---

[1] Lewin was co-scenarist on Marcel De Sano's MGM film *Blarney* which premiered 26 September 1926 (Felleman 274).

[2] Reznikoff published his mother's autobiography in his anthology *By the Waters of Manhattan: An Annual* (1929) and as the first part of his similarly entitled novel, *By the Waters of Manhattan* (1930). It would later be republished along with his father's "Early History of a Sewing-Machine Operator" and his own "Needle Trade" in *Family Chronicle* (1963).

Caligari again, and had a good deal of the old excitement. I saw *The Canadian* and thought the beginning good, but the end muddled.[1] There's a cross-eyed actress in it who plays the part of the sister-in-law and did excellent acting. I also saw the *Habima*, the Hebrew art theatre.[2] This is the most important production I have seen in years. They take a second rate play and by pantomime, singing, and dancing make it significant. Of books, if you care to read slowly, begin Gomperz' *Greek Thinkers*.[3]

Remember-me to Milly. And a happy New Year.

Charles

To Albert Lewin, [February–May 1927]

Monday

Dear Al,

I am too tired tonight to write you much, but Bill wrote me of your new job and I am very glad that the burden on you and Milly is lessened.[4] I can't write another word.

Charles Reznikoff

I got up at 5 this morning to make the 7 o'clock train and I have drummed this town until now. It is bitterly cold.

---

[1] *The Canadian* was a 1926 silent directed by William Beaudine and featured Thomas Meighan, Mona Palma, Wyndam Standing, and Dale Fuller (MPG).

[2] *Habima* was a Hebrew theatre company which was founded in Bialystok, Poland in 1912. Eventually one of the four studios of the Moscow Art Theatre, Habima traveled to the United States in 1926 (Britannica).

[3] Theodor Gomperz (1832–1912), *Greek Thinkers: A History Of Ancient Philosophy* (1901–1912).

[4] Lewin became head of MGM's story department in 1927 (Felleman 258).

To Albert and Mildred Lewin, March 19, 1927

Dear Al and Milly,

Just a note to thank you for your last letter—I am too tired to write more.

I bought a press (worked by a treadle) in January and had it set up in our basement. I have printed (the blackest of ink on glaring white paper) almost 32 pages of a book of verse and plays (to run about 200 pages).[1] I just blunder along. At present it takes me nine days to print eight pages (an edition of 375). However, I have just reached this point. Before that it took me much longer. I hope to be able to send you the book as a Christmas present. I am now printing the verse in the *Fourth Group* (that our mutual friend Josfu so kindly had printed for me). I have given the press a name and feel very kindly to it—and all machinery.

Give my sincerest regards to all of it in Los Angeles.

> Yours
> Charles Reznikoff

To Albert Lewin, June 3, 1927

1379 Union St., B'klyn, N.Y.

Dear Al,

I am sending you under separate cover the first book of my press.

I am sorry the dedication is so ambiguous, but in view of my importance and that of my press, a detailed dedication will have to be postponed until it will not seem ridiculous. The presswork is bad, the arrangement not very good, but I hope the next book will be better. I am working at it now.

The news about your father's accident is news; I expect to be in Newark soon and I'll try to see him. I'll also give him a book.

Dear Al, I'm in a terrible hurry; I have a lot of books to send out, the sun is shining—it's June in New York—I want to go to Manhattan Beach. By

---

[1] Reznikoff published two volumes, *Nine Plays* and *Five Groups of Verse*, in 1927. He printed 375 copies of the 67-page *Five Groups of Verse* and 400 copies of the 113-page *Nine Plays*.

the way, tell Millie I saw one of her friends today, no less than the Levine of P. 36, No XXVI—mind not P. 37!—She gave me the cut walking—that is tried not to see me, I greeted her aloud, very loud, so the poor thing had to smile, but walked on fast, very fast. How's that for a long good-bye?

I hope to be in California in 1929: by that time I hope you'll own Hollywood

C.R.

To Albert Lewin, July 31st 1927

Dear Al,

En route again—and head over heels in work. I don't suppose I'll be able to finish the book of plays until November.

Paul and I were sorry not to be able to see your mother, but we explained the circumstances to Will: Paul was leaving that afternoon for his vacation, and we were to have dinner home; we came to Newark in the morning to buy some special bread for my mother made by Wigler's of Prince Street, and we had only time to see either your father or mother. Now since your father was in the hospital at the time, that decided it. I'll see your mother as soon as she returns.

With my regards to her and Milly, I am

C.R.

Please let me know about the bookings of your picture and I'll go to see it.[1]

---

[1] Lewin was a writer on four MGM films in 1927: *A Little Journey*, *Altars of Desire*, *Spring Fever*, and *Quality Street* (Felleman 274).

To Albert Lewin, Oct 5, 1927

1379 Union St, Brooklyn N.Y.

Dear Al,

Under separate cover I am sending you the copy you asked for. I have plenty—and will gladly send you more.

I have worked hard today—finished Page 88 of the *Plays* and can hardly write or think just yet. In about two or three months I hope to be able to send you a copy of the next book of Nine Plays. It will run about 150 pages.[1]

I am glad you all—as they say down South I believe,—have had a pleasant summer. As for *Business Wives*—something good can be done with that—for example, I refer to the Bible—*Proverbs* XXXI 10 on.

C.

By the way, try
Hemingway *In Our Time*
Kuno Meyer's *Translations from the Irish*[2]

To Albert Lewin, January 12th 1928

1379 Union Street, Brooklyn, N.Y.

Dear Al,

It seems to me that I have much to tell you, but when I think about it a while, it all comes to nothing. I must wait until I can see you and can talk without thinking.

As for my plans, I do not intend to do any printing for nine or ten months, and then will probably do a play in verse and a sixth group. I am working at these now, but they may not be ready. I am not working at any prose. *The Menorah Journal*—my one and only—has taken a long story of mine—about 12,000 words—and if it appears, I'll ask them to send you a

---

[1] Reznikoff printed 400 copies of the 113-page *Nine Plays* (1927).
[2] Ernest Hemingway (1899-1961), *In Our Time* (1925). Kuno Meyer (1858-1919), *Translations from the Irish* (1909).

copy. My novel and my mother's book are also at the *Menorah*.[1] The have not definitely rejected them as serials, but most likely will take extracts. If they do not use them *in toto*, I'll have Nicolas Brown publish them for me and pay him for the printing. If I printed them myself, it would take me about a year, and this year I should like to establish myself in some business or other that would give me $25 or so a week.

I am glad Milly is coming to New York and that I'll be able to tell you through her how much I wish to at times—and do not—write.

By the way, have you heard that Michael Carr is dead? He died in France of pneumonia a few months ago. But I am sure you know all about it.

C.R.

To Marie Syrkin, January 31st 1928

Dear Marie,[2]

I suppose I ought to send you flowers to cheer you up. I went into the lots to look for some, but could not find any. I send you instead a scrap of cheerful verse—still in the rough—that I wrote when the weather was warm and I was not thinking of a job.

> The air is sweet:
> The hedge is in flower;
> At such an hour,
> Near such water, lawn and wood,
> The sage writing Genesis must have been:
> Lifting his eyes from the page he chanted,
> "And God saw the world—that it was good!"

I will call up tomorrow (Wednesday) at 5 or 6.

Charles Reznikoff

---

[1] Reznikoff's "Apocrypha" appeared in *The Menorah Journal* 14:2 (February 1928): 163-187. Sarah Reznikoff's autobiography "Early History of a Seamstress" would later become the first part of Reznikoff's novel *By the Waters of Manhattan* (1930) and *Family Chronicle* (1963).

[2] Marie Syrkin (1899-1989). See introduction.

To Albert and Mildred Lewin, March 21, 1928

1379 Union Street, Brooklyn, N. Y.

Dear Al and Milly,

Mother and I thank you for your gift. Mother (an ant) was surprised, delighted, and immediately began to plot some of her cookies for Milly—however, she's in bed with influenza, so that's off for a while—I was so touched that I was tempted to ride off to California to thank you in person, but one or two matters here detain me—as yet.

Things here are pretty much as Milly left them: I write a little, read a little, and in general lead so pleasant a life, my conscience is uneasy.

C.R. (a grasshopper)

To Albert and Mildred Lewin, June 17, 1928

1379 Union St, Brooklyn NY

Dear Al and Milly,

I am still working for the law book people—and hope to keep at it. Of course, the work is indoors and there is no physical exercise, but it is a good mental drill and $50—a week. Should I be able to save enough money, I'll have my mother's book printed, and my book of short stories, and two Biblical revisions in verse, none of which you have seen but heard enough about, and with these out of the way, will begin work on a sixth group of verse, which I hope to print on my press by next spring. So man proposes.

I hope your work is coming along, Al, and wish you would keep me posted on your pictures.

C.R.

To Editors, *The Menorah Journal*, June 24, 1928

1379 Union Street, Brooklyn, New York

Gentlemen:

Here is the revised King David which you now have as a play. I'd like to know, this week if possible, how *The Menorah Journal* stands on this and Israel, my stories, and my mother's autobiography. If I do not hear from you at all this week, I'll take it for granted that *The Menorah Journal* is not interested.

Very truly yours,
Charles Reznikoff

To Elliot Cohen, [July 1928]

1379 Union Street, Brooklyn, New York
Thursday Evening

Dear Elliot,[1]

The corrections in my mother's autobiography are mostly omissions. If you will leave the manuscript for me an hour or so, some evening after five, I can make all the changes—there are not so many.

There are no changes in Israel. I have been told that King David as revised is obscure, and I have added the following subtitles: for II, The Feast in Saul's House; for III, Michal; for IV, Ishbosheth and Abner; for IX, David and Michal.

If you do not care for the group of prose bits, will you please return it in the enclosed envelope? I should like to try them on *The Dial*. As for the two stories, I understand you, and will leave them with you for a while.

I really can't tell how I'm doing at my job. I like it, and I think I'm getting better at it. By the way, I've been reading hundreds of Alabama cases. I suggest a thesis on the decline of legal writing and thinking in Alabama since the Civil War. In this little mirror I seem to see a flash of what that war did to its best blood.

C.

---

[1] Elliot Cohen, an editor of *The Menorah Journal*.

To Henry Hurwitz, December 13th, 1928

1379 Union Street, Brooklyn, New York

My dear Mr. Hurwitz:[1]

I expect to be able to send you a copy of my new book soon. I am having only two hundred copies printed, but it will cost me more than I thought. It would be helpful if *The Menorah Journal* would pay me the balance due for my story used in February—very helpful.[2]

I know that you need the money too. Still, it seems to me that since *The Menorah Journal* has rejected all the material I am printing, I may with good conscience ask for what is due.

Very truly yours,
Charles Reznikoff

To Albert and Mildred Lewin, January 20, 1929

1379 Union Street, Brooklyn, New York

Dear Al and Milly,

At last I've managed to get rid of what I've been accumulating these years—and it's little enough at that. You'll probably get a copy this week: I mailed the book Friday.[3] My routine from now on is a lot of law, a snip of verse and a snip of reading.

How has your work, Al, been getting on? I saw *White Shadows* yesterday: it has excellencies and possibilities—it seems to me that a lot more could have been done to it.[4] For instance, when the doctor crawls out of the sea after the storm, and almost immediately afterwards plunges into the lagoon to swim to the huts, it seems to me that he should show some horror of the water, some reluctance to enter it; the bonfire that the doctor builds seems to me ridiculously small and instead of being on top of a mountain it seems well below the ridge in the rear; however the use of

---

[1] Henry Hurwitz, founder and editor of *The Menorah Journal*.

[2] "Apocrypha." *The Menorah Journal* 14:2 (February 1928): 163–187.

[3] Reznikoff published his anthology *By the Waters of Manhattan: An Annual* in 1929.

[4] *White Shadows in the South Seas*, a 1928 COS/MGM production, was directed by Woodbridge S. Van Dyke and starred Monte Blue, Raquel Torres, and Robert Anderson (MPG).

the stone image is good; but the essential weakness of the picture is in the failure to probe the doctor's character: the doctor's longing for civilization should not have been so crudely done—it was not mere greed. Well, we might talk on and on about this and that as we used to; perhaps we shall again.

Charles

To Henry Hurwitz, January 20, 1929

1379 Union Street, Brooklyn, New York

My dear Mr. Hurwitz,

Last Friday I sent you and Elliot Cohen each a copy of my book, containing the stories and verse you read and my mother's autobiography.[1] I had two hundred copies printed—a hundred more than I need. This will cost me close to a thousand dollars, and to pay for it I have been working at law since May. It would be a great help to me if you would send me the balance for my story in the February issue.

I suppose you think me a fool for printing the book myself and have no wish to send me this balance; but you know that you wanted neither the stories nor the verse, that not another magazine in the country would even consider them, that you wanted, if anything, only bits of my mother's story, and that I can find no publisher, though I have tried. I do not blame you: I know that O'Brien in his anthology for the year did not even give the story of mine that you liked and used one star, nor did Braithwaite, although he used some of the verse in the *Menorah*, use mine.[2] I say all this merely to make clear why I do print, why without hope of any complete or nearly complete publication, I cannot let work accumulate in my desk year after year until a stranger to it will burn it or throw it away as my grandmother after my grandfather's death burnt his verse.

Now I have a group of verse with Hebraic themes, but how can I send it to you?[3] It is disheartening to deal with people who will not answer letters and who have the discourtesies of Bohemians—or shall I say

---

[1] *By the Waters of Manhattan: An Annual* (1929).

[2] William Stanley Braithwaite (1878-1962), *Anthology of Magazine Verse 1913-29 and Yearbook of American Poetry* (1929).

[3] "By the Waters of Manhattan." *The Menorah Journal.* 16:4 (April 1929): 346-47.

Hebrews? I suppose it will be best to keep it, add to it, and print it myself at the end of the year.

Yours,
Charles Reznikoff

To Henry Hurwitz, January 27, 1929

1379 Union Street, Brooklyn, New York

Dear Mr. Hurwitz:

Thank you for your check. I notice that you write that there is a balance due me. I think you have paid me enough—at least all I expected. However, if you insist that there is more due me, please give it to me in a subscription to *The Menorah Journal*.

As for the group of verse, mailing books etc. has delayed me in my revision. When this is finished, I'll mail you what there is.

Very truly yours,
Charles Reznikoff

To Marie Syrkin, [February 14, 1929]

Thursday 10 P. M.

Marie:

I have just read a few more pages of the *Plato* you gave me: it is too late to call you up, so I write to thank you again. From now on, I suppose, I shall never think of Plato without thinking of you. There was a wise and beautiful woman—Hipparchia—among the cynics; now there is another in the Academy.

C.

I hope to see you Saturday.

A Valentine

> I hate—and now I hear you say
> Why that's no way to start a valentine!
> O well, I do dislike
> The ceremonies of a holiday.

I do admit it's fine
Of those who can do nothing better
To send their tokens on the stated days;
For me these are too formal and too few:
Time and again I'll sing your praise
And send my valentines to you.

To Albert Lewin, Sunday

En route from Brooklyn to 42nd Street and 5th Avenue.

Dear Al,

About two or three weeks ago I received Joseph Gaer's book—and am just writing him that I have been unable to read it.[1] So *your* letter was received by one who knows too well what it is to earn one's wages. In a month or two I hope to have more time. And will write you again.

There's a good play in New York—"Journey's End."[2] I hope you and Milly can come to see it. (Alas, I have just discovered a good restaurant—Viennese. Strawberry tarts! Cheese Cake! Alas! Alas!)

C. Reznikoff

To Henry Hurwitz, June 30, 1929

1379 Union Street, Brooklyn, New York
Sunday

Dear Mr. Hurwitz:

As you suggested I am putting down roughly what I said and was about to say. To begin with: the review of Doctor Levinthal's book was unfair,

---

[1] Joseph Gaer (1897–), *The Legend of Meryom* (1928). *The New York Times* praised the novel for Gaer's "skillfully painted pictures of the little lives [of his characters, calling them:] pathetic and humorous, interesting and informing" (15 January 1928): IV:8.

[2] R. G. Sherriff's *Journey's End*, directed by James Whale and starring Evelyn Roberts and Leon Quartermaine, was lauded in *The New York Times* as "one of the most powerful and somberly beautiful dramas of recent times" (23 March 1929): 23.

because the sermons were not judged as sermons.[1] A sermon, although learned and intelligent men and women may be in the audience, is usually addressed to a general assembly, the majority of which are housewives and men in business, people who have had little or no mental training—as a rule. It is clear, I think, that a sermon to be of use must be of the kind that its auditors can follow easily and understand: a profound philosophical discussion is not to be expected. Now then, considering those to whom it is addressed, a sermon must be interesting but should not be sensational or merely journalistic, it should stimulate or sustain or console simple people and yet must not be cheaply optimistic. It seemed to me, when I read them, that Doctor Levinthal's sermons were sermons like these; I know how they have moved those in the neighborhood in which we live, and I have heard other rabbis talk of them with respect and admiration. As for the technique of their construction, their use of Midrash, which I have heard praised by a number, I am not qualified to speak.

But if the reviewer's quarrel is with the rabbinate in general, you know that the average rabbi would above all else study and meditate upon and talk of matters profound and important, but among his duties, the sermons he must deliver, the speeches he must make, the funds he must raise, the classes in Hebrew etc. he must teach or supervise, what time or strength can he have for what many of them long to do? Unfortunately, they have their living to make, as so many others. Well, then, if these things are so, perhaps the future of Judaism is not in the rabbis, if by "rabbi" we mean what it seems the title has come to mean—the spiritual leader of a congregation of business men. Perhaps we may look to the rabbis to be at most guardians, but not creators—unless they are freed from their petty (but multitudinous) tasks.

Very truly yours,
Charles Reznikoff

---

[1] Philip S. Bernstein's review of *Steering or Drifting—Which?* by Israel H. Levinthal (NY: Funk & Wagnalls, 1929) appeared in *The Menorah Journal* 16:6 (June 1929): 569–571. In the review Bernstein concludes that Levinthal's sermons "cannot possibly meet the needs of modern intelligent Jews" (570).

To Albert Lewin, October 20th [1929]

1379 Union Street, Brooklyn, New York
Sunday

Dear Al,

You have not written for a long time, but neither have I written to you—so, I suppose, we are quits.

When Millie was in New York, I was out of a job; but shortly after she left, the *Corpus Juris* people, for whom I had been working, called me back, and permit me to work half days, 9 to 1, at $30 per week; so that now I have an income, rather agreeable work, and enough time to do my own work.

I have finished a small group of verse a la *Rhythms* and three short stories. One of these has been accepted by *The Menorah* (my one and only), one may be accepted by them, and one—the longest, about 5,000 words—is in *The Menorah* limbo. I am at work at a long short story, about 10,000 words, which is really an *olla podrida* of short short stories, and if I finish this, I'll begin a novel—I think.[1] I know I have told everybody time and again that I would do no more prose, both when I was sober and when I had a spoonful of peach melba, no, brandy, but this isn't going to be prose—it's just fooling.

I have seen—and heard—a number of motion pictures—some surprisingly good. I hope you like your new work and are still buying A. T. & T. If you can brush up on your Greek and would like to go into it for relaxation—like Gladstone—I should like to collaborate with you on a translation of *The Iliad*—in verse.[2] What purity of line and color. As for sound—I don't know enough Greek to get much of that. More about this another time, if you are interested.

Charles

---

[1] "By the Waters of Manhattan." *The Menorah Journal*. 16:4 (April 1929): 346–47. "Nudnick." *The Menorah Journal*. 17:2 (November 1929): 184-86. "Salesmen." *The Menorah Journal*. 17:3 (December 1929): 279–80. "Passage-At-Arms." *The Menorah Journal*. 19:1 (October 1930): 63–66.

[2] W. E. Gladstone (1809–1898), four-time Prime Minister of England.

To Elliot Cohen, December 1st [1929]

Sunday

Dear Elliot,

You know how I dislike hasty writing. Still, since there is no help for it—

The land that we Jews hold in common—free of any mandatory power—is ideas expressed in words: this is the only land of Israel. We have been in possession three thousand years and are a people only because of it. I think of the *The Menorah Journal* as a colony.

So much for rhetoric. I have two suggestions. 1. Become a quarterly. This will not abate one jot or tittle of any possible achievement. Moreover, you will be in the tradition of the great British quarterlies. 2. Change your format to resemble that of a book (again the British quarterlies). But at small cost you will be able to hold the type and have an annual printed and bound. This may mean income, but, above all, publicity, where you want it most—among the book reviews.

Unfortunately, I am working full time again and cannot write much—of anything. I am anxious to know how it all turns out. By the way, I sent that note up to *The New Yorker*, and they sent me a nice letter and $7.

Charles Reznikoff

To Elliot Cohen, [December 1929]

1379 Union Street, Brooklyn, New York
Sunday

Dear Elliot,

I like the idea of your society very much; I hope it prospers, and expect to be present Thursday.

I have finished the draft of a play in verse—*Jeremiah*, which in due time, after it is somewhat revised, will be sent to you. I have also written something (17 lines) about an Italian-Jewish mystic of the 18th century; this, too, in due time, after it is revised, will be sent to you. By this time, no doubt, *The Menorah Journal has* made up its mind about "Passage-at-Arms."[1] Please return it to me as soon as you conveniently can, if you do

---

[1] "Passage-at-Arms." *The Menorah Journal.* 19:1 (October 1930): 63–66. "By the Waters of Manhattan: 1930." *The Menorah Journal.* 18:5 (May 1930): 417–421.

not want it, and I will send it among the goyim or turn it into verse. At the same time, please include "By the Waters of Manhattan 1930."

Doctor Michael A. Cohn, of 1457 Eastern Parkway, whom you may have heard of, spoke to me this summer about David Bergelson whom he admires.[1] Now that you have a story of his, you might send him a copy of the December issue.

Charles

To Marie Syrkin, Feb 2, 1930

Sunday
1379 Union Street, Brooklyn, N.Y.

[Marie,]

It is 9 o'clock; there is still a lot to do, but I must scrawl a note. Thinking of you while at a lunch counter knocked over a glass of water. Man next to me was bending over to pick up his companion's gloves from the floor: all the water spilled on his head. Rather startled. Came home. Mother asked me where I had been—much worried. Thought my sister had met with an accident and that is why I had hurried away. Much relieved to find that it was only that you had left for Reno. Told her that when you had your divorce, the question of our marriage would come up. Did not seem surprised or worried; just said, Well, if you like her. So write all you like— when you like. And I think I'll write you everyday—or try to.

> Coming up the subway stairs, I thought the moon
> Only another street-light—a little crooked.

C.

To Marie Syrkin, Feb 3 [1930]

Monday 9:30

[Marie,]

I suppose you are now in the station waiting to go into the train.

I ought not to write you every day, because when I write these letters— after all my work is done more or less—I am tired; I throw down the words

---

[1] Bergelson, David. "The Revolution and the Zussmans." *The Menorah Journal.* 17:3 (December 1929): 239–257.

higgledy-piggledy; I hardly know what I am writing. But then it is pleasant to write to you—almost like a kiss stolen on the way downstairs or in a winding corridor. And you are so generous with my faults—you will forgive me.

To-day was a bad day—as I reckon bad days—the work at the office was troublesome—I made little headway. And I heard—in confidence—that they were thinking of selling the American Law Book Company to a concern in Chicago; but the deal is off. However, I cannot think it permanently off. Well, it may be a good thing for me to get into another kind of work; this is too strenuous mentally. But don't worry. Of course, you are thinking; my God! I'll have to support him, while he writes two stories a year for *The Menorah* and a little one about a boy refusing to buy a pickle for 2¢. But that is unkind of you; you never expected me to make $60 a week; and I ought to make much more in a law-office at the work I can do. However, I am still at The American Law Book Co and will probably be for some time to come.

I have finished typing the stories for *The Menorah,* and have practically a clean slate. Now for the novel, for the group of verse (maybe I'll print it myself, now that I have Saturday afternoon to myself and only the memory of you), and for what chance verse I can catch on the wing.

I spoke some more to my mother today about ourselves. She seems to think that you ought not to go back to teaching but should live on what I can make, assuming, of course that I make at least $60. Among other things, as I knew she would, she asked who is paying for your divorce, and I was glad to tell her how we are managing that.

I hope you are having a pleasant trip—full of wonders—and that you are having a much needed rest and change. One of these days I hope I'll be able to send you some verse to tell you accurately what I want to say.

C.

Do not be afraid to write me your flippant or moody letters; you see what mine are like. Besides, now that our relationship—that we will be married, if you still want to marry me, when you come back—is understood at home, no one will touch them.

To Marie Syrkin, Tuesday Feb 4 [1930]

At the station

[Marie,]

I just saw a Russian movie. Strange to say it wasn't good. Have also heard my father's stories.[1] They are good. He has written two (about a thousand words each) and is doing more. Perhaps if you become a member of my family, you too will write. I wonder if you will be angry if I print a volume of yours.

I hope to begin my novel in about a week. There is nothing new—nothing at all. Our hopes, our plans, our longings and our loves are still the same (editorial we).

C.

THE AMERICAN LAW BOOK COMPANY
Publishers of Corpus Juris-Cyc
272 FLATBUSH EXTENSION
BROOKLYN, N.Y.

To Marie Syrkin, Feb 6 (Thursday) [1930]

At the office—
noon.

[Marie,]

Meant to write you last night, but went to bed early—and this morning, woke up too late. To-night, am going to *Menorah* dinner. No news except

So you are going away, perhaps to California, perhaps to the South Seas;
Permit me to show you the twigs of our tree
In the light of the street-lamp when they are wet with rain.

C.

---

[1] Reznikoff published his father's autobiography, *Early History of a Sewing Machine Operator*, in 1936, and it was later included as part of Reznikoff's *Family Chronicle* (1963).

To Marie Syrkin, [February 6, 1930]

Thursday Evening

Darling: Of novels, if I can get to work again, I should like to begin work at two. The first I told you about time and again—the all-American. But I can't get the idea out of my head—all corners of the United States, many kinds of people. Did you read Gogol's *Dead Souls?* He must have had a similar problem to solve. The other is the first in a series I have referred to—at which no doubt you have smiled, snickered, or sighed. The idea of the series is this: to record day by day the petty events of that day, the daily, unmelodramatic events in delicate precise writing. Of course, such a thing can go on forever. Whether it's good or not, is completely in the writer; he has no story whatever to lean on. I like the idea. Darling, if I have time and life something may yet be done.

Darling girl, I love you so much. Before I met you, I found no one like you; and now that you are away, I feel a little like a stranded boat, a moving picture without music, an automobile that has been parked on a busy street, two slices of bread that have nothing to be a sandwich. Darling, I would like so much to make you happy; that as my wife you should do all you hoped to do and be all your father planned.

Charles

```
x    x      x      xxxx    x    xxxx
xxxx      x x    x   x    x    x
 x  x x    xxxx    xxxx    x    xxxx
 x  x  x   x    x  x   x    x    x
 x  x  x      x  x   x    x    xxxx
```

(now I understand why lovers cut names in trees).

To Marie Syrkin, [February 7, 1930]

[Marie,]

Your letter written on the train—I was glad to get it. I looked all over for x's, and was not pleased at finding none. But if I had, I would have thought it silly. In the midst of my work today—at the office—I suddenly thought of you: I wanted to cry—quite unmanly—and then I thought it would be nice if I could stop and write a poem—equally so. But of course, such things are not done in the office even by the ladies. And now I am too tired to write the poem. Of course, I don't call this writing at all. I feel that I am—isn't the word drooling?—the way I talked when I was very tired, seated on the sofa, the lights low and only you near to listen. I feel like a crab that has left its shell—utterly at the mercy of time and tide.

My mother has just called me over: I told her I was writing to you. Don't write to-night, she said; write tomorrow. If you write now in your mood, you will depress her; write a cheerful letter to-morrow to cheer her up. So that's the mother-in-law you will have. I feel cheerful at the thought.

Be brave and patient and very wise—I am really talking to myself now—and perhaps, if we really are brave and patient and wise, the future will make amends. I like to think of Goethe's saying, The things we long for when we are very young when we are older heap themselves all over us. By the way, in writing disjointedly and as I am to you I am not at all abashed but rather glad that you should know me as I am so that no stupidity, no silliness, no weakness on my part will dishearten you greatly or take you unawares; but what I may do otherwise, will please you all the more. I am glad that you did what you did in Chicago, but uneasy that advances were made and that you stress the fact that the young man was anaemic. However, of all my uneasiness, this is the least. I know you.

I wrote you that I went to *The Menorah* dinner last night. There was a gallon of wine for the ten of us; and we had a good time. Nothing new, otherwise. In two months time I hope to get back to half time; and then I hope to do something in my afternoons worth while. I hope to start a novel next week—early in the morning at 4 or 5; but you know how elusive my novels are. Well, we shall see. Anyway, you will not be here for me to be cranky at. I hope to write you again tomorrow. x I kiss your hand, Marie.

Charles

To Marie Syrkin, Feb 8th [1930]

Saturday

[Marie,]

Your letter of Feb 6th via air mail was received here this morning. I called up Mrs. Epstein to tell her what you had written (some of it), and ventured to ask about David.[1] Mrs. Epstein told me that he was fine and that he had perpetrated several witticisms: to-wit—well, they'll write you. But I was glad to hear that he was taking your absence manfully and that you seem to be getting along all right. Now, Marie, we have lots of money, so do not stint yourself on essentials—good lodging, good food etc. You must have a real vacation.

I am going to Elliot Cohen's for dinner tonight. Tomorrow I expect to see Zukofsky and will probably write you at night.[2] I am sending this air mail so at the rate it seems to take you probably will get it Monday morning. I wrote you last night and since then nothing new except your letter. I have a great longing to come out to see you; and this may crystallize into a plan, and then into a fact; as some of my longings do. I suppose I ought to fill up the rest of this page with x's. I hereby solemnly do.

Charles

To Marie Syrkin, Feb 8 [9, 1930]

Sunday

[Marie,]

To begin with, after I mailed your letter yesterday, I went to the library at 42d St. On the way I stopped at Charles & Co's grocery store to see if I could send you something. I thought of honey, often of cheese, of candy. Also stopped at a Russian store and saw woolen shawls (little ones) in colors. Wondered if I should send you one. Decided to lump all gifts in one (unless you want something special) and send it on your birthday next

---

[1] David Bodansky, Marie Syrkin's son.

[2] Louis Zukofsky (1904–1978), poet and literary critic, was a lifelong friend and colleague of Reznikoff's.

month, or rather send all gifts on your birthday. By the way, do you want a wrist watch? What do you want specially? I really would have to hear about this soon, if I am to get it to you on time. Did buy a jar of honey at Charles & Co's to bring Elliot Cohen's wife and went on to the library to wait for the dinner hour. While waiting wrote:

> It is stupid to be thinking about you
> As much as I do; for such thoughts
> Do nobody good: it is not even wool-gathering.
> I sat in the reading-room as I used to,
> But instead of reading, thought of you:
> I thought, If I should wait for you
> As in other days, I'd have to wait a long time.

And then:

> I meant to send you something cheerful; forgive me—
> But laughter is gone in a second, tears last a minute or two.

At Elliot's I found he had another guest for dinner—Maurice Samuel.[1] During the dinner Samuel was telling us about a book he was writing on culture: the theme, I understood him to say, was that culture must be divorced from government, and a general condemnation of the mob. He used big words and important names—Spinoza and the modern philosophers.[2] He was very glib. Elliot and I picked his argument to pieces: they were feeble stuff. We were all very good-natured about it; and he ended up by saying, that if he were not so sure of himself, we two might disturb him. He is furious at what he calls the mob and their idols—such as, Wise and Hillel Silver. "O no," I said, "these are very small idols, local gods: Herzl was a fraud."[3] The man is an out-and-out charlatan, Marie; I mean Samuel. But he told a beautiful story—of your father. We were talking of what stirs an audience most and I said "the unexpected." "When Dr. Syrkin," Samuel said "was once in Berlin, a communist was addressing a group of Jewish students. Communism *was* the solution; he pointed to

---

[1] Maurice Samuel (1895–1972), author of *The World of Sholom Aleichem*, first husband of Marie Syrkin. Their marriage was dissolved by her father because she was under the age of consent.

[2] Benedictus de Spinoza (1632–1677), Dutch-Jewish philosopher, foremost exponent of 17th-century Rationalism.

[3] Stephen Wise and Abba Hillel Silver, reform rabbis and strong and leading Zionists.

[4] Theodor Herzl (1860–1904), founder of the political form of Zionism.

76

his coat and said the collar had come from Angora, the cloth from England etc. As he did so, he showed a rent under the sleeve. Dr. Syrkin stood up, and said, "And that tear you got in a pogrom in Odessa!" You probably know the story. I won't go into Samuel's ideas: they are shallow and false as ideas and as history—well, I won't go into them. After Samuel was gone, Elliot said to me, "Do you still see Marie Syrkin?" I suppose we have been seen together. "Yes," I said. "Where is she now?" "In Reno," I answered. Then he talked about you for some time. I was uncertain whether or not to tell him that we were going to be married, but I decided not to, since that might make trouble now if it got about. But, on the other hand, I did not want him to say anything that would be embarrassing afterwards. However, he did not. But on the way home, I was very sorry I had told him that you were in Reno. When I thought that Samuel might come out to see you, by the anguish I felt and still feel I know how I feel about you. I am not jealous of him; but I am afraid that taking you by surprise in your loneliness—I think of it as of a snake creeping on its belly towards a dove. O, I know Samuel isn't a snake, but, sometimes, in your generosity, in your simplicity, you are such a dove. I cannot begin to tell you how I feel about you. Perhaps, it will take me the rest of my life. To begin with, I feel towards you like a father, I want desperately to shield you, to feed you, to clothe you, to take care of you—and yours; and then I feel towards you like a son, I want to tell you all my petty victories and my defeats, to have you reproach me and give me your advice; and then, of course, always, I think of you as companion and wife. (When we are married, we must be married by a rabbi: it would be intolerable to be married by a clerk.) You are all women in one to me—all women I ever saw, that ever passed me in the street, that I ever wanted to meet. I have only one wish: be wise, be wise, do the best for yourself. Now that you are away, I see clearly how much you mean, I see all your beauty, nobility, and innocence. When I think how often I used to say that my work meant more to me than anybody, I see how childish that was: I kiss your hand, the hem of your dress, the ground before your feet. Elliot said, "What a fool that supposedly great and wise man Dr. Syrkin was to break up the marriage of his daughter and Samuel. I wonder what he would say now if he saw what Samuel is now?" "What would he say," I answered, "what would a man trained in philosophy as Dr. Syrkin was say if he heard the twaddle Samuel was talking so pompously tonight?" By the way, Elliot Cohen told me that Samuel had told him that his father was not a butcher, but had been a cobbler. It seems he had been somewhat of a scamp, was in the Roumanian army, and then when he settled down in the village where he had met

Samuel's mother, since he knew how to sew harness, he became a cobbler. However, I am sure Dr. Syrkin would not have thought much of me either as a son-in-law—and he may be right.

C.

Marie, you must forgive me, if—according to your injunction—by writing without revision, just what comes into my head: I say, as I often will and have, stupidities. But I do not want to hide anything from you, including stupidities; and so, as I think I have written, I will obey. Whoever said anything against your letters? That person was a fool! They are yourself—and charming as yourself. I am now going to meet Zukofsky and hope to write you tomorrow. Take care of yourself, do not stint yourself in what you ought to have, rest, and have a good vacation. In New York I work for you; and think of you—pleasantly sad and sadly joyful thoughts. You understand.

C.

To Marie Syrkin, Feb 11th [1930]

Tuesday

[Marie,]

I thought I would have lots of time tonight (I did not write you yesterday); but I have to work tomorrow—at least half the day.

Sunday night I met Zukofsky—as I wrote you I would—and read his essay on me called "Objectivity and Sincerity"—about 25 pages (including quotations).[1] Well, I am sure *The Menorah* will not take it; for on Saturday Elliot told me that Zukofsky could not write, that he had done a poor piece of translation, etc. Zukofsky can write; and although I do not react to parts, to other parts I am—to say the least—attentive. In his essay on me he interpreted some things in a way new to me: for instance, in the thing to Athena, he showed the resemblance of the verse to the classic hexameter; in one about old men on stoops, he saw the lines of the steps of the stoops, the wrinkled faces etc. in a design of which I had only seen part. I told him

---

[1] Zukofsky's essay "Sincerity and Objectification: With Special Reference to the Work of Charles Reznikoff" was published in the February 1931 issue of *Poetry*. Zukofsky notes at the end of that article that it is "an extract from an essay written a year ago" (285).

so. However, I am sure *The Menorah* will not care for some of his work—and they will undoubtedly take Trilling instead.[1]

Now I have all of the finished group of my verse to type, including the set Elliot wants to see again; and then I'll be through. That is, I have ready 1. group of verse (By the Waters of Manhattan 1930). This may be printed by *The Menorah*, but that is unlikely.[2] If not, I will print or have printed 100 copies myself. (You sigh). 2. Not quite ready: 2 stories (which you have seen—Passage-at-arms and Greenwich Village; the play on Jeremiah 3. In work: a group of verse.[3] That is all. As to what I am going to devote myself after that, well, I have written you, I'll write you, and will probably change my mind, surely change my mind and write you again. But about one person I have not changed my mind; on the contrary, as time passes,—I see that this is becoming a valentine. If so, music! (I hope to write you every day; I want to. But I have not had a letter from you since Saturday, and now it is Tuesday. And now you have more time than I have.)

> The musicians enter, stand under her window, and sing:
> Watch over her who is still so trustful,
> The burnt child that will not dread the fire—
> Witch of En-dor, raise for me the spirit of her father
>
> Stars and wind,—
> Three have no compassion;
> Witch of En-dor, raise the spirit of her father.
>
> The cold light of the morn
> Do not harm her;
> Witches and wizards, go
> But leave the spirit of her father.

C.

---

[1] Lionel Trilling (1905–1975), literary critic and writer, taught at Columbia University for most of his adult life, beginning in 1931, and was the first Jew to be tenured in the English Department there.

Trilling's books include: *The Liberal Imagination* (1958) and *Beyond Culture: Essays on Literature and Learning* (1965). Trilling's review of *By the Waters of Manhattan* (1930), "Genuine Writing," praised Reznikoff's novel as "remarkable and original in American literature" (*The Menorah Journal.* 19:1 (October 1930): 88–92).

[2] Reznikoff's poem, "By the Waters of Manhattan: 1930" was published in *The Menorah Journal.* 18:5 (May 1930): 417–421.

[3] "Passage-At-Arms" was published in *The Menorah Journal.* 19:1 (October 1930): 63–66.

To Marie Syrkin, February 13th [1930]

1379 Union Street, Brooklyn, New York
Thursday Evening

[Marie,]

Your letter telling of your loneliness bothered and saddened me. I rush the result of a little meditation on the subject—special delivery because it may come Sunday.

Theory

A hasty or stupid person might conclude that your loneliness is due to inner insufficiency: that is, that you have nothing in yourself to fall back upon. I know that is not so; moreover, I realize that a person who has always lived practically in a mob would suffer until accustomed to the company of oneself alone. *Analogy*: A fat person, no matter how fat, if his food is cut down, would suffer for a day or two until his system became accustomed to tapping the reserves of food in himself—but then he feels fine.

Practice

By you. The Brittanica says the University of Nevada is in Reno. If so, excursions, courses, clubs, library, gymnasium. Furthermore, there must be a synagogue and its auxiliaries. *By me.* Much as I would like to, I ought not to come to Reno now—breaking off connections here and disappointing people who rely on me. Besides, it has been my observation, or rather yours, that the gallants that fly to pleasure, fly from the unpleasant. Therefore, I will try to write you daily; and I will try to send you weekly (each Saturday afternoon including this coming Saturday) a modest package of books and dainties.

Called up the Ludens, spoke to Mr. Ludens; he told me Tima has been out of bed for a week and is all better. They send their regards.

C.

To Marie Syrkin, Feb 14, 1930

Friday night

Darling girl, I read your charming letter of Feb 12th three times—I was so pleased to find that your stay in Reno was not so dreadful. I had hoped so that you would have a real vacation out of it, and it was disappointing. Now your letter has made Friday a holiday night, and given it some of the proper *simchah*. Your letter was so wise and lovely that I felt completely abashed. Darling! And you are writing stories and verse. Marie, you will never be completely happy unless you manage to keep at it for the rest of your life. I know. Please don't send any of it out until you let me see it. Of course, what I say may not be much help—but I let you see everything I do. And I have taken your suggestions—willy-nilly. Darling! I just feel like filling the rest of this letter up with darlings and letting it go like that. After all, that is the sum total of what I have to say just now. Talking of writing—or writing of writing—blessed word! I told you before you left that my father was at it. Well, he has written about 10,000 words—about 10 stories in continuity. I heard the first two—they are excellent, much better than my mother's—really stories. I advised him to continue until he brought his life up to about ten years ago—until he was 50. Then he will translate them into English and I will revise the translation and try to have it sold as a novel—it will run about 100,000 words. But whether it will be sold or not, or what happens is not so important; what is important is that he was beginning to find time very heavy on his hands, he wanted to try to talk to us who were still busy and we could not listen; now he is very happy, because he is busy, has a lot to do, and we all say that what he is doing is good—and it is. He loves to tell stories.

I see from your letter that you probably can get all the books you want. Therefore, I will not send you any tomorrow—just some eatables. However, if you want me to send you any books write me just what you want. Write me just what you want of other things and I'll include it in the weekly shipment (now don't expect a trunk, it will be a tiny shipment, "a few raisins, a few almonds, a handful of pistachio nuts, a date or two.") But you write me what you want—all that you want. I look forward to the intense pleasure of spending my Saturday afternoons—that sacred day sacred to us—to shopping for you, darling!

I will call up Mrs. Epstein tomorrow.

I sign my name in full so that you may know how to spell it.

Charles Reznikoff

I am going to my broker this evening—and am late.

To Marie Syrkin, [February 15]th

Saturday

[Marie,]

Your letter of the 11th came today. I will confess that the notion of your sticking your nose—short as it is—into the gullet of the tubercular woman to see her tonsils made me uncomfortable. At such a vision an injunction to wash your hands well seems of little good particularly at this late date.

I went to see my broker last night, and when we discussed income tax, he promised to give me a statement of my account. So by March 15th I ought to know how I stand. I feel that I ought to dedicate the present group of verse—if I print it—to him. It would please him, I think; and it is his due—at least.

I called up Mrs. Epstein at noon; and she tells me David is fine. His poetry is excellent; and I see that he has come at last to the muses. I know he would prefer to send you chemical formulas; but he stoops to talk to you in your speech.

I sent you assorted groceries today; and you may expect them by Thursday, I think. Next week I hope to send some assorted drug-store articles—soap, powder, etc.; but I will send you anything you prefer.

As for coming out west, here is the way things are: I have just received a friendly letter from Al Lewin urging me to come. I must work full time on my definitions until we reach a certain point (where the next volume ends). Now this may take two or three months. Then I will see. Of course, I'd like to come; and if I can only tie up matters neatly at the American Law Book Co., I'd leave at once. But I ought not to leave them in the lurch. Besides, I want to use them as a possible stepping stone for another connection. For this other connection is inevitable. I don't know whether or not I wrote you that I was told that Kaiser and Mack get $150—a week; and the highest paid subordinate (a man who has been with them 30 years) gets $125—a week. The job is insecure; men have been discharged after being with them 25 years and more when they can not turn out work like men of 30; Kaiser nearly lost his job, and would have if the concern would have been bought by Callahan of Chicago; it may be shifted anytime to St. Paul. Moreover, they squeeze the last drop of mental energy out of you: you are always behind the schedule, sometimes far behind—as I am now. You are always an employee and your immediate superiors are employees who have to make good by getting the most out of you. It seems to me that in the law proper, if I were to work as hard as I do, I should make $100 a week, with more security. However, as in all professions, such a connection is extremely hard to make—or any connection that would lead to what I could do well—briefing. However, I can negotiate best from my present connection. If I break it, it will be harder. As for part time, Kaiser is against it and he is very stubborn and is the rising star, if things stay as they are.

To go from one tedious matter to another, I have not started work on my novel, but it is assembling itself in my head. Nor have I any new verse, nor have I done anything for days. I hope to make fresh beginnings tomorrow—Sunday.

I am invited to Elliot Cohen's for this evening at nine. He told me over the telephone how much he liked my group of verse. I also sent it to the printer to get an estimate.

If my sister goes away Feb 22 and I get her tickets for the Philharmonic will take your aunt. Expect to write again tomorrow. Good bye, darling. Give my best regards to Mrs. Reznikoff.

C.

Forgive me for sending so much air-mail; it makes it seem that you are nearer.

To Marie Syrkin, [February 16, 1930]

Sunday Night

[Marie,]

I have just finished a pleasant day: a walk, seeing an exhibition of paintings by Indians of the Southwest, particularly a troop on horseback in a race and others hunting buffalo—I may see these again next Sunday—I did a little verse as follows:

> We have left the street and lots and are in the fields,
> Are deep in shining snow; the sky is blue as in early summer;
> But come, we must go back: here the wind is master.

Not so good, but I was glad to be back at the old music. I also began my novel (this is the historical one I used to talk you sick about, but, hitherto, the Wandering Jew has not appeared. Well, honey, I also read a little Ezekiel, quite good (chap. XVI), and Dante (centaurs and the river of blood, canto XII), Homer (Odysseus has reached Chrysa), Brittanica (practical applications of agriculture to English soil). Well, if you were beside me—it would have been more than pleasant. ("Be a lady and marry me," to misquote a young master).

Last night, at Elliot Cohen's—a young novelist who has just had a novel accepted by Longmans Green, Mr. and Mrs. Henry Hurwitz. Elliot, I gather is eager to print "By the Waters of Manhattan 1930" in toto; Henry Hurwitz is eager not to print it. However he is reading it again, and I suppose I'll hear soon one way or another—by Wednesday night, I suppose, when the society has a meeting. I asked the printer for a bid, anyway, but have not heard. My novel(?) will be hard work, lots of reading, and will take from 2 to 4 years, I think. But if it will be done as I plan it, although no more than 200 pages, it will be worth the time. Anyway, I can't get rid of the idea any other way.

I am terrified at all the blank space to the bottom of the sheet. Forgive me, although it was Sunday, I am somewhat tired and it is getting late. By the way, would you want a Shakespearean grammar? It looks a very learned book and costs only 75¢ (in a second-hand book-shop). Shall I send it? (I haven't bought it, so if you want it, tell me). It deals with English grammar as Shakespeare used it: lots of quotations. I would have sent it without asking you, but I don't want you to think of me as a taskmaster, as a grim father who snatches a light novel like Meredith from your hands and points to Aeschylus in Greek.

Everybody tells me that Sam Roth is going to Atlanta for six months, if he is not there now.[1]

I am thinking an awful lot of you "by day and by night"—even when I ought to be doing my work; perhaps, I am falling in love.

C.

To Marie Syrkin, [February 18, 1930]

Tuesday Night

Darling, beautiful as the new moon and the sunlight upon new-fallen snow, you must not read the verse I may send you—or have sent—as verse— read it only for the truth. To-night I have a dismal bit about myself:

---

[1] There was a federal penitentiary in Atlanta. (See note to letter of July 23, 1922.)

I have read too much; I shall begin to spit ink;
It has tinged my blood and is stored in my bones.

However, O illustration brilliant with gold and blue and ivory white! As I turn the leaves, I find you between the pages.

I do not complain of the infrequency of your letters; I complain of the infrequency of your presence. But I understand the first as I do the second. Use your own judgment; certainly, my family will not tell me now what they think. As for sending your letters airmail or otherwise—do as you like. I like to hear from you as soon as possible, but if it is any trouble, or if you think my family will think you extravagant and so prefer to spend 2¢ instead of 5¢—do what you like. If it would bring you back the sooner—but May will not come any sooner. By the way, maybe I can come out then; but we'll write about that in April.

And you must fill out a New York state Income Tax return due April 15th. You have no income tax to pay since as head of a family you are exempt $4000, I believe; but, since you received more than $2,500 you must make a return. The Board of Education, as required by law, has surely reported you. I believe you are exempt as a city school-teacher from Federal income tax, but not from the state.

It is almost 9 and my sister is waiting for me to go to a movie; and I am somewhat tired and would find it restful. Forgive this brief scrawl. More tomorrow, I hope. Dinner at The Menorah Society to-morrow night.

C.

To Marie Syrkin, [February 19, 1930]

Wednesday Evening.

[Marie,]

On my way to the *Menorah* dinner I have stopped at the post-office and am trying to write this with a post-office pen.

Coming home from the movies last night I wrote you this:

Marie, I said before you went away
A sonnet, regular in beat and rhyme,
Regularly would be sent you every day;
Indeed, I said it, and indeed it's time
Even that one were sent you; for, I say—

Ring, brazen bells, and, silver bells, now chime
Each joyfully, for Helicon I climb
Zealously at her feet my rhymes to lay—
No need for us to speak as others do
In prose or worse—of prose I've had enough—
Kisses are best, but if they must be few,
Or none—well, then I'll scribble rhyming stuff—
Forgive it if it's rough but it is true—
For you, a new Marie—soon Reznikoff.

This morning I received your air-mail letter of the 16th. I notice that you use Hotel Golden stationery. Therefore, this Saturday I intend to include in my packet a box of stationery (Darling, sending you a package is fun; what else shall I do Saturdays?) Will try a sonnet tomorrow on how many times to write me. It is selfish of me, but the notion of your going to bed at 8 o'clock pleases me—and your interest and work in Shakespeare. Darling Ph. D., the rest is crosses.

C.

To Marie Syrkin, [February 20, 1930]

Thursday.

[Marie,]

You ask and ask how often you're to write;
Why write as often—often as you please!
Do gentle women who with crumbs delight
A starving sparrow—do they number these?
And what if any other person sees?
How should it seem in such a person's sight?
That kindliness to him they love is right—
They won't mistake your generosities.
Then do not let what others may think matter;
And, if you please, each day another letter,
Letters, letters! these empty months to fill!—
Or if it seems to you that it is better
To write less often, I'll be grateful still;
Then ask no more, write when and what you will.

However, darling, no more sonnets—for a while. I care little for it as a verse form—as yet; besides, my sonnet writing time seems to be exactly at midnight 12-1, and that interferes with all the work to be done in the morning. I may say it is not too difficult a form, provided one is as careless and slipshod as I was. However, I like free verse much better.

Now, darling, as for your verse; for I received your letter of the 18th this evening. I cannot judge them now; I like the *Dyings*, but the other not so much. besides, the *Dyings* is precious because of you. I don't want to criticize it. It seems to me offhand that it is full of lovely music; I like it. Besides, I am too tired to criticize intelligently this evening. I just feel that it is very good. Darling, will you keep all you write until you return and then we'll go over it together. That will be better than writing about it. Besides, you do not plan to send anything out to magazines from Reno, do you? However, you are going to send me copies of all you do at once. Please! They are the most exquisite parts of a letter.

I have so much nonsense to tell you I don't know where to begin. Well, first: This Saturday the stores may be closed; if so, I may not be able to get a package off (including stationery, but no drug articles, as you say). However, I am pretty sure to find some shop open so I may have to send only "sweet comestibles." That Hotel Golden stationery bothers me. I know it's silly; but I don't like your using it, although you were a guest once. Well, I'm foolish; but I don't like to use hotel lobbies and stationery where I'm not a guest. If this sounds like a sermon, forgive me; I'm just writing as I think without premeditation or consideration—much.

I have tickets for Toscanini—I think—you know the box, and I'm going to ask your aunt—for this Saturday night.

My work in the place may ease up: Kiser got me some more assistance today. Both he and Mack are very nice.

The Menorah is at a standstill as far as I'm concerned. They've neither accepted nor rejected anything. Tomorrow I'm to see my printer about quotations for "By the Waters of Manhattan 1930." *The Menorah* will probably use Trilling's review—he's writing one—in this issue. Will tear it out and send it to you.

Darling, I love you so much. I regret terribly every unkind word or glance. It seems to me that I was always boorish or stupid; I remember the silliest things that I was always saying—and your gentleness, your great kindliness and beauty. Darling Marie

Charles

To Marie Syrkin, [February 21, 1930]

Friday

[Marie,]

This is really not Friday at all, but Saturday; for it is 12:30. However, I do not want a day to pass—if I can help it—without my writing to you; and I shall feel the better for it. But tomorrow is a holiday; and I am not working.

I received your exhortation not to send you anything weekly. I think I ought to and I will. It is a small extravagance—if you were here we would spend more Saturday—it gives me great pleasure, and (you can see by all this scratching out that it is late) it gives you some—certainly the prize bag effect which I want to convey ought to help pass the time slightly—Let's say no more about it, unless you want something particularly. Tomorrow the stores are closed; so I got a few things today at a shop near the office. In another place I bought a little stationery which will be packed with the other things. Later, I may be able to get you more and better things in the way of stationery, candy, etc. I am just learning now. I think I ought to try Macy's. By the way, it occurs to me that some stuff like the anchovy paste (or the *pate de foie gras* which is in this package) may spoil if kept. Use your best judgment and remember, if in doubt at all, *throw it away*. This package will not be shipped until Monday, so you will probably get it two days later.

Sunday, probably, by regular mail I will forward income tax blanks for New York State. As a married woman not living with her husband the law requires you to make a return if your income (as it was, I believe) was over $2,500. However, as the head of a family (your son David whose chief support you were last year) you are entitled to $4,000 exemption. However, you must make a return and swear to it before a notary. Anyway, read the blanks carefully, and I have no doubt you can fill them out. However, should you find it difficult send me all the necessary information and I will fill out a blank and sign it here as your agent. It seems to me that this ought to be taken care of. It is only a little trouble and may save a good deal.

I have had a little trouble at the place of the sort I wrote you, but now I believe it is all cleared up. A lot of pressure was brought upon me to hurry, and I did as much as I could and still had too much to do. Well, as a result, a good deal of mechanical work was lifted from me, a good deal of the more difficult and intensive work was no longer required; and now it seems to me that the work is fairly pleasant and endurable with my own.

Nevertheless, I ought to plan to better myself—excuse me, darling, ourselves. On one of these days I wrote:

This was a day of vexations;
I will go for a walk and visit my neighbors, the trees.

Fell's man was in to see me today with his bid for the printing of my little group of verse. His price is ridiculous—$165. I will not spend more than $50—so I think I will have to do it myself. Well, I will. It is relaxation; and besides, I will soon forget my printing, if I do not. I will do only a little a day. However, we shall see. He is going to make me a new bid; and I will let the Rumford Press (who is cheap, Elliot Cohen tells me) make a bid. If it is not near my price I will do it myself. I will become as good a printer as I am a typist. Toujours fou!

I called up your aunt tonight to take her to the concert tomorrow; but she was at the island with a slight sore throat. I am to call again tomorrow and she will see if her throat is all better whether or not she can go. I asked about David and was told that he was fine. (Now, Marie, don't write them about this sore throat. They will think me a fool, but I am simply telling you why after telling you that I am taking your aunt to the concert which I want to do badly, I may not after all. Your aunt spoke to me for some time and was cheerful and very pleasant so I suppose it's nothing. I am going to call her again tomorrow at 6. But don't say anything; they will think me an idiot for writing such trifles to you. If your aunt can't go, I'll take my mother.)

Darling, writing to you, even such stuff, is such pleasure I could write on until morning, but it is almost 1 o'clock. By the way, this morning my mother called up to me that there was a letter (yours) for me. When I came down to breakfast I said that I would probably get one almost every day from you. Yes, she said to me, I wanted to suggest to you that you ought to write her every day. It doesn't take long, and you ought to. So that is what my mother thinks, see!—why we love her.

C.

Marie, just as I told you it was not until I saw you that night with Tima that I realized how beautiful you are, so, now I see, it was not until you had gone that I realized how painfully in love with you I am. Before that I was joyfully in love: sometimes it was exhaltation; but this is different—it is almost always anguish. Darling, I love you so, it seems to me that I was only a child, and that compared to this, what I was feeling was calf-love.

Anyway, I recollect the Biblical "a most vehement flame." And yet I wait for you patiently because I hope when you return that you will be at last my wife—completely and everywhere, in the Bronx at Sherman Avenue and in Brooklyn on Union St.

Charles

To Marie Syrkin, [February 23, 1930]

Sunday.

[Marie,]

After all, I did not go to the concert with your aunt. She was home, but the weather had changed and become raw: so she thought it prudent not to go out. Nor for the same reason would my mother go. Well, I did not want to waste the ticket and thinking of men who might go tried to reach Melville Levy and another chap by telephone. In the end I went myself, but there in the lobby was our old acquaintance Samuel—you remember that nice old man who sat beside us at the concert in the C.C.N.Y. building and whom I afterwards met on a bus?—well, he was waiting for two ladies who always get him in. I gave him my spare ticket and he was thankful. Afterwards, a strange lady came into our box and he sat opposite with the other. I was glad I had no one with me, for I was tired and sleepy and the concert wasn't much. Toscanini was not conducting, but Molinari.

I meant to send you the state income tax blanks today, but find that I have blanks for residents and that non-residents must use another form. I will get this tomorrow or the day after; for, of course, you are now a non-resident, your official residence is in Nevada. Now, don't sigh about the blank, make believe it is a poem and decipher it; but, if you don't want to, I believe I can fill it out if you will send me all the information. Well, I'll ask for it in the letter with which I'll send the blank; and you choose between doing it yourself or having me do it. As a teacher, an employee of the city, you do not have to make out a Federal tax return, I believe.

I did not write you a letter yesterday; but I was so sleepy and tired when I got home, that anything I might have written would have been drivel. And why afflict a student of Shakespeare unduly?

I worked hard today, went through the regular procedure of writings and readings. And began again—the novel. Well, the fundamental idea is still the same except that instead of the last three hundred years, it is to be all in the present, instead of all the United States, it is to be all in New York, and instead of the Wandering Jew it is to be an old acquaintance—Joel Stein.[1] (Perhaps, this springs from a seed planted by you, farmerie!) I did 500 words or so including a beautiful description of the window of the restaurant that has been unoccupied for several months. Expect to write again tomorrow. Charles. x x x x x x x x x x x x x x x x x x x x x x x x x x x x x x x x x x x x x x x x x x x x x x x x x x x x x x x x x (You see, words fail me).

To Albert and Mildred Lewin, Feb 23, 1930

1379 Union Street, Brooklyn N.Y.

Dear Al and Milly,

Thank you for your invitation, which you have so often repeated—I may accept it. At present, I have to work at definitions for *Corpus Juris* until we reach "Public Lands." Perhaps in a month or two. As for my own work: I have a group of verse which I plan to publish soon as "By the Waters of Manhattan, 1930" (24 pages), and am at work upon other verse—and prose.[2] Of course, whenever I have anything that I care about, I'll send it.

I saw your friend Eddie Mayer's *Children of Darkness*.[3] A child of darkness sold me two seats at $2.50 each. They were away up at the very end of a row. Thereupon, another child of darkness offered me other seats in the mezzanine for another dollar. Despite this, I had rather an agreeable time. The play could stand some revision by cutting out all the soft spots— "the white birds flying"—but these are what Mr. Mayer probably likes best. And it would only be a one-acter, and not acted.

Several young men—ten years or so younger—are beginning to like what I do—also in spots. (One likes the prose and has no use for the verse, another likes the verse but only here and there. One has sent all I have done to Ezra Pound and has done a kind of Ph.D. study of my work— though, who will print it is beyond me.[4] However, that is none of my

---

[1] *By the Waters of Manhattan* (1930).

[2] Reznikoff's poem "By the Waters of Manhattan: 1930" appeared in *The Menorah Journal* 18:5 (May 19300: 417–421.

[3] Eddie Mayer's *Children of Darkness* was a failure in its initial production in 1930; however, according to the *Oxford Companion to the American Theatre* it achieved a greater success in 1958 when it was revived.

[4] Reznikoff is referring to Louis Zukofsky.

troubles: I warned him against it. I really must try to become thin and poetic; but I am fat again and look like a salesman—out of a job.)

C.

To Marie Syrkin, [February 24, 1930]

Monday Night

Darling,

I just called up your home and spoke to your aunt. She told me everything is "wonderful," and there is nothing at all to worry about. She herself is completely recovered, and, if I can get tickets for Saturday night (for a performance by a great Chinese actor who is now in this city) I will take her to make up for the concert. I will call twice a week *after this week* and write you.

Now, I am sending tonight by regular mail income tax blanks. I have filled one out in pencil—at a guess—to show how I think it ought to be done. But, of course, if you don't or can't do it, write me in time (April 15th); for it ought to be done. You use resident blanks, after all; for you were a resident, when the income was earned; but, be sure to give your present address to show that your Reno residence is bona fide. That is the important thing, as I see it. Now enough of that.

The result of a walk:

In front of the pigeon house the white pigeons are preening themselves,
And in the yard the white chickens with bright red combs bustle about;
At the pool in the lots six or seven brown wild birds are drinking.

Forgive my brevity, but I want to mail this at once so that you may get it the sooner. Darling, I love you so and long for you so, but I bear your absence somewhat patiently since it has shown me so overwhelmingly what I only, it seems, suspected and surmised—that you mean so much to me.

C.

To Marie Syrkin, [February 25, 1930]

Tuesday

[Marie,]

I did not receive a letter from you this morning. Well, perhaps you have spoiled me, but I miss it. Particularly, after your gloomy letter that I received last night.

I was up at 3:30 this morning and it is now 9 o'clock P.M.—so if some of this does not read just right, you'll know why. But I managed to do a little work. Of course, I've given up this idea of a novel and turned the description of the empty restaurant window into verse. On Sunday when I am fresh and rested I begin a novel, on Monday or Tuesday when I am tired I am through with prose forever—and I have a hundred or so good reasons— which I have told you and written you on divers Mondays and Tuesdays.

I have heard from Fell; he wants $125 for 100 copies bound. This is much too high. I am going to get a bid from a local printer near where I work, then one from the Rumford Press whom Elliot Cohen recommends. But I think I'll do it myself whatever they bid. I ought to work at printing 1 hour a day week-days and four on Sundays—just not to forget it. In a month I'll have this out—much better because hand-set.

I'll send you the "Restaurant Window" thing soon, when I am less tired.

The work at the place has become less difficult, and I think I do it better. But if I can get back into half time, I'll try for briefing or something lucrative or with a future. (These days Venus does not pal with Mars but with Mercury—or rather Hermes.)

Your aunt will probably write you that I have become fat. I hope you'll be able to recognize me. I went into a photomaton to take pictures thinking to send you one with each letter—but they were ghastly, each was different and on each I looked like a different kind of criminal. I liked the one in which I looked like a swindler best; I had my eyes up looking right through you at God in heaven—the very picture of Mr. Ponzi who promised his clients 500% on their money.

Marie darling, one month is almost gone and in a little while—darling, someday you will think of the mountains of Nevada and perhaps in a hot dusty street or in a street covered with ice and slush through which a bitter cold wind is blowing, you may regret them somewhat. So have a good look at them now. Darling, I hope you are having a good rest and a vacation you needed badly. Everything seems to be fine at your home. I have at this point only one word left in my vocabulary—darling!

Charles

Why only 3 x's, you stingy thing? In my letters every period and every dot over an I stands for an x.

To Marie Syrkin, [February 26, 1930]

The American Lawbook Company
Wednesday Evening

Darling,

The day before yesterday I received a letter from you in which you said that you were not so "peppy." Neither yesterday nor this morning have I heard from you (however, there may be a letter from you when I get home). Naturally, I am worried and anxious. (Especially since I remember that on occasions your notion of something digestible, wholesome, and refreshing is sausage, frankfurters, or salami.) *I would wire you at once but I am afraid that a telegram would scare you before you opened it.* Now you should receive this letter by Saturday, and if I do not hear from you by Saturday I will wire you and will expect a wire collect from you. I will wait for the answer at Grand Central Terminal from which I will send my telegram. *Should you be sick I will wire Milly Lewin in Los Angeles to come to you or send a friend or nurse and I will pay* all expenses. However, *if there is a competent, trained and registered nurse in Reno you are to have her stay with you* and I will pay all expenses. Please don't be penny wise and pound foolish.

I tried to get seats tonight for the Chinese actor to take your aunt to on Saturday but they are sold out (except for $4.40 seats).

I hardly feel like adding this but after my lugubrious notes it may cheer you—*The Menorah Journal* has accepted and will publish, this issue or next, most of the unpublished group of "By the Waters of Manhattan 1930" (all except 5).[1] I have put aside all thoughts of printing until then. They will also print—separately—the dialogue I called "Luzzatto" which you liked.[2]

My God, Marie darling, I must hear from you at least every other day after this.

Charles

---

[1] "By the Waters of Manhattan: 1930." *The Menorah Journal.* 18:5 (May 1930): 417–21.

[2] "A Dialogue: Padua 1727." *The Menorah Journal.* 18:3 (March 1930): 220.

I will send you a package this Saturday from the same place I sent you the first one—but will not include any fish. I hope by this time you have received the package from Brooklyn. *Darling, for my sake eat only what you would feed David.* When you come back, you can eat creamed Salami or rhinoceros stew.

To Marie Syrkin, [February 27,1930]

Thursday Evening.

My darling girl, beloved, I hold you and kiss you a thousand times! I know how you feel when you have not heard from David. This morning when the postman rang and there was no letter from you, I felt sick and stayed sick all day. I wanted to send you a telegram badly, but I was afraid I would scare you. All day I thought of calling you on the telephone. I had a hundred horrible surmises. I thought of throwing up everything and taking the train west; I thought of aeroplanes cheerfully. Marie, you made me very miserable. But I don't blame you. I know that you could not write, and your letter of Monday was delayed so that I only found it when I came home this evening. Now, Marie, it would have been so comforting to have been able to wire you and to hear from you in a few hours; so, after this, if you do get a wire, it is only from me—who, before you went away went doggedly (like a "Killer") about his work and saw you only twice a week and quarreled with you. Darling, it was against all my philosophy that a human being should be so precious to me, because I know how upsetting such a feeling might be and now I know how upsetting it is. Because I had not heard from you for three mornings—especially after you had written that you were not feeling well (true, spiritually because you had not heard from home)—well, I was on the verge of doing desperate things; I was sick, I could hardly eat—food was repulsive, and I had to force myself constantly to do my work. Well, thank God, that's over and that it were May! Marie dearest.

Now about sending you things. I like to do it; there is an exquisite pleasure about sending you something rare and pleasant. And it really costs little. However, *don't keep anything that may spoil and make you sick.* Please throw it away. So I am not even to send you candy just now. Well, darling, please please ask me for what you want in time to send it to you; and now I am *not* going to send you anything until you ask—except of course, for your birthday. Then, darling, you must have sweets and flowers and something very lovely. What shall it be? Give me time to look around. Listen, Marie, choose several [illegible] on the Saturdays I send you nothing will go to that. Darling, I cannot begin to describe the pleasure of giving to you—beloved. It seems to me that my love for you is like those terribly intoxicating liquors that go down like water and that do not act at once—but when they do you are terribly drunk. That is the way I feel now about you; I feel drunk, and yet, as if I were drunk, not ashamed to be drunk but happy at being so; I know how foolish it is to be so exuberant, but I feel glad that I am, glad that I am in love, glad that I love such a darling, glad that I received a letter from you, and glad that you send me "much, much love." Darling, I will turn poet and write verses.

C.

By the way, I have decided that I ought to make up the state-income tax for you (as agent). Please send me the amount of your earnings last year, itemizing them. That will free you from all responsibility and at the same time you will comply with the [illegible] part natural stupidity. There I am—inexperience, stupidity, timidity, blown by emotion into flame.

To Marie Syrkin, [February 28, 1930]

Friday Night

[Marie,]

I have written you letters from the post-office at Borough Hall and that at 32d St.; now I am trying the pens at City Hall post office

I have just spoken to your aunt and we are going out to dinner tomorrow night and then to theatre. Will write you all about it Sunday. I may be able to get off a letter Saturday afternoon; I know a nice little post-office near 171st St. I asked after everybody, and was told that all were fine. I am to come up to the house at 6 o'clock, and will probably meet your son David. Should I, expect the most detailed report possible.

I have thrown all my energy into the work at the place to break the jam, and am succeeding—but my own work! Silence! I am not sending you anything eatable tomorrow, because I want to husband all my resources for your aunt; I couldn't borrow a dollar from her very well. Sunday I will let you know just how much money I have in the savings bank, in my checking account, and that almost mythical amount at my broker's (that is, if I succeed in learning this at the broker's tonight—I am going there). Now—no, I was going to send you the poem on the restaurant window that had been empty (that is the restaurant) all winter. It is very sad and I may publish it in a little volume all by itself with the pickle story you know so well. If I do, I'll dedicate it to Longchamps or Alice Foote MacDongal (perhaps, in memory of a certain evening not so long ago).

I have just reread what I have written so far and I notice *Silence*! That is not an admonition to you, you know; I wanted to sum up practically all my own work for a week or two.

I should like to write you a sonnet just now—standing on one leg as it were—but I am so barren of rhymes that the only one that occurs to me is "love" and "tov"—the Hebrew "good," as in "Mazel tov." Darlingest, take care of yourself; I take off my hat and kiss your hand—perhaps, I bite it a little bit.

Charles

To Marie Syrkin, [March 1, 1930]

Saturday afternoon

[Marie,]

I am on the way to your house, and have stopped at the post-office at 169th St. to write you a note. There is nothing new, and I am just going to copy

> The fog lifted; the tops of the buildings stood out against the blue sky,
> And in the street a thousand automobiles speeding towards New York
>   were shining.

Pretty weak and perhaps I sent it to you. I'll try for the effect I want—a street jammed with speeding automobiles. Here is the restaurant window that I have been threatening you with:

> The store had been a restaurant, but had been empty for months.
> In the window there was still a dusty sign "All Kinds of Soft Drinks for
>   Sale";
> Bottles of "near" beer and soda had been grouped in a pattern about a
>   rubber plant.
> This had been taken away, and all that was left was a leaf, tightly
>   curled,

In two shades of brown, the darker brown spreading from the middle
    like a stain.
Most of the bottles, still tightly capped, had burst
And the liquid had run out and dried on the dusty oil-cloth.
Some had soaked into the gauze curtain in back that shut off the
    window from the store,
And there were the faint uneven marks along the dusty cloth where it
    had been wet.
The beer bottles burst into most pieces—even the thick bottoms of
    orange-colored soda were still whole and alive in the sunshine,
In their places. But the others were out of place,
And whatever the design might have been it was no more.
A bit of something dark was also on the oil-cloth, covered by a grey
    fungus of delicate hairs.

I am sorry that I haven't a beautiful bit of verse to send at present.

Charles

To Marie Syrkin, [March 2, 1930]

Sunday Morning.

Darling girl, I saw David and he is splendid—almost as tall as your sister, chubby, and full of fun. Now I'll tell you all about it.

I meant to write last night as soon as I came home, but I did not come home until 1 in the morning and was so sleepy I would have written only the barest and most unsatisfactory note.

To begin at the very beginning. I stopped at the post office and wrote you a letter which I did not mail, expecting to finish it when I got home—and here it is enclosed.

I walked up 169th St., and looked at all the familiar landmarks—the big chimney of the hospital—and then the school, and at last I rang the bell at 1114. (It seems that my coming was somewhat of a mistake; your aunt intended that I should call *up* at that hour, not call. However, it was a happy mistake.) Your aunt and Mrs. Epstein were at the head of the stairs, and I walked into the front-room. In bounced your little sister, tricked out with red cloth, a piece wound about her waist and another about her head, full of laughter. She stopped and looked at me with a slightly amused glance. Following her was a boy, almost as tall as she, and I knew, of course, that it was David. He is almost as tall as your sister, as I said, and round, and chubby. (I had expected a thin "puny" child, to use your expression). He wore a dark blue sweater with a thin red stripe in it (it seems he had just come back with Aaron), and yellow battered shoes (by "battered" I mean the upper leather seemed much pounded).[1] He had just had a haircut and his black hair (so much like yours) was neatly combed. His dark eyes—just like yours, too—were full of fun—he was very much amused at your sister's antics. He speaks in a full, strong voice (it isn't exactly loud—resonant is the word). Your aunt said, "Isn't she silly?", or—something like that of Sylvia.[2] Your aunt was much embarrassed, perhaps because Aaron was home. "No," I said, "not at all; why she looks like a little gypsy. She is very pretty in that red." "She is crazy, methinks," said David, laughing. I was wondering somewhat where he had picked up "methinks"; Mrs. Epstein was nodding significantly first at me and then at David to make me understand who he is. I shook hands with Mischa who had been lying down on his bed reading, but he got up to shake hands with me, and he is looking very well—much better than when I saw him last. Your aunt was walking towards the door, eager to get away; David, Sylvia, and I followed. "Who is this man?" asked David in a cheerful loud voice. "He is a doctor," whispered your aunt. "He is a doctor," repeated Sylvia, very much pleased at something or other. "He is a doctor," said David, and added, "I thought so." And with that Sylvia and he went romping away; and your aunt and I downstairs.

I asked her how he had managed to improve so? Did taking out the tonsils do it? Yes, she said, and we are giving him and she mentioned some kind of tonic. Is that a cod-liver oil? I asked. It is a hundred times better than cod-liver oil, she answered enthusiastically. So that is how I saw David for you.

Now, sweetheart, I made up with your aunt to call her at the hospital every Tuesday and Friday and she will be able to tell me all about David freely. So now you have another source of information. I will also, I expect, take your aunt out again—several times—and in this way I'll come up to the house and hope to see him.

Now, I had a very pleasant time with your aunt, and I hope she had too. She was charming. My sister has just bought a clavichord or spinet and

---

[1] Aaron Bodansky, second husband of Marie Syrkin, father of her son David.
[2] Sylvia Syrkin, half-sister of Marie Syrkin.

she reminds me of that. It is an instrument that preceded the piano and was used in the home. It has a faint singing tone and one would hardly notice its beauty unless one is attentive.

I asked her what she wanted to see and she—timidly, of course—suggested *Street Scene*.[1] Well, for Saturday night I managed to get excellent seats—about 14th row orchestra. (I bought tickets for the mezzanine, but they gave me that). Before that we had dinner at the Blue Ribbon and your aunt enjoyed that, I think. Well, you know the food is good. She had a modest salad—asparagus vinaigrette, coffee and cake. (Next time we go out, I arranged to take her to an Italian restaurant because she spoke of liking what would be antipasto—so we'll go to Luigino's). We both enjoyed the play very much; I wasn't a bit critical and thought of it more seriously than good vaudeville. Of course, it had to rain when we came out—only a drizzle. But, luckily, I had enough for a taxi. According to new regulations the taxi went almost two miles out of the direct way home; but still I had enough. (Though I was worried—a secret, *please*, dearest.) Now, darling, I want to post this letter as soon as possible. Your boy is doing splendidly, sweetheart, and, as the doctor told you, now take care of yourself. Write me what to send you this Saturday, loveliest, best dearest.

C.

To Marie Syrkin, [March 3, 1930]

Monday Evening.

Darling matron (to use your word) I hope you have received my letter of yesterday telling you how wonderful your son is. To-morrow, as I also wrote you, I call up your aunt for another report—so I ought to keep you well posted.

Yesterday afternoon I went first to "my broker," and discovered that I earned $814 last year in stocks and this is what I must report in my income tax returns. However, since the first of January I have lost some of this. I do not know how much, because I did not ask. He merely told me this. Of

---

[1] Elmer Rice's *Street Scene*, winner of the Pulitzer Prize, was described as "generally interesting, frequently amusing and extraordinarily authentic" (*New York Times*. [11 January 1929]: 20). The play, a popular success, began its second year, after 446 performances, in January, 1930 (*New York Times*. [10 January 1930]: 24).

course, the whole thing has an air of fairy land about it, and I don't count the money as mine—except for income tax purposes. By the way, I wrote you that I am going to make out your New York State tax as agent and you will please send me the amount of your earnings *last year* from January 1st 1929 to Dec. 31st 1929. Please figure it exactly. As for the money I do count—and *we* may count on—I have $550—in the savings bank, $260 in the checking account, $60 salary due me—in all we have here about $850.

From "my broker" I went to New York to meet Zukofsky (I am somewhat tired and can not write as clearly as I should like). Zukofsky has a letter from Ezra Pound in which he asks for some of my work. It seems that a French magazine has asked him to translate a number of Americans for an American number and he may use something of mine. Zukofsky suggested that I send him something new (Pound wanted something of mine that is "howling" for publication) well, you know my "still, small voice." However, I am sending him the two stories ("Passage-at-Arms" and "Evening in Greenwich Village"). *The Menorah* still has them, but if they appear at all, they appear in French—so that's all right, I guess. Besides, they are prose and much easier to translate. However, they may be too long. It is impossible for me to type them at present—even that—and I am having them done at a public stenographer's.

Darling, I am working as hard as I can at the place to sweep the work out of the way, and be able to ask to go back to half time, I found that I could not turn out enough work at the place with my earlier risings. If they do not let me go back to half time, I must look for something else to do, I think. Well, in a month or two I expect to know definitely. In the meantime, I will be able to do little, I expect, except for scraps of verse.

I am going out tonight—to see the Chinese actor who is here. I am anxious to see that type of play. It is possible to get a seat Monday night at a fair price. Tomorrow a troupe of Japanese actors open up in Japanese plays and I expect to see them—but my own work![1]

Darling, I am delighted with all the Shakespeare you send me and with your interest in your work. I am delighted with your letters—they are yourself. Sweetheart, I reach out for you many times. I can not think of you without a quickening of the pulse. But, darling, pollyannaish, I sometimes think that this separation is not so bad; it has given me, I think, the necessary perspective to see you—although, God knows, for years I have

---

[1] *The New York Times* announced the arrival of the Japanese Theatre in an article which predicted that "their Kan-Geki plays will bring an exotic and exciting drama form to New York" (2 March 1930): 9: 4.

loved you. Certainly, though, it has given me the perspective to see my feelings about you. Marie, I have always thought it silly to talk and write about love, and now it seems a sensible subject to your

Charles

To Marie Syrkin, [March 4, 1930]

Midnight
Tuesday–Wednesday

[Marie,]

I called up your aunt today and was duly informed that your son is wonderfully well. I will call again Friday and hope to hear the same.

I forgot in yesterday's letter two small pieces of news: the first, there is a chance that my *Uriel Acosta* will be played at the University of Wisconsin. So Elliot Cohen told me—but how much chance—I do not know. Second, Zukofsky is teaching at Textile High School, taking the place of a teacher who will be away for some time. I thought it was you, but said nothing. However, he told me it was a Miss Winter.

If I see by your Monday letter that you have not received the package I sent Feb 21st, I'll have it traced. Anyway, I'll send you another Saturday from the first place—the package that came so promptly. And, darling, how about your birthday. What do you want? Please, honey.

Received proofs from *The Menorah* today of my verse. Of course, as soon as it is printed I'll send you a copy, bone of my bone and flesh of my flesh. Especially, since they are printing the love poems (27 in all not counting those they have printed and the Luzzato Dialogue which they are going to print separately).[1]

Sweetheart, I never get enough of your letters—even though I read each several times. Darling, forgive me that I am not writing on; it is 10 past midnight now. Darling, I kiss you.

C.

---

[1] Reznikoff is referring to his "A Dialogue: Padua 1727" which appeared in *The Menorah Journal*. 18:3 (March 1930): 220.

Some day, when I am not so tired, I may write you some real sonnets—anyway, something that will tell you just what I feel for you—all that I feel.

To Marie Syrkin, [March 6, 1930]

Thursday Evening.

[Marie,]

I did not write you last night. I stopped at the post-office at 32d Street to do so, but I was too tired and sleepy to write sense—or even nonsense.

Darling, your Monday letter came this morning and I will make out your income tax, including the $90 from the Zionists, but not the money from Aaron—because this is not income, but a contribution.

I have asked the place where I bought the candy etc. (and where they were to include the stationery) to trace the shipment, but I hope you will have received it by the time this letter arrives. In any event, it is being traced. Because you may not get it, I am going to have a little package made up at Macy's for you and have that sent this Saturday (although it may not get off until Monday). However, this will be the last until your birthday. Now, darling, please tell me what to get. I was thinking of getting a wristwatch (a standard brand—Bulova or like that) but if you would prefer something else, why not tell me. Really, honey, we should not stand on ceremony.

I am mailing the two stories to Zukofsky tonight. The public stenographer did not make a good job of it: I found about ten mistakes and it is typed on the poorest paper. Well, it can't be helped: he must send it off this week, and I could not do it until Sunday. But no more public stenographers. Besides, they are expensive. This one charged me $3.00 for typing 15 pages (she brought it up to 19)—no carbon. When I gave the stories to her, she told me cheerfully that she would correct my punctuation and whatever faulty constructions she would find. I asked her—gently—not to trouble, but I don't think she liked that. I also stepped into a local printer tonight to find out what he wants for "By the Waters of Manhattan 1930." Only $125! I can do the job myself in about 40 hours—and I have the paper. Well, I won't have it printed nor printed myself just yet. *The Menorah*, as I wrote you, have taken all but 5 (and none of these 5 are very much.)

I have tripled my output of definitions. If I can keep it up—and I think I can—there is no question about my speed. But I can't do a thing of my own. Well, in about a month and a half I think I'll be through. Then, I'll talk half time and vacation. Darling, if only you could be divorced in May and I could marry you in Reno or California. Or, perhaps, I'd wait—if I can't get a vacation in time—until you come back and we would be married as soon as you did and go away to a quiet place somewhere near here. (Of course, you would see David first.) Well, darling, more than a month has gone, and it won't be long now, I hope.

Now that I haven't written a thing of my own for more than a week, I am full of ideas, of course. But I am not going to do anything until I smash those definitions.

Loveliest, dearest, darlingest—forgive me, I am lovesick.

Charles

I would like to write on and on to you. It is almost like talking to you. But it is late. Another day gone—but one day nearer to you—I hope! dearest.

To Marie Syrkin, [March 7, 1930?]

Friday evening

[Marie,]

I phoned your aunt today to ask about David, and she tells me that he is well. I also asked that he write to you frequently, and she promised to see that he would.

C.R.

To Marie Syrkin, [March 8, 1930]

Saturday Evening

Marie darling: It is a habit of writers, I suppose, to forget their own troubles by watching those of others; and so I want to tell you—I suppose you have seen in the papers that there is a lot of suffering in New York, many homeless men, many out of work. They are not like the professional beggars—they don't come up to you and beg, but pass you for the most part looking straight ahead. Last Sunday my cousin took us—father, sister and myself—to the Bronx in his automobile and he went through the Bowery. It was about 5 in the afternoon and there were many breadlines: the first I saw—the men were standing in squads of four or six close together and the line was all of a block long and turned around the corner. They were lined up next to the curb, and as we went swiftly past, I saw that one man was dead or had fainted. He was propped stiffly against a stoop— an old man, his hat was off, and I could see his white hair and face as white as limestone. No one was near him, he was all alone on the stoop, and the army of men in the breadline stood in their places alongside the curb.

This afternoon, I went to New York intending to go to the Chinese plays again (I asked your aunt to come Friday but she could not go; unfortunately, the plays end this week. But they were such a success, that they are sure, I think, to come back next year. Then, honey, you and I will see them together, I hope—). Well, darling, they were all sold out and no standing room, so I went on to 42d Street, uncertain what to do. I had had lunch, but I stepped into Folti's—Fischer and had a baked apple and cream, a large glass of milk and a cake. I could not make up my mind what to do— it was cold outside, sunny but a cold wind was blowing, and so I walked down 42d St., not particularly relishing the idea of a walk, tired with the week's work, and so I came to Bickford's cafeteria. I know they have good coffee and I was about to go in, when a man at the door murmured something about coffee. I put my hand in my pocket to give him a dime. "May I go in with you?" he said. "Certainly," I answered, and we went in together. He was a man of about fifty, his hair all grey, for he took his cap off as we went in, wearing rough clean clothes, his face extremely thin. We walked up to the counter, and I said to him, "What will you have?" He pointed to a cruller and said—timidly, the way a child might ask its father, "May I have one of these, sir, with my coffee?" "Don't you want something else first?" I said. "How about some soup?" "That would be fine, sir." Bickford's serve rolls instead of crackers with their soup. Now their soup is tasteless, I think, but their rolls are fine. I was thinking that heavier food might be bad for a hungry man, and, besides, I felt he ought to eat a little at a time. "Suppose you eat the soup now," I said, "and later we'll have something else." I ordered a cup of coffee and a slice of pineapple (thinking, here am I buying luxuries) and followed him to his table. "I'll be sitting over there," he said as he left with the soup. He was waiting for me, and he began eating in the greatest hurry. "Take your time," I said, "I can't, sir; I'm nervous," he answered. Then as he ate, he said to me, "I was at the waterfront all day trying to get on a boat to work my way home to Maine. I come from Portland. I never thought I'd come to this." "One can never tell," I said just to show that I was interested. "Oh, I'm going right home," he said. "How is the soup?" I asked knowing it was bad. "Fine. Fine, why this is nourishing, this is fine." I thought, he can sit on in Bickford's for hours and rest; as for me, it occurred to me that I wanted to go to the exhibit of paintings at 57th St. in the Modern Gallery (where you were with me once). "You must excuse me," I said, "but I have to go. You just take your time," and I stood up. "Now your check is 15¢, here is 50¢, and get a cup of coffee and whatever else you want," and I wished him better luck. He looked up at me and his face lit up and his dull blue Yankee eyes glowed. I felt a little ashamed of myself because I could have given him more than 50¢ (you would have); I felt cheap at having bought so much thankfulness for so little—and I went on to the pictures. You see, honey, there are so many petty fakers about; I don't mind giving anybody who asks a dime—beyond that, I hesitate. But, after I had given him the 50¢, I knew this man was genuinely in need; still, I could not at the moment think of how to give him a little more help gracefully; because, I was anxious to make him feel that I was just a friend, that it was only an accident that I was not in his place and he in mine and so I did nothing. Anyway, darling, I have felt loathsomely fat all afternoon; I must become lean as a lamppost not to be ashamed of myself.

By the way, Morrow, when he walked home with me pointed out that in the "Apocrypha" what he liked was that Lot had dignity.[1] People write of such scenes with contempt, or amusement, they belittle these people either sympathetically or humorously, I, he said, manage to give them size and dignity despite their circumstances. Now, I like that in Morrow's criticism, and if I can do this, I am glad to do this. Darling, I want to write and write, not only to you, but to everybody of a thousand things; I feel perfectly adolescent.

Darling, I wish so much that you were here again, or I with you; but, now, our old enemy Time has become my friend. Time flies; fly, Time!

Charles

Darling, here is all this space and I am tempted to start all over again and tell you how much I love you, how precious you are to me, that I kneel and kiss your hand, daughter of twenty-five generations of rabbis—but, I have

---

[1] Reznikoff's "Apocrypha" was published in *The Menorah Journal* 14:2 (February 1928): 163–87.

just bought 19 stamped envelopes, there will be other letters, and besides I will write to you for the rest of my life, even when we are married and living together.

To Marie Syrkin, [March 10, 1930]

Monday Evening

Darling: I received your letters of Thursday and Friday this morning. May 12 has become the most important day of the year—but, no, not as important as our wedding day.

What I sent Pound I did on Zukofsky's suggestion; after all, he is the "shatchen." Besides, Pound wrote that he preferred prose, since it is easier to translate. Zukofsky is writing him that he may use anything he has. I set nothing on it and don't you. If anything comes of it, so much the better. By the way, I never said a word to Zukofsky about you: so don't worry about Oscar. Zukofsky is still a substitute: he has not passed the exams.

I hope that for your reading in Shakespeare you are using the set at the library and not yours in fine print; of course, darling, I love you with or without glasses—but you won't like glasses—for a while.

I hope I get the ring card back from you by Saturday; because I should like to buy everything this Saturday that you may surely get it on time, for the Saturday after may be too late. I hope you won't mind getting your gifts a few days earlier: I think that's better than a few days late. If you want anything else than a ring and a wrist-watch, please let me know; because these are what I expect to get, but I do want to get just what you want; so please be frank as ever. I expect to buy at Macy's and they will be able to fix the size, if it is not just right, and also the watch. Darling, there is no pleasure like buying things for one you love: you know how it is when you buy things for David.

Yesterday being Sunday, and since I did not do a bit of my own work all week, I planned not one novel, but a series to last until the crack of doom—my doom. However, I do not intend to begin for at least a month—until I finish definitions up to the end of the volume (the objective). I am speedier every day (partly because I do nothing else but their work); and should I be through in a month or so—I'll talk vacation and half-time: that is, I hope to be through by April 15 or May 1st at this rate. Well, we'll see. My novel plan is quite feasible; and now I'll tell you about it—no,

I won't. If I do it, I'll surprise you. Certainly, you'll be surprised.

Darling, I hope you don't get tired of my affirmations of love—but, whenever I use the word, thinking of you, it seems to me new and holy. It always seems to me as if it is a word that I discovered, and the only word that I can think of to express all the emotion that wells up in me—always when I think of you, darling. I love you, Marie darling, I love you; the word does not seem a bit trite to me now.

Charles

To Marie Syrkin, [March 12,1930]

Wednesday Evening

Darling: I received your letter of Monday this evening (the air-mail is back to its old speed), and the piece of string you enclosed. Very well, it shall be a ring, candy, and flowers. I can buy you the wrist watch whenever you want it anyway. Why special days? But I did see some lovely models. Well, honey, even if we must buy gifts only on special days, I hope we shall have many such together. I intend to buy the ring at Macy's so that in case it will not fit—they can fix it—that is, if I can find a ring I think you'd like. However, I have a great respect for Macy's prices due to this, that a watch I priced in a jewelry shop for $35—(the standard net price) is—the same grade and model—$25 in Macy's. So, in the matter of rings, of which I know nothing, if in doubt, I shall certainly buy it there. I will order the flowers at Tripels—a new store at 5th Ave. and 47th St., and the candy will come from the first store I bought things for you (47th St. too, I think). So, darling, unless you hear to the contrary, these things will go out this Saturday (flowers will be ordered to be delivered on your birthday) and now no more about it.

It is curious, but I get—well, you might call it an electric shock—from the small piece of colored string you enclosed. Honestly, the thought that you touched it, that it was about your finger, gives me a curious sensation along the nerves of my fingers. I know this is horrible sentimentality—but it's true. This is how I felt and how I feel. As I look at it and feel its silky texture my heart turns in my bosom—alas, what a sentimentalist I have become. And, unashamed, I write this down, and add—many, many kisses, and that I love you very much, and all that old "drivel"—that is so deadly true to me, and, I hope, to you, darling, beloved, dearly beloved. Yours,

Charles

To Marie Syrkin, [March 14, 1930]

Friday Evening

[Marie,]

Called up your aunt today and she told me that David is fine. Asked her out, but she cannot go with me tomorrow because she has an appointment.

Received the card with ring measure today in time for tomorrow.

The Japanese players were terrible—a sort of mixed Ziegfeld follies, cheap melodrama, and acrobatics. Bah! But the Chinese! Well, the plays are very old, some from the 6th, some from the 9th centuries, I believe. The acting was exquisite—all idealized into almost a dance, the voices— when you got used to them—like soft drums and wooden hammers beating on brass or glass. I don't know whether or not you would have liked them as I did, but I came out anxious to do more plays—but you insist they are not plays. In other words, I don't want you to think that you have missed something: it meant something to me because it handled certain aesthetic problems as I should like to handle them.

I have finished a difficult piece of work at the office today; from now on I hope it will go on easier. I have still about 21 pages to do and hope to do it in 21 working days. (I should like to write—now—much more, but there is a terrific clatter (well, terrific is exaggeration) going on: my sister is giving a party, doorbell ringing, people are talking—you know.)

I am feeling exceedingly cheerful today, principally, I think, because I finished that difficult tract of work. (It is impossible to go on now: people are walking about, using the telephone—the party is on.)

Darling, I was tired last night and had a headache; I went to bed and perhaps thinking of you as much as I did cured me, because I woke up fresh and chipper. Good night, sweetheart. (There goes the door-bell again, and again. It is impossible to write more. I steal a kiss from you, and go down to meet the folks.)

Charles

To Marie Syrkin, [March 15, 1930]

Saturday afternoon

Marie, lovely and darling one! I regret that I have to talk so much (as it were) to you about your birthday gift (slight as it is) but—well, if you were here it would be simpler and pleasanter, not that it is anything but simple or pleasant (this reads as if I had been reading Henry James, but I assure you it is natural).

Today—a glorious, sunny day—brought such a mob of shoppers out, that Macy's, never uncrowded, was like New Year's Eve at Times Square. I regretted that my shopping had to be done on this afternoon, particularly as rings should be studied long and carefully—even inexpensive ones. The shopgirl, however was very nice and when I told her—as I had to—that it was going to Reno became all the more so, since she had recently come from there. She knew where Island Avenue is and said that Reno was an unpleasant place. She said people like it very much or not at all; clearly, you and she are in the same class—the respectable. Before that I selected a ring of white gold, the stone a genuine aqua-marine (it seems that even of this inexpensive stone there is a synthetic variety). The stone looks (in the gloom of Macy's) like the sky on a bright Spring morning; it is a rather long oblong and ought to look well on your kind of finger. The size will be 5¼ and I hope it will be just right; if not, you can have it fixed. It will take about a week to have the size made right and then it should be sent to you special delivery. You ought to receive it just in time; I hope you will like it and, if not, I am sure Macy will exchange it. I have receipts, and should it not be delivered, we are protected.

Then I went to the candy department and saw a pound box from Hungary (a variety I had never seen) and it did look interesting. So I had that sent to you. Unfortunately, there is a fuss about getting candy sent—innumerable slips. I meekly suggested that it be insured, since that seems to be the routine in the other stores, but that seems to educe so much trouble in Macy's that the manager or floor-walker (a stupid person) told me not to have it done. Well, then I asked to have it sent special handling (so you ought to get it this week). In any event, if you don't want to, you need not open it until your birthday.

Then, darling, I went to a new florist's on 5th Ave. and ordered two doz. red roses to be delivered to you March 25th. They will probably be as nice as any I would select, little as I know about flowers. And with that, darling, the pleasant business of the afternoon ended for me; but you, I hope, will receive everything as I hope and plan.

The party last night lasted until late; I expect to spend this evening taking a long walk.

I am glad that I write verse sometimes, because sometime I may be able to put into that kind of music how much I love you, how much happiness I wish for you, and how lucky for me that I found you among all these millions.

Charles

To Marie Syrkin, [March 16, 1930]

Sunday afternoon

[Marie,]

I spent all morning riding around with "my broker" and he informed me that I have been losing money—that I might draw some of it. It seems there is a new kind of ticker used now and his customer's man (who is taking care of my account) is not quite used to it. I told him I would draw none of it, because I did not need it now. Very well, he answered, let it be a nest egg. It did not seem to me good sportsmanship to grab and run the moment things were not going favorably; besides, I am sure should the losses continue, my broker would stop all future speculation so that I would probably have as much saved as if I draw on it; and, moreover, I am with him and not out of it. I think he simply told me this that I might not expect additional profits for a while.

I have 21 pages of definitions to write—that will probably take me a month, if I do no work of my own—and I intend to do none until I clear that up. In this month, too, I hope I can lose about ten pounds, for I am getting too fat. I weighed myself this morning and stripped weigh 174. When I met you first I weighed in my clothes about 154. Love, is this a man in love? Yes, this is a man happily in love. But, darling confessor, I am going to report my weight to you from now on that I may become slender again.

The sun is shining, my sister is playing the clavichord she bought in Germany—playing the music written for it two centuries or so ago; everything is peaceful and Sunday like here. Darling, I hope you have become accustomed to Reno and find it as peaceful and restful as I hoped. I wish you would think of it as a vacation—a vacation from getting up at 5 in the morning, a vacation from a lot of useless worry and fretting and irritation, and the quiet prelude to joy and happiness with your husband

Charles

To Marie Syrkin, [March 17, 1930]

Monday Evening

[Marie,]

To your hopes for our happiness, including David's permit me to add "amen." Please do not regard your birthday dolefully: on the contrary, think of it as the beginning of a *vita nuova*. You are serving three months in Reno; with that I hope all the liabilities of the past canceled, and only the assets brought forward.

I see from your letter that your birthday is on the 22d. It was stupid of me to think it was the 25th. Now, your flowers are supposed to be delivered on this day, your candy ought to come about the middle of this week, and your ring about the middle of next. Well, then you must think of your birthday not as a holiday, but as holidays, a holiday season—like Passover or other Jewish feasts.

I am very glad that the matter of the seal seems settled; it seems to me that your divorce will be good and unquestioned anywhere, including New York. I don't think you ought to leave Reno until you get your divorce, even though the trip west will take another week. You ought to leave Reno quietly, without the uneasiness attendant upon a return; and ought, it seems to me, stay in Reno until your divorce is granted. However, it still seems so far off that I cannot make plans. I would prefer, I think, if I cannot leave in time, that you stay in Reno until May 12th, then go West and stay there at ease, as long, or as little as you like, and then come home and see David. And then we would marry and go away together for a while. I think, if you were to see David first, you would be happier. However, it may be a better plan for me to be in Reno by the 12th of May, marry you there, go with you to the coast and back. Well, that seems so far off now, darling; but it will come soon. In fact the second plan seems far better to me; then, perhaps, we could stop off at a number of places instead of coming right home. I hope I will be able to work this out.

I was out with Zukofsky last night. The Guggenheim people have rejected him (I am convinced they give these scholarships practically only to people with academic or what might be considered important editorial connections—they play safe); he also failed in his examination for a high-school teacher's position. He is no longer at Textile—was there only four days. One of the questions on the exam was on modern poetry—now he did not have to take it and if I were Zukofsky that is one of the questions I would avoid if I wanted to pass the exam. However, he took it and got only 3 out of 10 etc.

That reminds me, how is your work on Shakespeare and your own work?

Darling, it is almost 11 and I am afraid I have lost the last mail tonight. Good-night, darling; I kiss you again and again.

Charles

To Marie Syrkin, [March 18, 1930]

Tuesday Evening

[Marie,]

Called up your aunt today and she told me David was fine; will call again Friday, as you asked me to.

No letter from you today, we had some people to dinner last night; they stayed until midnight. Today was dark (now it is raining); my stenographer did not come in this morning. All in all, my work did not go smoothly today. I expect to be in bed by 9; and hope to do more tomorrow. I am very sleepy, and if it were not to let you know about David, I would not write this evening and afflict you with my "vapours."

The Menorah dinner will be Thursday this week. Zukofsky, last Sunday, told me that "Cliff" Fadiman has informed Trilling and Cohen that he has no use for any of my writing, including the prose; I gathered as much from his manner which has been hostile—as if I were pestering him for something. *The New Freeman* (No. 1.) has a review of Stendhal by Fadiman and I read most of it; it was interesting to me as a sidelight on Fadiman's thinking and writing. However, if I make any comments, even you, I am afraid, will think there is something personal in my attitude, and I might keep on protesting that I am talking of ideas only—neither my mother, my sister, nor you would believe me. I am glad, however, Zukofsky told me of Fadiman, because now I understand what in his manner has always puzzled me—for he never spoke directly to me. He has, I believe, a great respect for Zukofsky—they were at college together. Well, well, what does it matter—if I could only work. And I hope to. Good night, darling.

C.

To Marie Syrkin, [March 19, 1930]

Wednesday Evening

Marie: I have had no letter from you for two days, and am beginning to feel worried about you. I hope I get a letter tomorrow morning.

I have had to make a character affidavit for an old friend who is about to be admitted to the bar, and this has taken up most of the evening; now it is growing late.

The work in the place is as hard as ever, but I am whittling it down: 18 pages of definitions left—at least 18 days of work—and then? But, really, I am not thinking about it; I have put my nose to the grindstone and see no farther.

Darling, I was sure I would get a letter from you today. Even if you have nothing to write, you might just say, Hello! These sudden silences (the 2d) are very disturbing: I understand, of course, that there may be a storm over the Rockies and no air mail going. Well, I hope I get a letter tomorrow morning. And now, good night, loveliest. It is very late—for me; good night, beloved—until tomorrow.

Charles

To Marie Syrkin, [March 20, 1930]

Thursday

[Marie,]

Your letter of St. Patrick's day came this morning; and I was glad to know that your not writing (if you did miss a day) was simply due to having nothing to write about. Long ago I became convinced that you are beautiful, wise, and good; and it will take a good deal to convince me of the contrary—if ever. Of course, if your letter happens to be particularly

114

good, I am all the more pleased; but I am pleased at any letter—glad to know that you are. If you are ever too tired to write, or better yet, have nothing to write about, just say hello!—you know there is no need to write me witty or clever letters or wise letters or even letters full of affection. I love you as you are—and you are all of these, wise, witty, and clever, at times—but the variations of the day have not made any difference to me. However, if you do not write at all, I begin to think that you are sick or hurt or—something or other, and that does concern me.

I am writing this at a post office on the way to *The Menorah* dinner, and have just finished wading through hundreds of books defining "provide," "providing," "provided," "proviso," "provision"; therefore, no doubt, I have not made my point as clear as I should like—but you will understand.

Very often, darling, I think how we will soon be together again—alone together—and I with no other beauty to look at than your beauty, no other voice to hear but your voice. At this moment, I see, that if I could sing, I would begin to sing—to the disturbance of those writing about me, nor can you hear me—as yet. I hope to write you tomorrow.

Charles

To Marie Syrkin, [March 23, 1930]

Sunday morning.

Marie, loveliest and best, darling wife and my Sunday girl: I did not write you yesterday. I was going over to a post-office to do so in the evening, but I called up home and was told that your special delivery letter had come. I could not write you until I had read your letter; there is no air mail collection after 4:30; there is no mail collection in this neighborhood at all on Sunday until the afternoon—so, reluctantly, I put off your letter until this morning. Besides, there is so much I want to write you about, and I was up at 4 o'clock Saturday morning. As for the Lewin letter, I wrote you that I would write them today, so, as you see, your letter came before I wrote at all. I do not want to speculate about whether your fears as to Aaron's reaction are groundless or not—and as to whether he would hear or not. I am not going to take any chances at all. I know the Lewins are constantly meeting, talking, and writing to people who know you and me and may know Aaron or one of his brothers. Why take the chance? So I'll not write at all now. I cannot write of you as "a very good friend"; that will have only one meaning in their gossip. Besides, you will probably get the best reception from them as the woman I am to marry. However, I plan to do this: as soon as you have your divorce, I will send night-letters to both Lewins and the Gaers—that will be quite *à la* Hollywood—and it will get to them before you will be able to telephone them. By the way, I urge you to get in touch with the Gaers before you engage a room (though you ought to *reserve* one by mail); Fay Gaer is a lovely girl, simple, natural, very intelligent, very good. She is very poor, but she will share all she has with such simple friendliness, that I have always enjoyed their society much more than that of the Lewins when they came to town. For instance, when Al took me to a play, he never thought of taking me to a play I would want to see, such as *Journey's End*, but any play, one of those he had to see. He had to see and did see "Journey's End" too. All I mean to say is he felt he ought to take me to some play, but he never thought twice what. Well, such hospitality doesn't please me very much. Of course, Al may be away on location, Milly may be out-of-town, too; Joseph Gaer may be working on a farm etc. Fay Gaer has just had a one-man show of her sculpture in San Francisco.

I notice that you ask me about the humanist controversy that is "raging." I haven't read much these days: I suppose the pupils of that Harvard "prof," whose name I can't think of this moment but whose book on French criticism I read ten years or so ago, have begun to discuss his theory in the journals.[1] I did not think it particularly illuminating at the time—his name is Babbitt—he is anti-romanticism etc. Well, as far as I am concerned, romanticism of the early 19th century, is so thoroughly dead, that only a college professor and his boys, could think it alive. If the humanistic controversy rages about Babbitt, I care little about—but, perhaps, only because I know—as yet—little about it. However, you might read Babbitt yourself—he has a book called the New Humanism, I believe.

To come to a more immediate problem, I saw Bergman yesterday afternoon. He tells me that "the novel" is practically accepted by Charles Boni—of course, that is only Bergman's story—that he would give me an advance if I wanted it, that Boni will pay me $1000 outright for the paper cover rights, if he takes it, royalty on the bound copies, motion picture

---

[1] Irving Babbitt (1865–1933), was a leader of the "New Humanism" movement in American letters. His books include: *Literature and the American College* (1908), *The New Laokoön* (1910), *Rousseau and Romanticism* (1919), and *Democracy and Leadership* (1924).

116

rights etc., and that I ought to get to work as energetically and as soon as possible; that Kitty Parrotts, whom I know, made $60,000 out of "Ex-wife" etc., etc.[1] In the evening I went to Elliot Cohen's and met Fadiman there; he seemed friendly and we had a long and animated dialogue, in which I was voluble and he indissoluble, in which I was eccentric and he concentric, in which I was fireworks, and he, simply, a bonfire. From this, O my hunter of moths, you conclude no doubt that I was pinned, pricked, and stuck on the dinner-table as a mere curiosity. You are mistaken: my self-esteem escaped their pin-pricks and still buzzes loudly. By the way, Elliot told me they are considering seriously the Greenwich Village story (you know, the Iceland saga, bookshop etc.) for next month's *Menorah*, but he wants a few changes. I may make them during the first of the week, if not too tired, perhaps to-day. Marie, darling, I think I am going to talk to Kiser about half time work at once; I shall have finished all the unfinished work by Monday or Tuesday, and it seems the merest cowardice to hang on to a full-time job without saying a word, while I may be able to do much better, for the sake of a possible and rather poor half-time job. I have done all that I should in finishing my work; from now on to work full time, when I have my own work of such urgency and opportunity, seems almost incomprehensible timidity and stupidity. Marie, it's like going into business, there are some risks to be taken, but the rewards are great. I see this clearly: if I work hard enough, have time and energy enough, I can write novels that will sell. If I do, it means freedom from drudgery, travel together, children etc. I burn no bridges behind me: I have a thousand dollars saved, my stockbroker has for me say about five hundred dollars; I ought to be able to make about $30 a week at some kind of writing or selling, if Kiser lets me go. Now, I ought to delay no longer—both for your sake and my own: I ought to talk to Kiser this week about half time at once. I ought to be prepared to be fired or to quit, if he does not let me. Otherwise, it is two or three months more, surely. I owe them nothing. Why should I let them grab more than they originally planned at the expense of—perhaps—my future? our future? I know this is a reversal of my previous position, but whereas then I thought the Boni plan was merely favorable, now I think his attitude much more so—the novel almost accepted. In any event, darling, do not agitate yourself about this matter: it is my problem to solve, and I must solve such problems again and again. It is true that the road to Zion lay through the deserts; nevertheless, our

---

[1] Katherine Ursula Parrott's (1902–) novel *Ex-Wife* was in its ninth printing by April 1930.

ancestors refused to be slaves in Egypt. I take your hand, daughter of Israel, and hold it firmly; you shall beat your timbrel yet and dance before the Lord in Zion.

Charles

To Marie Syrkin, [March 23, 1930?]

Sunday Evening

[Marie,]

I have come home early—I wrote and mailed you (from New York) a letter this morning, but now, the house silent, for I am alone, I am thinking of you and hoping that you will not be worried about my leaving or losing my job (I assure you, Marie, I will do my best to stay on—at half time) and I cannot help writing you again just to tell you, darling girl, that I love you and that I can not think of my happiness without thinking of yours. x

Charles

To Marie Syrkin, [March 24, 1930]

Monday Evening

Darling and best! Under separate cover I am sending you a copy of this month's *Menorah*.[1]

If my letter yesterday was too stupid, forgive me; I have a notion that it was idiotic. But all the walk I kept thinking of you (3 hours twilight and night) and when I reached home I was almost in a frenzy of love and gloom; if I had been less tired, the mood might have resulted in two or three good lines.

I hope you have received the candy and ring by this; in any event let me know by Saturday that I may start inquiries, if you haven't; the flowers will not come until tomorrow.

---

[1] The March 1930 issue of *The Menorah Journal* contained Reznikoff's poem "A Dialogue: Padua 1727" referred to as "the Luzzato Dialogue" in Reznikoff's February 26 and March 4 letters to Syrkin.

118

I have at least three more weeks full time work at the place—full steam ahead—and maybe four. As I wrote you, I am not doing a thing of my own—but exercise, long walks etc. I have lost 3 pounds since last week.

Darling, if by the time I can leave, if I have a hat to sell, I may sell my way across to the coast. (My cousin sometimes has a hat that sells like wildfire to the department stores; if he has, he will let me sell it and the commission ought to pay my way). However, May may be too early; September is the usual month. Well, it's a month off, and we have lots of time.

My father has been busy at his writing and has 50,000 words of his autobiography in short chapters—a story in each. He has written an independent short story (1000 words) and I promised to begin to translate it this Sunday. I suppose I won't finish it for a week; as soon as I do, if its any good, I will send a copy to *The Menorah* (Nathan Reznikoff, author), and another to you—daughter-in-law!

Darling, won't you like to keep an orthodox Jewish home? Bless candles on Friday, keep all the holidays? I like to think of you blessing the candles in our home. I kiss you a hundred times. Good night until tomorrow.

Charles

To Marie Syrkin, [March 25, 1930]

Tuesday Evening

[Marie,]

Spoke to your aunt today and she tells me that David is getting along "fine." Last time we were out I had promised to take her to an Italian restaurant (I had Luigino's in mind), and today I arranged to take her Saturday, if she wants to go. I will try to meet her downtown—but, of course, it is as she wishes.

I am glad you liked the candy, and I hope the ring and flowers will please you. As for what I'll do when the definitions are ended—of course, I'll ask for half-time. Should I get it, I plan to resume all my old activities and write 500 words a day of a novel—the first of a series—I have in mind (didn't tell you of this, I think). In addition, I plan another source of income to make up the loss—advertising or journalism or law. I must do this in case the law writing is out—and there is no future at it. However,

I have always liked the proverb—*mann tracht und Gott lacht.*[1]

As for your Ph.D. in Shakespeare, I suppose if you work steadily at it something will occur to you—besides, you do enjoy the work. I wonder if there is anything in this: The Shakespearean dramatis personae—the hero, the heroine, the villain, the clown—for instance, Hamlet and Macbeth are very much alike—is it possible to build up a composite hero, heroine etc? Are not the hesitations of Brutus like that of Hamlet? It is the vaguest idea—perhaps, you see something in it—I wonder if the multitude of Shakespeare's characters cannot be reduced to three or four—perhaps to one! Ah, to show Iago and Hamlet one! A very interesting job—if true. Darling Marie, Marya, Miriam, Mariechen, darling wife, good night until tomorrow's light will bring another night and I may write again to my delight. (This is what the Hebrew [illegible] must be like). In all seriousness, darling, good night, and—shall I whisper it?—I love you.

Charles

To Marie Syrkin, [March 26, 1930]

Wednesday Evening.

[Marie,]

If you are marking off days on your calendar, I am marking off pages of definitions. I have 13 more. I ought to finish by April 15th. Then, 2 weeks for writing up the material and revising the stenographer's work. By May 1st I ought to be through. Now by May 15th the railroads offer reduced rates to the Coast and back (including stop-overs) but those reduced rates ($120), exclusive of pullmans, do not go into effect until May 15th. We have several courses: 1st you go to the coast after the 12th and I meet you on your return and we go somewhere (after marrying you in New Jersey); 2d I leave New York May 1st (assume that I get a vacation to begin then) and selling to department stores (if my cousin has a good selling hat by that time) make my way (and most of my expenses) to the Coast, stopping off at Reno (after the 12th) and marrying you there and going on together. 3rd You wait in Reno until the 19th; I will leave on the 15th and

---

[1] "Man strives and God laughs."

120

go straight to Reno by train (this will cost me about $250 including stop-overs).[1] Now I should very much like to go to the Coast together; I think you will be able to see much more and it will be our honeymoon: If conditions here will warrant it, I intend to meet you in Reno. However, there is no use writing about it for a month at least. If I can earn my expenses, I shall certainly go; particularly, if I can earn some of yours. If— well, in a month. I have sunk myself completely into the definitions; I even think of them at home. I want to take work home; I want to get rid of them. It is too bad I did not begin with "love"; I would be so learned in that subject. By the way, I do not know why I assume so "blithely," as you say, that you are going to marry me. I notice that you said nothing of the Marie Reznikoff sonnet—even the fact that it made exactly 14 lines did not seem to please you overmuch.[2] Honey, darling, will you marry me?

Charles

To Marie Syrkin, [March 28, 1930]

Friday Evening.

[Marie,]

Your aunt tells me that David is getting along "wonderfully"; he has gained ½ lb. Your aunt has postponed our visit to an Italian restaurant to a future date; she is very cordial, however, and—I flatter myself—is very friendly. Well, I do like and respect her much more than I did—due to our evening out and our talk then. In fact I respect her immensely.

I am glad your ring and flowers came. As for the ring, wait until you get back. I'll keep the receipts, and they'll fix it for you. And I was afraid it would be too small because I asked them to make it 5¼.

I have about 10½ pages of definitions to do—about 2 weeks work—and I begin to sniff the fresh air of freedom.

I hope you sun yourself a good deal and have lots of the fresh mountain air.

I suppose Tolstoi did have—what might be called—a romantic view of war. I don't think, after the war books that are being written now, that those who inherit this civilization will ever have that view again—as

---

[1] $250 would have been about half the price of a new automobile.
[2] See Reznikoff's letter to Syrkin dated February 19, 1930.

everybody in the west prior to this generation had it. The Chinese poets, however, thousands of years ago, had a view like this generation's. À propos of the starving man—you underestimate the romanticism in "isms," and equally so the power of the "word." However, that is an old quarrel between us; and I refuse to quarrel with you when I cannot kiss at once and make it up. Besides, I don't want to quarrel with you at all—and, by the living god, as King David used to swear, I do want to kiss you.

Charles

To Marie Syrkin, [March 30, 1930]

Sunday afternoon

Darling Mahout (I think this is the technical term for an elephant driver) I have your letter explaining all your tender ministrations of the saleslady forlorn, and was duly amused.

At this point let me explain that I did not write you yesterday for the following bad reason: I left the office to go to New York to buy a spring suit (as I am almost in tatters), and one of my co-workers who comes from a farm in Iowa was anxious to come along to help in the selection; so we walked, and talked of farm life in Iowa and Jewish life in New York City, and I bought apparel befitting one who hopes to take you about in the not so distant future, and before I knew it it was six o'clock, Thereupon, I left my ex-farmer and present law editor and hurried home where my mother was waiting for me to take her to a concert (Toscanini—my sister's tickets). Thereupon I went with my mother to said concert (which interested me slightly), my mother coughing, sneezing, wheezing, whistling etc. during the subway trip, but very quiet during the concert due—perhaps—to will power, or better air—and so I got home at 12 midnight and went to bed feeling very guilty at not writing you—but all the mail in the corner box is not collected until the afternoon Sundays—so it was no use, anyway.

At this point—in this coherent document—permit me to inform you that I called up the Ludins' this morning and asked after the book and was informed that the matter is now in charge of another set of relatives. I spoke to Tima, and she seemed cheerful as usual. I will call them again soon and expect to pay them a visit—when a due report will be forwarded to you in the minutest detail. Tima will no doubt send you a report in the minutest detail and so you will probably know how everything is when I visit the Ludins.

Now I take this sticky post-office pen in hand to inform you of something disagreeable and upsetting at my place of work. On Friday I began the definition "public"; now I was supposed to go as far as the article "Public Lands"—10 pages beyond. In other words, I could clearly see that I would be through by about May 1st. After working at "public" I realized clearly that all the definitions beginning with "public" ought logically to be listed under that word—now there are 11 pages of such definitions after "public lands"—so that instead of having 10 more pages to do I had 21 plus 2 pages of another definition ("proximate cause") which was supposed to be done by someone else but was returned to me. So without going into more shop talk, I have now, about April 1st, work which will take at least six weeks—allowing for writing and revising the stenographer's typing. Now, darling, I have carried the load so far; I don't want to kick over the traces now. But I see my trip west vanishing. Dearest, I see this plan very clearly: you will have completed your Nevada residence by May 5th. It seems to me that it would be safer and avoid any possible question to stay in Reno until the 12th; however, if your lawyer advises you that you may and you feel like it, go to the Coast in the meantime and return to Reno; but I think you ought to stay in Reno until the 12th and then go to the Coast and then come directly to New York since this would be simpler and less bothersome and eliminate any question of residence—no matter what your lawyer says. Now when you get here, and have seen David, I want you to marry me, and, unless the seashore is intolerable to you, we ought to take a place together for the summer—where I could get to my work and you could bring David when you want to. However, if you don't want the seashore we can rent a place in the country from which I can commute. Do you intend to go away for the summer without me? I don't like that at all. But if we had a nice place at the seashore or in the country we could be alone there during the end of May and all of June, and then (the place would be more than one room, I take it) you could bring David there for the summer—and why not in June? Darling, I could marry you as soon as you arrive, and we could arrange for the summer at once.

Charles

To Marie Syrkin, [March 31, 1930]

Darling: I have just come home from meeting Zukofsky, and though it is 11:15 I must write you. Zukofsky had nothing of interest to say this time: so that's that.

Your letter, received this morning, about what the children wrote you was delightful. Sylvia's straw bathtub (this no doubt occurred to you) was suggested, I suppose, by a manger and the Jesus story.

As for my plans—darling, I am tired, excuse me if I am too dull but I wish to be as explicit as possible—I wrote you yesterday that instead of having about 10½ pages more to do, I would have 21½ pages to do. Now, today, I discovered from Kiser that the volume instead of closing at "Public Lands" will continue to "Quieting Title" and that instead of 21½ pages more to do, I have 59½ pages—which, working as hard as I do—I cannot finish in less than three months full time work. And, moreover, Kiser is against part time—as much as ever—but thinking that I might quit on the spot, I suppose, at the very end of our talk said that though half time was impossible until the volume is finished, that, after that, he and Mack would be willing to have me go on at ½ time. I doubt whether if he can keep it, that he will let me. I do not relish at all the idea of working without doing a bit of my own work. If I had the prospect of a steady half-time job, it might be worth it. But I don't think Kiser will let me alone; however, he might. Darling, I will work on until I can think my way out. Of course, the way things have turned out I am a fool for ever letting the half-time go. But it seemed reasonable at the time. Well, I suppose I am a fool. Darling, I am very tired tonight; I can hardly write. I will not change the status quo just yet; I am inclined—well, *this* week, anyway, things, as far as I am concerned, will continue as they are.

Now, darling, as for my plans about ourselves. Don't worry about my giving up this work, if I do; I ought to be able to make at least as much as I would be making on *half-time*. And don't worry, as you have at times intimated, that I would ask you for anything of yours; you know how much I want to give you, and that you should have such ideas—. I plan this: as soon as you return, we marry; you take a place in the country or at least a seashore as you always do for the summer (I pay for this, of course); this seems to me sensible, inexpensive, and with you—blissful. Darling and sweetest girl, I hope this letter does not discourage you; you are not of such flimsy stuff. We must not be afraid of such trivial squalls, I have mastered worse, and you certainly have. Darling, I don't want our marriage to hamper you in the slightest; I mean it to help you in every possible way it can; certainly, I expect it to help me greatly—as knowing you has helped me. Darling, I have about $900 in the bank, I see nothing to worry about. Will you let me kiss you good-night?

Charles

To Marie Syrkin, [April 2, 1930?]

To Marie

1

If you are my wife you are cruel to me, if you are my friend you are kind;
If you are my friend be cruel for all I care, but if you are my wife be kind.

2

I wrote you that I loved you, that when I thought of you I sighed;
Perhaps it merely pleased your vanity and putting the letter down
You went up to the mirror and smiled at your pretty face.

3

I can think of names that would cause your heart to leap;
But at mine you would merely turn your head and smile a welcome—
You try to be kind to me and in your kindness call your kindness love.

I am glad to learn from today's letter that you are all better and have recovered from your overeating (by the way, I could not send anything this Saturday); and I try to think that it is remorse for Tony's dance hall etc. that caused you to overeat. However, I may learn more from tomorrow's letter—that is the letter I expect tomorrow.

Love but no kisses

Charles

To Marie Syrkin, [April 3, 1930]

Thursday morning

[Marie,]

I lay awake most of last night thinking of you at Tony's dance hall, of you on the automobile trip Monday with your landlady picking violets. If you love me somewhat as you loved Maurice a good deal, my unhappiness will not displease you; if you do not care about Aaron, it will merely annoy you. If you love me you would not do what would hurt me, if I knew about it, even though I may never know about it. I used to love your frankness and always forgave you; please do not learn all from the salesladies; be frank now.

C.

To Marie Syrkin, [April 3,1930]

Thursday Evening.

[Marie,]

I had no letter from you today, nor yesterday. It has been stormy these two days, and I suppose the air mail has not been flying. However, if I do not hear from you by tomorrow, I will wire you and you must answer by wire *collect*. (I write this—quite uselessly, because you will not receive this letter until Saturday, I suppose. Perhaps, not until Monday. How I wish you were back.) I am too uneasy to write. I might write you more about yesterday: there were a number of moderately funny incidents—but, really, I can't, Marie. I don't feel jocular at all. I feel black and gloomy because I have not heard from you. I would not mind so much if I did not know you were not well. You used to laugh at me and call me a *"vögele."* Do you know the old German ballad *"Wine Ich ein vögel wöre, Flieh ich zu dir"*?[1] One does not have to be a bird to fly to you, but if I were not trying to hold down a job, if I were not anxious to have money for myself and you!—such money as it is. I can only end on the old saying, now strangely cheerful, *"Time flies."* Dear wife, good night!—a strange wife that one must say good-night

---

[1] "Wenn ich ein Vöglein wär / und auch zwei Flüglein hätt, / flög ich zu dir." ("If I were a bird and had two wings I would fly to you.")

126

to—but, now, only for a little while, and then good day—and good days and years, I hope.

Charles

To Marie Syrkin, [April 7, 1930]

Monday Evening

My darling girl: I have finished—not quite to my satisfaction—about 25 pages of my mother's autobiography and have about 90 left to do. I consider this the hardest part of the job—except, perhaps, finishing off the Joel.[1] However, that will not be forced; it must live and move of its own accord. I am now completely "a *vögele*". Please do not sigh. I see myself now in the business of writing fiction: that is, not writing to order, I do not think that necessary, but writing what I see and feel. I think of myself as one of a hundred thousand Jews who is an operator, a peddler, and goes into business and faces laborious and uncertain and meagre years—at last to have everything. When I went to law school I was really quite stupid at first, but driven on, perhaps by conceit, I ranked second in the class (and in my own judgment first). When I began to work for the American Law Book Co you remember how I trembled from week to week. Well, I worked hard, but I was bad. However, in one year's time I felt the ground firmly under my feet and I was both swift and good. The same thing was true of definitions. I feel that way now about writing. I am slow, clumsy, timid; I commit a thousand gaucheries. But I feel as if there were a gigantic motor within me—whirling a propeller—the hum of a small lonely aeroplane that fills the great vault of heaven. Of course, I may plunge to earth—but I think most of them reach their fields. The whole point is, I think, one must work long enough, hard enough, with enough enthusiasm to become competent. Then, success is only a matter of time. In writing of myself so much, I do so with less diffidence because it seems to me that only by freeing my mouth and hands can I hope to free yours. I hate the notion of your drudgery at least as much, I think, as I hated my drudgery—but I have said

---

[1] "Joel" seems to refer to Reznikoff's novel, *By the Waters of Manhattan* (1930), which he refers to as a work based on an acquaintance Joel Stein in his letter to Syrkin dated February 23, 1930.

this a thousand times. At the end of the term, dear teacher, I hope you will not flunk me.

Charles

To Marie Syrkin, [April 8, 1930]

Tuesday Evening

[Marie,]

I called your aunt today and she told me that "David is fine."

I received my note with your comments this morning. I had never intended to "heap insults on you." In fact, in all my letters to you your essential integrity was never questioned. I don't see how I could have questioned in my writing what I had—and have—never questioned in my mind.

I suppose I have been very stupid about it all; please forgive me. Perhaps, the letters you have received since have shown you more fully what I felt and thought; I have only been conscious of love, misery, and anxiety, but never of insulting.

Charles

To Marie Syrkin, [April 10, 1930]

The American Lawbook Company
Thursday noon

Marie dear:

By this time you have no doubt received two letters of apology. Let's forget all about it, except that when on Saturday I send you a parcel I'll include a pound box of candy for your landlady.

Charles

To Marie Syrkin, [April 10, 1930]

Thursday Evening

Darling,

I have just sent you a telegram which I hope will reach you (as promised) by 8 o'clock tonight. Dearest, your letters came today and I feel dreadfully sorry that in my frenzy I hurt you so. Sweetheart, I have never doubted anything you said *deliberately*. But your letters had become so brief and cut and dried and then your casual remarks—well, please let us forget all about it. I love you dearly, and believe you implicitly. I don't want to write about this misunderstanding and stupidity of mine anymore; I love you and trust you completely. I always have trusted you, but I was worried. Darling, if I could only kiss you. I know that you love me and I know that I love you; as for the rest, our love will find the way.

Now, sweetheart, Kiser stopped yesterday at the door to tell me that the volume may stop at "Public Service," which is only a few pages beyond "Public Lands." So I may be through after all by June 1st, if not sooner. At home, we are all well. My sister has just bought a Victor victrola and radio (the victrola for her music). Tomorrow, I will only be able to write you a brief note because I have to go to a friend of the family after supper. Saturday, as I wrote you today, I hope to send you a parcel. Darling, I hope I could include some Passover dainties, but I suppose the stores where I buy these things do not carry them. I am really including a box of candy which I want you to give to the landlady for taking you on rides. Darling, even in my angriest letters you must have seen how I love you. Very soon now I hope we will be husband and wife, and if any differences should arise, God forbid! we will be able to settle them at once, and not through the medium of letters and intolerable delays and what "a sick fancy" may feed on. Dear wife, I kiss you good-night—if you will let me.

Charles

To Marie Syrkin, [April 11, 1930]

Friday Evening

Dear Wife:

I spoke to your aunt at noon and she was very cheerful: the children and she are feeling fine, and tomorrow Mrs. Epstein is having "a big seder." Perhaps to please me your aunt added that the only thing about it she does not like is that Aaron is invited. (Of course, Mrs. Epstein could not do otherwise.)

Your letter telling me about your physical pain came today (I hope it is nothing worse than a nerve strain.) *Please keep me posted on this.*

In about a month I hope you will be divorced. Until then, darling, for my sake, rest yourself, sun yourself, do as little work as possible, go to bed early, and eat the simplest food (what you would feed David!). For you are my David.

When you are back here, darling, I promise you as much fun as I can give you—and as much as you want. (Darling, I promise: you can go to all the dances you want to, provided you have a respectable escort—even if it isn't me. Now, I am beginning to skirt the fringe of nonsense.)

Marie, tell me when you want Al Lewin's address (Los Angeles) and Gaer's (San Francisco). Also give me a Sunday on which to write them. However, I am not going to write them until you tell me so that I may be able to tell them about when you are coming. Darling, how I hope you are all better when this reaches you. And now, good *shabbas*, good *yomtov*!

Charles

To Marie Syrkin, [April 12, 1930]

Saturday Afternoon

Marie dearest:

I have just had sent you from "Glass" some Droste's *crème de caraque*, some French nougat (ready cut), and some candied grapefruit peel (memories of Mrs. Epstein's!). I have also included a box of French chocolate intended for your landlady. However, if you wish to give her the nougat instead, do as you like. You ought to receive it Wednesday or Thursday. Now, darling, I do not understand what is going on at the place. I wrote you how Kiser told me that we were only going as far as "Public Service Companies." Yesterday, he took all the definitions following "Public" away (saying, "he would get me help"). Now I have about 3 weeks work ahead of me to finish what I have started; and it may be that he cannot wait for me, or that he is breaking in some one else. I don't know; I have said nothing, but have worked steadily. Still, I know that he did not like my statement that I wanted to go back to half-time after I had finished the volume; and his promise that I could was given grudgingly. As a matter of fact, if he had put me on definitions as soon as I had gotten back instead of keeping me for months on "Tables," I might have been through in time—half time. However, I say nothing, but work on, and we shall see. I am a very poor sort, if I cannot earn as much as we would be content with if I were working half time and still doing my own work. With you, I am full of zest and energy; and I think I can accomplish something. Darling, I hope you are all better. I am going home to the Seder and next year, sweetheart, I hope we shall go there together.

Charles

To Marie Syrkin, April 12th [1930]

Saturday.

[Marie,]

I have just sent you a letter from the post-office, and have come home to find your letter of April 10th and your telegram. I suppose I will not receive your explanatory letter until Monday. However, whatever that letter contains, good news or bad news, *you are my wife*, your troubles are mine, and what you say about not considering marriage, because of this, whatever it is, is nonsense: you are married. If you are running no risk by staying until you get your divorce, stay on *by all means*, but if you do, come back at once. Certainly, you do not intend to have anything surgical in any event done to you in Reno, do you? Marie, to use a Yiddish expression, I feel "as if with a hammer on my head."

Dear wife, I want to send you a telegram, but I understand your reluctance to wire me details, and I do not like to write you, what I have just written you, in a telegram. But, know this, Marie, you are my wife now, and nothing that happens to you can alter that—except what may happen to your feelings.

My poor girl, how I wish I could be with you now. And, unless your letter to be received Monday is more reassuring, I may be able to be with you in two weeks or so—or sooner if you want me. I can think of nothing else.

I want you to understand this, Marie, that I am your husband now—and only one thing can divorce us, your real wish, but nothing that happens to you can: you are my wife, my money is your money, your sickness is mine.

It is agony to be away from you now.

[Charles]

131

To Marie Syrkin, April 13th [1930]

Sunday Morning.

Darling wife: I want to be with you as I never wanted to be with you before. The thought of you in pain and I not there to tend you and to try to comfort you is poisoning. I am writing for the explanatory letter which I hope will come tomorrow. I would drop everything and go to you today, were I not restrained by several considerations. First, if your sickness will continue, we may need every possible cent, and unless you need me and call me, I may not be justified in spending a good fraction of what we have on what in the last analysis may be merely sentimental and of no essential good to you. Again, unless you need me, I ought to finish my unfinished work here at the American Law Book Co, a great deal of it is merely in notes, not much good to anyone else. Now I have merely to finish this, for, as I wrote, I have not a single new definition to write. Again, due to my expressed desire to Kiser to go back to half time as soon as this volume is finished, and his insistence at first upon my working full time (I think now that if I had not gone back to full time myself, he was going to get rid of me) and his actions lately, my job is precarious and it may be all time or nothing. However, that may be, to leave now completely will be to leave for good. These really petty reasons will not hold me if you need me. Darling, I cannot begin to tell you how much I love you, how my love for you has become my blood and marrow. I am filled with a calm fury against any circumstance against us, and will fling myself against it or try to circumvent it until death. I know your courage, too, and how in the past you have been victorious against many evils. I look forward to our future calmly, whatever it may be, with the elation of battle against all that is hostile—man or nature. Now, darling and brave girl, dear companion-in-arms, if you can stay without harm until you get your divorce, by all means do so that we may be married when you come back and that I may be able to be with you and to nurse you night and day without the petty annoyances of being unconventional. In any event, since you should be able to get the best of New York medical ability to help you, it seems, unless really unavoidable, rash to do anything in Reno. However, unless I misunderstand you, you do not intend to. As for myself, I will do none of my own work until I finish the rush work at the place (I estimate it now at about two weeks more). I wait anxiously for news from you. Please write me daily, no matter what, it is infinitely worse than not to hear from you at all. Please take the best care of yourself, be careful of what you eat, sun yourself as much as possible, eat sparingly of the candy I sent you, make your body as strong as possible that it may be a good ally to us. Maybe, your pain (and I remember having heard that pain is a good sign; dangerous growths are never painful at first, I believe)—maybe, it is only a cold, or strain as the first doctor said, and will pass. Dear wife, dear girl, brave girl, good-by until I write again—at the first opportunity.

Charles

Sweetheart, I am so happy in the consciousness that you love me so completely, that even, forgive me! the pain at your pain is somehow mixed and transfused with my love.

To Marie Syrkin, [April 14, 1930]

Monday Evening

Dear Wife: I came home expecting to find the explanatory letter of your telegram, but it has not come as yet. Perhaps tomorrow. Your letter of the 11th did come, and I am glad that by that time you were not as despondent as the day before. Please don't worry, darling. I think it very unlikely that you have anything really the matter with you. In any event, when you come to New York you will have the best advice available. Dearest, I have a great faith in the power of emotions: at one time hate enabled me to do what I would otherwise have found impossible. Likewise, love for you at one time helped me over some stumbling blocks. My love for you has grown so great that I feel strong enough to climb—and carry you—anywhere. Darling, our love should make us unafraid and joyful in the face of anything. Darling, how I wish that I were in pain instead of you—at least I am home among friends. Dearest, when you come home and we marry, we shall never be parted again! I kiss you, and writing this, my heart beats faster. Hand in hand through everything!

I hope you do not find this too idiotic. I am very tired; I am floundering about for words to express my love and sorrow, my love and joy. Dearest, you understand me and will forgive my clumsiness—as you have forgiven it.

C.

To Marie Syrkin, April 15th [1930]

Tuesday Evening

[Marie,]

I called your aunt at noon and she told me that David was fine, but how worried she is about you. She is afraid, I think, that you may have a breast cut off just like that and come back like an old Greek statue. I tried to reassure her, and told her of the "explanatory" letter I got this morning and the three doctors. When I got home, I found your rather cheerful letter written Sunday, and I called her again at the hospital and read it to her. She seemed somewhat cheered—especially by the prospect that your trial may come off May 6th. And so am I, darling. And by the thought that next year we may have our own "seder." Darling wife! I am so anxious to make you happy that even if I blunder sometimes, blunder badly as lately, I think that on the whole I shall not do so badly. *On the whole*, darling and with the years, more wisdom, perhaps.

In about a week I expect to have finished all my work in the place—the unfinished work I have been writing you about—say about May 1st and then I shall know whether they want me to go on at full time until the end of the volume. I have been working as hard and as fast as possible, and, as I think I wrote you, have done no work on my book except to try a few pages of rewriting the autobiography. I have said nothing to Boni as yet; but today he called me at the place and said that Horace Kallen (one of his editors) wants to meet me.[1] I am to spend tomorrow evening with them. If I get home early enough, will write you a long letter; if not, just a note. It was very kind of you to send the telegram, else these days would have been dreadful, to think of you in pain and so far away. Dearest, I hope that you are better when this reaches you; take things easy and don't worry about anything. I have great faith in our love and in its strength. Good night, sweetheart.

---

[1] Horace Kallen (1882–1974), pupil of William James known for his conception of America as a symphony rather than a melting pot. Charles Boni (1894–1969), publisher of Reznikoff's first novel *By the Waters of Manhattan* (1930).

To Marie Syrkin, [April 16, 1930]

Wednesday Evening

[Marie,]

I am writing this in the subway, en route to Boni—hence the pencil.

Darling, I had no letter from you today; since you are not well, this makes me very uneasy. I hope to goodness I hear from you tomorrow.

At the place, Kiser made the next move: he gave the new definitions to one of the old-timers to do. If he had given them to one of the new men, I would judge that he is breaking in someone to take my place.

Midnight. In the subway en route from Boni. Met Horace Kallen and he likes the autobiography very much, but is inclined to dismiss the Joel as adolescent. Boni, on the other hand, likes the Joel and sees quality in it. The upshot of the matter is that I am to get to work as soon as I can and carry out the Boni idea.

In about a week or two, Marie, I expect to get back to half time, and to begin on my own work. In about three weeks you will be divorced, I hope, and on your way home. Darling, spring, *vita nuova*; I think we are in tune with the season and our spirits move in harmony with the spheres. Dear wife, I kiss you good-night—or rather good morning!

Charles

To Marie Syrkin, [April 18, 1930]

Friday

[Marie,]

I spoke to both your aunt and Mrs. Epstein today, and everybody is "fine." I am to meet your aunt tomorrow, and we are to have dinner together. Your letter of Monday only came today; but your aunt had received your letter of Tuesday, and told me it was not so cheerful. Though your letter to me was not cheerful, since you were still in pain, it was so sweetly scented with your loveliness that I saw for the ten thousandth time why you have been "grappled to my soul with hoops of steel."

When I left home, your letter had not come, and I had a miserable day all day at the place, and was prepared to send you a telegram tonight, if your letter had not come. At noon, I tried to talk to your aunt, but the operator at the hospital told me she was off. I then called Mrs. Epstein and she told me that everybody was fine. Tonight I called your aunt, who was home, and arranged to have dinner with her tomorrow. But she must be back at the hospital by the 7:30 boat. I will write you in full Saturday night. I hope that you are much better; I suppose it is too much to hope that your pain should be all gone. Take things as easily as you can; do not read too much in bed. You will soon be home, dear wife, with David and among friends.

Charles

To Marie Syrkin, [April 19, 1930]

Saturday Evening

Dearest:

I have just had dinner with your aunt. I called for her at the foot of 125th Street at about 4 o'clock, and we went to Luigino's Italian Restaurant together. On the way I told her of my last letters from you, and that cheered her a good deal, for she had been very much worried (I received yours of Thursday and Wednesday this morning). I asked about David and was told that he had grown so that visitors can hardly recognize him, and that when he was told the other day by your aunt that his mother was expected back in about a month his eyes lit up and he became very happy. Your aunt, however, is somewhat annoyed at Aaron because he thinks that David's improvement is due to his own presence, and ignores all that your aunt, Mrs. Epstein (to say nothing of yourself) have done and are doing for David. Your aunt told me a good deal about herself and her brothers; I feel flattered that she should be talkative when she is with me, and I trust that she had a good time. The meal wasn't much—you remember that you were fed up with Luigino's last time—but your aunt said she liked it—perhaps, merely out of politeness. We took a taxi back to get to the 7:30 boat on time; and we drove through Central park in the twilight and saw the lawns covered with flowers, many bushes in flower etc. I am afraid that your aunt thinks me disgustingly fat, because I haven't lost much, if anything, for months. However, she did say as I left her that she always found the night duty extremely long, but that tonight she would not find it so, because she had been out that afternoon. Anyway, darling, she loves you very much, and she told me how Sylvia loves you—but that she stoutly declares that she will never act otherwise towards you than she has acted.

The man who is writing definitions from "Public" on has—upon instructions—been consulting me now and then, and so I know that *all week* he has merely managed to do ½ a page. Of course, he is now at it, but he has been with the company for 10 or 20 years and is getting $85 to $100 a week I should guess. This amuses me. In the same time I would have done about 5 pages, but have worked like the very devil. He takes it quite easily. Well, I expect to finish my work at the end of next week or the first of the week after that. Then we shall see. I am afraid they may give me all the definitions (that they took away) to do.

Dearest, I am so glad that you are better; and I hope you will soon forget all about it. If you can do it at all, I wish you would go to Los Angeles; not that I think there is so much to see there, but you may think you have missed something, if you don't. However, use your own judgment. But, still, I think you ought not to leave Reno until you get your divorce, even if you have to wait a week. What is another week when you have been there so long?

When I begin thinking that within a month you will be back, I find myself so anxious to see you, so excited—that I find I must not think of it, or the wait of a few weeks will be unbearable—so I say to myself, you will be divorced on the 12th, you will go to the Coast, you won't be back until about the 20th—all to allay my fever. Dear girl, dear wife, I love you so. I hope I will be able to do so much and to repay you in happiness sevenfold for all your years of unhappiness, to repay you in companionship for all your nights and years of loneliness, to repay you in love for all your years of bitterness. Dearest, I am quite conscious of my great weakness but also of my great love—and this, it is written, will find a way.

Charles

To Marie Syrkin, April 20th [1930]

Sunday morning

Dear Wife,

I have been doing nothing but legal definitions these days and have become stupid. We have had four days of fog and rain, but today the sky is cloudless, everything is brilliant in sunshine, and the bear is about to become a bird.

I wrote you last night; now it is almost noon; and in the meantime I have done nothing but sleep a good deal, eat a little, and listen to the radio for a while, and sleep again. And I have not even had dreams to write you about.

For the next week or two, until I am back at half time, I expect to do nothing of my own. I want to be through with full time definitions as soon and as well as possible. In all my spare time I shall walk and exercise that I may not be hideous in your eyes. Perhaps I shall write a poem or two, or a story or two, in the meantime.

Darling, how miserable I would be in this glorious weather, if my thoughts did not have you to turn to, you to hope for. In just about two weeks, I hope, you will be leaving Reno. (By the way, if you are going to the Coast, as I think you should, I ought to write to the Lewins next Sunday, and, if you are going to San Francisco, to the Gaers).

Do you recognize this beautiful paper?

Charles

To Marie Syrkin, [April 21, 1930]

Monday

[Marie,]

I have come home very tired—and, of course, I have tossed the novel overboard to lighten the load. Now it seems to me that I ought to do the lyric only. I could put in eight hours a day reading for the novel and must read at least four—and when I get through reading law I can't look at a book for a while. Well, it's a very old story for you and no doubt annoys you as much as the rest of my family. If I work at law—well, I turned the prose I wrote last night into verse, as follows:

The English in Virginia April 1607

They landed and could see nothing but meadows and tall trees—
Cypress, nearly three fathoms about at the roots,
Rising straight for sixty or eighty feet without a branch.
In the woods were cedars, oaks, and walnut-trees;
Some beech, some elm, black walnut, ash, and sassafras; mulberry trees
    in groves;
Honey-suckle and other vines hanging in clusters on many trees.
They stepped on violets and other sweet flowers,
Many kinds in many colors; strawberries and raspberries were on the
    ground.
Blackbirds with red shoulders were flying about
And many small birds, some red, some blue;

The woods were full of deer;
And running everywhere fresh water—brooks, rundles, springs, and
    creeks.
In the twilight, through the thickets and the tall grass,
The savages came creeping upon all fours, their bows in their mouths.[1]

It isn't quite right, but I think I have something. However, none of it is
invented, all drawn from the sources, put together, a word changed here
and there, the order completely changed. But no more. From now on, the
lyric only. You smile, or worst still, laugh. But why should I tread so
laboriously through prose, when verse is easy for me and pleases me much
more. Besides, I will not be able to sell my prose faster than my verse and it
costs so much more to print. You know this argument so well, darling,
don't you. Well, I am sorry. But, darling, this is me. I don't want you to
forget me as I am, and be unpleasantly reminded. But, darling, I see
possibilities in verse that it seems to me no one has done in English, that
only I can do; and in prose I am no better than a hundred others—worse.
How much better to let all my energies—such as they are—flow into my
verse, publish my booklet year by year, live joyfully in my work—come, my
Lesbia, let us sing and love—than to laboriously construct a novel in two
years or more, which I may have to print myself, and which in another few
years a few arty critics will praise—not for my characters, the sweep of my
story, but for my delicate style, the moods—which I do much better in verse
with all its music to help me. *À bas*, prose! At the very thought I am joyful
and rested. I hug you.

C.

To Marie Syrkin, April 22d [1930]

Tuesday

Dearest: I have been struggling all day with a behemoth of a definition
"proximate cause," but when I finish this I will have little left. However,
Mack told me this evening, that I will probably get the other definitions

---

[1] This poem was eventually published in Reznikoff's *Jerusalem the Golden* (1934).
The published poem is essentially the same, except that Reznikoff has shortened
the lines to increase the poetic rhythm of the stanzas.

back; for the man who has them (as I knew and wrote you) is not doing well at all. Mack had a grim and pleased smile on his face, and I know he is on my side against Kiser, and also he is on my side for half-time. So I may have a month or so of hard work full time, and then, I hope, half time. Then, too, I hope, my novels, my verse,—and my wife—or rather, our novels, our verse, and our life. I spoke to your aunt at noon: she is well and the children are fine. I began to do some verse this evening and only did the first stanza—one of the bald kind you dislike. However, here it is:

> The days are long again, the skies are blue,
> The hedges are green again, the leaves are out on the trees,
> Only the twigs of the elms are dark against the sky.

This is really going to be something quite cheerful, if I finish it.

Darling and sweetest, the cold snow of your absence is melting under the spring sun; take comfort from the proverb: April showers bring May flowers. Be patient; the earth turns from day to night, from night to day—swiftly, and soon you will be here—and we shall go to May parties together, Queen of the May.

Your servitor,
Charles

I have $1025 in the bank—in trust for ourselves.

To Marie Syrkin, [April 22, 1930?]

Tuesday Evening.

Dearest: I called up your aunt today, but this afternoon she was given, or had taken, off. I call her at the hospital or island or whatever it is (Harlem 6764) at noon, and so I called the house, but she had not arrived. However, I spoke to Mrs. Epstein and she told me all are "fine": Sylvia, David, Judith, Mischa etc. She sounded very cheerful, asked me up etc. This evening, at 6, I called Tima, as I was invited to do on Sunday, and made an appointment to go up there this Friday at 8:30.

Zukofsky did not like my verse in *The Menorah* at all (the Dialogue) and thought it full of "little thoughts." I know what he means; he also does not like its rhythm. He may be right. I met Bergman who used to be editor of the *Tribune* and he seemed glad to see me. He is working—among others—for Charles Boni and told me he lent him *By the Waters of Manhattan*, also told

Boni of "Apocrypha" etc. urged him to print it, etc. Expect nothing of this.

To go back to what I was thinking most of today: what to do at my place. I am inclined to do nothing at all, but go back to my old schedule of doing my own work too. This will cut down my production at the place heavily, but I can not reconcile myself to do nothing at all of my own work for about three months more—for it will take me all that to reach the new "end of the volume." My mother urges me to give up everything and just write: she thinks I should do only one thing and do my damnedest at it. Kiser, too, has that in mind; but partly by threats, partly by wheedling, he wants me to do nothing but my work for them (and I had gotten to the point where I could do more and better work for less than anyone they had, I believe). He will undoubtedly get rid of me as soon as he can if I ever go back to half time; for he is a stubborn man, and has none of the "individual freedom" notion of Anglo-Saxons, such as Mack. Of course, he has definitely promised to let me go on half-time as soon as the volume is finished. But, after all, he is only an employee and can always shift responsibility or, in fact, have none. Darling, I am sorry to trouble you with all these plans and counterplans in this little game I am playing at *Corpus Juris*—but, of course, you share the winnings (and losing)—small as they are. I will do nothing rash. If I am lost, it will be because of too much caution. If my allies—the years—were not leaving me, I should be nothing but a Fabian. As I write, it occurs to me, that perhaps it would be wiser, since I have invested so much full time and expected to invest all my time and energy until May 1st, to do so until Aug. 1st, cinch the half time job, as they have promised, and then go back to half time and never shift from it. But then, I think, the job is never cinched; as soon as I am back at half time Kiser will edge me out of it, if he can; he could have put me right at definitions at the beginning instead of keeping me for months at other work, and how much will half time pay me—$30 or $35. So I keep thinking about the matter. Well, whatever conclusion I come to will not matter much I suppose. I ought to be able to earn about $50 a week at something or other sooner or later; if I live, I'll write whatever I have to, I suppose.

It's a long time since I sent you a box of eatables, and I'd like to send you a box this Saturday. Darling, as a sign of how much I have come to love you—but I have for a long time—anyway, it is curious how much satisfaction your most casual notes give me. I begin to understand what it is to love a woman not for her goodness, her wit, for her wisdom, for her beauty,—though you have all these—but for herself—for what she is as she is—for what you are, Marie.

Charles

To Marie Syrkin, [April 23, 1930]

[Marie,]

> The days are long again, the skies are blue;
> The hedges are green again, the trees are green;
> Only the twigs of the elms are dark against the sky.
> At night the wind is cold again;
> But by day the snow of your absence is melting,
> Soon May will be here again and you will be the May queen!

Forgive me the repetition. Today, too, I have been continuing the struggle with the leviathan definition "proximate cause," and have swallowed about half. Naturally, I am torpid.

I have your letter of Monday and see that you are beginning to worry again about your pain. Now, Marie, that is nonsense; the doctors discharged you; there is nothing the matter with you. I know a cure for that pain—kisses! and I will apply these as soon as I can. It's an old remedy. Among your other thoughts I note this: did I tell my mother that you were sick? No. However, your telegram might have started questions—for that was opened—naturally. But your added wish for a happy Passover somehow gave my mother the impression that it was the holiday that caused such exuberance, and she said to me, "I suppose Passover is a great holiday for Marie, since her father was a Zionist." And the dear soul was puzzled and pleased. Incidentally, your aunt asked me the very same question when we were out Saturday. Why, Marie, if anything were the matter with you, my mother would be the first to be with you, for you, beside you. However, I have told her nothing—*and there is nothing to tell*! I also note that you are bothered by what I am going to do to the autobiography, Joel, etc. Now, Marie, I do not expect that the whole matter, whatever I do, will take me more than a few months. Besides, I don't think I'll be able to start until you are back; because I won't be through with full time definitions, I suppose, until then. Now, darling, I have a number of things to do, and even if the Joel as rewritten should not go, what of it? On stepping-stones of our dead writing etc. Dear wife, dearest girl!

Charles

To Marie Syrkin, [April 24, 1930]

Thursday Evening

Marie dearest: Today, God be thanked. I finished "proximate cause," and you'll hear no more about it. Tomorrow I expect to finish writing all the definitions I have, in two days or so I shall have checked the stenographer's work, but I am not through. Today Kiser stopped at the door of the office and informed me that I am to have the definitions (that he took away) back. However, Skyles (who is working on them) has finished two or three pages, and there will be about ten pages more left for both of us. So in about two weeks, unless their plans change, and they want to go on to "Quieting Title" instead of "Public Service Corporations," I shall be through. And back to half time, as we plan, I hope. I am glad now I did not kick over the traces, though it was a little tempting. I have an exciting theme for a novel (one you haven't heard); so now I have to do 1. the Joel 2. Apocrypha (that's really the first half or quarter of a novel) 3. my all American theme 4. the new theme. The new theme is a business theme—a father, 2 sons, a great business which disappears in ten years. It's a theme I ought to be able to do something with.

Dearest, I keep thinking of you all day—in every way. I glance at the paper and see a sale of fur coats and think how nice it would be if I could buy you one. I listen to our radio and think how nice it would be if we had one—a good one. I think Plato has a myth which he puts into the mouth of Aristophanes (at the Banquet) of the origin of love—how originally man and woman were in pairs, but now severed, each half hunts the other and is not satisfied until together.[1] Something like that, but very beautiful. Well, I feel like that; I am all branches and roots reaching out for you—for nourishment, black loam and white sunshine. We have been playing hide and seek, as it were, with each other, you hidden in Reno, and I hunting for you—but in New York; well, in a few weeks I hope to find you, and then we will play at other games—at house, for instance.

Charles

---

[1] Aristophanes' myth of the hermaphrodite appears in Plato's *Symposium*.

143

To Marie Syrkin, [April 28, 1930]

Monday Evening

Dear Wife:

This morning I received your letters of Thursday and Friday; I am glad that you are thinking of going to the Coast, because if you do not go, you may feel that you have missed something.

This is Al Lewin's address:

1823 Courtney Ave

Hollywood, Calif.

Should you go to San Francisco, and feel like seeing the Gaers, this is their address:

1525 Arch Street

Berkeley, Calif.

I will write Al Lewin this Sunday and tell him and Milly that Marie Syrkin, whom I expect to marry as soon as she returns to New York, will leave Reno for Los Angeles about the 6th or the 12th of May, and whatever courtesy they will show you will be greatly appreciated by etc.

Now, honey, of course I want you back as soon as possible; nevertheless for your sake I think that if you feel like it at all you ought to see the Coast. And for the same dear sake, I think your plan of leaving Reno and returning for your divorce is not good. It is one of those plans that sound fine on paper and that friends say, Of course! to, but it cannot work out well for several reasons. First, the long rides, change of climate, hurry and bustle, will tire and exhaust you. Second, if by merest chance the Lewins are going away and want to take you along on a trip you will not be able to go. Dearest, you will enjoy your trip to the Coast ten times as much when you have had your divorce and do not have to return to Reno. Please, darling, stay and rest in Reno, if need be (and I hope not) one week more, and then leave it completely at ease. It may be somewhat premature, but I suggest that you go by an early train, so as to see the scenery, *that you go by Pullman*, that you may use the observation car etc., that before you go you reserve by letter for the night you expect to arrive in Los Angeles the lowest priced room and bath in the *best* hotel in town. About this let me say that you can find the name of such hotel in the best hotel in Reno, that such reservation will not obligate you at all, that such room, if you use it, will cost very little more than a second rate hotel, but that the difference is tremendous. As soon as you arrive in Los Angeles, call up the Lewins. Now they may invite you to stay at their house; again, they may not. Expect absolutely nothing. Our relation, I am afraid, has long ago become mere phrases. If I were in a position to do anything for them, they would give you a wonderful time. As it is, I don't know what time you will have. However, be your own dear self and expect nothing.

Sweetheart, my mother timidly suggested that after marriage you live with them, but I ruled that out flatly. I merely write it to show you that you need not think twice about your welcome—if you do. Darling, please make the most of the [illegible] air, watch your food carefully, and be at ease. I suppose it is silly to do so, but it gives me pleasure to say that I love you and exquisite pleasure to read that you love me.

Charles

By the way, if you need money, my money is ours.

To Marie Syrkin, [April 29, 1930]

Tuesday Evening

[Marie,]

I called up your aunt this noon: "the children are fine"—so is she.

Tomorrow I speak to Kiser about my future at the company. I shall have finished all my work that was in notes etc.; from now on new work, if any. If he lets me go on half time at once, well and good; if not, he will simply string me along for 2 months until this rush is over, and then refuse to let me go on half time—so I think. Well, we shall see tomorrow. I am not at all anxious to leave; on the other hand, unless I can do my own work, no good will come out of anything; and out of my work, I expect all kinds of good for both of us.

Darling, your last two letters were your old bright, cheerful self—the Indian school and my bald head. The *Shelburne Essays* by Paul Elmer More, I understand, is the bible of the new Humanism.[1] You might read some.

The sun is shining—we have daylight savings time—and I am anxious to take a walk and be fresh and keen tomorrow. So good-night. Tomorrow morning I hope to have a cheerful letter from you, and tomorrow evening

---

[1] Paul Elmer More (1864–1937), *Shelburne Essays* (7th Series, 1905).

145

to write you a cheerful one. I am tired of making xs and talking of kisses; I long for the reality.

Charles

To Marie Syrkin, April 30th 1930

Wednesday Evening

Dearest and Darling: I am very tired tonight, and would much rather write tomorrow, but I do not want to keep you in suspense. To begin with, darling, if you will not get your divorce until the 12th, stay on quietly, if you can, enjoying as best you can the Nevada spring, and do not hop about to Los Angeles etc. until you are through. Again, do not try to write Solmic? or Solmmic? letters; I like your letters as they have been lately immensely; in other words no letters can appeal to me as much as Marie Syrkin letters—I want you as you are, not otherwise, the simple unadorned Marie Syrkin—the more Marie Syrkin the better. Now as for myself: this morning I finished my work and went in to see Mr. Kiser. Very well, he said, now work with Mr. Skyles. Very well, I said, but am I to understand Mr. Kiser that when we are through with the definitions for this volume (about 1 or 2 months more) that I am to go on half time? No, he said, we will talk about it then; I cannot commit myself now. I may want to put you on other work which will have to be done full time. In that event, Mr. Kiser, I said, am I to understand that I am not to go on half time? No, I will not commit myself. Well, I said, knowing what your feelings are about half-time and that you are always more or less in a hurry for work, I am sure that you will not let me go on half-time. If that is so, I cannot write another definition. Well, I am through, Marie. I left on the friendliest terms with all, I gave my stenographer a box of candy, and I can come back at any time—at full time. Darling, I do not regret it one bit: the work, even at half time, was very hard, it was affecting my health, particularly my eyes, and it had no future. Marie, dearest, I have no doubt that I can earn thirty or so dollars ($1500 a year) at much easier ways. To begin with, I am going to rest for a few days and do nothing, for I have been working at a pretty good pace for months. Then I am going to do nothing but work at the novel for Boni. Dearest, do not worry in the slightest; you know how prudent, if not timid, I am, and I see no reason for any worry. As for our plans, unless you change them, I see no reason for any change—but for the better. I expect, of course, to

146

provide for myself, for you, too, if necessary; for you, necessary or not, soon; I love you and I love my work, neither, as I see it, interferes with each other; on the contrary, I expect my love for you to feed my work—and my love for my work to feed you.

Charles

Dear wife, I kiss you a thousand times. My hunger for your presence these ninety-odd days will take ninety-odd years to quench. A little mixed—but I am intoxicated with thinking of you while writing this letter.

To Marie Syrkin, [May 1, 1930]

Thursday Evening

Dear Exile,

Whose days of exile are almost completed, I congratulate you; and from now on may you be exiled only from the cities of misfortune. With which oriental greeting permit me to proceed, strewing promises and hopes in your path—may they bear seed, which mere flowers no longer can!—to-day I spent gloriously—loafing. (Enter a sextette who sing in very unjazzlike strains)

Holiday

What tree is this that bears only light-green blossoms,
What bird is this that hidden in it chirps so cheerfully,
What bush is that red upon the lawn?
I recognize the [illegible]
I used to see them in the park
Splendid in cloth of gold among the commonfolk—the grass.

Audience, consisting of a certain Marie, mutters, not so hot, and O how sweet, and other derogatory expressions, thinking sadly, for this he gave up $60 a week, woe! woe!

I have written to Boni promising him a manuscript in about a month.

I have weighed myself and find that despite the loss of some hair from the top of my head—the lean gods of the Greeks protect us! Buddha get up and avaunt!—almost 180 Ibs. But this month, Adonoi, the one, true, and only God help us! I expect to exercise, write, and read, I expect to grow lean and brown, and I expect to welcome and

147

marry a certain Marie Syrkin, whom Mrs. Bodansky may remember.

There was a good deal more to the conversation with Mack and Kiser than I was able to write you. Both admitted virtually that half-time from now on is out of the question—it is too upsetting to the other men who work all day. Now, Marie, I must strain every muscle to get into business for myself—and this is the business: to write, write, write. I ought to make as much as I could half-time very soon, and very soon, perhaps, more than I could earn at several times full-time. We have a little money—under any circumstances, however, I will never touch a cent of yours—and I am mindful of my obligation to Tima, and that you may need some money for the trip to the Coast and return—nevertheless, we still have some money, and, I think, great love for each other. Darling, I am not afraid of the future, and with you to share it, I look forward cheerfully. I cannot help quoting again that quotation I like, "Hitherto hath the Lord helped me."

Charles

To Marie Syrkin, [May 2, 1930]

Friday Evening

Dearest:

I spoke to your aunt today: David is "fine." I arranged to call her at the hospital a little after 11 o'clock this Sunday in reference to any telegram I may receive.

This afternoon I received your letter mailed in Reno Wednesday, and am accordingly writing to the Lewins today as follows:

Dear Al and Millie:

Marie Syrkin will probably be in Los Angeles the first of this coming week. Millie might remember her from Hunter's; anyway, they have a number of friends in common. I am very much attached to her, and any courtesy you can show her will be deeply appreciated.

The rest of the letter is about myself. Dear Marie, I could add a good deal, of course, but if I wrote of your father they would not know of him; if I said you were a writer they might expect someone who is trying to sell scenarios. And so, perhaps, I have written, as so frequently, too little.

However, I hope they will give you the pleasantest of times; but you know, of course, how hard-worked Al is and Millie may be having troubles of her own.

This, unless your request otherwise, is my last letter to this Reno address. Tomorrow's letter goes to Mrs. Bodansky, General Delivery, Los Angeles, as per your letter of Tuesday.

Darling, I have begun to work at the Boni book. I think it will take me a month. Now, if I were working half-time, I would earn only $120—; as you see, as a business investment, I think it worth while, and it will be, I hope, a better book.

At the latest, then, I hope you will be home in about 2 weeks—and then, I hope, we will be able to talk to each other to our heart's content. In the meantime, have a pleasant trip, take good care of yourself, and have the best of times, my love.

Charles

To Albert and Mildred Lewin, May 2, 1930

1379 Union Street, Brooklyn, N.Y.

Dear Al and Milly,

Marie Syrkin will probably be in Los Angeles the first of this coming week. Millie may remember her from Hunter's; anyway, they have a number of friends in common. I am very much attached to her, and any courtesy you can show her will be deeply appreciated.

Bergman showed Charles Boni (for whom he is doing publicity) my Joel etc book. Boni likes it and suggested an idea that I am working on now. I have given up my law work because I could do nothing of my own, and they would not let me go on half time. However, I managed to save a little money, and I have a good deal of writing to do.

Dear Al and Milly, I hope that when Al is forty—only a few more years, but no later—that he will retire with his booty from Hollywood and catch up with all of us who have been trying to do two things at once. Down with fur coats and automobiles, but hurray for ivory towers.

Charles Reznikoff

To Marie Syrkin, [May 3, 1930]

Saturday Noon

[Marie,]

I am sending this letter to Reno, because I think it will reach there by Monday—before you leave.

I have just finished the first 15 pages of the Boni book and at this rate I should be finished in about a month. In about four hours a day I can do all the writing I want to do, in two hours all the reading. I know that I can do some kind of work—such as selling—that will give me a steady income and not interfere with my work, as any brain work does. When I got through this morning with my work, I couldn't do another stroke of *mental* work. However, I shall not look for anything this month; and, if Boni takes my book, perhaps, I shall not have to. At present, my future work is as follows: in verse, a book a year (the one that is ready will probably be published mostly by *The Menorah* sooner or later; I told you that I corrected the proof). *In prose,* 1 this book I am working on 2 a millinery novel to include "Apocrypha" and the new theme 3 the "United States" novel—all times and places, still to be crystallized 4 a record of a long walk, day by day, the Coast etc. Of course, this is years off. Then, a translation and rewriting of my father's book of which about 80,000 words are ready. As for you, I consider you my wife, my duty and delight to do all you want me to. I am very happy since I am at my own work; may you be too very soon. The next letter to Los Angeles.

Charles

To Marie Syrkin, [May 6, 1930]

Tuesday

[Marie,]

This, Marie darling, is the last letter I expect to write you for a long time, I hope. I am all for glances, whispers and hand clasps as a mode of communication between us.

I called your aunt today about David; and he is "fine."

From now on, darling, I wait to hear from you—as to how you are enjoying yourself, and above all as to when you are to be expected in New York.

150

I hope—need I add this?—that your divorce went off as you expected today and that you are free to become my wife, to be married by a rabbi, according to the ancient rites, for health or sickness, for better or worse, for prosperity or poverty.

I did 30 pages today; I may be through with the novel in 2 weeks—maybe.

Marie, we have known each other somewhat for two years; and though I thought I loved you a long time ago, I know that was a mere candle to what I feel for you now. If you are going to be sick or in trouble, I want to be with you even more than if you are well and prosperous—that may happen—want you—above all—to share it. Darling, I cannot close this series of letters on any other words than these: I love you.

Charles

To Albert and Mildred Lewin, June 14, 1930

225 McClellan St., Bronx N.Y.

Dear Al and Milly,

Charles Boni is publishing *By the Waters of Manhattan* as his next paper book. Of course, I'll send you a copy.

I married Marie Syrkin on her return from Reno a few weeks ago, and we are living at the above address—3 rooms, $45 a month. I am reminded of your home in Harlem where I was your boarder Saturdays.

Charles Reznikoff

To Albert Lewin, [June 22, 1930]

225 McClellan St, Bronx, N.Y.C.
Sunday

Dear Al,

I sent you the following telegram last night:
Paul somewhere in England. Sinai surgeon my friend says of doctor

diagnostic and surgical skill good, but heartless as regards money and treatment.

I hope this answers your inquiry somewhat. Paul is still in Europe, now in England or Scotland. We usually write him care of American Express Company, London, but he may be at Cambridge, Oxford, or for that matter, Edinborough.

To get some information, I called up an old chum of mine who served his internship as a surgeon at Sinai and has been for some time a visiting surgeon there. He was somewhat sleepy, and all he would tell me of the doctor in question was "He is a son of a bitch." This was not explicit enough, it seemed to me, and when I asked for details, he added that though diagnostic and surgical skill was good, the doctor would extract all the money he could reach. When I suggested writing "heartless as regards money," after reiterating "son of a bitch" as the best expression, he added "heartless in treatment too."

I am assuming that neither you nor Milly are sick, and that this information is for a friend of yours. Please write me if this is not so.

Charles

To Albert and Mildred Lewin, July 26th [1930]

225 McClellan St, Bronx, N.Y.C.

Dear Al and Milly,

I have been uneasy for some time because of your silence. How are you?

Charles Reznikoff

To Albert Lewin, [August 1930]

225 McClellan St, Bronx, N.Y.C.
Sunday.

Dear Al,

I was glad and relieved to learn that you are better.
No doubt you saw the notice in *The Times* of *By the Water's* etc—not

good, but *The Post* and *Herald-Tribune* were better.[1] I am at work on another book—prose—but that will take a year or so. *The Menorah Journal* for May had a group of verse (non-Jewish), and *Pagany* will print something sooner or later—dear Al and Milly, Marie, who exclaims at my laborious and dull composition is going to finish this letter to show me how letters should be written. Marie!

The foregoing is not true. I said merely that letters were not necessarily models of stylistic grace and should be written simply and effortlessly as one talks. But Charles ponders and ponders. Now he has made me nervous and I ponder too. Anyhow, I was awfully sorry that I didn't get a chance to see you two when I was in Los Angeles. I spent a dismal two days and departed after having had only a glimpse (from an automobile) of the Hollywood boulevards and divers enchantments.

We have an excellent apartment full of splendid new furniture. I emphasize the new because that was unexpected. When Charles finishes his great work in progress we will go in for antiques. I hope we will see you before then.

So now you see the severest critic in action. Lights!

Charles

To Henry Hurwitz and Elliot Cohen, September 1st. [1930?]

225 McClellan Street, Bronx, New York City

The Menorah Journal, 63 Fifth Avenue, New York City

Dear Editors:

Enclosed please find *Jeremiah in the Stocks* and *In the Country*.[2]
Please discard the play *Jeremiah* which I sent you. Mr. Cohen told me that he thought only the beginning and the end effective. I have come to think that he is right: *Jeremiah in the Stocks* is the beginning rewritten.

---

[1] A review of Reznikoff's novel, *By the Waters of Manhattan* (1930), appeared in *The New York Times* on 27 July 1930.
[2] "In the Country" was published by *The Menorah Journal*. 19:2 (November–December 1930): 185–188.

Please note my new address—and telephone number: Jerome 2348.
Marie Syrkin and I were married the end of May.

Very truly yours
Charles Reznikoff

To Harriet Monroe, Dec 4th [1930]

3900 Greystone Ave, Bronx, N.Y.C.

Dear Miss Monroe,

I am enclosing proof of "Winter Sketches." Thank you for your
suggestion—which I have accepted—that I omit one of the subtitles.

If *Poetry* is still paying for contributions, please deduct one subscription for me. If not, please send me a bill.

Very truly yours,
Charles Reznikoff

Charles Reznikoff,
3615 Greystone Ave.,
Bronx, N.Y.C.
[December 4, 1930]

WINTER SKETCHES

I

Now that black ground and bushes—
saplings, trees,
each twig and limb—are suddenly white with snow,
and earth becomes brighter than the sky,

that intricate shrub
of nerves, veins, arteries—
myself—uncurls its knotted leaves
to the shining air.

II

Upon this wooded hillside,
pied with snow, I hear
only the melting snow
drop from the twigs.

III

From the middle of the pool
in the concrete pavement a fountain
in neat jets; the wind scatters it
upon the water. The untidy trees
drop their leaves upon the pavement.

IV

Along the flat roofs beneath our window,
in the morning sunshine,
I read the signature of last night's rain.

V

The squads, platoons, and regiments
of lighted windows,
ephemeral under the evening star—

feast, you who cross the bridge
this cold twilight
on these honeycombs of light, the buildings of Manhattan.

To Albert and Mildred Lewin, Dec 27th. [1930]

Dear Al and Milly,

We thank you for your telegram of good wishes and for the candlesticks. It is unnecessary, of course, for me to say that these are beautiful. Long ago, I think I have learnt—not without your help—to know simplicity;

now, still instructed by you, watching the lovely ornate pattern of the candlesticks, I am learning to understand ornament.

We wish you a very happy New Year.

Charles

The candlesticks look stunning. They occupy a place of honor on a side-table together with a silver plate donated by Paul. The effect is choice and precious and will prove a great convenience to highwaymen, robbers and pawn-brokers who can now concentrate on articles of value without being distracted by the Woolworth motifs which ornament the rest of the room. Thank you very much. Best of luck for the new year!

Marie

To Albert and Mildred Lewin, Feb 4th [1931]

225 McClellan St, Bronx

Dear Al and Milly,

A month or so ago I weakened my constitution with persimmons and brie cheese. I realized this when I had some Boston cream pie (two kinds of cream—custard and whipped cream) yesterday and felt sick after it. Luckily, I could get spaghetti and anchovy sauce in an Italian restaurant nearby to fix me up. I am all right now and I hope both of you are.

There is a learned article about my verse in *Poetry* for this month from which I learn that I am "an objectivist."[1] I have received my last check (and several small notes) from Boni, my book (booklet) will not be ready for two or three months, and I am about to diet.

Charles

Marie sends her love.

---

[1] Louis Zukofsky, "Program: 'Objectivists' 1931." *Poetry*. (February 1931): 268–275. [See Reznikoff's letter of 11 February 1930.]

To Marie Syrkin, [April 16, 1931]

The Harrisburger, Harrisburg, Penna.
Thursday Eve.

Dearest,

Bus riding is fine—but there's a little too much of it. And, of course, there will be much more—I hope.

When I see something beautiful—and I have seen so much—I think of you and reach for your hand, dearest. I am tired tonight and must be up very early. I kiss you a thousand times, dear wife, and hope that our separation will not be useless.

Charles

I sent Freed, the insurance agent, the policy: Santini's address is, I hope, 1407 Jerome Av.

To Marie Syrkin, [April 21, 1931]

The Pittsburgher, Pittsburgh, Pa.
Tuesday Morning

Dearest,

I have a minute or two before the business day begins, and have addressed a card to David, another to Sylvia—with this letter the important correspondence of the day is concluded. (By the way, it is not easy to find cards that are *good*.)

I received your letter and thank you. Darling, the trip is at times exciting—mountains (Pa. variety), forests, wind. I feel fine and enthusiastic —if we could only make such a trip together. Well, we may, and soon.

I may not be able to write from Pittsburgh again, because I should like to catch the 12:30 bus. That would land me in Columbus at 9. Otherwise, I may stay over here.

Darling, please remember me to Mrs. Epstein, tell Mischa I am sorry I did not get a chance to say good-by. Of course, remember me to your aunt. I shall drop a note to all of them when I get a chance.

I thought of you for many hours yesterday and separation from you lessens my pleasure in seeing all I do.

It is 9 o'clock and I must take my hats.

Charles

157

To Marie Syrkin, [April 21, 1931]

The Pittsburgher, Pittsburgh, Pa.

Dearest,

I worked hard this morning—sold 4 doz. hats, but have to stay this afternoon—I have an appointment at 4. I expect to take the 6 o'clock bus which will land me in Columbus at 2 in the morning.

I am feeling fine—except for your absence. I hope that you and David are fine, your Aunt, Mrs. Epstein etc. I feel too businesslike to write a line of verse, or even copy what I have. Perhaps, I will not be able to write a love poem until I reach the coast, where some more leisure and the terrible distance from you will overwhelm me.

> If my blood were ink
> I would write you all I think;
> If my heart were paper,
> I would send it,
> You would read it, laugh, and caper.

Charles

To Marie Syrkin, [April 22, 1931]

Hotel Fort Hayes, Columbus, Ohio

Dearest,

I didn't get into this town until after 2, did no business and am leaving at 4 for Indianapolis. When the bus is due at 10:20. I asked at the post office for a letter; there was none, but I'll ask again before I leave. It has become cold here, but not cold enough for an overcoat; it is raining, and I am tired.

> If I were Edna St. Vincent Millay,[1]
> I'd write a song ending alack-a-day—
> A song with this burden alack-a-day;
> For I can rhyme

---

[1] Edna St. Vincent Millay (1892–1950), American poet whose 1923 volume *The Harp-Weaver and Other Poems* won the Pulitzer Prize (CGLE).

As well as Edna any old time—
Despite anything you may say;
But since I am Charles Reznikoff,
I've written eight lines and that's enough,
Enough, enough,
I've written ten lines and that's enough.

But I am seeing a lot—have the *sensation* of being alive—motion—speed—sights. I kiss your lips and hand and am

Charles

To Marie Syrkin, [April 23, 1931]

Claypool Hotel, Indianapolis
Thursday

Dearest,

Received your letter addressed to me here.

No business here. I do not think I will do much more, if any, until I get to the coast, but there I hope to make up all my expenses. These are as follows: a room in a hotel costs about $2.50 to 3.00, food about $1.50 to 2.00, in all my expenses are about $5.00 a day. I plan in all about 15 stops—that will be about $75. Plus fare about $135. If I had gone by train that would have been $100 (round trip ticket now—$60 after May 15th). Plus Pullman and meals (about $35) = the same.

In addition I see much more of the country, get my hand into the selling end, and it is pleasanter to sleep and bathe in a good hotel than to sleep in a berth. As for bus riding, it is much more enjoyable and exciting than going by train, but it took me a day or two to be used to it.

The bus leaves for St. Louis at 3 P.M. It is now 1. There are still two customers to see—and I may do some business after all. Good-by, sweetheart, until tomorrow. From your loving salesman husband

Charles

To Marie Syrkin, [April 24, 1931]

Hotel Statler, St. Louis
Friday

Dearest:

From now on write to General Delivery, Los Angeles or no others will reach me. I leave here tomorrow morning at 8 for Springfield, Mo., then next day at Tulsa, then through Clinton, Okl., to Amarillo, Tex; then through New Mexico to El Paso, Texas. Stopping at night at hotels, I expect to be in El Paso by Wednesday night. I have seen much, expect to see more, and feel richly repaid by the bus mode of travel. At El Paso they route me to Los Angeles.

The jubilation about the millinery business has been quite premature, as you no doubt realize. It was cold and rainy in Columbus, Indianapolis, and here and I could do no business whatever. Besides, I do not know how good the hat is outside the New York radius. Well, will see. I have never felt better. Of course, I'll write each day—if only to scrawl a line. It is funny I should have mentioned Edna St. Vincent etc. in the doggerel I sent you a day or two ago, at the same time you were writing your letter.

> Beside the road the flowering shrubs
> Are white or purple, the blossoming trees—
> The countryside is green;
> I should be happy, but I love you so—
> Between us now a thousand miles
> And I have twice as far to go.

Charles

To Marie Syrkin, [April 25, 1931]

Hotel Connor, Joplin, Missouri
Saturday Night

Dearest,

arrived at Joplin tonight. Will stay over and in the morning expect to leave for Oklahoma City. Have changed my plans—I ride all day and sleep in a hotel at night. I do not try to sell hats or write or anything—I just try to soak in as much as I can. Dearest, I think I have learnt to make these trips most enjoyable. If only you could be with me, darling. I think of you a thousand times a day. We could have such good times together. I hope this separation will be the last and after this we will see everything together and have twice as good a time. I am too sleepy to go on like this—because I could go on forever. Good night, dearest.

Charles

To Marie Syrkin, [April 29, 1931]

Hilton Hotel, El Paso, Texas
Wednesday Evening

Darling,

I am very lonely and think of you often; I am afraid that I am thoroughly wedded, and I hope that this parting will be our last. Life without you just isn't right.

The bus due here last night came in this afternoon; we laid over en route because of rain and bad roads. But all the inconvenience was worth it: the Southwest is so new to me that I just stared and gaped. I feel fine. Tomorrow at 7 I leave for Phoenix, and the morning after for Los Angeles, due there Friday night.

I tried to buy you a little Mexican token, but couldn't see a thing except a brightly colored basket—I am having it sent (only $1). I am also sending my mother a little filigree pin (90¢). I should like to send little gifts to my sister, your aunt and Mrs. Epstein, but I am waiting until I sell hats in Los Angeles. (I sold 1 doz in Amarillo, but none here).

I hope to rent a cheap room near Los Angeles and first clean up my father's book. Incidentally, of course, I expect to sell hats, keep my eyes open etc.

I saw *Front Page* in this town—and I am not like Benziger: I would not put my fingers to my mouth![1]

Dearest, good night—good old Mouky! I hope to have many letters from you when I reach Los Angeles.

Charles

---

[1] The 1931 film version of Ben Hecht and Charles MacArthur's play, *The Front Page*, was produced by Howard Hughes and directed by Lewis Milestone.

161

To Marie Syrkin, May 3rd [1931]

Sunday morning
714 N. Roxbury Drive, Beverly Hills, Calif.

Dearest and best of darlings,

To begin at the beginning: the ride from El Paso to Phoenix was, in places, over the mountains—by daylight and moonlight—the ride from Phoenix to Los Angeles was through desert—all kinds—and we arrived at Los Angeles at 1 in the morning. The next day I called up Al Lewin and he asked me over to the studio. He is leaving tonight for the East and will be gone 10 days or so. Milly is going with him. They both were so friendly and urged me to stay here at their home at least until they return. There is a maid, a cook, a chauffeur. I am in a sort of wing, all to myself and have a private bath—a kind of Hollywood bath. Last night Jim Tully[1] was in and talked—at times well. I met Boris Pilniak at the studio and he talked Russian to me. Joe Freeman has been telling him of me and wants him to translate *By the Waters* etc. I hope to get down to work on Father's book by tomorrow.

Darling, when I think of what a good time you would have here I feel miserable and selfish. Dearest, I feel very unhappy at you slaving in the city and myself out here. I will write you every day by airmail and you write when you can. Need I tell you how much I love you? How I long for you and think of you? My dear wife, I owe you a lot of happiness and feel like a bankrupt.

Charles

---

[1] Jim Tully, mentioned above in the letter of September 13, 1925, was the author of *Beggars of Life* (1924) and co-author of the screenplay of the movie version. He appeared as an actor in MGM's *Way for a Sailor* (1930, directed by Sam Wood). Later he was a writer on *The Raven* (1935), produced by Universal.

[2] Joseph Freeman (1897-1965).

To Marie Syrkin, [May 5, 1931]

Tuesday Evening.

Dearest:

I had no letter from you today; I hope to have one tomorrow.

I went to Los Angeles today and tried to sell hats—but did nothing. I have an appointment for tomorrow at 9; but it is too late here for Panamas and I am afraid it will be hard to sell anything. I'll know more tomorrow. In the meantime I managed to do a few pages of Pa's book and I'll work at it again this evening.

Last night I called up Joe Freeman—I went down to Santa Monica to see the ocean—and he wants me to have lunch or dinner with him and Pilniak[1]—I think he said. If the selling of hats is out, I'll work at Pa's book from 6 to 6 out in the patio and clean that up—maybe in a month or two. When Al comes back in ten days or so, I suppose the evenings will be busy.

The weather here is like this: early morning a cold damp fog, at about 9 it begins to get warm and it gets hot and sticky—sun shining brightly—until 5 or 6 in the evening; then it becomes cool and at night it is chilly. That's Los Angeles: later on, I am told it gets much hotter in the daytime. Now it is like a warm July day in New York but not so heavy.

I am leading a fantastic life and since you saw Charlie Chaplin in *City Lights*—the beggar in the automobile, you'll understand.[2] I am served dinner—alone—every evening in style by a butler in a white coat. I have a large touring car to ride wherever I please. The whole thing is Arabian nightish, but I really don't care much because I prefer the bus—the top out in the open air—to the closed limousine. Anyway, I feel silly. When Al comes back, I'll find a cheap room and a good cafeteria.

My darling, I think with longing of our year in the Bronx and I hope soon that we shall be together again never more to part. I think of you with tears in my eyes and with great longing. And now to work. I kiss you. Your husband,

Charles

---

[1] Boris Pilniak (1894–1937), prolific Russian novelist and short story writer. See, for example, Vera T. Reck, *Boris Pilniak: a Soviet Writer in Conflict with the State* (Montreal: McGill, Queen's University Press, 1975).

[2] Charles Chaplin (1889–1972) wrote, directed and starred in the 1931 silent comedy *City Lights*, which also starred Virginia Cherril, Florence Lee, and Harry Myers.

To Marie Syrkin, [May 6, 1931]

714 N. Roxbury Drive, Beverly Hills, Calif.
Wednesday Evening

Darling,

I have arranged to write the folks once a week, but I'll write you every day. However, don't feel obliged to write me every day, because I know how often you come home fagged out—but do write me at least once a week and let me know the day you write so that I may know when to expect your precious letter.

I spent almost all day in Los Angeles trying to sell hats and could do nothing: this is the deadest town I ever struck: the buyers look but have as much interest as I have in—anything I have no interest in at all. It may be too early for the ribbon hats, because one or two told me to come around next week; but from my experience of Los Angeles weather I think these hats too heavy for this part of the country. The climate here is vile, I think; it is chill and raw in the morning, chilly in the evening, and blazing hot in the daytime. This rapid alternation of temperature I find tiring, and I am told everybody complains until they are used to it.

From now on I expect to spend all day in the patio—which is an enclosed lawn with flowers, palm trees, birds, sunshine and shade—with the other birds; I expect to begin work at 7 and work until 7 at my father's book—to-date I have only finished the first thousand words, and I have 74,000 more to go. I hope to do about 2,000 a day in time.

I expect to send your aunt and Mrs. Epstein a slight gift and you some ornament that I really like—also Lilly and Dorothy one as soon as I feel I have the money to spare. I drew $197 from the Corn Exchange to open an account in a bank here (the Lewins' bank). That leaves $200 in the Corn Exchange (I think) and I have some money with me. Now, darling, if you need any draw against the $200 in the Corn Exchange. My plans are uncertain, but I expect to stay here for some time—I am told I can get a room in Santa Monica for $10 or 15 a month and food is cheap. In any event I am certain of only one thing—that I love you dearly, I am very glad that you are my wife and, I hope, mine forever, just as I hope that you are not sorry I am yours. Darling and loveliest, dearest and best.

I hope David is well; I hope the school work is not too hard for you; I hope and I hope. (Darling, you will keep writing me just what Lillian is doing—just as you have. I rely on you.)

Goodnight, sweetheart. I could write I love you a thousand thousand times just like kids have to do when they write one sentence over and over when they have been bad or late to school.

164

To Marie Syrkin, [May 7, 1931]

Thursday afternoon

Dearest,

I see in Sunday's paper (*N. Y. Times*) that we are required to file some kind of paper for our claim against the Bank of U. S. This amounts to $46 I believe. I am sorry, dearest, that you must go to this trouble—for since it is a joint account, you may file the claim in your name, I suppose—but I suppose they will tell you in the bank Saturday morning just what they owe us (if you cannot find it in the papers I left you) and fill out the papers for you. This is rather important, I suppose, but if you cannot do it this week or next, I am sure you have more time.

I have just finished revising about 1200 words of father's book and if I go no slower—and I should go faster—I ought to be through by July 10th Last night a young chap River who wrote *Death of a Young Man* and his wife came to see me,[1] we stayed up late, and they are arranging a party for me Saturday at which I am to meet all the Russians and some of the Russian Jews etc. in pictures, Pilniak etc. I am becoming quite black in the sun. I kiss you again and again, darling.

Charles

(No letter from you today).

To Marie Syrkin, [May 8, 1931]

Friday afternoon

Darling,

Your letter written Tuesday came today and I was sorry to read that the new building was not all that was anticipated—particularly, that the work was more tiring than ever. Sweetheart, I know your labours and your weariness. I think of that as I think of my sister's illness and my parents' troubles, and I feel—at times—ineffectual—mud beneath these charging hoofs. I flatter myself—at times—that some day I will do something somewhat lucrative, that you, at least, and that soon, will not have to work as you do. But, dearest, I have nothing but hopes and wishes. For the present, there are no hats to sell; I work at my father's book in the patio—

---

[1] Walter Leslie River (b. 1902), *Death of a Young Man* (New York: Simon and Schuster, 1927).

revising about six pages a day—that takes me almost the day, and I ought to be through in about two months—all but the typing. It is pleasant enough here, but, when I think of you and Lilly, it is not so pleasant, and I am still an alien among these palm trees and this cactus. Before I met you I think you were alone except for David, and now you are alone except for David—and except that somewhere there is a man—a kind of man—who calls himself your husband, who if he should get anywhere at all will help you get somewhere too, who loves you very much. None of this, however, is coin of the realm. However, May will be soon over, and June is not so hard a month for you; whether I do anything else or not, I do expect to have this book off my hands (at least written); your love is pleasant and lovely to think upon, without you I should be in a desert and even the sunshine tiresome. Do not be utterly discouraged, darling; next year in Jerusalem—that kept us going two thousand years.

Tonight I am going to visit Herman, Nathan's brother; I will not write you tomorrow, because tomorrow's party with Pilniak, Joe Freeman, River etc. may be interesting.[1] In any event I'll write about it Sunday.

Until then your knight in far *paynim* countries,

Charles

I am glad you like the basket. I couldn't find any ornaments for you or any young person—that's why I left Lilly and Dorothy out. But I did not want to send my mother the pin I liked for her without something for you—if only an empty basket.

> I would send my darling a poem;
> I think of her and am tearful,
> But song is dried up in me.

To Marie Syrkin, [May 9, 1931]

Sunday evening.

Darling:

I received the telegram this noon. I hope that—as it reads—all is well. I was afraid to send the folks a wire for fear that for a minute or two they might think it from the hospital—so I sent an air-letter special delivery. I

---

[1] Herman Reznikoff, Charles's uncle and the brother of his father Nathan.

asked them if they want me back; of course, if I thought they would need me, I would not have gone—but they may need me.

In a way I was relieved when the telegram came, because I knew that one kind of suspense—the first—had ended, and the second begun. I feel in a way as if I ran away, but I could not see that I would be any good—and it was awful, that first suspense, with my mother not saying anything, just looking absent-minded. I suppose you think it ironical that I should be at a party yesterday—but though important people were there Pilniak and Van Dyke (director of *Trader Horn*) among others, it was only so so—as such parties always are, unless you liquor up.[1] Of course, I don't and am disgustingly abstemious. Van Dyke took me back here in his car, so I don't think I offended anybody—in fact I don't think anybody minds a person who doesn't drink—it leaves more for the others. Incidentally, Pilniak drank almost nothing.

I am working all day at my father's book—but do no more than 6 pages—and am now waiting for news. Darling, please do not go to the hospital often—do not exhaust yourself.

Charles

To Marie Syrkin, [May 11, 1931]

714 N. Roxbury Drive
Beverly Hills, Calif.
Monday

Dearest,

Your annoyance at the brevity and vagueness of my notes is completely justified—all I can say is that after struggling all day with my father's manuscript—for I want to finish it as soon as possible, and yet can do no more than 6 pages a day, 36 to-date and 350 to go—I can hardly read, let alone write. And I do not write to give you information—all of which I hope to give you sooner or later—but to tell you that I love you, even though this writer has only a weak twitter by nightfall and that damned repetitious and monotonous. But, really, darling, the news here is not startling, the new things are in slight close detail which to be interesting

---

[1] W. S. Van Dyke (1899–1943) was the director of MGM's 1930 film, *Trader Horn*, produced by Irving Thalberg, about an African trader starring Harry Carey, Edwina Booth, and Duncan Renaldo (HFG).

would be difficult to do and I have no strength for it now—but hope to have.

I am sorry that you are finding the schoolwork so tiring and so tedious. I implore you to look at the calendar—you probably do a hundred times a day—but May is almost half over and June is easier. Just think how angry you would be if you were left in the annex. Perhaps, you could be transferred back there, on the plea that it is nearer home?

As for the Bank of U. S. blank, if your signature alone will not do (ask them, if you can) there is nothing to be done but to put it in a large envelope and send it to me. As for the telephone bill, I believe I paid every bill I got, but, of course, the bills cover a period about half a month prior to date and probably a month prior to payment. However, I can get the vouchers and I can straighten the matter out when I return (the vouchers are in the bank in Flatbush and you could get them, but, darling, don't; wait until I come back, a mistake is quite unlikely.)

Now, dearest, I have written to Lillian, to Paul, it is almost nine o'clock, I have a long walk to the post-office and I am tired. The variation—daily—from cool morning to hot day and cool evening is still tiring to me.

Al will probably be here by the first of next week; Milly will stay on in New York.

I kiss you goodnight. Please write me—Saturday night when you are not so tired—all about Lillian.

Charles

It is nice here, but it was also nice in Brooklyn—and the Bronx. Perhaps, nicer (not counting you, of course). Anyway, I have all the leisure I want to do my work and am thankful—profoundly.

To Marie Syrkin, [May 13, 1931]

Wednesday

Dearest:

I did not write you yesterday—nor did I hear from you or anybody for two days (I do not know whether this is a good sign or not—I suppose you have been to see Lillian and have been too tired to write, or have been too tired to write without seeing Lillian. Anyway, even if Lillian is recovering as fast as may be, I know she is not out of danger as yet. Perhaps, by tomorrow—). I did not write you because I was called to a gathering at Pilniak's room—the usual group—Joe Freeman, the Rivers, a female

168

stenographer, and in addition Mrs. Peretz Hirschbein.[1] Pilniak speaks very little German or French, I speak less, and for the most part—as River says—we look at each other like two strange dogs. Pilniak is about my age and has written ten novels—the first at 25 and about one a year after that. In Russia, Freeman tells me, if you are a writer you do practically nothing else: your work is passed upon by a board of what might be called the union of writers. If you belong to the literary division, you are guaranteed the sale of 10,000 copies. Pilniak writes no more than two pages a day—I suppose about six hundred words—that takes him about two hours, and the rest of the day he does work of a commercial nature, teach etc, or reads, talks etc. Pilniak, Freeman, & Co are going to Redlands (?) tomorrow to see a noted mission there, and I am cordially invited to tag along—it will mean the loss of a day's work and I am not yet decided about going. I have finished about ⅛ of Father's book (48 pages)—it is not bad so far. I am to go to dinner at the home of a composer of very successful musical comedies tonight—Stoddard—and will write you about it tomorrow or the day after.[2] I find nothing of great interest or importance here but the book I am working at—until Al is back probably by Sunday. Joe Freeman has been very friendly and he is planning some kind of a magazine. Rivers works for the motion-pictures but is thinking of quitting to do some work of his own. Everybody agrees that Pilniak is the real thing, but, of course, all I can see is that he looks it. We had dinner in his room—served by the Hotel Mirimar at Santa Monica—and it was poisonous. However, I feel fine today. If this breezy inconsequential writing at this time offends you, you know that that is not how I feel. I find myself always thinking of Lillian and the others and of you; I feel often restless and unhappy and, even though you think me a fool, I often wonder why the devil I came. But then I did see the hinterland of the country—which I began to feel important, I tested this and that—and the trip may still prove wise. However, I am, more than ever, yours.

Charles

Don't be uneasy about "testing this and that"; all I mean is selling hats, etc., looking at desert and mountains etc. I see a lot of pretty girls—kind of magazine-cover-like—in the streets and about the Metro Goldwyn studio (on my 2 visits). But I know none of them, and if I did, who would be like

---

[1] Peretz Hirschbein (1880–1948), Yiddish writer.

[2] This could refer to Harry Stoddard (1892–1951). But the next letter suggests that the reference is really to Herbert Stothard (1885–1949), who wrote the music for many MGM films.

you, dark-eyed one, speaker of honeyed malice, but kind of heart, noble of soul, you who are not merely pretty but beautiful, who are not merely beautiful but intelligent and noble-minded, my dear wife.

To Marie Syrkin, [May 15, 1931]

Friday morning

Darling: I received your letter about Lillian, and I hope by this time she is much better. I hope, too, that you have become somewhat used to the main building—certainly, your vacation is somewhat nearer.

I did not write you yesterday and, as you read the chronicle of parties that are the reason for it, you will think I am having a wonderful time—which is not true. But then, as I was told yesterday by a Bolshevist lady, I am a "yeshiva bucher." To begin with the night before last, I went to the party I told you about—at the home of the composer. He is the man who wrote the music for *Rose Marie* and many others.[1] The Rivers were there and a couple who came from New York—the man Sydney Phillips has been an actor and seems important in theatrical circles, the woman was exceedingly good-looking and has been an actress. They were very affectionate towards each other, and very good company. Our acquaintance—mine and the important man in theatrical circles, who seems to be some kind of agent now,—was exceedingly limited, although it turned out that we were graduates from the same public school. (I did not tell him the story of my life.) Anyway, the party broke up late and I did not get home until 2:30. Now Mrs. River was planning a trip to what was supposed to be a mission (old Spanish mission) in Redlands through the fruit country. I did not want to go, but they insisted they would call for me. So I got up at 6 in the morning, and did as much of my own work as I could. At eleven the party appeared: Mrs. River, Pilniak, his secretary, and a lady who has just come from Russia, a Ph.D. in farm economics, whose husband is an assistant to Pavlov, and whose son is a "pioneer"—Bolshevik "boy-scout." She is the lady who insisted that I am a "yeshiva bucher"—which was never a compliment and is less so in the mouth of a Bolshevik. Well, the ride was nice, but the mission, as Pilniak's secretary brightly remarked, was not a

---

[1] Stothard collaborated with Rudolf Friml (1879–1972) and others on the 1924 musical, *Rose Marie*.

mission but a restaurant. In fact, the building is modern with bits of old missions gathered about and a museum full of trash—including a picture of Nicholas II. The meal was vile, and expensive. Pilniak paid. (Mrs. River told me he is getting three thousand dollars a week, and so nobody seems to give a damn about his paying.) Then we walked about the stuffy corridors, Pilniak saying "Padom! Padom!" We rode back to Los Angeles, where the secretary left us, and we went to the Bolshevist lady's room—Mrs. River, Pilniak, and myself, to wait for Mr. River and Joe Freeman. Here Mr. Pilniak drank most of a pint of whiskey and lay on the bed and delivered in a long harangue at me what he thought of Hollywood, particularly of the way he is treated. This was translated sentence by sentence by the Ph.D. in farm economics, Pilniak waiting very obligingly. It was an excellent speech, to which I could only make some feeble remarks. However, Pilniak is not quite right; however, it was difficult to engage in a subtle argument, especially since just as I began Joe Freeman and *les* Rivers appeared. It was 9 o'clock. They took us to a Mexican restaurant—a swell place for Hollywoodists, expensive, but good. Here I saw a number of good-looking women, Mexican and American, and tasted a lot of Mexican dishes—special dinner which everybody had. (Pilniak paid.) I got home at 1 in the morning, taken here in Mr. Pilniak's new Ford car in which he is about to cross the continent or go to Japan. It's now about 6:30, the starlings are making a racket outside the window, and I am writing this before I do anything else—feeling guilty about not writing yesterday. Pilniak and Joe Freeman are leaving in a day or two, and Al Lewin is coming back, it is said, Sunday or tomorrow night. I like Joe Freeman very much; he is a very clever Jew—"a mazick," and since he is going to be in New York, I'll look him up there (by invitation). The Rivers are fine, genuine people, Americans, that is she is of German parents, and he of French-Irish. They are very good friends of Mr. and Mrs. Lewin, and will no doubt appear often in these notes, as for Pilniak—well, I have no idols. Dearest girl, if you were here you might have a good time, but I should have a bad one, for Mr. Pilniak is very free with his hands and his kisses (for females). (This is not why Pilniak is not an idol, though a goddam clever man—at least.) However, I suppose I am a "yeshiva bucher"; however, other kinds of people too used to object to having their wives kissed. However, this subject, because of my inability to kiss you which I so long to do, is painful. Permit me then to say good-morning and to assure you, that in addition to my sister's illness and your absence, I am not having such a good time. (Darling, I love you.) Charles loves Marie!

Charles

To Marie Syrkin, [May 17, 1931]

Sunday

Dearest,

Al Lewin came home last night and since then we have been going out and people have been coming here—I have stolen away to write you just a line. Pilniak is downstairs and others—I will write you again tomorrow. Dearest, I have taken you into a corner to whisper that I love you—that it will be impossible to live through the summer without you—I will probably go to Berkeley in a few weeks (details later) and if it is pleasant you must come there with David; if not I will have to go to you and David. But life without you, Marie, simply isn't. Darling, I just have time for this note. More—or less—tomorrow.

Charles

To Marie Syrkin, [May 18, 1931]

714 N. Roxbury Drive, Beverly Hills, Calif.
Monday Afternoon

Darling,

I hope this will prove to be a long letter, for I have much to tell you, and yet nothing of consequence or very new. But I may not get a chance to write you a *letter*, as you would say, instead of a note, for some time, for with Al's return I have no time at all evenings, and during the day I want to do my work. Yesterday, Sunday, I had no time to write at all, and could merely jot down a line to my parents; I hope to write them before next Sunday again—in any event, I see this will be a rambling letter with much repetition of what you know too well, perhaps.

To begin with my work: I have managed to do sixty-five pages of manuscript of my father's book: this leaves 320 to do which should take me from a solid month to a month and a half—most likely the latter. By "do," I mean, as you surmise, writing in a little, striking out a lot; and yet I think I have something readable. In all the book will probably be 50,000 words (about ⅓ of the original). I am doing nothing else. As for selling hats— perhaps I wrote you that the taffeta hats Nathan gave me—as I knew—were not his, but copied from the hat of another manufacturer, in fact, there was a window-display of the hats in Stern's or Best's.[1] That is where Nathan got the hat, and so, no doubt, did others. But not only this—the original manufacturer, who has been making the hat for four years, so I was told in Pittsburgh, is selling it for $3 a dozen less than what Nathan wants. I do not blame Nathan, because even at his price, his profit is not large, but that is the problem of the salesman to get a good house—one that creates or sells cheaply. I doubt that Nathan's is either—as yet. As for the panamas he sent me, Los Angeles uses for the most part, since it has a large poorly-paid population, cheap hats—to sell retail at $1.98, and I have none such. I spent, I suppose $25 more on the trip because of the hats, and made more uncomfortable jumps at first, not taking the best trips—those that begin early in the morning. I shall try to sell the taffeta hats in San Francisco, which is a better market for them, but should I not do anything, I will waste no more time with them.

Now as to the motion pictures: the salaries, although large, are exaggerated. For instance, Pilniak does not get three thousand a week as Mrs. River told me, but five hundred; however, he has been hired only for a few weeks—perhaps, a month. In addition, in his case, he is very much annoyed, because he has been given a scenario which he thinks stupid and false, and his job is to fill in the realistic detail. Moreover, the picture will be anti-bolshevik, and the consequences for Pilniak are bound to be unpleasant. River, for instance, gets $150 a week; Lewin, who gets $1250, is one of the important figures in the industry. Thalberg, who is manager of Metro-Goldwyn, the most successful, financially and artistically of the motion-picture companies, has now six or seven assistants of whom Lewin is one.[2] His work is most important: for instance, he went east chiefly to arrange matters with Alfred Lunt and Lynn Fontanne.[3] I find Al Lewin clever as ever and the most intelligent man I ever met; but he and I feel he is wasted in the work he does and we discussed in detail the plans he is making for himself and if these work out his work will be somewhat more creative—and though he will make much less, he will be far happier. All I

---

[1] Nathan Reznikoff, Charles's cousin.

[2] Irving Grant Thalberg (1899-1936), film producer and studio executive. Thalberg was Al Lewin's superior at MGM. Married to Academy Award winning actress, Norma Shearer, Thalberg is said to be the model for the protagonist of F. Scott Fitzgerald's final novel, The Last Tycoon (1941) (IDFF).

[3] Alfred Lunt (1892-1977) and his wife Lynn Fontanne (1892-1982), primarily stage actors, appeared in just two films together: Second Youth (1924) and The Guardsman (1931) (Katz).

have surmised about motion-picture business I have found true: the pay is large but uncertain, the work exhausting, most exhausting of any for writers, because none of them, even those who wrote when they were advertising men or what not, can do nothing of their own—because they are constantly attempting to do imaginative work. And this work is of a particularly degrading kind, because everything, of course, must have box-office value above all. Now, as to what this box-office value is—as far as I can judge from listening to Al Lewin, it is more or less codified in formulae, so that the writer must not only be a prostitute, but he cannot even, unless he is very successful, be a prostitute in his own way. Anyway, I hear of this and that man who has come here because of a literary success and none has done anything more of his own—nor is any as great a financial success, say as Al Lewin. The most successful by far are those who have done only their own work, writing their own books, and their profit from the motion-pictures has been simply sales of the rights. We knew all this, still it is important to talk with men actually writing for the movies and live here for a while. To begin with the climate here is enervating; I have been told this, but one must experience it to know just how and why. I believe it is due to the rapid alternation of hot and cold, for, as I wrote you, the mornings and evenings are cool—as our autumn or spring, the days are hot as in summer. This sounds very pleasant in advertisements, but the result is tiring—and, after a year or two, very tiring. This is why this place is a kind of lotus land for creative people, they talk and live pleasantly, but very little, if anything, is done here. However, this may be, I see no likelihood of—and have no wish to—doing anything for the motion-pictures here. At this you may feel exasperated at my having spent so much—well, I have so far spent about $200, perhaps a dollar or so less, have lived one month and seen the country. I feel tremendously refreshed and have stored up, I believe, many sights and sounds. I have tested some of my ideas—and found them no good; well, I count it a gain to be rid of them.

Now then, for my future plans: I expect to stay here—unless there should be reason for a change, and if so, it will be by way of extension of my stay most likely—another week. That is, I expect to leave next Monday morning so as to spend another Sunday with Al. Milly will not be back for another week, or so; but these are my reasons for leaving: Al has been as friendly, if not friendlier than ever. He urges me to stay for months. Still, I can hardly do that in all decency. Besides, it is hard for me to work here. I have not gone to bed before 2 o'clock for a week. Whether friendly or not, and when they get drunk some—like Jim Tully—become unfriendly (though none to me because I am still a guest), everybody is extremely sociable: there are always the people of your circle—which is usually a small one— dropping in or inviting you out. Now, last night we went to a Chinese restaurant where the food was most disgusting and then we picked up a gang of strangers—negroes—male and female—and went to their house. I, as you imagine, was not the life of the party—and I don't give a damn. During the day, I sit in the patio: here it is pleasant, though no pleasanter than many other places. It is very hot until evening, there is a palm tree, flowers etc, enclosed by a high whitewashed wall, it belongs to the house and no one enters it all day but I—green turf, easy chairs—however, there are also flies: some bite, others just crawl on your hands and neck and face. However, I prefer it to the house, which is cool and screened. Well then, if I cannot stay on and on decently, I should get a room. But every place is so far from every other place in this city—Beverly Hills is 6 miles from Santa Monica, 4 from Culver City, 10 from Los Angeles, 4 from Hollywood. I thought of stopping at one of the beaches, bathing is best during the middle of the day, but I am not so keen about it. In other words, in another week I should have had enough of Los Angeles, and I would leave today were it not for my friendship for Al Lewin and the feeling that to leave almost as soon as he returns would be unfriendly. We have talked a good deal together, in fact we spent all of the day yesterday talking until Pilniak, Freeman, and River came, and I feel more than ever that he has a lovely mind. Pilniak has become friendly, for some reason or other, and insisted on my autographing for him a copy of "By the Waters etc." He told me that his grandmother was a Jewess.

I plan then to leave for San Francisco. Here I expect to see and spend some time with Gaer. If I find Berkeley as pleasant as I am told it is, I shall compare it with Riverdale, for instance, and we can then discuss your coming out here with David for the summer. In any event, in San Francisco (Berkeley, you know, is 20 minutes on the ferry across the bay), I expect to see a large law publishing house and I may be able to make some arrangement with them—half time or outside work, but I expect nothing. When I shall have spent a few days in San Francisco, or rather Berkeley, this discussion of plans—my plans—will be continued. In the meantime, I know very well I have said nothing about you. I do not like to speak of *our* happiness, because I consider myself as happy as I can reasonably be. I am well-fed (very well fed, just now), sufficiently clothed, married to a woman I love and who, I think, loves me (although separated, I hope it will not be for more than another month or so), for the most part I manage to do the work I want to and receive for it as much recognition as I merit. But, I am very conscious that you want leisure, an opportunity to do your work, amusement and *children*. In other words, though I may be fairly happy and have reason to be, you have reason to be dissatisfied. And since I love you and crave your happiness, I think about it often and hope that all those promissory notes I gave and give you will be paid.

Sometimes, just out of the blue sky or the starry sky, I think of you and then I imagine that I put my arms about you and hold you very close and kiss you for a long long time.

Charles

To Marie Syrkin, [May 20, 1931]

Wednesday

Dearest:

Monday night I went to a pre-view at Santa Monica with Al. There was a crowd to see the notables come out and Al and I were scrutinized as we walked to his car. It is not an unpleasant sensation—you look completely glassy and unaware, but inside of you you are not displeased. Last night Pilniak came here with his friends to say good-by: he was very friendly, called me "friend Reznikoff," and invited me to visit him in Moscow. Some of the party got drunk—not the Russians and not the Jews—but we had to take one who was neither home—who was too drunk to drive his car. So I could not write you. To-night Al is going out alone—that is without me: I shall go early to bed thankfully.

I notice in the papers (*N. Y. Times*) that the U. S. bank paper (claim) must be filed by June 30th. I have not received any and I suppose they accepted yours as sufficient—as I think it is. In your last letter you comment on the mystery about Lilly that is being manufactured. Of course, I agree with you—and I suppose it is their innocence. But it is too late for me to do anything. I never expected that the hospital as well as the disease would be a mystery, or I certainly should have objected. I have been working hard all day on Father's book and am tired. Forgive me for writing no more. Dearest and dearest—will this tell you how much I love you, how my thoughts play about your image as I see you in my mind. Dear Marie, I love you very much; I become a little drunk when I think of you—but my legs are sober enough, only my heart staggers.

Charles

Charles and his younger brother, Paul (1896).

From left to right: Father (Nathan), Charles, Lillian, Paul, Mother
(Sarah) (ca. 1908).

Charles at the University of Missouri, compulsory ROTC
(ca. 1910–1911).

Albert Lewin portrait on occasion of his New York University
graduation (1915).

Marie Syrkin, age 18 (ca. 1920).

Albert Lewin (ca. 1927).

SAGETRIEB

CHARLES REZNIKOFF ISSUE

Volume 13, Numbers 1 & 2 • Spring & Fall 1994

Charles Reznikoff and his niece, Camilla (1932–1933).

Charles Reznikoff (ca. 1935).

Charles and his father, Nathan Reznikoff, on the streets of Brooklyn
(ca. 1939).

Marie Syrkin (1940s).

Marie Syrkin (ca. 1950).

Marie's favorite study of Charles in his later years (1950s).

Albert Lewin (ca. 1950).

Marie Syrkin (1980s).

To Marie Syrkin, [May 22, 1931]

Friday

Darling,

I did not write you yesterday—there was nothing new to write about. The night before I went to bed early, and during the day worked in the patio. In the evening Al and I went to another preview. He is anxious that I stay on all summer in his house, but I feel that I should not. We have now resumed our ancient harmony of mind, but it is not easy for me to work here—during the day it is so hot and at night, there is almost a constant round of entertainment—and the only way I'll ever make money is through the sale of my books—if and when. To-night, for instance we are going to a dinner-party at the house of the musician I wrote you about—whose music we heard at yesterday's pre-view—and I suppose we'll be back at 2 in the morning. Then the summer without you would be very unpleasant. I do not feel justified in asking you to come without David and I do not think you ought to bring David to Los Angeles for two months—I do not know how this change of climate, food, etc, might affect him. From all I gather, if you come to California, Berkeley will be much better for all of us. Well, I shall see; for I plan to leave here Monday morning. On the whole I have had an exceedingly pleasant time here, but, in my opinion, this is the time to leave. I am buying a ticket only to Berkeley—but I do not intend to spend the summer away from you—I have spent too many years away from you. But that was before I knew you or before we were married, darling.

Charles

To Marie Syrkin, [May 23, 1931]

Saturday Evening

Dearest,

I am spending this at home—quietly. Last night's dinner-party was so so: I am tired of dinner-parties—the rich food, the drinks, the small talk. I am afraid I am not a social being. Al has gone away, but tomorrow we shall spend all day together and Monday morning I leave for San Francisco (Fresno Monday night)—San Francisco Tuesday.

I have finished about one fourth of my father's book, but it is becoming harder to work here as this lazy weather gets you. At least everybody says it is lazy weather—but San Francisco—they all say—is cool and bracing.

Al has been extremely friendly to me—so have his friends—and we have had a number of our old time talks. I would stay if I saw any future: but I see worse as far as I am concerned. Even this letter seems to me the worst yet: forgive me, darling, dearly beloved and most precious. Marie, if others have gone west to be divorced; I have gone west to feel myself completely and absolutely married, now and forever. I kiss your hand and your mouth (I have no cold).

Charles

~~I am enclosing cards for the children.~~
(I mailed them separately).

To Marie Syrkin, [May 27, 1931]

Pickwick Hotel, San Francisco
Wednesday Evening

Dearest:

Your letter to Beverly Hills, dated May 24th, was forwarded to Berkeley. I found Berkeley a pleasant suburb—nothing wonderful, and San Francisco much pleasanter than Los Angeles. Still, I do not think I ought to spend more time here and I am going on. Riverdale is much better for us—in every way.

It costs very little more to go up to the Far North and this is the way I expect to go home:

<blockquote>
Thurs. Eve.—Eureka, Calif.
Fri Eve—Grants Pass, Ore.
Sat. Eve—Portland, Ore.
Sunday—Seattle and back to Portland.
Mon. Eve—Pendleton, Ore.
Tues. Eve—Boise, Ida.
Thurs. Eve—Denver, Colo.
Fri Eve—North Platte, Neb.
Sat Eve—Omaha, Neb.
Sun Eve. St. Paul, Minn.
Mon Eve. Waupaca, Wis.
Tues. Eve.—South Bend, Ind.
</blockquote>

Wed. Eve–Toledo, Ohio.
Thurs. Eve. Pittsburgh, Pa.
Fri. Eve (midnight)–Philadelphia.
Sat.–New York

[Marie,]

Of course, this is tentative and may be changed. I'll advise you from almost every stop (sometimes, when arrival is at midnight, this *will* be postponed a day).

This should bring me home about the middle of June and will give us lots of time to clean up the Bank of U. S. claim, summer plans etc.

I bought some gifts today for your folks and mine and they are being sent from here. They are slight, because I cannot spend much. I am having sent to you three necklaces (I hope they go over your heads), one each for you, your aunt and Mrs. Epstein. The chain is supposed to be sterling silver and the pendant is a bead of genuine crystal. There are three shapes to the head–so take your choice. I prefer the square one for you. It is a trifle–so do not expect much. I am also having sent a kind of necklace of imitation jade in a little box for Sylvia and a safe of wood for David. This is a trick box–if you slide a panel you will find a key hole and if another panel is moved in two directions you will find the key. I sent other things to my mother, sister, and Dorothy–which they will show you no doubt.

I am somewhat worried about my mother because in my father's last letter he did not mention her. I hope she is in good health and all of you. You might write General Delivery–*Chicago*. (I shall stop there en route).

Charles

To Marie Syrkin, [May 30, 1931]

Heathman Hotels, Portland, Oregon
Saturday Night

Dearest,

I could not write last night, because I did not stop at Grant's Pass–it is quite hot now throughout the West–but went on to Eugene. I arrived at 12:45 A.M. and had to be up early to catch the bus for Portland that left at 7.

179

Today I went about 100 miles on the way to Seattle—the most interesting part—and came back to Portland. I leave tomorrow morning for the East. I expect to stop at Pendleton, Ore., tomorrow night; Boise, Ida, Monday night; and Cheyenne or Denver Wednesday—that is I expect to ride all night through the desert.

Sweetheart, I am well—"feeling fine"—and I hope all of you are so too. I am somewhat sleepy—you must forgive brevity and clumsiness while on my way. Good night, dearest. I hope to be with you soon.

Charles

Please write Chicago, General Delivery.

To Marie Syrkin, [June 1, 1931]

Hotel Boise, Boise, Idaho
Monday noon

Dearest,

morning star in the east, towards which the buses I ride in travel, I suppose my schedules are as uncertain as my mother's recipes. Well, Pendleton was too hot to stay in, so I came on to Boise and arrived at dawn. I am leaving at 1 o'clock for Twin Falls and expect to be in Salt Lake City by 1 tomorrow afternoon. Still, I may stop over elsewhere for the night.

I am fine and hope to hear from you in Chicago. (I am satisfied that the climate in New York is no hotter than elsewhere in summer. Portland was hot. It is cooler in Boise.)

Charles

To Albert and Mildred Lewin, June 28th [1931]

Dear Al and Milly,

We are at 3615 Greystone Av., Bronx, N.Y.C. I am back at the American Law Books Company this Monday on, but I hope to be able to do some of my own work. Many thanks for forwarding the letter: the first was of no value, but the second was a request to include some of the old verse in a new edition of the *The New Poetry*.[1]

Please remember me to the Rivers and to the people down the street (composer of *Rose Marie* and wife). Marie and I hope to see you in New York this fall.

Charles Reznikoff

To Albert Lewin, Aug 30th, [1931]

3615 Greystone Av, Bronx NYC

Dear Al,

I am sorry to hear that Milly is not well. Should she come to New York, I hope that she will call me up (Halifax 5-2947) as soon as she can, if I can be of any service—or Paul.

I have gone back to the American Law Book Company for a while—a long while this time, I think. So far I have managed to do my own work mornings and evenings: this year I hope to finish the two books I have been working at—such as they are; and then I have the usual plans, another book, verse, and so forth.

I hope that you will soon be free to do your own work—in pictures and in writing. I hope too that you will come to New York this autumn as you planned.

Marie sends you and Milly her love, and please remember me to your friends who were so kind to me.

Charles

---

[1] Reznikoff's "A Group of Verse, I–VI" was included in Harriet Monroe and Alice Corbin Henderson's anthology *The New Poetry* (1932).

To Albert Lewin, [September 1931]

3615 Greystone Av, Bronx N.Y.C.
Sunday

Dear Al,

Please don't mind my not writing often—or just a scrawl when I do; but I have less time than ever now. However, I am managing to do some of my own work, and am thankful for that.

I saw Milly at the hospital yesterday. She was looking very well, was very cheerful, has books, candy, flowers, and a very nice room. We expect to go out some day next week—Milly, Marie and I—probably just to a restaurant, for there is almost nothing to see. Marie and I saw *The Guardsman* and though the audience seemed to like it immensely and so did Marie—the play is so bad, I suppose they did the best they could.[1] Of course, it is better as a play than a picture; for, as I think you said, a picture must be closer to reality, at least when all the furniture and people are photographs of reality, the fable itself cannot be so improbable. Well, I am too tired to go into that; besides, I have no enthusiasm for abstraction in these matters.

Your mother told me that you lost your father.[2] I felt sad remembering his cheerful aloofness. I knew him hardly at all. Well, it's as if one is walking along the street and a light in a house goes out—just one of the rooms—but it's a room in your house. I'll try to write again soon, and write me when you can.

Charles

Remember me to the Rivers and Stothards.

---

[1] *The Guardsman*, Alfred Lunt and Lynn Fontanne's only talking picture, was a 1931 MGM production produced by Albert Lewin and directed by Sidney Franklin.
[2] Lewin's father died on 4 September 1931 (Felleman 260).

To Albert and Mildred Lewin, Nov 14, 1931

3615 Greystone Av, Bronx NY

Dear Al and Milly,

Back home and somewhat weak—but strong enough to go to work this Monday or next, I hope.

Thank you very much for your inquiries and for your flowers which brightened the room for quite a few days and impressed the nurses by the size of the box in which they came—"like a casket," the head nurse said. Please thank the Rivers, the Stothards, and Jim Tully for their kind wishes.

I am afraid a trip to California to recuperate would require a special recuperation of its own—but I thank you. I hope you will soon be able to come to New York to recuperate from California and that we shall be able to see each other often in libraries and restaurants, as we used to, and in each other's homes, and not in hospitals.

Marie sends her love.

Charles

To Mildred Lewin, [December 1931]

Sunday

Dear Milly;

I saw Kling yesterday afternoon and he promised to send your picture off last night. He asked $15—so I endorsed your check and gave it to him. He seemed very anxious to sell to Beverly Hills and I hope you and Al will be pleased—but if not, please let me know and I'll drop in on Mr. Kling.

There is no news. A new magazine *Contact* may run the book I was working at last year—at least the first number is supposed to have the first part of the first part.[1] If it does come out and so forth, I'll send a copy. I am still working at the American Law Books Company and still at my father's book—probably for the rest of the winter.

---

[1] An excerpt from Reznikoff's "My Country Tis of Thee" appeared in *Contact: An American Quarterly Review*. 1:1 (February 1932):14–34. A second excerpt appeared in the May 1932 edition of *Contact*.

Marie sends her love and we both wish you and Al and all our friends a merry Christmas and a happy New Year.

Charles

To Albert Lewin, Feb 22 [1932]

2165 Greystone Av, Bronx

Dear Al,

I am reading a rather informative and interesting book you might look at—*The European Caravan*, an anthology by Samuel Putnam and others, published by Brewer, Warren and Putnam, N.Y.[1]

Marie sends her love to you and Millie, and we hope she is fully recovered.

Charles Reznikoff

To Albert Lewin, [March 1932]

3900 Greystone Ave
Tuesday.

Dear Al,

This is the second day of my vacation and I feel restless—anxious to be out walking, out in the open, before the subway and the office door is closed upon me for another year, and yet, if I don't write you this letter, it will bother me for a long time. But, don't mind, if I am not orderly, if I empty what I have to say upon the floor any old way, just as I might be talking to you in your living room while the maid clears the dishes away in the next room and before Jim Tully or the Rivers or Pilniak and Joe Freeman or all of them together come riding up. Well, then, to begin with, I feel somewhat responsible for the *European Caravan* since I got you to buy it. I have been reading in it very slowly, not because it's so good but

---

[1] Samuel Putnam (1892–1950), *The European Caravan* (1931).

because I haven't had much time. I know you haven't either: so let me tell you that I have found the following so far: the end of Paul Morand's "Another Jew Dead" p. 107, some of Georges Ribémont-Dessaignes "The Coffee-Cup" p. 178, Ramón Perez de Ayala "Dón Guillén and La Pinta" p. 344, and Jose Ortega y Gossart's "Time, Distance and Form in Proust" p. 355.[1] I am now at p. 377. So much for that. Milly's visit raised again the whole problem of work—our own and others—jobs and leisure. As for me I have managed to become somewhat better at my work for the legal encyclopedia, I do much more and I don't meditate upon it and polish it. I'm not supposed to. Kiser, my chief, said to me, If I hire a man to make me a crate, I don't expect him to finish it like a piano. Well, I'm making crates; what they want is speed and accuracy; we are not writing a philosophical treatise nor literature; it is a reference book to the law, to the opinions of judges. As for my own work, at present it is this: I divide it into work horizontal and vertical. The "vertical" is the moment, the as/ is; if possible from the top of the sky to the bottom of the earth. For that my instrument is the poem,—and, of course, I rarely succeed. But I try to write some verse every day, to keep up whatever skill I have—for which I don't give a damn—and, above all, the seeing eye, "the haiku spirit." Many days, of course, I don't do anything; many days it's just rubbish; but at the end of these months or so I have a group of ten or twelve. Some of these drop away, and at the end of a year I might have two dozen bits of verse I would print myself. Well, I don't print them myself anymore because there are some magazines that take them—not magazines of any consequence, if there are any, and I think that if I get a publisher for my prose he will do my verse too. So I keep putting off a privately printed book or booklet of verse. That brings me to the "horizontal"—the succession of events, the story, the years. As for that I work at the "novel"—in prose. I have just finished my father's book and given it to an agent. I have a novel, partly on paper and partly in my mind, which I am working at. The book I had just finished when I came out to see you is very far from this horizontal treatment—it is closer to the "vertical," the poem," and is more like a poem in prose. It is now running serially in a magazine—a sort of little magazine, *Contact*, and I am very doubtful; of a publisher, or that the magazine will print it all.[2] In other words, I haven't written a satisfactory book in prose at all, but I think the one I'm at work on is on the right track. Now I find that I can put down four or five or six hundred words a day, almost every day

---

[1] Reznikoff is listing typographical errors, such as "Gossart" for "Gasset."
[2] See note to Reznikoff's letter dated December 1931.

and I can revise almost that many each day—that means a book a year. I try to do it in the morning before I go to work and in the subway or elevated— I take the cream off the day for myself. Of course, if I had evolved this system years ago, I might have done much better and more; and then, too, I may not be able to keep it up, but "hitherto hath the Lord helped me." Looking back, I find that two principles or axioms of conduct that I started out with have been confirmed by experience; first, that human beings are capable of improvement as a result of application and second that change brings as many disadvantages as advantages and is seldom worth while. Like all generalizations they are easily made fun of and are capable of ludicrous applications, but à propos of the first I like to think of Gilbert Murray's sentence about the Athenians that their achievements were not as remarkable as the fact that within a century they raised themselves from barbarism to Athens, and though I know well the proverbs that one cannot make a silk purse out of a sow's ear or a silk girdle out of a pig's tail, secretly I think better of myself than that.[1] Now, as for you, I urge you again, as I used to urge you years ago, not to wait—to leave Hollywood, of course you will, when you will have nothing to surrender, nothing to lose but your chains, but why not begin your own work now. It will take you a long time to get into it again. If, as part of your duties, you had to write a novel a year, you could, of course: you have in Hollywood a theme, an endless series of themes, you can get rid of all your bile, your malice, your humor and wit; you will feel tremendously relieved and your job will no longer be as close and chafing, you will become observer as well as protagonist as far as your job is concerned and protagonist as well as observer in the fights you care about. Al, you have merely to set down a few words a day, fifty or a hundred, daily you will do more and more; just as you spoke French at the breakfast table when I visited you, you might try writing English. Do it in the morning before you go to work, do it as you take a shower or shave or urinate—empty the bladder of your mind daily. Forgive the hortatory tone—the successful alumnus at the graduation exercises. But I am against postponement—I always hear a clock ticking—I am against change where nothing is changed but unpleasantness, the unpleasantness of one kind of work for that of another (how often I imagine that), the unpleasantness of distasteful work for the boredom of nothing to do (I have done that too). At this point we will wring the neck of rhetoric, even though the neck be that of

Charles Reznikoff

---

[1] Gilbert Murray (1866–1957), well-known classicist.

Of course, this is based on the assumption that you still consider the written word as your private medium—as I hope you do. Excellent and compelling as the screen is, you know the money it takes, the people you have to interest. As for a novel, even if you had to pay for the printing, which I don't expect, it won't be more than a week's salary (yours not mine). You will need no designers, no actors etc. (One result of working for an encyclopedia is that one is always stating the obvious—it's safe). Well, now, I hear the Rivers' automobile on the stones outside. Now, the bell rings. Please remember me to them and Millie. Marie sends her regards. By the way, I have received a letter that an anthology (by "a group") is mailed to me with some of my stuff (six copies) and I'll send you one as soon as it comes.[1]

To Henry Hurwitz, [August 2, 1932]

3900 Greystone Ave., Bronx
Tuesday afternoon

Dear Mr. Hurwitz:

Here it is the second day of my vacation, a warm sunny day, and I am still indoors with pen and paper, typewriter etc., my companions all this year and I suppose all of next year and for years to come. I meant to read *The Menorah* from cover to cover, carefully, and write you a detailed letter, but I cannot—I must get into the open.[2] I dipped into the first article—in fact into everything. You were right about Shuster—he is good, straightforward, unpretentious, and yet the reader gets a notion of what it's all about and a bit of nostalgia. Bransten's *High Destiny* is a little overdrawn—his hand is too heavy at times—but it's interesting. Lowenthal is always that, but more like pastry than bread. I won't go on—I haven't time, the sun is sinking. As for the adaptation I am sending you, it consists of almost all that moved me in *Jeremiah*—boiled down. If it moves you, *The Menorah* is welcome to it: if not, in a world where there is so much being written a few lines won't come between us—especially as I can't help thinking, how long ago and far away.

Charles Reznikoff

---

[1] Louis Zukofsky, ed. *An "Objectivists" Anthology,* published in France in 1932.

[2] *The Menorah Journal.* 20:2 (Summer 1932) included contributions from Marvin Lowenthal, "Paris—That Great City" (123–34), Richard Bransten, "High Destiny: Sketch for a Novel" (151–57), and Zachariah Shuster, "Letters from Abroad: Tel-Aviv: Progress and Problems in Palestine" (159–66).

To Henry Hurwitz, September 5th, [1932?]

3900 Greystone Av, Bronx N. Y. C.

Dear Henry,

When I first got your note I was anxious to accept your invitation to be at Mt. Vernon; but thinking about what to say, I realized that I could give no talk of any merit off hand. The preparation of even the most informal of talks would take me probably a week, for as you know I work all day until late. It would give me great pleasure to be of some service to the *Journal*, but I must postpone these luxuries until I have more time.

Yours
Charles

To Albert and Mildred Lewin, Dec 25th [1932]

3900 Greystone Av, Bronx, N.Y.C.

Dear Al and Milly,

Marie and I thank you for your Christmas greetings and book of drawings. The drawings are particularly amusing as Christmas greetings—in this season of powdered sugar. I wonder if they are like the drawings of Michael Carr which he would not show me for fear of corrupting an innocent whose thoughts were still all of food.

We hope to see you in New York soon and send our wishes for a happy New Year.

Yours
Charles R. (mistake).

To Henry Hurwitz, February 24th [1933]

3615 Greystone Avenue, Bronx, New York City

Dear Mr. Hurwitz,

I thought the verse of mine you are thinking of running in the next issue was safely dead. If you care to run it in the form attached, I'd be very glad; but if not, please forget about it.

As for the prose, the little stories etc., proofs of which I corrected, I wonder if you can let me know now if you have decided to scrap them, or which you have decided to scrap. I should very much like to send those you don't want elsewhere.

In any event, I hope to finish the revision of the novel I was telling you about and to show it to you in a month or so: it deals with Jews in business here and in Russia—the small traders we heard about last night.[1]

Very truly yours,
Charles Reznikoff

To Henry Hurwitz, February 28th [1933?]

3615 Greystone Avenue, Bronx, New York City.

Dear Henry,

As for the prose stories, if you want them, of course they are yours. I am returning the proofs uncorrected and will correct them when you are ready for them.

As for Exodus, if you prefer, let the first two stanzas stand as you have them—I like them well enough. However, I do not like the end of the last stanza. Please do not use it. I submit the attached stanza in its place as more in keeping with the language and mood of the first two stanzas.

Very truly yours,
Charles Reznikoff

To Marie Syrkin, April 1st. [1933]

Saturday evening

Darling wife,

I have just come from Sylvia's birthday party where I saw David who was very busy romping and having a glorious time. He looked to be in perfect health and was as cheerful as I ever saw him. I tried to talk to him

---

[1] *Early History of a Sewing Machine Operator* (1936).

but he seemed shy and I didn't want to make myself a nuisance. Sylvia is becoming quite beautiful and seemed in the best of spirits and health. Your aunt and Mrs. Epstein are well too, and the household seems the same as ever.

As for the tasks you set me, they are all done: your shoes are in the hanger on your door, I sent all the blankets but those I use to the laundry and tonight I am wrapping them in tar paper and putting them in the paper box. I have also sent your clothes to the cleaner, that is a red scarf attached, and your black coat and white fur; all of this is going into paper bags with mothballs as directed. Monday I call up Marian for your check. Now one more thing. The state department took over the Globe and Rutgers Insurance Company in which Eisner insured your luggage. I called him up and he told me that he secured similar insurance in another company for you, but you must return the Globe and Rutgers policy. I believe you have it with you. If so, return it to me at your convenience and I'll send it on to Eisner. I have also secured burglary and theft insurance as you suggested. There is no real news here otherwise. I have begun to lose weight and am feeling fine. Definitions are going on as always. I have had a few very friendly talks with Mr. Kiser, which he initiated, about the German situation. The press here has been extremely friendly to the Jews and the general feeling among those of German descent is one of embarrassment. However, I feel very uneasy about the Jews, and the ludicrous fire-eating announcements that are printed, while they make the Germans ridiculous in the eyes of Americans, are probably lapped up in Germany. It is easy to diet when I think that one of the most cultured nations of the west is in the hands of such barbarous and unjust stupidity. Forgive me, for these vaporings, but I am going to write a long lament for Israel, and though that will do nobody but me any good, I suppose, I feel the compulsion like a task set me by a boss.

The spring issue of *The Menorah* appeared without your poem and without my Jeremiah. Well, just as well. I am not too keen about it, and may drop it completely. Otherwise, I have worked at verse this week, at the prose, read a little of the book of Daniel in that cursed Aramaic, and a little of Marx. Have not heard from Lieber about that $200.

Darling, this "bundle of contradictions" sits at this desk; it is very quiet here, very clean and delightful. No one talks to me as I typewrite or read, and yet I do not think of your absence at all gladly, though I am very glad that you have gone, for your sake and because of all the sights you will see and all the pleasant excitements you will have. I know that you will throw this letter up to me some time, but nevertheless I must tell you that I love you very much, that the thought of you and the memory of you seems as much part of me as my breath and blood. My nerves are tied to you. But do not hurry back. However, I need not warn *you* to see the Grand Canyon. Forgive me if I do not close with the customary xs and kisses, but the thought of these is too disquieting. Have a good time. Have a glorious time. Be your glorious self. Shalom.

Charles

To Marie Syrkin, April 8th [1933]

Saturday

Dearest wife,

I was beginning to get worried about you, but last night at my folks I found your postal and when I came home your cable and two letters, one from the boat and the other from Paris. I called up Aaron at once and gave him the address and also called up Mrs. Epstein to let your aunt and Sylvia know.

Everything here is going on as always. I asked about David and was told he was fine. I got your check ($81) from Marion. I took some pictures in the photomoton, but they are like nobody I know. I received a curious letter this week from John Gould Fletcher in which he writes that he bought a copy of Chatterton etc. ten years ago and likes it immensely and was moved to write me when he saw my name in Monroe's anthology.[1] I have tried to reach Lieber to find out what there was to his remark about selling my father's book for two hundred dollars, but have not been able to do so nor have heard from him. I have done a little work on verse, but nothing on the prose nor will for a time. I feel a compulsion, which I shall not resist, to write my lament for Israel. I am thinking of nothing else in my spare time, and though nothing may come of it, I must do what I can. I have been losing weight slowly, but it is tiring at first, as you know. When you were here I weighed 170 and now weigh 162. I hope to get down to 148, a pound or so a week. I got Lillian to go to an obesity doctor and she lost five pounds the first week and is slowly becoming normal, I hope; this doctor was recommended by Paul and Lillian seems to be very pleased.

---

[1] John Gould Fletcher (1886–1950), American poet. His 1938 volume, *Selected Poems* won the Pulitzer Prize (CGLE).

As for you, darling, though I wish you here, I also wish you to see everything and enjoy everything slowly, *unhurriedly*, to soak in as much as possible. Somehow, I feel as if I, as well as you, am in Palestine, that is, that you are my alter ego, and so I know that we have really become one flesh. As I sit here thinking of you and looking at times at your picture on the desk, I am very thankful that after so many delays, so many twists and turns, we have found each other, at least I have found you, and curiously enough, alone in our house I do not feel lonely. I have still much to do tonight. Good night.

I have come to think that of all states of human happiness that of being happily married is not to be despised, as I once despised it—before I knew you; there is quiet glow in me whenever I think of you, I feel its warmth to my fingertips, to the roots of my thoughts. Sometimes, I think of your beautiful face; sometimes, of that lovely spirit of yours; you are bread and flowers, you are wine and you are water. You are not a blaze that burns the house down, but you are the fire in the hearth, from which comes food, warmth and light daily, dear wife; you blaze, indeed, but on hearth and altar. I see that I have become a bad poet but a better lover.

Charles

To Marie Syrkin, April 15th [1933]

Saturday night

Dearest—darling wife

Forgive me for writing this in long hand but the Boston Symphony Orchestra is going full blast and I don't want the typewriter to bang. Well dearest I'm still at definitions and no immediate end in sight. You aunt just called me up. She had just spoken to David on the telephone and he was very cheerful. She and Sylvia are going to see him this Wednesday. Mr. Ludins also called me this evening. He and Mrs. Ludins are delighted with their home and very well. They had 39 persons at their home for Passover. Ryah is in Mexico—she is very happy there. Tima is still in Russia. I got a card from Halper—asking me to go walking some time.[1] Dorothy and Paul were at the *seder* of my father and mother: it was very pleasant. My mother and Dorothy are growing very close together. Paul took an excellent

---

[1] Albert Halper (1904–1984), American novelist whose books include: *Union Square* (1933), *On the Shore* (1934) and *The Foundry* (1934) (CGLE).

photograph of me beside Camilla's carriage and as soon as I get a copy I'll send it to you.[1]

I think of you often; not only at home when I think of you always but on walks and sometimes even at work. Of course I expect you back in two three or four months; and so am not unhappy believing you very happy. But it seems to me that if I were not to see you and be with you again in two three or four months your absence would be unendurable that nothing could assuage my pain then not even writing about it. I know nobody like you and all the women I see in the street in the subway at the place are but shadows of yourself.

Charles

To Marie Syrkin, April 22d [1933]

My darling wife:

Your letter, including enclosure for *The Nation*, dated April 2d on board the steamer going to Palestine, came Thursday and your letter from Haifa, your uncle's house, today. I am writing to Paris, because you see it takes three weeks for a letter to get to Palestine and I suppose you will be on your way to France by that time. And I am writing, instead of typing, because I am listening to the Boston Symphony broadcast.

To begin at the beginning, David is fine, splendid, in the pink of condition. Mashette saw him last Wednesday and so found him.[2] I haven't seen him, but I met Aaron on the bus two or three days ago and he says the same. As for me, I am fine, working and walking and reading and writing, but no news. I am enclosing a picture of Camilla and me—I am the one standing *beside* the carriage.

This week the U.S. went off the gold standard, as you know; but although this means you will probably get less francs for the dollar and less English money, you will probably not lose more than ten percent and you must not let that spoil your trip. But go wherever you want to and stay as long as you like. As for your letter to the *Nation*, it is much too mild. Both the *Nation* and *New Republic* have been printing letters beside which yours

---

[1] Paul Reznikoff, Charles's brother. Camilla was Paul's daughter, Charles's niece. The photograph graces the cover of *Sagetrieb: Charles Reznikoff Issue*. 13: 1&2 (Spring & Fall 1994).

[2] Mashette Syrkin was the stepmother of Marie Syrkin, second wife of Marie's father, and mother of Sylvia Syrkin, Marie's half-sister.

descries a May party (Brooklyn style). *The Evening Post* and other papers have been printing stories and the Hitler administrative measures, the "cold pogrom," have given German "shrecklichkeit"[1] a good deal of publicity—the feeling in the United States is not at all friendly to Germany. But who knows? It was not at all friendly to Mussolini.

You have been gone a month now. I do not know how you feel about me, but as for you, I feel that you are my wife for all eternity. If to think of your absence with regret and of your presence with joy, if to see your old clothes hanging in the closet and to be almost moved to tears, if to feel happy at the thought of you, a little drunken, with a quicker heart beat, is to be in love with you, then I must be very much in love. I love you very much, Marie. The thought of you is like perfume and music. Some day, I hope, I will write you love poems that will phrase somewhat of what I feel.

If you feel like going to England, I hope you will. I am afraid you will be sorry if you don't. Dearest, be as careful as you were on the French boat; be greedy only with your eyes.

Charles

April 29th [1933]

Darling wife,

I had no letter from you this week, but I suppose I'll get one Monday. I called up Mrs. Epstein this evening. Mashette is on duty this weekend and Sylvia is spending it with her. Mrs. Epstein is well and told me that Mashette had seen David yesterday and he is splendid. I think of you often and miss you greatly, but I am very anxious that you see all you want to see and stay as long as you like and go wherever you like. Do not worry about the fluctuation of the dollar; it won't add much to the cost of your trip and the increase of the cost of commodities here which seems to result means much to this country. I have been having quite a good time in your absence—walking until all hours of the night and all day Sunday from dawn and all Saturday afternoon. I have lost ten pounds since your absence and feel fine. I am finishing turning "My country" into verse—don't be vexed! some of it is better so and as for the rest, it is no better in prose. I hope to be through by next week or the week after. Then I shall probably put it aside until your arrival or type it or have it typed. When I get it out of the way, I am going to construct, first of all, a detailed analysis. In this way I shall have structure and climax, both of which are now wanting.

---

[1] "Horror, frightfulness."

Then I shall write all the missing parts. And, lastly, revise. Now this will take some time, but it will be good fun. I have a second book on my chest—a novel, and this bothers me, but I must first clean up all the verse, then this half finished novel which you read. (I believe I wrote you that I was going to do verse only, but now, having done no prose for a month and having glanced at some novels greatly praised, I am full of contempt, ideas and enthusiasm.) As for the job, I am still doing definitions and find it easy and pleasant. I suppose that as soon as I become really good at it, the work will end and I shall be looking for a job. But I think I am good for at least half a year as yet. (Halper has just called me up for a walk tomorrow morning, and the clock is set ahead an hour, daylight savings time, so I must bathe and to bed—it is half past eleven new time.) Thursday night, by the way, I heard T. S. Eliot speak about his own verse and read lots of it and had a thoroughly good time. That was at the New School for Social Research and the hall was jammed.[1] So you see, darling, everything is going on very placidly here, may it continue! I console myself for your absence by thinking of your return and cannot help "nashing" some of the pleasure of that by so thinking. By the way, Eliot spoke of the recognition scene in *Pericles*, and I opened it at random and ran across an excellent phrase—that which Pericles addresses to his daughter Marina—"Are you a fairy motion?" Well, dearest, for me you are now only "a fairy motion," but that motion is bringing you eventually homeward to your delight-anticipating, not love-sick but love-anxious husband

Charles

To Marie Syrkin, May 6th [1933]

Darling,

I received two letters from you this week—one from Tel Aviv and the other from Rehoboth. I found them charming—interesting and delightful. I visited the Epsteins—for a few minutes—and read them extracts from the first (the only one that had arrived at that time). They are all well and your sister Sylvia has grown and is looking splendid. Your aunt sees David about once a week and he is in splendid condition—has never been better.

---

[1] T. S. Eliot (1888–1965) was briefly in New York "to deliver two lectures and to call on his American publishers" (*New York Times*. [22 April 1933]: 16). The *Times* article noted that it was Eliot's "first visit to the United States in eighteen years."

(Aaron Bodansky just called me up to get the French address I am writing to and he tells me the same.) There is no news. Everything is just as you left us except that I walk more—in fact, except for the hours at my job and the hours in the subway am almost a *voegele*. My walk with Halper last Sunday was very pleasant and informative. He told me where I could get printing very cheap—I'll investigate in due time—and of a loft on Fifth Avenue that I can get for $17.50 a month should I want to set up my press. Only 7,000 copies of his book have been sold so far—people are not buying much, but he has enough to live on for four years at the scale he is living now. We became as friendly as ever. When I left him I went to the library and read an excellent book he had praised—*The Sculptor Speaks* (Epstein).[1] I bought a copy that was being remaindered and sent it to Al Lewin. By the way, I got your check for last month and it is unexpectedly large—$148. I suppose that is the Easter vacation, but Marian tells me it is only part of the vacation money. The dollar has been dropping, as you know too well no doubt, and by the time you reach Paris and read this letter, it may be worth as much as 25 per cent less than its gold standard. Still, I hope you are too wise to be stampeded into spoiling your stay or any intended trip because of a few extra dollars. Suppose the trip costs fifty dollars or so more. Or a hundred. Your cards from Jerusalem dated April 20th have also come. I am working steadily at my verse and hope to have it ready for the printer in a week or so. The work at the American Law Book Company has become much easier and I, unless I flatter myself, swifter and better. But though we are all pretty sure it will last for a while, no one knows what will happen when the work is ended in a year or less. I suppose by the summer we will know. Forgive me for the random way this letter is written, but I am writing to you just as if we were at our little table together talking over the steak and buttered potatoes. I notice that in your letters you say very little about loving me, but I suppose you are too busy reveling in all the strange sights. I forgive you. However, as for me in the routine which we both were in together, I think of you, darling; and who could be happier than a man in love with his wife and believing, as I do, that his wife is not indifferent to him? Now remember, stay in Paris until you are completely ready to go home, and if you have the least desire to do so, visit England.

Charles

---

[1] Jacob Epstein (1880–1959), *The Sculptor Speaks* (1932).

To Albert Lewin, May 6th. [1933]

Bronx, New York City

Dear Al,

I sent you today a copy of *The Sculptor Speaks* (Epstein) which I picked up at a "remainder" sale. I read it and found it stimulating. I thought you'd like it.

Marie is still abroad and finds Palestine exciting. I expect her back in June. No news. Remember me to Milly.

Charles

To Marie Syrkin, May 13th. [1933]

Saturday night

Dear wife,

To begin with, I just saw David. I met him and Aaron at 231st Street and we took the same bus. He is—that is David—is looking splendidly (*kein ein ohra*), tanned, active, and cheerful—and impudent—to his father. David greeted me warmly and Aaron and I had a pleasant chat about the date of your probable return. They have just sent you a letter c/o American Express Co. Mashette called me up as soon as I got home. She, Sylvia, and the Epsteins are all well. Mashette too is sending you a letter c/o American Express Company.

I received your cable from Naples Tuesday night and your letter from Palestine in which you write that you are going directly to Brindisi Friday night. I took your policy this afternoon to Eisner. He assures me that you are covered and will mail me the new policy in a week or so. I told him that you were going—or had gone—direct to Brindisi on the Martha Washington. Upon which I was told that the Martha Washington was a worse boat than the French boat that took you to Palestine and about which you had no enthusiasm and that the trip from Brindisi to Naples is absolutely the worst in Italy. At which news I was and am worried, but since it is all over by this time, my uneasy feeling is as useless, no doubt, as such feelings usually are. I also asked them what a trip to London and the Shakespeare country from Paris and back would cost if bought through the American Express and they tell me about $45. Darling, if you feel at all like going, go; but don't go if you are tired or have seen all you want to

197

for the present. Perhaps, you may arrange to take the steamer back to America from England. I leave all this to your good sense, and only urge you not to let the fifteen per cent or so drop of the dollar (if by the time you get this France too has not gone off the gold standard, which is unlikely) worry you or spoil your trip in the slightest. However, don't exhaust yourself.

As for things here, there is a feeling of optimism in the country, stocks are going up, but this is merely anticipation of the future for the most part. However, we are no doubt much better off than any other country and certainly you and I, when we think of the Jews of Russia, Poland, and Germany, of the Jews you saw in Palestine, may even be ashamed of our prosperity. I am still working at my definitions by day and my verse by night, I feel as well and as energetic as I ever felt. My father has paid off the last of the Pollack money and in two months or so, my contributions may either be cut or end. But this depends on the renting, the mortgage etc.

Your last letter was better than ever, and genuinely exciting. I hope you have enjoyed the trip through Italy as much as you seem to have enjoyed the trip through Palestine. Don't hurry. Don't tire yourself. Take it easy. But I say this for your sake, Marie; as for me I hunger for your presence, but then, I think, our love is not a fire of straw; it will keep; it will burn—until our bodies, I think, are burnt away. In the meantime, don't be stampeded into leaving France until you are good and ready.

Charles

To Marie Syrkin, May 20th. [1933]

Dearest,

I just spoke to your aunt on the telephone. David is fine; so is Sylvia and your aunt. My people are all well, except my grandmother (Father's mother) who is very sick and not expected to recover. She is seventy-nine, but she was active until this Monday. In fact she became sick in my aunt Gertrude's house minding her children for the evening. She is there now and has not been fully conscious since Tuesday.

The flowers you sent me have a beautiful dark red, and I gave them to my mother to keep in her prayerbook—where they belong. She was somewhat reluctant to take them fearing you would be displeased, but I know you won't be. As for the wrist-watch you lost, I called up Eisner and was told that unless your baggage was broken into you are not covered by his policy. However, when I get your policy from him, I shall read it myself. In any event, except for the fact that your father gave it to you, a value no insurance company can replace, the actual loss is small. Forget about it, and when you are back, I'll buy you another. (I didn't buy you a birthday present.)

I have not done as much of my own work as I hoped to do this week—my grandmother's sickness. My work at the place seems to be going along smoothly. There has been a slight change—we are to work until 5:30 daily through the summer (except for two weeks' vacation) but are to have all day Saturday during July and August. An improvement. As soon as I get my present work out of the way, I am going to begin a series of novels—real novels. I hear you snicker. Well, we shall see. Live and learn—that's for me! I suppose it will take this letter about a week to get to Paris, and by that time I hope to hear from you. Unless you feel like going to England, don't go. You can always go again, and it may be too much of a strain. Just rest in Paris until you are ready to come home. However, whatever you do, I hope you will have much pleasure out of it.

It is true that I do not bear our wedding anniversary much in mind; but I do not like to think of one day as especially important; I like to think of our wedded days—all of them—as holidays, particularly as I think I have grown in my understanding of you—and, if I may change the old maxim, to understand you is to love you.

Charles

To Marie Syrkin, Aug. 8th [1933]

Saturday evening

Darling,

I have been working steadily this week and have turned most of the outline of the play into dialogue; I have only the last act to do and hope to complete this next week. Then will begin reading for accuracy and amplification, and then revision. At least, I hope to get some of this done before Al comes East. I wish you were here next week to hear the completed play (roughest draft).

I am reading the papers eagerly these days to find some mention of you at the Congress. Certainly, they will make you give your impressions of Palestine. However, when I come across a name we both know well, my heart burns with anguish. To boot, I have had only that very skimpy letter from the Aquitania and two postal cards from you (one from Trieste and the other from Palestine). I do not blame you, because I suppose you have written to California and the letter is not yet returned.

I suppose I must be very much in love with you because I can torment myself so easily with jealousy. I suppose I could stab certain gentlemen with the greatest pleasure. If I did not, living with you these years, come to have implicit faith in your candor and sense of honor, I could go crazy. As it is, I am damnably uncomfortable waiting to hear from you, at least by letter, that you love me. I wish I could hear you say it and force your head back under my kisses.

Charles

To Albert Lewin, [September 17, 1933]

3900 Greystone Avenue, Bronx, New York City
Sunday morning
Dear Al,

Marie and I are glad to hear that you are both well and still swimming, although in a maelstrom. I suppose we are merely floating in a pool. I am glad you found something in the Epstein book. I saw an exhibition of Brancusi at the same time as Epstein's exhibition and could not see Epstein at all; I was glad then to find the artist himself, as it were, showing me about, and thought you might be too.[1] As for Pound, I read the cantos with care, and found the first, a translation of a Latin translation of the Greek, excellent, the second, a translation from Ovid, I believe, good, and the rest more or less a failure, except for a small part from the Cid.[2] But when little work has any value, this may be a good deal. There are some

---

[1] According to *The New York Times*, sculptor Constantin Brancusi's (1876–1957) exhibit at the Brummer Gallery consisted of "fifty-eight pieces—impressive feats of a poet's imagination" (18 November 1933): 13.

[2] Ezra Pound (1885–1972) published his epic *Cantos* in several parts during his life, beginning with *A Draft of XVI Cantos* (1925), continuing with *A Draft of XXX Cantos* (1934) and *Eleven New Cantos* (1934) and finally concluding with *The Cantos of Ezra Pound (I–CXVII)* in 1970 (CGLE).

200

English names appearing, Auden and Spender.[1] I find the first interesting, but not exciting. Other than Pound, I know no one except T. S. Eliot who is genuine. As for my work, I am still working for the legal publishers, just now writing definitions, and because this gives me little freedom, I have had to choose between my verse and prose. I had been working at a novel for about a year and still a great deal of work to do on it, but have grown tired of the people and their small talk. Verse, however, I still find exciting and there is much to be done, for both Eliot and Pound are in high-grade furnished rooms in good neighborhoods, but I think myself on the highway—with little done and very far to go. And at present, I have the time it takes me to get to work and to get home from work and Saturdays off (NRA)[2] and Sundays—time enough to write something and money enough to print. Louis Zukofsky, with whom I disagree as to both form and content of verse but to whom I am obliged for placing some of my things here and there, is planning, or was planning, to form some kind of a publishing firm, and I promised to let him have the book of verse and another of prose which I have ready, if and when anything comes of his plans, provided I do not have to wait beyond the middle of September. Well, I shall see him this week (he's just back from Europe and Ezra Pound). If nothing comes of his plans, as I expect, I shall print both books privately, as I used to years ago, and will be glad to send you copies for yourself and as gifts to as many of your friends as you think might care for them. That will be in a month or so. I hope we will soon meet and that you will have more leisure than you have been having—a crust of bread (toast, well-buttered and jam) and quietness. Marie is teaching this year. She sends her love to you and Millie. As for me, whenever I walk along 57th Street, I think of it as your and Millie's habitat: let's hope soon.

Charles

---

[1] W. H. Auden (1907–1973) and Stephen Spender (1909–1995). Interestingly, both Auden and Spender are mentioned as "promising young English poets" by T. S. Eliot, whom Reznikoff had seen in a lecture several months before, in an interview noted in *The New York Times* (24 April 1933): 14.

[2] The National Recovery Act and the National Recovery Administration (1933–36) imposed compulsory fair-practice codes on businesses before being declared unconstitutional by the Supreme Court.

To Albert Lewin, [Jan 1934?]

3900 Greystone Ave, Bronx N.Y.C.

Dear Al,

I received your outline for the first two acts and will mull over it. "The triumph of greatness over humiliation, torment, calumny, condemnation" is a theme worthy of all we have. In about two weeks, I expect to complete preliminary readings and will begin writing. As soon as I finish the draft of an act (probably one a month) I'll send it on to you.

If you have received my books and want any for anybody, I'll be glad to send as gifts as many copies as you'd like.

Charles

We hope Milly will come to New York.

To Harriet Monroe, May 8, 1934

3900 Greystone Avenue, Bronx, New York City.

Dear Miss Monroe,

The Nazi triumph set me to writing the enclosed which neither in length nor theme, I am afraid, is quite suitable for *Poetry*.[1] If you care to use it, I should not mind if you printed it in the smallest type you have.

Sincerely yours,
Charles Reznikoff

To Albert Lewin, May 15, 1934

3900 Greystone Avenue, Bronx, New York City

Dear Al,

I received your letter of April 30th on Monday of last week and intended to answer it last Saturday, but on Saturday I had a cold, fever, etc.,

---

[1] Reznikoff is referring to his poem "In Memoriam: 1933" which was eventually published in *The Menorah Journal*. 22:2 (Autumn 1934):103–133.

and have been in bed until today (Tuesday). I am staying at home today to see if the temperature will stay flat, and expect to go to work tomorrow.

When you first wrote me about Abélard, my work at the law book company consisted of writing definitions, which I had become used to and was good at and was not finding difficult; as for my own work, I was about to commence the revision of about fifteen hundred lines of verse all about Jews in the play form I used in "Nine Plays" (perhaps, it would be more accurate to say libretto form, for ever since I saw a production of *The Habimah*, the Moscow Hebrew theatre, I believe this form capable of production in conjunction with music, dancing, and pantomime—wasn't that the Greek play?). Now, I couldn't stop that revision, not only because it was somewhat timely, but because I was working Hitler off my chest. Still, I saw no reason why I could not get to work on the Abélard theme at once. However, about the time Milly came here—shortly after—I was taken off definitions and put on straight legal writing, which is more difficult for me. It seemed best to me then to put all my spare strength into the revision, finish that as soon as possible, and in the meantime do what reading and thinking I could about Abélard. I think I told this to Milly. However, unless one has all one's time at one's disposal, these things are usually behind schedule. But in the meantime I did not write you, not because of any lack of interest, but because the only interesting thing would be a good draft. I could hardly expect you to be interested in more plans and schedules.

I finished the revision of the verse last week, and began to think about Abélard seriously. I find the outline of the first two acts, in your letter of January 22d, somewhat too tight for me as yet. I see the century breaking into three streams—after Henry Adams—Godfrey of Bouillon, standing for the strength of arms, St. Bernard, for the strength of faith, and Abélard, for the strength of the mind.[1] The first takes form in the crusades, the second in monasticism, and the last in scholasticism. Now keeping the first two in the background, I could see the Abélard story breaking into, say, six—not acts—but episodes. Of course, I realize that if the matter ends there, this is not a "well-made" play and certainly no vehicle for a recognized actress. However, if I do about two hundred and fifty words a day, in about a month and a half or so I ought to have the draft of the Abélard theme. If you find the draft worth fooling with, you can then get to work and on the basis of your reading and thinking about the theme, tear the draft to bits, pointing out what should be amplified and what cut

---

[1] Henry Adams (1838–1918), *Mont-Saint-Michel and Chartres* (1904).

out. The method is analogous to color printing in which each color is imposed separately.

I am sorry about the delay and hope in a month or two to have a complete draft for you to put your teeth in. If, in the meantime, I find it impossible to have the theme come alive in my hands, I'll write you at once. I am glad that you have found it increasingly interesting and that it has had the immediate effect of putting your daily work in its proper perspective. This, if you extend "daily work" to include "daily life," has been the chief value of my own work to me. I like your use of the word "perspective": it is not an escape.

I hope Milly enjoyed her trip. We had a very good time when we went out with Milly except once, when waiting in Milly's room in the St. Moritz to go to the theatre, we heard a great noise outside and going to the window saw thousands of strikers in the street booing us for being in the hotel. The three of us stood at the window looking down at the crowd: I have a sneaking pleasure at the thought of being mistaken for a patron of the place and playing the part of French aristocrat with no immediate danger of guillotine or pike, but Marie, daughter of the founder of the Zionist labor party, terribly abashed. But, really, there we were, three very cheerful people, in a warm bright room, about to go out to a very good dinner and to see a very good show (Henry Hull in *Tobacco Road*) and there, outside, was a howling mob of hungry, bitter people.[1] Boy, those are the moments when you catch cold; when the eleventh century seems exactly nine centuries away, and that unless one can reach such fundamentals that what was true then is just as true now, one might as well write triolets.

Our love to you and Milly.

Charles

---

[1] *The New York Times* reviewer writes that Jack Kirkland's adaptation of Erskine Caldwell's *Tobacco Road*, starring Henry Hull, Sam Byrd and Margaret Wycherly, "reels around the stage like a drunken stranger to the theatre, [yet] it has spasmodic moments of merciless power when truth is flung into your face with all the slime that truth contains" (5 December 1933): 31.

To Henry Hurwitz, June 17, 1934

                  3900 Greystone Avenue, Bronx, New York City

Dear Mr. Hurwitz,

    I thank you for the Spring issue of *The Menorah*. Both Marie and I were glad to see it, and found it interesting and alive. I expect to drop into your office one of these days with manuscript.

                              Cordially yours,
                              Charles

To Harriet Monroe, July 7, 1934

                  3900 Greystone Avenue, Bronx, N.Y.C.

Dear Miss Monroe,

    About two months ago, I sent you a bulky manuscript "If I forget you, Jerusalem; In Memoriam 1933." I am in no hurry about a reply, but, knowing your promptness, I cannot help wondering if the manuscript ever reached you.

                              Very truly yours,
                              Charles Reznikoff

To Henry Hurwitz, November 7, 1934

                  3900 Greystone Avenue, Bronx, New York City

Dear Henry,

    Will you have a copy of the *Journal* sent to:
Dr. Haym Greenberg c/o The Jewish Frontier, 1225 Broadway, N. Y. C.
Dr. M. Syrkin c/o Epstein, 310 West 95th St., N. Y. C.
Albert Lewin, 714 North Roxbury Drive, Beverly Hills, California
Dr. Chas. H. Wolf, 1379 Union St., Brooklyn, N.Y.
Nathan Reznikoff, 765 Eastern Parkway, Brooklyn, N.Y.
Nathan Reznikoff c/o Felon-Storm Co., 10 West 36th St., N. Y. C.
Dr. Paul Reznikoff, 114 East 81st St., N. Y. C.
Hyman Reznikoff, 5801 Julian Av., St. Louis, Mo.

Charles Reznikoff, 3900 Greystone Av., Bronx, N. Y. C.

As you see, I have put myself down for an extra copy. I have read Lowenthal and Ginsburg to date, and find the former as good as ever and the latter putting up a good case, which Marie assures me, should be shattered.[1]

Cordially yours,
Charles

To Albert Lewin, November 9th. [1934]

3900 Greystone Avenue, Bronx New York City

Dear Al,

I have asked that a copy of *The Menorah Journal* with "In Memoriam: 1933" be sent to you, and no doubt you will receive it soon. I am having it reprinted in book form and will send you a copy and as many more as you like.

"Abélard" has been on my mind, but I have done very little with it since I wrote you last—more than three months ago. I thought I would do a good deal during my vacation (first two weeks in August) but I was still tired and didn't do a thing; and then I kept putting off the writing from week to week until all this time has gone. The work of completing *Corpus Juris* is still going on, and though I have no trouble throwing off verse now and then, I find it hard to do any "muscle" work, as I must with Abélard or any prose.

You have been unreasonably patient, considering how little I have done (I am dissatisfied with all of it except a little of the first scene) and how slowly, and if you want to go ahead you are welcome to any of the lines, and I will be glad to read the work, when finished, making what suggestions (as to diction) I can. Otherwise, I will wait until the pressure has eased off, which should be by the end of the year. I wish you would do what suits you best having your own interest solely in mind, for I have lost nothing and if you can only begin to do your own work, you have much to gain.

Remember me to Milly. Marie sends her love.

Charles

---

[1] Marvin Lowenthal's essay "The First Jews in Germany" and Elias Ginsburg's discussion "Is Revision-Zionism Fascist?" both appeared, along with Reznikoff's "In Memoriam: 1933," in *The Menorah Journal* 22:2 (Autumn 1934).

To Albert and Mildred Lewin, December 15 [1934]

3900 Greystone Avenue, Bronx, New York City

Dear Al and Milly,

We received your beautiful bowl and thank you for it, stopping every now and then to admire the hare racing in the desert.

I am sending you three copies of "In Memoriam," and you may have more if you have any use for them. Your "Abélard" is still in my mind, but only in the background at present; however, I hope to get back to it.

We wish you both a very happy New Year.

Charles

To Henry Hurwitz, [Mar. 23, 1935]

Dear Mr. Hurwitz:

I suppose it is too late for the insertion in this issue of the ¼ page ad which you so kindly promised me, but, as you know, I had no material available until this morning. This morning I found the attached in this week's issue of the *Saturday Review*. This review, I think, is quotable and especially since it mentions *The Menorah J'l*. In addition the *Jewish Chronicle of England* in their issue of Feb. 22/35 has this to say: "After a prolonged, and somewhat unseasonal hibernation, *The Menorah Journal* has again put in an appearance with a range of contents which shows no falling-off from the former high standard. Of particular significance are 'In Memoriam: 1933'—a long narrative poem of almost epic quality, by Charles Reznikoff; and 'The Economic Picture in Palestine' by J. L. Cohen."

Of course if you think neither notice (the *Chronicle* notice cut of course to eliminate the introductory remarks about hibernation) is particularly effective, we can just forget about the ad for this issue. Perhaps by the next issue there may be other notices and an entirely different ad. may be advisable.

[Charles]

To Henry Hurwitz, March 31, 1935

3900 Greystone Avenue, Bronx, New York City

Dear Henry,

Thank you very much. I am impressed by the selection, arrangement, and general appearance. If not too late, the deletion indicated would obviate any necessity of registration as a "retailer," which the Objectivist Press might incur.[1] In addition, if the size of "by" (second line) can be reduced to the type size, say, of the address at the bottom, and the spacing rearranged accordingly, the appearance of the "ad," otherwise excellent, might be improved. However, if too late or troublesome, please forget about these trifles. I appreciate what you have done in this matter.

Cordially yours
Charles

To Albert Lewin, April 13th [1935]

Dear Al,

Your poem came Monday but I had to wait for the week-end to answer it. I suppose you might send it to Joe Freeman and, if he has turned Trotskyite, he will, no doubt, print it gladly. I am keeping it, for I suppose you have a copy.

When you left you were resigned, and I hope you have not yet become impatient, about *Abélard*: I am living with the idea—very pleasantly; we take walks together, sometimes, and sometimes read together. I hope when Pegasus does get into labor, it will produce, at least, a foal.

I bought Arthur Waley's new book on Taoism called *The Way and its Power* and feel very much at home in some of it. If a copy has come to Los Angeles, you might look into it. I hope Milly likes the pictures you bought. Marie and I send our love.

Charles

---

[1] In 1934 the Objectivist Press had published three Reznikoff titles: *In Memoriam: 1933, Jerusalem the Golden,* and *Testimony.*

I think at times of the ear-exercising machine and hope it has proved helpful—at least. We are still struggling as the Mice to crawl out of "Corpus Juris" and begin the new work which, I hope, will give me a little more time.

To Albert Lewin, Aug 17th [1935]

3900 Greystone Av, Bronx N.Y.C.

Dear Al,

Marie and I went to see *China Seas* last Saturday, and we found your name across the screen more exciting than storm or pirates.[1] The audience, however, responded warmly at all the proper moments and, for that matter, Marie and I were not unmoved, although I expected that the cast would mean no more to me than their faces on the racks of a magazine-stand.

I have had a vacation and am going back to work Monday. I told you, at times, of my father's book, which I worked at when I was in your house. Well, after it had been lying around all this while, I saw clearly what I could do with it—such as it is—and spent most of the vacation putting what is left of it in shape for the stenographer. I expect to print it this autumn. With this, and working at a longish poem which managed to accumulate this spring, a little walking, and a little bathing, the two weeks are gone.

We completed *Corpus Juris* (71 volumes) a few months ago, after almost a year of pressure, and were immediately plunged into writing law for a new work, which is still in an experimental stage. On this the continuation of our company, which has become a subsidiary of a much larger company, and our own jobs depend. Naturally, we do our best.

My own way of living (week-days) is now something like this: I must leave the house at seven to get to my job in Brooklyn at eight forty-five. We work under constant supervision, which is kept for the most part in velvet gloves, until five thirty, reading and writing law steadily, with an interval for lunch, of course. Every once in a while—every other week or so—if our pace seems to slacken, pressure is put upon us to raise our blood pressure,

---

[1] Lewin was Associate Producer of the 1935 MGM film *China Seas*, directed by Tay Garnett and starring Clark Gable and Jean Harlow (Felleman 274; HFG).

and we have to step lively or find our heels stepped on; but, since the NRA and for the time being, we have our Saturdays free. Our place of work was originally in a fairly quiet neighborhood which has since become the busiest and noisiest in Brooklyn, since it is on the best way from Manhattan. The steady analysis of cases and careful writing beside the traffic is—if you can remember your days on Fifth Avenue—pretty tiring; it takes me an hour or so in the evening to rest up. This I do while eating, reading the newspaper, and riding part of the way home. I usually get off at 72nd Street at about seven o'clock and walk along Riverside Drive as far as I can go—usually all the way. This is the time I do my own work, and when I reach home after ten, I am usually too tired to do more than glance at some Hebrew, if I do that. On this walk I find it easiest to do verse, which more or less writes itself or not at all, and does not bulk; for even a thousand lines, enough to make a small volume, will have no more than about five thousand words. Perhaps, this will partly explain why I have been so dilatory with Abélard. I had hoped for a period in which to soak myself in it, and thought my vacation, if I should get any, a good time—at the latest, but now have used it for my father's book, which has older claims and, besides, the book, such as it is, would mean a good deal to him. (Our organization has become so strict and jobs so desirable that to ask for a leave of absence is to quit.) You have made it quite clear to me that I am not to consider the play an obligation in the least, and I have made it equally clear to you, I believe that you are not to consider me in the least in doing whatever you wish with your theme; nevertheless, it would be so great a pleasure for me to work with you on it that, for my part, as long as it is a possibility, I cannot forget it. And so I continue to hope that, somehow or other, it will accumulate. In the meantime, I try to do what I can at whatever themes I carry—or rather sit at the helm and let the wind carry me—and though I always thought there was a lot of nonsense in talk of inspiration, I must admit that after all day at the law I can do little rowing in the evening. Sitting at *China Seas*, I could not help thinking how difficult your work must be—to weave all these stubborn threads into a saleable pattern—and I know under what pressure you must work when any delay is so expensive. I suppose you smile when an unimportant employee in a leisurely business, such as writing law, talks of pressure and weariness. However, at one time—not so long ago—I found it impossible to do any work of my own while holding such a job as I have now, and now I can do almost as much as if I were selling. I hope then for still more strength. And if, in the meantime, the wind does blow from the France of Abélard and Héloïse, we shall have our play the sooner.

Marie sends her love to you and Milly. We hope you are both well. Your new honors please Milly, I am sure, more than you.

Charles

P.S. Charles has confessed to me that the most fascinating figure in the Abélard Héloïse imbroglio was, as far as he was concerned, St. Bernard! Send Jean Harlow.[1]

Marie

To Albert Lewin, October 19th [1935]

3900 Greystone Avenue, Bronx New York City
Saturday

Dear Al,

My neighbors began eating their shoes at last.[2] Noticed that they had hoofs and realized that they were only a small harmless herd—constantly chewing. But fear they have come to harm in Chicago.

Arrived safe, slightly unsound (as shipped), and fearfully sleepy. Found your letter of September 7th (your last) which must have been considerably delayed and missed me. Most of your suggestions in this, however, were in your notes, which I used, and in your talk; and the new version, I hope, will have the rest—acted upon and actable.

Marie sends her love to you and Millie. When I told Marie that she might have to live in Los Angeles, she said that she could not give up her job, particularly because she has her boy to think of. But, in any event, there is no need for her to give up her job in New York. I can come out to Los Angeles in the spring, if you wish it, and she can get a leave of absence for the next year, and have it renewed, if necessary. I think this should amplify my answer with respect to Marie's teaching in California. I realize, of course, that our talk was merely exploratory and need go no further.

---

[1] Jean Harlow (1911–1937), actress whose films included *Hell's Angels* (1930), *Public Enemy* (1931), *Bombshell* (1933) and *China Seas* (1935) (IDFF).

[2] Reznikoff seems to be referring to a famous scene in Chaplin's 1925 film *The Gold Rush* in which Chaplin in his role as the tramp eats his shoe.

Please remember me to Millie. I hope you both find the trip east restful and pleasant.

Charles

To Albert and Mildred Lewin, Dec 29, 1935

3900 Greystone Av

Dear Milly and Al,

We feel quite showered and dowered. You have us Jews completely benighted—Arabian. We wish you a very happy new year.

Charles

You have this Jew completely overwhelmed. What a swanky bag! and what pajamas! Charles was all dressed, ready for one of his gruesome hikes, when they arrived on Xmas morning, and—this is the gospel truth— he promptly undressed, took a bath (to be worthy of Jean Harlow) and spent the day at home in the pajamas. This being the first thing I have ever encountered powerful enough to deflect Charles from a projected hike, you can judge how generally overcome the Reznikoff household is.

Thank you both very, very much, and I should like to thank you again for that very beautiful silver *lever.*

Greetings of the season, including Chanukah!

Marie

To Albert and Mildred Lewin, [February 16, 1936]

3900 Greystone Avenue, Bronx NYC
Saturday

Dear Al and Milly,

I met Milly's niece on Fifth Avenue this afternoon and, when I asked after you, she told me that you, Milly, have broken your arm and that she read in one of the trade papers that Al is away for a vacation because he is not well. Marie and I hope that when this reaches you, you are both fully recovered. If I can be of any service here to either of you, please let me know. (If Al feels like reading, he might read Trotsky's *History of the Russian Revolution*, 3 vols.)[1]

Charles

To Albert Lewin, June 24, 1936

3900 Greystone Avenue, Bronx New York City

Dear Al,

I hope you and Milly are completely recovered. I am sending you today a couple of copies each of a new book of verse and the first part of my father's book.[2] I have done all I could with this and, whatever age may do to it, it will no longer improve it. Besides, my father is anxious to see in print a memorial of at least a part of his life.

I have been, I believed, on excellent terms with both my immediate superiors. However that may be, in this week's clash of executive wills, I am out—"at liberty" if that is the phrase for it. Of course, they would let me stay a while until I make some other "connection," but I have no stomach nor urgent need for a couple of weeks' salary on such terms. Luckily, despite my ill-timed printing, I have some money saved and, of course, Marie has a job with "tenure of office." (She is leaving this Saturday for a trip abroad from which she is not due to return until September.) I have made no plans for the future other than to get at the accumulation of my own work—of which your play is not the least.

Charles

---

[1] Leon Trotsky (1879–1940), *History of the Russian Revolution* (1932).

[2] The book of verse would have been *Separate Way* (Objectivist Press, 1936) and the other *Early History of a Sewing Machine Operator,* which Reznikoff published himself.

To Albert Lewin, July 4th [1936]

3900 Greystone Avenue, Bronx New York City

Dear Al,

As soon as I read your letter it was clear to me that I must work at nothing but the play and that I cannot take any money from you for doing so. I appreciate, not only your offer itself, but the manner in which you made it: you could not have made it any easier for me to accept it. However, I believe that I am as serious about the play as you; it is certainly as much to my interest as yours; and I have enough to carry me for quite a while and to pay for any transportation.

This brings me to the part of your letter that bothers me. I know how tired I was after a day's work at writing law. Even if I did not remember, I should know, considering your vastly greater responsibility, how worn out you must be after your work. I feel that it will be harmful for you to add the strain of consultation with me to the burden you carry. I flatter myself that you may, at present, think of it as recreation, but it will certainly not be that always.

I propose to begin work at the play immediately and as seriously as if I were in Beverly Hills. I am at last free to do so and have nothing else as urgent. I propose to put into the work as many hours, at least, as I put into the law and by the first of next month, "with luck," I expect to have a complete rough draft for you. I have, of course, whatever suggestions you have made; if you are disposed to make others in the meantime, well and good; in any event, when you have the first draft, you can pour as many broadsides into it as you have ammunition. (If it will be easier for you, I'll bring this first draft so that you may talk your comments.) And I will have another draft ready for you when you come through New York on your vacation.

This arrangement, I think, will enable me to do no less and minimize the strain on you until you, too, are free. In any event, without waiting to hear from you, I begin work, and with a full day, and every day, at my disposal for the first time in five years, I feel that this summer, except for the unexpected, will not be fruitless.

Please remember me to Milly. I imagine that she will agree with me.

Charles

To Albert Lewin, Sept. 10th [1936]

Dear Al,

Marie duly arrived Monday, instantly developed a cold, fever, etc., but is better now. My mother has pneumonia which set in Sunday but it is taking and, I hope, will continue to take a favorable course. I expect to leave Friday and should be in Beverly Hills by the first of next week.

Love to you and Milly from Marie and

Charles

To Albert Lewin, March 13, 1937

3900 Greystone Avenue, Bronx, New York City

Dear Al,

Your letter came yesterday. I expect to be in Los Angeles Saturday. It was kind of you to offer to advance the fare, but I still can manage.

If you were a stranger, I would work for you as well as I could. I should do no less for you. On the other hand, I expect you to be candid and ruthless, if I am to be of best service to you—and myself.

Thank you, and love to Milly and you from Marie and me.

Charles

To Henry Hurwitz, [April 1937]

Hotel Carmel, Santa Monica, California
Saturday Night

Dear Henry,

The job came through after all. Will send you some verse, or what I have, when I come to. In the meantime, hard at work but find it exciting—and very pleasant.

Best wishes
Charles

To Henry Hurwitz, May 20, 1937

1147 Sixth Street, Santa Monica, Cal.

Dear Henry,

It will take me some time, perhaps years, for me to see this group objectively. However I like it well enough now to send it on to you; but you, of course, must not, out of kindness, hesitate to reject it all or in part.

Charles

To Henry Hurwitz, September 22d [1937]

3900 Greystone Avenue, Bronx, New York City

Dear Henry,

I am sending the group I spoke about (if you care for some, forget about the rest) and the first part of the American poem.

I have reread *Kaddish* (which you have) and think the first line of the last stanza would be better as:

> Upon Israel,
> and upon their children etc.

Cordially,
Charles

To Marie Syrkin, [September 1938]

Carmel Hotel, Santa Monica
Saturday

Dearest,

Yesterday Doctor Margoshes invited me to go to Reinhardt's *Faust* but I begged off.[1] Sunday I am to go to Al's for lunch—the lunch is for

---

[1] Max Reinhardt (1873–1943), Austrian theatrical director of international stature.

Nazimova, Cukor, Helen Westley, etc.[1] He suggested that I might prefer to walk but I accepted. *Zaza* should be a superb picture—of real, as well as mere box-office, value.[2] I saw the first rough assembling (in the august presence of Zoë Akins—another luncheon guest) and was profoundly impressed by its quality. It will be ready in three weeks or so. A number of what seems to my unpracticed eye perfect. *Spawn of the North* is proving its box-office value, with few exceptions, throughout the country.[3] On the whole, I imagine Al has done very well in the year and a half on his own.

As for my own work, I am still revising the verse I managed to accumulate and still have about two months' work just revising to do. However, gathering up the new and the old (last year's work is still in manuscript) should make a fairly sizable work. What to do with it is still to be considered. As for the prose, I am trying to finish the rough draft. I have perhaps another week's work at this. It is the first to suffer, if I have too much to do, and I cannot work at it as steadily as I do at the verse. The rough draft, however, will only be the beginning. It is in such bad shape that it will require a long and slow revision until it is anything at all. This revision will take from four to six months but no more than two or three hours a day. I should also have the time to write the rough draft of another book while I am at it. However, man plans and God pans.

I suppose I will be able to leave about October 1st, the way things look now. I hope you and David are well, my love.

Charles

---

[1] Alla Nazimova (1879–1945), Russian-American stage and screen actress and pupil of Stanislavsky. George Cukor (1899–1953), director whose credits include: *Zaza* (1939), *The Philadelphia Story* (1941), *Gaslight* (1944) and *My Fair Lady* (1964) (BDF). Helen Westley (1875–1942) was a member of the cast of *Zaza.* Zoë Akins (1886–1958), writer whose films include: *Camille* (1936) and *Zaza* (1939). Akins won the Pulitzer Prize for *Drama for The Old Maid* (1935) (IDFF).

[2] Al Lewin produced George Cukor's 1939 film *Zaza* for Paramount. The film starred Claudette Colbert in the title role, and Herbert Marshall (HFG).

[3] Al Lewin produced Paramount's 1938 action film *Spawn of the North* directed by Henry Hathaway, written by Talbot Jennings and starring George Raft, Henry Fonda, Dorothy Lamour and John Barrymore (HFG).

To Marie Syrkin, [September 1938]

Carmel Hotel, Santa Monica
Wednesday

Dearest,

I received your letter yesterday and was very glad to get it for it seems to me a very long time before I heard from you and a very long time indeed since I heard from my father and sister. I am sure they missed a week completely.

To begin with trifles, the grand party on Sunday was all right. Cukor and Helen Westley and even Nazimova were amusing. Milly served champagne to begin with. I had none because I had had some sherry and was a little afraid of getting sick inopportunely. They told some funny stories: of Tallulah Bankhead who insisted that cocaine was not habit-forming and who said she knew because she had been taking it for seventeen years; there were several others but I have forgotten them.[1] Helen Westley kept asking Cukor to put her in his next picture which he kept refusing because it called for a sweet old lady until she quoted the New Testament to the fact that "knock and it shall be answered you" and hit him three times on his leg, aiming higher I believe, but the blows were so solid I thought he would be unable to walk. Nazimova had lived for a while near Fourth Street where I once lived and Cukor had actually lived on Fourth Street when a boy so the three of us were "landsleute" after a fashion. Well, the party was all right, but I like walking better. Still, if you had been there, I'd have liked it much better, getting some pleasure out of your pleasure.

Spawn of the North is doing excellent business, the reviews in New York quite good, despite your say-so to the contrary and better than expected. The picture is excellent as a "show" and proves Al's showmanship to the studio, if it needed proof. It will, except for something quite unforeseen, prove to be a money-maker and, after all, that is what counts with money-payers.

What you say about Paul and Dorothy's attitude toward Judaism makes me sad, of course, but it is no news obviously. The Jews must always lose a large percentage of "joiners," of people who are uncomfortable in a minority because they are weak or, to be candid, because they do not see the

---

[1] Tallulah Bankhead (1902–1968), actress whose most famous film role was in Alfred Hitchcock's 1944 *Lifeboat* (BDF).

218

sense of it. As for me, I so despise majorities, whether they call themselves Nazis or Bolsheviks, Christians or Mohammedans, that I am ready to burst with rage when I think of their stupidities and injustice. The notion that under communism, Jews will be treated any better than under capitalism is ridiculous: will there not always be competition for place within the bureaucracy, within the shop, in the theatre, on the field and difference in race will always play a part as long as similarity of race will form a bond and by race I mean a similarity of manners and viewpoint due to similar environment and pressure. I know I am right but I am in too great a hurry just now to choose my words and elaborate what is obvious. The answer of the communist is really intermarriage. That is the answer given for many centuries on one ground or other but it is of course no answer to us. I see in the papers that there have been pogroms in the Ukraine. Of course, the Jews have the best places.

I am here, as you are, of course, greatly excited by the news from abroad. I feel that England is right in trying to postpone war in every possible way and, providing it piles up its strength in the meantime so that there can be no question about the outcome and so ultimately no issue by force, England can afford to give ground little by little only to regain it all and much more at once. They will probably give the Sudeten to Germany after they have stripped the territory of all that can be beneficial immediately to Germany, but though this is a setback it is not a defeat. A war is as destructive to the winner as to the loser unless it is brief and the conquest of Germany will not be brief so that even if, as I think, Germany will lose in a long war, England and France will probably win only a victory that will not last in the face of an inevitable third war waged by an angrier and greater Germany with a population then greater than both England and France put together. As for me, I am for England and for France and am very skeptical of the future of humanity generally or of the Jews in particular in Russia; whatever victories for humanity have been won there are fine but the future under the present leadership is uncertain. Whatever civilization they have is, and has always been, chiefly a hot-house product: the Jews there are civilized and so is a small, very small, proportion of the general population—as for the rest, who knows. Perhaps only noble savages, at best. Intelligent, often enough, but essentially savages.

Well, having gotten a lot of vaporings out, which I may think wrong, that is all. War would certainly change Al's plans to go abroad and may change mine. If Germany is given the Sudeten region, which, at present looks likely, there will be no war, of course. Things continuing as they are, I ought to leave early or in the middle of October but the matter has not been discussed at all. I hope you and yours are well. I am very sorry that you have to be going back to teach and I hope with David in college you will feel able to take the plunge of giving up work and salary. Love, as they say in the telegrams.

Charles

I am no humanitarian. At the moment, I prefer the six Jewish constables that were killed in ambush to all Arabia. The dogs have been well taken care of by England who freed them from the Turks and by the Jews too, always only too anxious to be friendly, until they have answered like the savages that they are. O yes, picturesque. Of course, it is wrong to indict a people for perhaps only a handful. But the people must take its color from the potent handful. Just as today, Italy is *virtually* (using the word in its original sense) Fascist and Germany Nazi and the Jews still humanitarians and defenders of the liberty of the individualistic Blum and Trotsky, even Brandeis.[1] Of course, to share in the glory of being a Jew, means sharing its burden (same word in Hebrew). Why am I so platitudinous? It must be the fact that the afternoon is drawing to a close and I am tired.

To Marie Syrkin, [September 1938]

Carmel Hotel, Santa Monica
Friday afternoon

Dearest,

September is surely the hottest month out here. It's been hot as blazes for a week—hotter than August. If you walk a block you are soaked. Evenings are warm. However, it is nevertheless livable and, I suppose, even pleasant. I just write you this little detail to let you know how easy it is to soften and, after a while, how hard to leave the rouge-pots of Hollywood.

Spawn is continuing its own excellent business and strengthening Al's position here. (*Zaza* should be the "kudos" getter.) My own position is as it was—somewhat mysterious to outsiders and decidedly uncertain to myself. No word, yet, of when I leave. I am beginning, I think (knock wood!) to get a little better grip on my bank account. Maybe I'll land in New York with

---

[1] Louis Dembitz Brandeis (1856–1941), Supreme Court Justice.

five hundred dollars. Hush! Hush! I hear a birthday and a visitor, the landlord and the insurance man.

I have finished the rough draft of the novel.[1] The end is thrown together anyway at all. It runs well over a hundred thousand words and will take me from six to eight months to revise in my best revising. And then what have you? At the moment, I am discouraged about it. I hate to think of it. It has some good bits, I suppose, but lacks completely the drive a novel should have. On the other hand, my verse pleases me. I have never written as much but then I don't want much. A couple of good poems a year that will wear well and are easy to carry about. The novel has much more about me than about my father and much more about my father than my mother. As for me, the validity of what I do revolves completely about the value of my verse and unless that is taken for granted, my plans are of real interest to no one—and that value cannot be taken for granted. Well, why go into that again.*

I suppose even if war breaks out Al will go to New York. He really wants a vacation and it would be a very good thing before beginning as difficult a picture as *Knights of the Round Table*.[2]

I looked through a list of possible telegrams for Rosh Hashonnah, thinking to send you one; but of all the list, the only one they didn't have was "happy new year." So I write it now instead. I wish you a happy new year and David and your aunt and sister and all your friends.

Charles

*I'll just leave it lie around for a while until my interest re-awakens.

To Marie Syrkin, [September 1938]

Saturday morning

[Marie,]

I didn't get a chance to mail your letter last night.

The Czech situation looks very dark this morning. Hitler wants too much and England seems ready to concede it. If Russia backs the Czechs

---

[1] *The Lionhearted* (1944).

[2] Lewin's planned *Knights of the Round Table* was never completed. According to Felleman, "growing hostilities in Europe and anxieties about the expenses led Paramount executives to call it off" (278).

sufficiently, it may present the only obstacle to a complete surrender. In this way, Russia will act as it did in Spain. It is impossible not to keep thinking about the matter. Even Chamberlain on his trip to Hitler was "preoccupied."

This morning, I awoke fresh and eager about the novel. What I said on the other page is perfectly right. But! If I can succeed in treating the matter with humour and irony, the situation is saved, I take the curse off it and yet say my say. I begin revision today.

No notion at all when I go back. Will let you know just as soon as I do. Again, a happy new year!

C.

To Marie Syrkin, September 24 [1938]

Carmel Hotel, Santa Monica
Saturday

Dearest,

Of course, I stick my chin out when I discuss foreign affairs in these letters. By the time you get them, you have read the morning paper and are much smarter than I. However, the events going now are so astonishing that it is hard to keep still. I wonder why Hitler is taking the attitude that he does since everything will be in his hands in a few weeks or months, if he will only be that have brought the Nazis so high will bring them to their doom [*sic*]. In the light of last night's news, which will be old stuff when you get this letter, Chamberlain's moves show up very well and, in the event of peace, they will show up very badly.

I suppose Al will go to New York whatever happens. *Spawn of the North* is proving to be very profitable, although not as profitable as *In Old Chicago*.[1] *Zaza* is completed, except for the music, which will take another two weeks. It is generally conceded that this is a really fine picture and no

---

[1] *In Old Chicago*, a 1937 melodrama directed by Henry King, starred Tyrone Power, Alice Faye, and Don Ameche (HFG). *Zaza*, written by Zoë Akins, directed by George Cukor, and produced by Albert Lewin for Paramount, was released in 1939. "A 1904 French chanteuse is in love with a married aristocrat," Leslie Halliwell summarizes, commenting: "Rather flat period romantic drama with interested credits" (HFG).

"hokum." If the preview takes place in a couple of weeks, I should know where I am by that time.

I have had to drop all my own work for a couple of days to present my view of "knights" as forcefully as possible. That will be through this morning—that is, a nineteen-page summary of my conception of the proper theme and though it will be probably ignored, that is off my chest and I have done my duty. I find that I am unable to do more than about 300 words a day by way of revision, when I can revise, of my novel, but I like to do it that way. However, it will take a year and more at going, in the rough, at the same time.

Tonight there is a party at the Marx's to celebrate Al's birthday and I must go, of course. However, today I hope to do some of my own work and begin that again.

A happy new year! Long live the Czech republic!

Love
Charles

To Marie Syrkin, [October 1, 1938]

Carmel Hotel, Santa Monica
Saturday night—late

Dearest,

In the utmost confidence, the censorship board banned *Zaza* in toto. Nobody must know. Any cuts or additions will only spoil it; however, this may have to be done. If it is done, it will delay matters here. But the head of the board refuses to be specific about his objections, refuses to pin himself down to particulars. He is being urged to do this. If he does, and if his objections can be met without spoiling the picture too much, they will be; but if he refuses, it may be best to appeal to his chiefs in New York. Should this take some time, we may leave on our leaves at once. Naturally, I cannot bring the matter up now. To begin with, we will not know where we stand until next week—if then. Zukor likes the picture very much and is all in favor of refusing any changes and appealing.[1] So you see, dearest, how hard it is to make any plans. Of course, Al wants his leave and it is all set that he will leave as soon as possible. All we can do is to lean back about

---

[1] Adolph Zukor (1873–1976), Chairman of the Board at Paramount Studios (IDFF).

this matter and see how things develop. In the meantime, I do my work, as I have been doing it, save what I can, and, generally speaking, lie low. Will write you again just as soon as I have anything definite. Be well and cheerful, dearest. My book of verse is almost ready, my prose is getting along, slowly, slowly, but steadily. I suppose I ought dedicate them to "Paramount Studio." Hush, hush!

Charles

To Marie Syrkin, [October 4, 1938]

Carmel Hotel, Santa Monica
Tuesday

Dearest,

Newspapers these days, what with the Arabs revolting in Palestine right after the Czech mess, are so exciting that it is hard to think of one's private affairs. However, here goes:

To begin with, while walking through Hermosa beach the other day, I ran into a Russian who is in the candy business. His people came originally from Rostov where they were in the wholesale woolen and silk goods business. From Rostov they moved to Harbin with two million rubles and ended up in the United States with much less—if anything. Our hero was in medical school for four years and studied philosophy and the like, but that's all over now for a "while," and he is in the candy business. He takes it very seriously, studies it, and tells me that all he wants to do is to live—he is no longer interested, so he says, in politics, etc. A very interesting chap about whom I might write you more. Anyway, he is specializing for the present in fudge and taffy, has a very clean store, handles each piece of candy with exquisite care. I bought a couple of pounds of fudge for you and I suppose you will get it by the end of the week—unless our Russian has forgotten or is postponing the matter.

Zaza censorship is no longer a secret, but it makes my immediate plans uncertain. I may not be able to leave until the end of November: it all depends on what happens to *Zaza*. Cuts and retakes, if they decide to make them, will certainly take a week and then recording the sound will certainly take another week. I do not suppose I can leave for three weeks, if then. The best thing to do is to pay no attention to it but go about our work as well as we can and when I can leave, I leave pronto. It's like counting my money here: every time I count it, something pops up. I don't think about it anymore but save what I can and let it go at that. By the way, I got a letter from Bunting. He is safely ensconced in Tauoin's apartment for the time being and wants me to get in touch with him when I return.

I ought to know in a day or two just what is planned about *Zaza*. That is, if they don't appeal to the board in New York.

I received the last number of *The Jewish Frontier*. I read it with interest but have no particular comments to make.

I hope you are well and hope to see you by Thanksgiving, at the latest.

Love
Charles

To Marie Syrkin, October 6 [1938]

Carmel Hotel, Santa Monica
Thursday

Dearest,

I have been, and am, very busy. A lot of reacting for *Knights of Round Table* seems suddenly to have heaped itself on my desk and I am expected to do it. I have let my own work go for a couple of days until I wade through these early plays about King Arthur and sources of Malory. I don't know what great good this will do but it seems to be my job and I think I ought to pass from the scene in a great stir of business and accomplishment.

The foreign news is bound to be depressing for a while as Hitler consolidates his victory and Mussolini tries for a slice of victory too. The papers will be full of a great number of articles written by experts like ourselves. When you see the position of the Czechs on the map, I think you must realize that Hitler's victory was inevitable and that the English and French could not challenge him there. I feel that Chamberlain did the wisest thing in minimizing that victory. All the states of the middle of Europe, Poland, Roumania, and the like, will now woo Hitler. There are, of course, irreconcilable differences between these, such as the differences between Hungary and Roumania, but, for the time being, the Fascists are certainly in the ascendancy. In thinking about Europe, we ought to determine our own position first, that is, our position as Jews and that may make a change in our attitude; for example, a war between Poland and

225

Russia might be a great defeat for Jewry whichever side won. I have always been pro-English and am still. I feel that the interests of Jewry, as well as the interests of the United States, are identical with England's. I should very much like to talk this all over with you and it will be easier than writing.

I have no notion just when I am to leave or how long Al will stay away or even if he will want me back. However, all this will be settled this month—at least when we leave and for about how long. I hope you are well and that this is true of all your family. Now I must get to work cleaning up my desk—if I am ever to get to my own work. Love.

Charles

To Marie Syrkin, October 8th [1938]

Carmel Hotel, Santa Monica
Saturday night

Dearest,

Well, I bought a big valise today. It will go under a seat in a Pullman. But I don't know just when I'm leaving. I'm pretty sure, though, it will be the last week of this month.

In a way, although you are the lonelier, it is much better for David to be uptown and avoid the subway rides. I think it should be easier for you, too. One of these days I think I'll ship the little radio home. There is no use taking it with me because it will probably be broken in a suitcase. I understand the express company will pack it for me. If they do, I'll ship it next Saturday probably. Maybe the Saturday after.

Scoring for *Zaza* should be completed by Wednesday of next week. Recording the score should take another week or so. Then the preview (sneak). Then, if it is all right, the official preview. About three weeks, I suppose.

Knights of the Round Table is a long, and not particularly pleasant, story for me as yet. I was going to write you all about it at the time but it was too long and I had too much to do. You must know (confidentially) that I have not been consulted at all about *Knights*. Al and Talbot Jennings have been working it out by themselves.[1] When the first two sequences were ready,

---

[1] Talbot Jennings (1905–1985), screenwriter whose films include: *Mutiny on the Bounty* (1935), *The Good Earth* (1937), *Spawn of the North* (1938) and *So Ends Our Night* (1941) (IDFF).

226

that is, mimeographed for everybody to read, and about two-thirds of the play finished, I read it, of course, as carefully as I could and found it completely uninteresting. I wondered whether or not to tell Al so at once or wait. Thinking it over, I decided it would be stupid to wait since the sequences were complete. I told him that I found them uninteresting and that the trouble was, I thought, in not beginning at the point where the "Round Table" fellowship breaks up, for, obviously, that must be included and all the rest is merely introduction. That, too, is where Malory begins to be interesting and I suggested that I make a brief summary, twenty pages or so, of all that is interesting in Malory. I felt that would make a powerful play. Al told me to go ahead. I worked my head off for three days and boiled the last hundred pages or so of Malory—with a few changes—into a powerful and, to me, profoundly moving, and yet simple, story. Al read it and came into my office saying sarcastically that he had read my "effort" and found it impossibly dull and quite unimportant. He was quite bitter about it. I was very quiet and merely said I was sorry. I knew, of course, I had hurt him by saying that I did not care for the first two sequences as they are, for they have been working at them for three months. Still, I am not really a "yes man." I say what I have to say as tactfully as I can but my value at all to Al, and to the studio, is to give my reaction truthfully and if that reaction is displeasing, or is not worthy of notice, well, I am sorry, but I have no business to be here, and, indeed, will not last here, on any other terms. Now, my summary, which I did in three days, was not as bad as all that, and the first two sequences are dull. Al knows that and is worried; so is Talbot Jennings. Well, then, Al was hurt at my lack of appreciation and I was somewhat hurt at his lack of appreciation. Hell's bells, I thought, so it is over. I will leave when *Zaza* is finished and he will not have me back. So that's that. That evening I had to go to a birthday party in honor of Al. It was given by Dr. Marx. I had sent Al a print (the Hindu dancer and chorus we have). I had it framed and it cost me almost $10. Our little talk was on Friday (his birthday) and the print was delivered to his home that day. I saw him Saturday briefly but he did not thank me or mention it. Well, I thought, he does not like it, or does not like the frame. Too bad, but I can't help it; I did my best. That night at the party, however, he thanked me very pleasantly; later, Talbot Jennings came up to me, as I was sitting near Milly, and he asked me, "How do you like the script of King Arthur as far as I've gone." Milly, of course, sitting right beside me, listened with both ears. I knew, of course, Al would regard any statement of mine that might be construed as derogatory with great hostility, especially since I had every reason to believe that Jennings was working along the line Al had chosen against his (T. J.'s) own opinion. Still, I could not praise it. As I was silent for a moment, Jennings, who was a little drunk and, accordingly, all on edge and very observant, said, "I see you don't like it because you are silent." There was a bitter note in his voice. "What do you really think of it?" he asked. "I must read it once more at least," I said pleasantly, and so it all passed pleasantly enough. I had made no false statement and yet had said nothing Al could find unpleasant. I knew Milly would tell him all about it and that he would like the way the incident had turned out. So it proved. He became very pleasant again. I was glad that he knows that though I respect his opinion I am not afraid of voicing my own. On this ground my position has somewhat more stability. At any event, he has just confided to me there is very much work to be done. So there is. In the end, I feel there will be a good script. Certainly, while I can, I shall fight for it as pleasantly and as tactfully as I can. No word of this to anyone, however.

I am very sorry that you are so tired teaching. But that is an old story. I sympathize with you completely. I hope that this is your last year of it and that, somehow or other, you will be free of it and free to do your own work. It is high time. I certainly think we ought to be prepared to face hardships for the sake of freedom. However, we will talk this over when I come home. By the way, I have managed to do the first five thousand words, revised of my novel. I like it—so far.

By the way, if you are the least bit sick, please get a nurse. Don't try to stay by yourself. That would be a foolish saving. However, I hope you are well. My love, dearest.

Charles

To Marie Syrkin, October 22, 1938

Carmel Hotel, Santa Monica
Saturday

Dearest,

I meant to write you a long letter but I have just been invited to Al's for dinner and now I am somewhat rushed.

Al has been working on *Zaza* and they have written some new lines and decided to cut out others and it may be approved. If so, there would be only a couple of days shooting, a week of sound recording, and then in a few days more the picture would be ready for previewing. I think we may get away by November 15th or, at the latest December 1st. If so, Al counts on being back at work in three months. He will go to Europe but his operation may be in New York.

I have reached the point where I am arranging my verse, in preparation for typing, and that is going along much more slowly than I expected. It will take me all of next week, at least, to arrange it, and a couple of weeks to type it. I expect to have about eighty pages, pretty close.

I have been working at my "novel" pretty steadily. I can manage to put in a couple of hours a day at revision. That is probably all I could do if I had nothing else to do, for nothing takes the edge off one's mind as fast as revising. I have about seven or eight thousand words in shape. However, there are about three hundred sheets still to revise and I have only revised about thirty, so you see I have about ten times as much to do. In any event, at this rate, and I don't see how under any circumstances I could, or should, go faster, it would take at least half a year before I am ready with a book.

In addition to this revision which, after all, is only two or three hours a day, I should like to gather the material for a historical novel, digesting it and writing it very roughly at the rate of about a thousand words a day. This would take about six hours a day and with the revision of the book I have in hand make a full day's work for the time I spend in New York, assuming that it will only last about two and a half months. In this way, I hope to have another book in the rough, with all the research done, for revision when the present book is out of the way.

Well, dearest, I hope you enjoy your Baltimore trip and do a lot of good. It is needless to add how exasperating all these postponements of my returns are to me and how I hope to be with you just as soon as I can.

Charles

To Marie Syrkin, October 27 [1938]

Carmel Hotel, Santa Monica
Thursday

Dearest,

Zaza is out of the woods. I think. The censors will approve it—probably. Yesterday they "shot," I hope, the last of it. Little was done to the picture but, my how adroitly. We may have a "sneak" preview by the end of next week and I may be on my way in another week. The music department is now at work on it.

The tentative script of *Knights* is also finished. I was mistaken about the first two sequences; as I read them now I find them justified by the end. It is a good play and, perhaps, in view of the motion-picture audience (and the censors!), the only possible play at present.

I hope your trip to Baltimore will not prove tiring. Now I really expect to see you soon.

Love
Charles

To Marie Syrkin, December 2, 1938

Carmel Hotel, Santa Monica
Friday

Dearest,

Zaza is proving to be a terrible headache. After the first previews about $40,000 was spent on retakes, and last night's preview audience kidded the picture. Of course, it needs only a few kids to stampede the audience. But there are always a few kids in the audience. A million and a quarter has been spent on the picture to date. I found the picture, as I wrote you, profoundly moving in the projection room; so did everybody who has seen it there. I think I know the answer. It is not the fault of the censorship. The censorship really helped the picture by bringing out what was in Zaza's heart, namely, marriage and children. The fault is this: the first third of the picture is loud and funny; this part is excellent and goes over very well; then the picture turns deadly serious and romantic. Well, the audience is at first slightly bored, uncertain whether they are supposed to laugh, and then decides to keep right on laughing but now at the characters instead of with them. That is the younger element does; older people are more sympathetic but even they are swept along. Now Al is doing more cutting and rearranging in preparation for another sneak. My suggestion is to put back everything and in addition have a long sequence at the very beginning in which we see Zaza as the little girl with the tin cup singing at street corners before we see her as the loud frivolous good-natured singer in cheap music-halls. Of course, that early life is talked

230

about but that is not enough: it must be seen and felt by the audience, which it never is, and must set the tone of the picture. The audience must feel that they are not to see a comedy but that the excellent comedy is only a welcome relief. This is so clear to me and so sound that I am surprised that Al dismissed it. He did. I did my duty and that's that. We'll see what the next preview, probably the early part of next week, will show. Of course, you will tell no one what is delaying us. It is surprising how malice will make news like this agile. In the end it will all come out but at present only those in the group here know what is what. I am sorry to be delayed in my return, not only because I want to be with you but because I think I can be of some help in little things like the affidavit and the income tax, for example. Well, it can't be helped. I must stand by. We have a release date to meet soon for *Zaza* and the picture may be released anyway. Well, Cukor is beginning to work at *Gone with the Wind*, everybody has other things on their minds, and *Zaza* has outworn her welcome.[1]

I have finished my verse (typing it) and put it aside to forget it for a while. Al has been asked to write on the function of the producer for the *Encyclopedia Brittanica* and I spent two days revising it—not the complete days but enough of the day to give me no enthusiasm for my own prose revision. I expect to go back to that tomorrow: I have about a quarter (or a sixth) of the novel finished and like it very much this far. It seems to me it has just the right tone—humorous compassion and the clarity and precision I like. Well, I have about three hundred pages still to boil down to that consistency. I think it will be done.

I have become so exasperated at the delays in leaving that I can't think of it. I was sure this week was the last. Well, let's hope it's next week.

Love
Charles

I have just spoken to Zoë Akins. She has just seen the picture with the quarrel scene cut out and is jubilant: thinks the picture greatly improved. I hope so. Al seems pleased. Well, if cutting will do it, I can get away all the sooner—so let's hope it solves our difficulties.

---

[1] Victor Fleming was ultimately the principal director of the 1939 classic MGM film, *Gone with the Wind*, starring Clark Gable and Vivien Leigh, although Cukor and Sam Wood also received credit as directors of the film. (HFG).

To Marie Syrkin, December 8, 1938

Carmel Hotel, Santa Monica
Thursday

Dearest,

I have received no letter as yet from you this week, but take it one is on the way.

Last night's "sneak" preview was, I believe, quite successful. At least, there was no ill-natured laughter, no mocking, and a round of applause at the end. I found the picture, in spite of the cuts, moving and still good. The cards this morning are about ninety per cent favorable instead of almost unanimously unfavorable as they were after the Oakland preview. So much has been done—by Al. The picture has lost, of course, depth, intensity, and much that would stir adult audiences to tears and the proud adolescents of all ages that form most of the picture audiences to mocking laughter. So I think it will get by very well—still a good picture as pictures go. This means, of course, I ought to be able to leave soon—just how soon I do not know. Now that they know they are on the right track, there will be a resolute move to polish and round off corners and, probably, though not necessarily, another "sneak" preview the first of next week and then the official preview next week, too. However, I am not certain of this. But, anyhow, we see daylight and will be "out of the trenches by Christmas," as one of the cutters said last night after the preview.

In case you have not heard of it, there was a letter in last week's issue of *The New Republic* stating the Arab position on Palestine. If any of you are capable of writing a calm, lucid answer, it would probably be published and might do some good. But, no doubt, the magazine by this time has been overwhelmed by letters, none of which has the coherence and clarity which Jews devote constantly to alien causes. You, of course, have both the intelligence and emotion to write such a letter admirably; unfortunately, you have not the third element—leisure. I am afraid that this is to be obtained, by those not born to it, only by the surrender of comfort or face. The leisure I have had to quite an extent this past year has been at the expense of face. I think it was worth it for it enabled me to clarify many thoughts I have had about my writing. I keep thinking about your lack of leisure very often and think the solution very simple, if we assume that leisure is more important than comfort, and life more than money.

Charles

To Marie Syrkin, December 13, 1938

Carmel Hotel, Santa Monica

Dearest,

It is now nine o'clock Tuesday night and I have had a difficult day and am tired; but tomorrow will be harder and I should like to write you (I am still at the office) before going home.

To begin with *Zaza*: retakes are difficult. The actors are scattered, the director is doing this and the writer that. They must be all gathered again for a day or two. Well, that has been done and the retakes will be finished tomorrow or Thursday or tomorrow and Thursday. Then we must have the "sneak" preview, the very last, I hope. Once that is over, and a little extra work ready for the last preview (although we need not wait for this) and are ready to go each our several ways.

I need not tell you how anxious I am to be with you—certainly for every day of your holiday; how much I want to plan with you; and this delay has tormented me. Of course, I could leave instanter, but this would not merely be impolite, it would be an impolitic, thing to do, and I owe Al at least the courtesy and ourselves the good sense of leaving just as soon as I can—all things considered. Well, that will probably be next week at the latest. I hope it will be the early part of the week so that I may arrive at the end— just when your holiday begins. In case I am delayed I have reserved a seat on the streamliner that leaves Friday night and is in Chicago Sunday morning: Friday the 23rd. I expect to write you again Saturday or this Friday with more details. I may know by then when the final "sneak" will take place. It will probably take place next Tuesday. Well, I must not think about it; neither must you; as soon as I can we shall be together again.

I have bought two books about the Jews in Spain and expect to study them on my way back—not to waste all that time. I notice that Ezra Pound has dedicated his latest book *Culture* to "Louis Zukofsky and Basil Bunting strugglers in the desert."[1] I am bringing it with me. I have some detailed plans for my work as soon as I get back—certainly for the two months before any question of return can come up. If you feel about me as you once did, I do not think we ought to be separated again, certainly not for

---

[1] Ezra Pound (1885–1972), *Culture* (1938). The book was published in London under the title *Guide to Kulchur*. Basil Bunting (1900–1985).

such a long period and should plan to be together, either here or in New York.

Charles

Received a copy of *The Jewish Frontier* late last night. Skimmed it. Shaved myself this morning with an "Ohava" razor blade, made in Palestine (bought a package here). Very good blade. Will certainly try to get away on that Friday (Dec. 23rd) train—at the latest. Hear that we are shooting today and may finish today—and what a relief—everything was too dry, skins and nostrils and throats. I finish today the first part of my novel (about 20,000 words)—closely written but not dry, rhythmic and humorous. Hai Judah!

Wednesday morning.

To Marie Syrkin, [April 17/18, 1939]

April 17/18. Leaving New York. We leave the hotel for a walk but A gets into a taxi and we drive to the park. We walk a little distance and find a seat in the sunlight. The bench is at an angle with Fifty-ninth Street and we talk of going to California—trains, time-tables, etc. The towers along Fifty-ninth Street make a brave show against the blue sky and heavy white clouds. Then A begins talking of Byzantium, of the strange empresses chosen in beauty contests. Back in the hotel, A, remembering a visit, speaks with annoyance of people who pay calls that seem to be social but are really in search of a job. This offends his vanity, he explains, for the visit is not to see him but the producer. He would rather a man or woman asked point blank for a business interview and, if recommended by the person whose recommendation earned the supposedly social visit, he would certainly grant it.

* * *

M's stomach is upset and she feeds it strangely. Goes into Child's with me and orders "chopped steak." Fed to children, she explains, but adds "if fresh." At night brings up a "Napoleon" for supper. This for me supposedly. And yet I have not eaten that pastry since I was sixteen and became deathly sick on two I bought in a cheap bakery on Fulton Street and bolted on the way from school. By this time she is quite sick. She insists on going

234

with me to see me off and, after we have parted, I watch her going upstairs slowly. She turns at the very top and smiles wanly. I go into the train uneasy.

* * *

The train leaves the tunnel and I see the houses like so many paper toys along the great ridge behind us. Later, I look up from my newspaper and see clumps of tall trees standing in pools of water. There is a blind girl on the train. She sits by herself in the club car, her head to one side as if she were listening closely to something we cannot hear, a disagreeable leer on her face.

I drive right to the Carmel Hotel. I expect to find it empty but it is almost full. The gambling ship that used to be off Redondo Beach has moved three miles off Santa Monica and those who work on it, take care of the gaming tables, etc., are stopping at the Carmel. Nice place for "an intellectual," as Mrs. Morris calls me, but I'll stay and see what's what. I have had to take a better room and pay forty dollars a month for it, instead of thirty-five, but it was the only room available other than an inner one level with the roof over the dining hall. However, my room fronts the ocean and used to be forty-five or fifty.

* * *

Monday morning I am early at the office and have moved all my things over. Have my old office. Get the scripts of the two comedies A may produce and read them. Come back to finish reading at night to prepare for similar stays when I am doing my own work. Read in the "Bulletin" issued by the studio an amusing story of an official who has spent his life in U.S. Public Health Service. He has accomplished much, particularly in fighting typhoid, and this involved much education of farmers and others. He had a difficult time explaining some simple preventive measures to a farmer or other and the man seemed stupid and unable to understand even the simplest explanation. But the official, a Doctor Lumsden, was very patient and finally, to make some point or other, said, "Now there are some people who believe the earth is flat." At this the man he was talking to brightened up for the first time and said, "By God, I do!"

A = Al Lewin
M = Marie Syrkin

To Marie Syrkin, [April 19, 1939]

April 19. The weather here has been as warm as in summer. One must keep flogging oneself to keep at work; nothing is easier than to go at one's slowest gait in this warm sunshine—stewing in boredom over a low fire.

* * *

At a quarter after one yesterday, A, as he used to do, put his head into the doorway and we went off to lunch together. At least he went to lunch but I had had mine an hour before and merely went to talk and listen. "I don't want to go to the commissary," he said. "I'll have to shake hands with too many people." "Yes," I said cheerfully, "they have even shaken hands with me." So we went to Lucey's. No sooner are we seated than A begins bitterly: his hearing is no better; in fact, it is getting worse and he may have to have another operation; but this, so the surgeon assured him, if necessary, will be a minor operation lasting no more than twenty minutes—to reopen the opening; *Knights* is through—they are all frightened about the conditions abroad: business in this country has been none too good; the chief men are going about with heads hanging; if Z does not make a success of GWTW he is through as a producer; MGM is producing only a single picture and all is at sixes and sevens over there; and over here they are frightened stiff; a reorganization is inevitable; LeB told him right out this is not the place for you—said it most friendly (but I remembered how he had glared at me over the table at the last "sneak" of *Zaza* and said, "What is he waiting for? Why doesn't he leave?"); and he would leave at once if he did not need his salary until next March because of his new house. From this we went on to discuss the comedy the office wants him to produce. "You had better get a copy of the script and read it," he says. "I read it last night," I answer. "What did you think of it?" he asks in a flat "dead pan" voice. I can tell he doesn't like it any too well but I say, "I liked it." He looks at me sharply. This is the story: a girl stole a necklace, is on trial, everybody is anxious to leave on Christmas vacations, assistant district attorney is afraid girl will be acquitted in general spirit of Christmas; gets adjournment but feels sorry for girl, gets her out on bail; finds girl on his hands; takes her with him to his mother; falls in love with her; decides to get her acquitted by cross-examining her roughly; but girl pleads guilty; sentence suspended; marriage.[1] "Do you believe it?" A asks.

---

[1] This film was eventually produced by Paramount and released in 1940 as *Remember the Night*, directed by Mitchell Leisen, written by Preston Sturges, and starring Barbara Stanwyck and Fred MacMurray (HFG).

"And that old hokum about mother pleading with girl not to damage son's career. And all that old Christmas hokum." I defend the story. Christmas may be hokum but it is sound hokum; Christmas does come every year, after all; besides, integral part of story. A admits this. Then assistant-district-attorney taking up with girl is done plausibly; really edged into situation, step by step, and reluctantly—for instance, the girl came to him in the first place because the cheap bondsman who got her out, solely as a favor to the D.A., thought he wanted her. But the mother pleading for her son's career? That is not necessary. It can go. Mother's suspicion of girl is indicated. And the early scene where they go to the girl's home for her Christmas (why D.A. took her along at first)—home of poverty and brutality—is good. A agrees emphatically. He suggested it to writer. Remembered article in *Harper's* called "Delinquent Girl." Yes, the story has possibilities, but girl must not know D.A. loves her until end and thinks rough cross-examination hostile instead surest way to acquit her. Must get title "Delinquent Girl." All characters must be harder...a bird has just alighted on the tree outside my window. A sparrow with speckled feathers. Moves its head sideways like the blind girl on train.

To Marie Syrkin, [April 20, 1939]

Apr. 20. I have had little lunch and by three o'clock am hungry. I run across the street and drink a glass of port. No sooner am I back in my office than I feel quite dizzy. I am drunk and I sit down in the large arm-chair to get over it. I take my glasses off and close my eyes but place a magazine open on my lap to give an impression of reading should the door open suddenly. It does and in comes A. He analyzes the story we had been discussing at lunch in the old clear way: a hard-boiled man for the law, a hard-boiled girl against it; he is humanized by her home; she is humanized by his; he tries to get her acquitted by his tactics in court (rough cross-examination); when she learns from her lawyer what he is about she pleads guilty to save his career. Office wants him to do it.

A = Al Lewin

Z = Zanuck?

GWTW = *Gone With the Wind*

LeB = William LeBaron, producer at Paramount Studios, LeBaron produced Paramount's 1939 film *Television Spy* directed by Edward Dmytryk (MPG).

Barbara Stanwyck the girl, Melvyn Douglas the man.[1] I object to Douglas. Too soft. A agrees that casting for type (which is right) Douglas too soft. Spencer Tracy would be better. Try and get him. Begin production in June. Hope script will be in shape by then. We talk loudly. Two boys who have been loitering across the street hear us and look up at my window grinning. (My head is clear; my tongue exact; but my eyes are swimming. A, however, sees—or if he does—says nothing.) That was yesterday. Today as we go to lunch A cannot hear me though I talk loudly as ever. I ask him if he has been to see the doctor today. Not yet, he says, and then tells me the opening is closing up. He is sure of it. A new operation will be necessary but it cannot be performed for three or four months. However, it will take only twenty minutes and is not as dangerous. If the opening closes up, this is the time it closes. Surgeon told him that just before he left. The question now is how many re-openings stay open. Surgeon had minimized proportion of cases in which openings close and had said nothing of much more dangerous situation that occasionally develops right after operation when hearing is totally lost. As we go into Lucey's, we meet LeB face to face. It is marvelous how he looks right through me as if I were just air. "Hello Al," he says coldly, and walks on.

To Marie Syrkin, [April 21, 1939]

April 21. The mist this morning was so heavy it felt like a drizzle and I did not walk part of the way to work. Now I shall have plenty of time for all I want to do, I thought.

As I passed the lawn in front of the cemetery I passed a white pocket-book and a white poodle near it; about twenty or so feet away, watching her dog and pocketbook, a Mexican girl was walking up and down with

---

[1] Barbara Stanwyck (1907–1990), actress whose credits include: *Stella Dallas* (1937). Melvyn Douglas (1901–1981) Academy Award-winning Best Supporting Actor for *Hud* (1963), also starred with Greta Garbo in *Ninotchka* (1939). Spencer Tracy (1900–1967), two time Academy Award-winning Best Actor for *Captains Courageous* (1937) and *Boys Town* (1938), made his stage debut in 1922 as a robot in Karel Capek's *R. U. R.* (BDF).

bandy legs and a bright spot of rouge on each cheek. We stared at each other as I passed. I saw, further on, a cocky young father bring his little daughter to school. When they reached the gate, he stopped and, taking his cigar out of his mouth, wiped at the corners of his mouth with his thumb and bent over to be kissed by his daughter. Then he kissed her on the forehead and he walked jauntily away but the little girl walked into the schoolyard with an unhappy look as if she had not read, or had not understood, her lessons.

***

As it turned out I have very little time for myself today. No sooner did A come than he sent for me and showed me the draft of a letter he was planning to send his surgeon in NY. It asked a series of questions on the assumption that the opening had closed. But his physician here will not admit that it has. But even if it has, a second (and if necessary a third) operation will be much less difficult. Even a fourth may be necessary. But the original French operation contemplated three operations so that, except that the first was much more painful and risky, now that it is over, A is really no worse off than if he tried the French one (which would have taken all of six months). I read the letter and suggested that he wait a week until his LA physician tells him definitely the "fistula" is closed. He has nothing to lose for he must wait three or four months at least before he can be operated on again and beyond that can wait as long as he likes (for the worst is over and the difficult part of the opening will stay open). Incidentally, he wants this unfavorable result kept secret in the office, although it will be (and is) obvious that he can hear no better. But perhaps, he wants to hear no comment other than that which he invites. That broke up the morning.

After lunch, A came in to say he had just had a long talk with TJ. Talbot Jennings is not looking for another motion-picture assignment just yet and would like to write a play with A's help (another secret). A spoke of *Abélard*, and asked me if I had the copy I kept. I said I'd bring it in. Luckily, I had in my desk the copy of the three sets we did together, and the first set which I had revised by myself (when he stopped me), and the rather voluminous notes I had taken from Taylor's *Medieval Mind* and a note of A's last suggestion. I turned this all over to him and suggested that he go through it before turning it over to J, "a real playwright," A said. I suppose whatever interest I have in the matter will be taken care of, if anything comes of it, which I doubt; I am really quite indifferent. I feel that my real work is to finish the autobiographical book which I am working on steadily and which, despite forty or fifty thousand words, is only half finished, if that much.[1] My other real interest is the historical novel I am planning and as for *Abélard*, let be what will.[2]

To Marie Syrkin, [April 22, 1939]

April 22. Another reason for aloofness in Hollywood. Before I left for New York, I used to eat in the coffee shop of the commissary—the cheaper side where the cheap help ate—electricians, extras, stenographers, and the like. I was somewhat of a mystery because afterwards I would be seen with A on the side where the important people were, even on the porch where only the most important of all dared enter; but I was used to the cheaper side and liked the crowd and liked the small table at which I sat alone. At another such table, next to mine, I used to notice a man of about sixty, who had the same waitress as I, and now and then I would overhear some of his speech to her (he spoke slowly and pontifically) and smile at it. For example, I would hear him say, "My wife tells me you must be an excellent waitress to take such good care of me," and the waitress, who was really excellent, a mature sensible woman of forty, would blush and smile.

When I came back, I found the commissary changed, the small tables taken away, and very large ones, seating six or more easily—really circular counters—in their place. My old waitress was in charge of three and I found a seat I liked best (I eat at 11:30 before the rest). The first day I finished rather early and walking to the gate I met the old fellow walking to the commissary. I felt rather chipper—the old familiar place, face, and sunshine—and I said to him (we crossed each other in an alley between two stages), "Well, I see they have taken your table away but left you your waitress." "Yes, yes," he said, smiling vaguely and went on. The next day, when he came to lunch, I was still seated at my table; the other two were empty. He hesitated and finally seated himself at the table to my left. But yesterday he came right up to me, although the table at the left was empty. "I don't want to sit at the table with girls or boys," he mumbled. "May I sit

---

TJ = Talbot Jennings

[1] *Family Chronicle* (1963)

[2] Reznikoff's historical novel was *The Lionhearted* (1944).

here?" "With pleasure," I said politely and he sat right next to me, although there were all the other seats. He instantly began to talk. Saw a motion picture which he liked and earnestly recommended to everybody. *Stagecoach*.[1] I agreed—briefly—that it was good. Am I from New York? He had lived there when a boy. Born in England. Was in the war. Would like to go back to New York for a visit. Accordingly, we talked about New York. He would not stop even to let me order the dessert. I could see that our good waitress was uneasy for she was afraid he would frighten me away—perhaps that we should frighten each other away and she would lose two customers.

Then at last he leaned forward and said, "May I ask you a personal question? What do you do in the studio?" I tell him I am an editorial assistant. Do I know so and so? So and so? I gather that he is an electrician but I talk as briefly as I can. In fact, there is no need to talk at all for he is going full blast. As soon as I have had my dessert, I excuse myself and leave.

Today is Saturday and he was not there, but I look forward to lunch at the commissary next week with uneasiness.

To Marie Syrkin, [April 24, 1939]

April 24 (*before A's talk with treasurer as per last letter*).[2] Negro washing window outside of drug-store. Radio going inside and negro moving brush and body in tune... Man working on gambling ship going up with me in elevator—young man grown fat with pale face. Says gently, "How I hate these Saturdays and Sundays!" I say just to answer, "Most people like them." "I hate them," he says sadly... Of LeB's failure to greet me. Miss B told me how Th once turned on a mail-boy who had said, "Good morning, Mr. T," to say, "When I want you to speak to me, I'll ask you." ... The party soon hit its stride. Mrs. T, who is really a capable woman, said of this

---

Miss B = Lewin's secretary

Th = Irving Thalberg

Mrs. T = Albertina (Rasch) Tiomkin, ballerina and choreographer, wife of Dmitri Tiomkin (IDFF).

[1] John Ford's classic 1939 western, *Stagecoach* starred John Wayne and Claire Trevor (HFG).

[2] See letter following, dated April 25, 1939. This parenthetical comment was a handwritten insertion to the typewritten April 24 entry, which Reznikoff obviously added after he had written his letter to Syrkin the next day.

picture and of that, "It stinks!" Of Tyrone Power, who had never done her any harm, she said, "When I look at this face, I feel like spitting on his nose."[1] A added brightly, "The only trouble with Power is that he has a nose." Mr. T got up to imitate how an important person at the studio walks—flat footed, belly stuck out; and A did his imitation of another who shakes each foot before putting it down. We left late, much pleased (I hope) with each other but certainly displeased with the rest of the world (or most of it)... As we walked together to Lucey's, where A eats now, he said, "Do you find it plausible that a man should drive all the way to Indiana in winter? That cows should be in the fields in winter? That threshing machines should be out in the fields?" And so on. So we discuss the script and on the way back he says, "This is what I have that is plausible, the adjournment by the district attorney to prevent acquittal, because of Christmas," and he goes on, step by step. "But I cannot have the man tell his mother that the girl he has brought along for Christmas is a criminal. He must be embarrassed when he sees that his folks think he is engaged and it is the girl who tells the mother what she is." This sounds like a good scene and we feel pleased at it.

To Marie Syrkin, April 25, 1939

Carmel Hotel, Santa Monica

Dearest,

Al walked into my office before noon and told me he had just come from a talk with the treasurer of the company who used to be stationed in New York and for some time has been here in Hollywood to take over command. As you know we have been working on a comedy which is basically sound but needs a good deal of working over to be Grade "A." This is what Al told the treasurer. The treasurer answered that he was not prepared to spend another cent on it. In that event, Al answered he was not prepared to make it. In other words, an impasse. We believe that the

---

Mr. T = Dmitri Tiomkin (1899–1979), wrote the score for Lewin's *The Moon and Sixpence* (1942) as well as such Hollywood classics as *It's a Wonderful Life* (1946), *Strangers on a Train* (1951), *Giant* (1956), *Rio Bravo* (1959) and *High Noon* (1951) for which he won an Academy Award (IDFF).

[1] Tyrone Power (1913–1958), romantic leading man in such films as *Lloyds of London* (1936) and *Marie Antoinette* (1938).

position of the treasurer (which is arbitrary and unreasonable) was assumed to get Al to resign. At least that is a possible explanation. Of course, he will not. His contract protects him and there is a clause in it which requires that he make only important pictures with important stars and writers. Should they really want to get him out, they may offer him some kind of settlement, and if it is substantial enough of course he will take it.

On the way back from lunch, as we entered the studio, Al said to me, "I am surprised that they don't fire you. If I have nothing to do, obviously I don't need an assistant." "That is the next step," I answered cheerfully. "What will you do?" he asked. I took my checkbook (the Bank of America one) out of my pocket and tapped it. "I will draw a check and go home," I said. We were going upstairs and I looked—and felt—cheerful. "It is a shame to have made you take that trip," he said. "Oh, that's nothing," I said. "I have only four suitcases here." I feel that my attitude was correct. Obviously, I must eliminate myself even as a source of the slightest vexation. If he will want me to stay or has any plans for me, he will make them in good time. Of course, even scientific weather-reports prove misleading and all this may blow over. But I am hastening to let you know what's what. It may even be desirable that I go back. We were agreed, I believe, that I am in a blind alley, from which I can only escape by my own work. The only advantage of this job (outside the not considerable salary considering trips and a double household) is that I get about half of the work done that I would do if I had nothing else to do. Should I lose this job, it would mean that I must finish my autobiographical novel in five months instead of the year and a half which would be needed (at least) if I hold down this job, such as it is.[1] Accordingly, I am really quite at ease whatever happens, and I trust you are. It was obvious, also, that out of decency and good fellowship, if not common sense, I had to return as I did.

I will keep you promptly posted on all developments and hope you are well. (Love and kisses—very soon perhaps.)

Charles

(please keep this all secret—to protect Al—even from my family *for the present.*)

---

[1] *Family Chronicle* (1963).

To Marie Syrkin, [April 26, 1939]

April 26. At noon, A came into the room and asked me if I would see an exhibition of modern French tapestries with him at the art museum. "Right now?" I asked. "This minute," he answered. It is quite a way to the museum and I suspected that once we were clear of the studio and the neighboring streets he would talk about his status. Instead, he spoke about *Abélard*. "You did a lot of work on it," he said. "The second act is not as good as I thought, but the last act is much better. There are a number of moving speeches in it, but it is too stiff for any company to act." I agreed cheerfully, for I want to do no more work on it (it has served its function for me which was to get me whatever job Al could give me); besides, it is not my subject and I can afford to spend no more time on it, especially since production is most unlikely. However, if he wants to spend time on it and amuse himself with it, I certainly won't stand in his way. As a matter of fact, I am somewhat pleased that he has found anything in it to praise. "Yes, the dialogue must be broken down," I agree. "It would be interesting to see what Talbot J. does with it." "He may think too much has been done on it already to do anything with it." "Why, I make no claims to it. He can do what he likes." (Certainly, as it stands the play will get nowhere; if, with T J's help, it does get somewhere, A will probably see I get something; in any event, I may gain something by being generous and cannot gain anything by being otherwise.) ... On the way back, we step into a restaurant (A, having first asked me if I had my lunch—which I had) and there A tells me of his conference with his agent. (He left early last night for that.) A needs for taxes, his house, furnishings, etc., unless he is to sell some of his stock, almost as much as the studio will pay him until his contract is up in March. Accordingly, any settlement that the studio will consent to is unlikely, for A cannot agree to any substantial reduction of his claims. Now the agent thinks he may be able to effect a settlement involving a substantial reduction and at the same time effect a new contract with another studio for A for the production of *Gettysburg* and *Knights*.[1] This would take about a year to produce, A's prestige would be restored, he would get a year's salary plus whatever he got from his studio for settling his contract, and the agent would get commission on salary and settlement. Pretty smart agent. Unfortunately, he is sick and has to go off

---

Talbot J = Talbot Jennings

[1] Neither of Lewin's plans for films of *Knights of the Round Table* or *Gettysburg* came to fruition (Felleman 278–79).

244

to the Springs to recuperate. But he will be back by Monday. As for me, I got my first check for my full salary today and no notice (as yet) to quit. MGM would have fired me yesterday but if these people here have not the guts of some of their competitors, they have the virtues of their weaknesses—some hesitation to be ruthless ... Something or other reminds me of different standards and the pretty girl in the cheap store in Santa Monica selling me a pair of pants for $1 which I wanted for walking on Sunday. The choice narrowed down to two—one a lighter shade than the other. "I always think that this color with a dark shirt is very smart—a dark shirt and a black tie," she said. How to be "smart" for $2 or less. Well, the store sells workingmen, farm hands, and the like, who wear overalls all week, and can't afford more than a couple of dollars to dress up on Sunday. She had genuine interest in the "style" of such Sunday clothes ...

To Marie Syrkin, [April 27, 1939]

April 27. Mrs. Z, EG's sister whom I promised to visit, is dressed in black, a thin gold chain about the high collar of her black dress. Her eyes bulge somewhat and as she shakes her head staring into the distance dismally and moves her lips in a peculiar way as if she were chewing something unpleasant and which she would like to spit out. Her father had been a physician, I think, a colonel in the Russian army, she never had to wash a tea-cup. She has been a soloist with the old Berlin Philharmonic orchestra and with great orchestras throughout the world. A few years ago she and her husband came to Hollywood on a tour. They were received as equals by all the great and promised great things by BM and others (I can see his fat jovial face giving away the world). She had a number of pupils in New York (graduate of the St. Petersburg Conservatory) but her husband, caught by all the glitter here, persuaded her to store her things and come to Hollywood and then to bring her things here from storage. There were a few jobs at first (her little daughter made $75 in three days as a musical extra three years ago) and then—nothing. Now she has three pupils and she cannot teach in a school because she must have a degree from a local

---

Mrs. Z = ?
EG = ?
BM = ?

institution (M.A.—there really is some such state law). Her girl is studying desperately for a scholarship and is doing her music too; her little boy, who is gifted as an illustrator and wants to be a cartoonist or commercial artist, sells newspapers after school. There are people here whom her father entertained in Riga when they came there penniless and they won't do a thing for her husband; she played when a child with JS, the actor. His mother gave her his private telephone but when she called a woman answered rudely and she was told to call in half an hour when she explained who she was and that his mother had given her the number. When she called in half an hour, the butler told her Mr. and Mrs. S had gone out. (But what can S do for her financially? I remember his unhappy scowl at Dr. M's as he ignored him—or greeted him curtly. And the long letter he wrote praising A's picture, really trying to get his attention.) She hopes to get to meet T. Oh, he could do a lot for her husband. She knows his step-father well and through him met T's mother, although they are no longer living together because of T, but T's mother, a sweet cultured woman, refused to introduce her to the son. (But what could T do for her? I know very well how he was pushed about when he wrote the music for *Spawn*. And now he is out of work—said so himself the very night before at the dinner at A's.) But she does not want to meet these people and ask them for favors; her husband keeps urging her and it is all so distasteful. Useless, I add. But, no, not useless; jobs here are given through friends, through recommendations, she says earnestly, making that motion of jaws and lips as if she were chewing a big lump of something disgusting which she would gladly spit out.

To Marie Syrkin, [April 28, 1939]

April 28. Yesterday, as I was standing in front of the administration building, talking to the cutter on *Spawn*, out came B. He is LeB's assistant, gets a thousand a week, and was the one I had to see when I was hired before I could become part of the organization. He has always ignored

---

JS = ?
Mr. and Mrs. S = Herbert and Mary Stothart
Dr. M = Dr. Rudolph Marx
T = Dmitri Tiomkin
B = ?

me, in keeping with his lofty post (in fact, Miss B tells me he will never wait to be announced but bursts into a producer's office). This time he looks at me, does not greet me, but smiles. It is not an unpleasant smile but I do not like it. And in a moment he has looked away... I have nothing to do, even ostensibly. I spent all morning typing my own book. After lunch, my neighbor comes in. He has a subordinate post in the studio administration but knows all that is brewing. "Are you busy?" he says. "Not at all," I say. (In fact, I am just calculating how long it would take me to finish my book of which there are still 157 pages to revise. If I go at the rate of a page (of four hundred words) a day, as I have been going, and take Sunday off, it will take me until November 1st; if I do nothing else, and manage to do two pages a day, it will take me three months.) My desk luckily is clear of all pages, written and typed, and there is only the calendar on it. "I am just working at the calendar," I say ambiguously. He laughs and sits down. We talk about Hitler's speech and Warner's picture, *Nazi Spy*.[1] I wait for him to say or ask something pertinent to my own situation. But he says nothing. Perhaps he knows of nothing. Perhaps it is really to talk about Hitler, for he is a German Jew. I look up, after he is gone, and see Damocles sword hanging above my head. It is really only a sprinkler head and, really, I expect to take my dismissal calmly enough but it is—if not serious—certainly as exciting as watching a big firecracker about to explode.

To Marie Syrkin, [April 29, 1939]

April 29. A, talking of *If I were King*, says the trouble with it is that the script was written as a farce and directed as melodrama...[2] Yesterday afternoon he told me that in talking about the script he refused to make as it was, he said he would be glad to send his comments and criticism to LeB, if he wanted them. He heard nothing from LeB, but, nevertheless, wrote his comments and criticism in six closely typed pages and sent it to him ... Today told me that I am invited to dinner tonight. Had planned to stay and work but must now leave early.

---

[1] *Confessions of a Nazi Spy* (1939), directed by Anatole Litvak.

[2] *If I Were King*, a 1938 Paramount production starring Ronald Coleman and Basil Rathbone was written by Preston Sturges and directed by Frank Lloyd (HFG).

To Marie Syrkin, April 29th [1939]

Carmel Hotel, Santa Monica
Saturday

Dearest,

As you can see by the enclosed there is really nothing new just yet. However, next week ought to tell another story—unless negotiations are quite prolonged. If Al goes to another studio, he may take me along—although he is quite unwilling to go and prefers to sit tight here. If he does, I see no assisting at nothing—not even ostensibly. My personal relations with everybody, I believe, are as good as can be expected, but that does not matter now. However, it may all blow over; in any event, keep mum and I shall let you know whatever news there is as fast as I can.

Do not buy Joyce's new book, *Finnegans Wake*, since I had to buy it.[1] You won't like it, anyway; at a glance it looks short and long-distance punning—verbal music and all the sense in overtones, some of which are very faint: "horns of (Ireland) ... faint blowing."[2]

I hope you are well and cheerful. Love and kisses.

Charles

To Marie Syrkin, [May 1, 1939]

May 1. Saturday night at A's. C told of a party to which she had gone the night before "where I danced like mad." "It sounds like a witches' Sabbath," said A pleasantly. They are trying out a new cook. The dessert was some kind of white of egg whipped up in a sauce of custard and lemon. C's comment was "that it was without imagination."

I had great trouble finishing the stint I had set myself Saturday. I decided that a solution might be to be up at four, allow an hour or so for shaving, bathing, etc., try to do some work before taking the street-car at six, work in the street-car, and then finish up all my work in the morning. I did get up at four this morning and caught an earlier street-car than the

---

[1] James Joyce (1882–1941), *Finnegans Wake* (1939).

[2] "The horns of Elfland faintly blowing!"—Tennyson, "Introductory Song" to *The Princess*.

C = Cecilia Ager?

one that left at six, but read the newspaper all the way; however, by half past ten with time out for breakfast, reading the trade papers before A takes them, I managed to revise about four hundred words of my novel—which is the minimum I set for myself. The plan is sound. Under the earlier way, I was immersed in the day's work and distractions before I could get well under way and constantly interrupted.

To Marie Syrkin, [May 2, 1939]

May 2. There has been a change in my relationship with A—very slight but perceptible. Now that the position of master and man is about to be terminated, if not this week this year, but most likely in a week or two, we have become equals again; in fact, I act the superior when it comes to writing—give suggestions as to practical methods, "daily dozen," etc. At lunch, and we go to lunch together every day, I am silent for long stretches and obviously comfortably so; now he makes conversation, tells stories I have heard before, and which he feels, somewhat uncomfortably that I have heard him tell; they are not particularly good stories, for example, how he dined with a certain friend and this friend engaged in a quarrel with somebody at another table, who was then insignificant but is now the head of a studio—a great man; I listen politely and think with some satisfaction that now I can make a suitable reply. (Certainly, people who are good at "staircase repartee" should welcome such friends; there is ample opportunity to redeem themselves. Now I thought of a good answer a few months after I heard it first.)...Marie says that I am always uncomfortable in new surroundings—"terrified," she says. In a sense this is true. For example, when I go walking on a Sunday, I go to the place where I have gone for about two years: I know the transportation problems, where to eat, when I am going to feel tired, where chilly, where overheated—I know the first faint symptom of discomfort that will mean a blister if I don't do something about it right away and I know what to do, how to pad it with cotton, and I know how fast to walk not to be stiff on the morrow; in other words, I know how to meet the terrors of nature, the fatal chill, the sunstroke, but only because I am on my own ground. When I get off it, I am not so good. Now this Sunday, for example. I am all better, I feel fine, but—. On Sunday I went to the beach. A beach I knew, of course. I decided not to bathe because it was rather early for that, but I will stand about in the sun (if it will only shine—the morning is misty), run up and down, do setting up exercises, skip lunch, if need be; in other words, exercise and reduce. The sun begins to shine during the afternoon; it seems mild and beneficent; the skin on my body and legs turns pink but does not feel burnt. And at the end of the day, so well spent supposedly, a Sabbath truly, I decide to eat lightly—a little fruit, a little cheese, a little port wine; I have it all in my room. I am tired and might as well go to bed, although it is only seven (one advantage of living alone in a hotel-room); because to tell you the truth I am beginning to feel a little stiff, a little chilly, and yet my skin is burnt and burning, yes, the sun out here seems to be hot, for all its mildness, even in April. I fall asleep almost at once and wake in the night. I know it is early for I hear voices in the hall, in the rooms, and in the street. I feel for my watch, light the lamp: half-past ten. I am thirsty—not very thirsty. I think I'll go to the bath-room. How stiff my legs are, how burnt the skin; as I stand on them, the pain grows worse as the blood rushes into them. By this time I am in the bathroom, but I can hardly stand. I think I had better go right back to bed. I leave the light burning behind me and step towards the bed-room—the bed to my left, the armchair in the corner to my right, and I hear someone falling on the floor. I wake up to find myself lying on the carpet, face down on it, between bed and chair. I am really very comfortable, not chilly at all as I have been when I fainted before, and the almost excruciating pain in my legs that had made me feel so weak is gone—almost. My legs are a little stiff, the skin a little burnt; but I am really feeling quite well, lying there face down on the carpet. I get up and slip into bed and in the morning, for I lie awake for the rest of the night, I manage to shave and bathe. I get up at four and go at it very slowly, taking long rests—quite needlessly but pleasantly. I get to work very early and feel perfectly well, except that I am very stiff and my legs and breast and neck are burnt. Today I am not at all stiff and only my shoulders are a little burnt. I am perfectly well only a little darker but next Sunday I think I'll go walking again. It got pretty tiresome standing around at the beach and I didn't lose any weight there, after all, in spite of doing without lunch. Maybe it was the little cheese at night. Anyway, I gained a pound in spite of everything.

To Marie Syrkin, [May 3, 1939]

May 3. I have heard nothing at all about my job but this uncertainty is uncomfortable. It would be childish to ask A, "Shall I resign?" for he will have no hesitancy in telling me what I should do. I am even tempted to ask his secretary, who knows all about studios, just how one learns that he is fired when not under contract. But that would be sillier still. Of course, I will sit tight and wait. Last night, my neighbor, who though quite unimportant himself knows what is going on because of his position in charge of the wire to New York came in. He asked me somewhat gloomily how things were and I answered briefly, "All right." Something was on his mind but he did not speak of it—if it was. We spoke about the studio's new picture *Union Pacific* which A tells me is intolerably dull and he asked me if I had seen it.[1] There had been a private showing at the studio theatre to which I could have gone. I'll see it downtown where I can get the audience re-action, I said. Then we spoke about Miranda's picture which is to be released. It will be pre-viewed Saturday night but you may not be able to get tickets, he said. Since I never get tickets for a preview and do not rate them, this means little to me. Perhaps there is a warning in it? Today I got paid—the usual check without notice of any kind. At lunch we sat opposite LeB—at least in opposite booths—and when he got up to go he looked at me for a long moment. I felt his unfriendly eyes but did not look up. I wonder if he thought, Is he still here? Still on the payroll? We must see about it! Perhaps I am too unimportant for so great a man to bother about. After all he does get about three thousand dollars a week ... I hope no one listens to what A and I talk about at lunch—and yet how can they help hearing it? Our talk today began well enough about Elie Faure and *The Spirit of Forms* but it ended about barbershops and the difficulty of getting a haircut in the neighborhood and how good and cheap the shops in New York are.[2]

---

[1] Paramount's 1939 film *Union Pacific* was produced and directed by Cecil B. de Mille (with William LeBaron as executive producer) and starred Barbara Stanwyck and Joel McCrea (MPG).

[2] Elie Faure (1873–1937), *History of Art*, vol. 5: *The Spirit of the Forms* (New York: Harper, 1930).

To Marie Syrkin, May 4th [1939]

Paramount Pictures, Hollywood, Calif.
Thursday noon

Dearest,

I am very sorry to hear about David's mumps but hope by the time you receive this it will be all better—if not forgotten. The sunburn which I have described in the attached sheets (too graphically except that I want it for future reference) is all better and my only damage seems to be that because of it I did not walk to work. However, tomorrow I expect to walk as always (unless I have to bring a valise to work to cart off my papers). However, *that matter* is still where it was last week.

I am keeping the information with respect to your uncle and aunt but am afraid to broach the subject of an affidavit just now. As soon as I can I'll do so but, as you can gather from the attached sheets and those I sent you, I am completely up in the air. However, this weekend ought to clear matters up—and probably terminate my job. I shall let you know as soon as there is anything definite.

I hope you are well. Love and kisses.

Charles

To Marie Syrkin, [May 4, 1939]

May 4. We were talking about T. You know how ebullient he is, I said, mispronouncing the word by accenting the first syllable. A corrected me. When we spoke about him again yesterday, A said, He is absolutely unreliable. Pay no attention to him. At least, I said, he taught me how to pronounce "ebullient." He as the remote cause, I explained. You looked it up, said A with mock accusation. Why, I would not trust my own father in the matter of pronunciation, I might have said, but did not think of it until afterwards. So, going home and waiting for a bus, along came a stenographer who had been in an adjoining office last year and whom I had greeted with the courtesy expected by a loyal daughter of the South (we were about to do *Gettysburg* and she had a few things to say which Miss B and I listened to with amusement). Now I greeted her again and we went into the bus together. She has dyed her hair and dieted but was not good-

252

looking, even last year. She waits for me to sit down ("because I am getting out before you") and sits beside me. If people saw us leaving together, she says, there might be a scandal. Not leaving in a bus—in a car or a taxi but not in a bus, I might have said, and so laughed off the remark which annoyed me. But instead I said coldly, I don't care. She waited a moment to digest it and then said cheerfully, Well, if you don't, I don't. It was not very bright of either of us and in another couple of blocks she had to get off ... Miss B is worried. Mr. L has no conferences, is not working on anything, he sent down six pages of comment on *Amazing Marriage* to LeB and has not heard a word.[1] I look at her blankly and say nothing. Suddenly, as I sit in my room, I hear very clearly a railroad whistle—shrill, clear, several times. Now I never heard that before. I go in to find out if A will go to lunch with me—if he is still in his office and has made no appointment, he will; and Miss B tells me he has gone off the lot, taken his gloves with him—which means that he is driving somewhere for lunch. Mr. F (vice-pres. of the studio) called him this morning and Mr. L said he was going to have lunch with *him* today, Miss B tells me. She guesses "him" is P. S., author of "Amazing Marriage." Oh, how I hope we get started, she says. I guess "him" is D, A's agent, who will represent him in his quarrel with the studio, but I say nothing, of course.

To Marie Syrkin, [May 9, 1939]

May 9. Saturday I took a street-car to the city. Waiting for it, I saw a man come up, eager about something, his clothes old and yet not ragged, his shoes old and yet sound. "Have you got a match?" he asked. No, I answered. He is a man of thirty. Now he walks up to a man of fifty and says, "Have you got a match, son?" The man gives it to him and walks away to the very end of the platform. The car comes in. Will they let me smoke there? he asks me, afraid of authority—even that of a conductor. I suppose

---

T = Dmitri Tiomkin

Mr. L= Al Lewin

Mr. F = ?

PS = Preston Sturges, director and screenwriter.

D = ? (Al Lewin's agent)

[1] "Amazing Marriage" was eventually released with the title *Remember the Night* (1940).

they will order me off, he adds bitterly. He is jovial, uneasy, anxious to be friendly—an equal. He looks at me again and recognizes a Jew. I wonder what Hitler will do next, he asks friendly as ever. But there is an invention—airplanes that will fly without motors—it will stop him. I know a man paroled from the pen who invented it. Yes, I do not doubt he knows many men paroled from the pen and some who are not... Today is Tuesday and I have heard nothing except this: Miss B tells me that yesterday a reporter from V, the trade paper, came into the office. Say, but are they disgruntled with your boss downstairs, he said. They're stuck with him, all right. Took him for prestige pictures and now want to make program pictures. Made three pictures and they did not make a dime.[1] Of course, I can't print that. A hard man to get along with unless he has his own way. She said nothing except to deny that he was hard to get along with.

To Marie Syrkin, Friday May 12th [1939]

Carmel Hotel, Santa Monica

My little darling,

I am sending you the original this time and keeping the carbon:

To begin with, I had dinner at A's last night. At the table, the conversation went around to their house and their claims against the architect: he had made a mistake in his plans so that a wall came right in the middle of a window; the windows were too narrow so that a row of them looked like a prison (which A had foreseen and feared but had been persuaded by the architect to allow); the dressing-tables were too narrow to conceal the plumbing underneath; all of which, and other matters, had to be changed.[2] A is going to incorporate all of these grievances in a letter which the architect will not like. (I cannot feel that A is unjustified because they have already given their architect more than five thousand dollars in fees and surely they ought not to pay him for changes due to his errors of

---

V = *Variety*

[1] Lewin's three productions at Paramount were *True Confession* (1937), *Spawn of the North* (1938), and *Zaza* (1939).

[2] Lewin's architect was Richard Neutra (1892–1970), who built the Lewin home in Santa Monica (Felleman 261).

judgment or taste). M then explained to me her troubles with her cook. It seems that a really good cook does not want to clean; on the other hand, M does not feel that she ought to enlarge her establishment just now; so she has been trying out boys who are neither very good cooks nor very good cleaners; one of them broke a very precious vase and tripped over an electric light cord and broke a very expensive lamp (he was a good cook); the cook who made the dinner we had was clearly not good—the green pea soup which should have been thick was thin, he had made potatoes as well as wild rice to go with the duck, and his lemon pie was too thick and heavy. Now since M must invite people to dinner, having a really good cook is no simple matter. Having discussed these troubles, we passed to another. You must know that they are collecting in the studio for the relief of the refugees. I asked what was expected of me and was told one day's salary would be ample. So I sent $15. This was returned to me yesterday by the head of the committee for Paramount Studio because in his judgment I had contributed, considering my salary, *too much*; if I would give $5, it would be ample, but I could give less without any criticism. I sent $5 at once with a letter saying that I appreciated the motive behind his letter. On the other hand, A had contributed two days' salary (about $750), and this was returned to him as insufficient, the head of the committee feeling that he ought to contribute a week's salary. Now, considering that he had been out for three months with all its incidental and perhaps useless expenses, and the certainty that the studio would not renew his contract, he felt that two days' salary was ample (and so do I) but, naturally, he could hardly explain all this. All this, however, brought us around to what was uppermost in my mind and when M went upstairs, which she did, I said to him that if my position in the studio embarrassed him, since obviously I was doing nothing, I would do whatever he thought best. He replied that I was part of his unit, that I should sit tight, that his agent had obtained two weeks in which to try to sell *Gettysburg* and *Knights of the Round Table*; that he had not been successful as yet although there was a possibility that Samuel Goldwyn might be interested,[1] at least he was reading the scripts; that he himself, however, did not bank on this; that when the two weeks were up (this week? the middle of next?) his agent would have a conference with the studio; that Paramount would, no doubt, try to settle his contract,

---

M = Millie Lewin

[1] Samuel Goldwyn (1884–1974), independent producer, founded Samuel Goldwyn Productions in 1922 and produced many Hollywood films including: *Greed* (1924), *Ben-Hur* (1926), *The Little Foxes* (1941) and *The Best Years of Our Lives* (1946) (IDFF).

but he would make no concessions; in fact, he could not because he needed all the money due him under the contract to pay off his house, complete the furnishing of it, and pay his taxes next year; that he was, as I knew, indifferent about the renewal since he wanted to devote himself to writing, etc., but he could not abate a jot of the contract; under the circumstances, any settlement could hardly be effected, but he would be willing to make a picture for them for the rest of the time, holding strictly even to a budget of half a million, make it, if necessary, by going out on location himself; and that he had several ideas in his mind which it was unnecessary to mention until he was ready to present them; and that, finally, I was not obviously doing nothing but engaged in the search of suitable material. This was the gist of what he said and from this you can see that matters will probably come to a head next week; that A may go to another studio but this is unlikely; that A will probably stay at Paramount until his contract expires or at least for some time; that he will not be allowed to stay here idly but will be given a picture to produce—a small picture but still an "A" picture—which he will probably, most likely, undertake and bring in within the budget and, probably to the satisfaction of everybody; that, in that event, they will probably try to hold him but it is unlikely that he will care to stay; finally, that I shall probably stay as long as he does and go when he goes and, should he go to another studio, probably or possibly go with him. This is how the matter stands today with all the "if" and "buts."

Now I like a business where a salary like mine is considered so small that a contribution of $15 is rejected as beyond my means. I should certainly like to work up from this position, if I can, but if I am not allowed to do more than I am doing it is a blind alley. I can get back here as a writer provided I have a novel or two published. However, the type of novel that will win me a position I want must be one that has the best I've got—not one in which I aim at Hollywood but one which is so good that Hollywood aims at me. This is undoubtedly true. I have been working at my autobiographical novel steadily.[1] I have completed more than 150 pages of three or four hundred each. I have still about the same number of pages to revise. It takes me from three to five hours to revise a page for I find that I must add much as well as take away. As long as I am here I think I can do a page a day which means that I should finish the revision of the draft I made last year in about six months. However, I have about one hundred pages more, some printed, some written, some briefly noted, to

---

[1] *Family Chronicle* (1963).

go through and add in the proper places. This should take about another two months, for most of this additional material is in excellent shape. Should this book be completed as I plan, I ought to have a good book with the presentation of three major characters, my father, my mother, and myself, a period in American Jewish industry, and the pilgrimage of a spirit from confusion, more or less, to a sort of equilibrium among the changing circumstances of the world, a kind of warranty. The book is certainly worth doing and I feel this more and more each day. Should I lose my job, I plan to go right back home and try to do *two* pages a day, cutting down the time of completion to about four months. I think I can do this if I finish one page and then allow a long interval, say about four or five hours, before completing the second. I'll be able to do nothing else but I think the time will be well spent. As for the other books, the historical one, the one based on current life, they must wait the completion of this which is becoming all engrossing.[1] I will try to keep the diary going, however, but I will not spend any real time on it. I will also try to do some verse but in this case, too, I find the autobiographical novel too absorbing. I hope it will bring us somewhere.

Now, as for your summer. It looks, although tomorrow may change all this and I may be on my way to New York, that I will be here for the summer if things work out as they seem to be tending. In that event you should come here, of course. Going to Europe or Palestine now is taking quite a chance of being marooned there for four years although, if there is no war this year, I think the chances for peace are good as England and France grow in strength and allies. I think, too, you should allow your aunt and sister to have the apartment, if they want to, so that they may save a little money and have whatever conveniences they may. In any event, I don't see how you can renew your lease or do anything until we know where we are. They will, no doubt, allow you to renew the lease by mail as you did last time.

I hope you are well and all yours. Love and kisses.

Charles

---

1 Reznikoff's "historical" novel is *The Lionhearted* (1944); "the one based on current life" could refer to an early version of Reznikoff's postumously published *The Manner MUSIC* (1977).

To Marie Syrkin, [May 14, 1939]

May 14. We are sitting in the restaurant together and Al is telling me about a professor of his who was a great walker. The man taught philosophy and among other things said religion had nothing to do with ethics—at least did not spring from it. With which I agreed. It sprang, said Al, from vanity—from the desire of man, overwhelmed by the size of the universe, to identify himself with a superior power. I had always thought it sprang from fear—from the desire of man to win the protection of a superior power. Al did not agree and I sat there wondering if we had not both uncovered the emotional springs of our being, what makes us tick, vanity, perhaps, in his case, fear, perhaps, in mine ... I sat looking at the fire for the restaurant had a great chimney and there was a fire blazing in it, for the day was raw. Every good restaurant should be equipped with a fire, I said. Yes, said Al, especially in the kitchen, at which we both began to laugh ...

To Marie Syrkin, [May 15, 1939]

May 15. Yesterday it was cloudy and chill—a gloomy Sunday. I went to the office and worked most of the day, slowly and leisurely in the utter quiet. Walking up the stairs of the hotel, I heard a light firm step descending and looked up to see a girl coming from my floor. (I have seen some fairly good-looking girls about the hotel. Al tells me that he was told in one of the homes he visited that they had a pretty maid but had to let her go because she would wink at the guests when she gave them a cocktail. She did not seem to mind losing her job and told them she had another on the gambling boat as a "come-on" girl—one who plays and wins and gets others to play. Perhaps, some "come-on" girls are living at the hotel, too.) This girl is rather pretty, nothing to faint at, but fairly so, and she walks gravely and gracefully. I step aside to let her pass and she never glances at me. Later in the evening, when I go out, I see her in the farthest corner of the parlor reading a book and when I come back she is in earnest conversation with a man. She was probably waiting for him. I go upstairs and go to bed, my mind busy with calculation: if I have a hundred and forty pages of my autobiography to revise and I do it at the rate of a page a day, slowly, carefully, filling in all the chinks and crannies, and if in the meantime I manage to do my research for my historical novel, slowly, carefully, soaking myself in the time and place, and meanwhile, too, jot down these notes for a novel of the life swirling about me—and so fall asleep.[1]

To Marie Syrkin, [May 16, 1939]

May 16. Miss B came in at noon to show me the afternoon paper with a statement by one of the columnists that he hears that A is trying to settle his contract with Par. A came in afterwards to show me a long letter he is sending his architect, listing a number of items on which he thinks (properly, I think) he should not be charged a commission according to their contract. After I had approved the letter, although one phrase by which A characterized a change in the building due to an "absurdity" in the plans worried me but still I felt I could not cut all the tang out of the letter, having carefully removed all statements as to negligence and the like, I spoke of the item in the newspaper. A's face clouded. "I have spoken freely," he said. I showed him the paper. "O, that's all right," he said. "It says I am trying to settle the contract." Just as long as it does not say, they are—which is the truth … I stayed in the office until ten last night, finishing all I wanted to do, and did not get home until midnight. Now I am dull and heavy-handed.

To Marie Syrkin, [May 17, 1939]

May 17. Today we were paid. As I took my check I remembered the voice of the prophet: "How long, Israel." … I had breakfast in the Ontra Cafeteria. One orders and receives a number on a little stand—if food is to be cooked. Then, when ready, a boy brings it to one's table. This morning the boy with my order walked about the tables looking for my number and at last saw it and brought my order (no small one) and placed it before me. "Alas, my sins have found me out." I said, but, unfortunately, there was no one to say it to but the busboy; however, we both enjoyed it … I went to bed at nine o'clock to be up bright and early this morning. I was up at eleven-thirty at night—even before the morning began. I lay awake for three or

---

Par = Paramount Studios

[1] *Family Chronicles* (1963), *The Lionhearted* (1944), *The Manner MUSIC* (1977).

four hours and woke at six, as tired as if I had gone to bed at two which is just about the sleep I had. However, I did not mind lying in the dark and resting: I felt utterly serene and at peace—whatever troubles I had were still sleeping soundly.

To Marie Syrkin, May 18 [1939]

Carmel Hotel, Santa Monica

Dearest,

There is really nothing definite yet—as you can see from the enclosed.

I am glad you liked the nougat and will send you a larger box when I am near the place again. The newspapers, even in California, are almost as exciting as in New York: the good news about England and Russia's approchement (if that is correct) is balanced by the news from Palestine. However, it is clear that the Moslems are more important for England than the Jews and will win out every time in Palestine. I hope the Jews will be able to wangle a better territory than British Guiana out of England for settling besides Palestine.

Love and kisses
Charles

To Marie Syrkin, [May 19, 1939]

May 19. I heard one waitress ask another (in the commissary) for "teaspoons." Now they serve very little tea but the term still persists. Such is the conservation of speech. For a long time, the national drink has been coffee but the spoon is a "tea spoon." This morning's newspaper had in one of the columns a note to the effect that the studio will do *Gettysburg* and is trying to exchange the script of *Knights* for the services of a certain director. Miss B read this, too. So did A. I said nothing but Miss B tells me that he asked to see Mr. LeB (who has been too busy to see him all morning) and that Mr. LeB's secretary, at noon, told her that the report was ridiculous...Last night, went to dinner at A's. Tonight I expect to be free to work. Find revision of my book, as I expected, slow but am doing it steadily and with pleasure.

To Marie Syrkin, [May 22, 1939]

May 22. A study in tempo of conversation: a pretty big boy and a little boy are walking together. The little boy is really tagging after the other one—eager to be a fellow. The older fellow is wearing a peculiar hat and the younger fellow asks, "What kind of hat is that?" No answer. "What kind of hat is that, *Stanley?*" emphasizing the name. Stanley answers cheerfully, "A monkey hat." "What kind of hat is that?" the little fellow asks again, not what kind of hat is *that* (namely a "monkey hat") but *what kind of a hat is that* (namely, the hat you have on). And again Stanley says curtly and cheerfully, pleased with his own wit, "A monkey hat." But, after a pause he adds, "A small round sailor hat." Specific enough, to be sure, but the little fellow now says aloud to himself, "A monkey hat," wondering, perhaps, if it is really a kind of hat and if so what an attractive name for a hat and could he get one ... I go into an Italian restaurant—a cheap kind of place, counter, stools, not very dear for dinner. On the walls are posters—beautiful posters issued by the Italian government to encourage tourists, the leaning tower of Pisa, an arch in Rome, a column in Florence. I see that they are beautiful but do not admire them; in fact, my dislike for them grows so great I am almost nauseated and am sorry I came in. I will not come again...

I walk along the sea on Sunday. It is a beautiful day—cool and sunny. The cottages that were closed are now being opened and those for rent occupied. Out of one cottage tumbles a family of Jews—mamma and three or four assorted children and papa himself stands in front of the door to his neighbor's cottage—planted in the very middle of the sidewalk, right in front of the door. Mamma is on the stairs of her cottage and talking to her chicks; one is going back into the house, another to the sea, still another up the street. She does not talk too loudly, considering the circumstances but her English is Jewish, distinctly and, alas, somewhat unpleasantly so. But Papa has something else on his mind. He looks, unfortunately, a little like the Jew the Germans use for their caricature on the "Buy Christian" stickers: the fat belly, the heavy jowls, the long nose. On this he is wearing two pairs of eyeglasses—his regular glasses, thick and heavy and a pair of dark glasses against the sunlight. And he is smiling, a smile of friendship and deep happiness—for the beautiful day, for his own cottage right on the sea; a smile of deep benevolence for all his neighbors, particularly the handsome Gentile couple who are just going into their house in front of which he is standing, gazing at them, smiling, eager to speak. The Gentile couple (a dark young man and a slender blonde girl) are trying their best not to see him, although he has placed himself, big belly, big smile and all, right in the middle of the sidewalk in front of the door. They enter the house, gazing intently at a dog in a neighbor's yard and when they reach their door they almost hop into the house and close the door quickly behind them ... A's barber-shop has closed and for a few days he had tried another. He did not like it and now does not go there. But we pass it on the way to lunch. Now Al is decidedly a good customer, gets shaved every day, tips as only a producer must and can, and the owner of the shop and his barber smile at A as we pass, almost fawn at him, and he looks away coldly, his face set. They raise their hands in greeting through the pane of glass and, embarrassed, I raise mine a little by way of answer—but of course they are not greeting me at all.

To Marie Syrkin, [May 23, 1939]

May 23. I was invited to A's house last Saturday. We had just come back from lunch, at least my escort of A to lunch, and I was about to sit down snugly for a long afternoon of work, when the telephone rang and M asked me to the house for dinner. Thank you, I said. But the matter did not end there. A will probably be leaving in few minutes, she said, and you can come with him. Thank you, I will, I said, too dull to think of what to say, and seeing all the blue afternoon in ruins. Of course, I should have said, I have some chores to do this afternoon and will be over at seven. No, it would not have been clever to be candid. I went in to tell A I was leaving with him and he looked distressed. I expect to read this afternoon, he said. I will leave in a few minutes but I will spend all afternoon reading. However, I could not retreat so I said simply, Then I'll take my work along too. He was just going to read his magazine but perhaps he was afraid that I would talk about the story he has been writing in M's presence (which I have too much sense to do). Perhaps, there was some other matter, certainly there must have been, because he has never made any bones about reading when I was there. However, on the way out he was pleasant enough. He read his magazine and I tried to so some work (I took my brief-case along) but did nothing—no longer used to working in the open air with the noise of the sea in my ears. Unfortunately, too, to add to the wasted afternoon, I met MS there. You must come to the house for dinner, she said. Tuesday night. No, said M, Tuesday night you and Herb are

---

MS = Mary Stothart

invited here and you, too, she said, turning to me. I bow. Well, then, said MS, you will come to our house Wednesday night—alone without the Lewins. "Two dinners—one right after the other," I expostulate mildly. I think to myself, If I can get out of it graciously Tuesday night. Perhaps I shall say, May I drop in after dinner instead of coming to dinner. I am afraid I'll be too late. Yes, I suppose if I were to say simply, Listen, I have a lot to do and it is moving so slowly, how can I spend an evening just eating and talking nonsense, you must excuse me, they would be offended. It is simpler to say, Thank you, and look grateful. Well, tonight is Tuesday night and I am going to the first dinner—now I must go to the barber and get shaved ... This morning I saw a blind girl come to the street corner with her dog. I asked her if she wanted to cross and she said she was waiting to take the car. When the car was still a block away, sounding its bell, she said to her dog, Up, Up! as if ordering it to get up in the street-car. The dog looked at her, puzzled. I wondered if despite the keen hearing the blind are supposed to have she thought the street-car had actually reached our corner or whether because of that keen hearing, the bell a block away sounded as if at the corner.

To Marie Syrkin, May 24 [1939]

I watch two women in the bus. The elder has a sharp face, grey hair; the younger is almost pretty—small pert nose, large blue eyes. The elder is talking in a low flat voice without gestures but whatever she is saying is of great interest to the younger woman who does not take her eyes away from her companion's face and only speaks to say, softly too, My goodness! or just Goodness! or some other expression of shocked gentility and as the elder woman talks on, scoring point after point, a brighter light comes into her grey eyes and her speech is slightly more emphatic but still flat, still low ... I watch three men waiting for a bus. They are talking Italian, at least only two are talking and the third listens. They stand away from the others waiting for the bus, against the large plate glass window of the store, and talk: first one of them talks, a fast stream of words that seems endless, and all the while, the points of his fingers gathered to a blunt point, he keeps gesticulating at the second man with the back of the hand; all his talk is directed at the second man who listens patiently, never stirring; and the third man, who is not being addressed at all, listens too, a short heavy man (the other two are tall and lean) he listens intently, his fat face mirroring despair. Then the second man begins to talk, the same long stream of words, the same intense speech and now the short fat man turns to him to listen and his fat face shows the same intense despair; so the two talk, making long uninterrupted speeches at each other and their silent auditor turns to each speaker in turn, never opening his own mouth, his eyes fixed in despair, the corners of his mouth drooping.

To Marie Syrkin, [May 25, 1939]

May 25. Yesterday and today have been very warm: the temperature does not go up very high—perhaps 82 or 83 degrees, but one can hardly move for the heat—at least one walks slowly and with lassitude. Going to breakfast along one of the alleys of the studio, I find a row of actresses waiting on camp chairs and benches outside one of the stages. They are young girls, mostly, and as I look at the faces I see (unsurprised) that they are very good-looking—I think one of them would create a stir in a restaurant or a bus, but all strung out like that, with their heavy make-up on, they mean no more than a lot of slick magazine covers. They are every bit as good-looking.

To Marie Syrkin, May 25 [1939]

Carmel Hotel, Santa Monica
Thursday

Dearest,

I am sorry that I have no news for you, but things are unchanged either for the better or worse. However, this cannot go on much longer. This very week may change matters. However, we must learn, as I have learnt somewhat, to live completely in the present and confident of the future, if the present is used wisely. I have systematized my novel-writing to my satisfaction and feel confident that, given time enough, not an extravagant amount, I shall do something in this field. My method now is to revise about a page of the draft I have finished; I revise it with some care and it usually takes me two, three, or even four hours, depending how early I can get to it, for the longer I wait the longer it takes. I type this revision the next day and then set about revising the following day's work.

In all, it takes about three or four hours and is a big chunk of the day. I have about four hundred words a day. To date, I have completed more than 60,000 words and have still, working at this rate, enough to keep me revising my draft through October. I have then additional writing to do, some now written and revised, some written and unrevised, some not even written, and some printed; in all, I think the book will run about 150,000 words and take the rest of the year. I do not doubt that these statistics bore you but my own plans must be based on them.

As you gather from the above and the attached, I spend most of the day serenely typing. I wish you were doing your own work too—not too far away, say in the next room with the door closed until evening. Well, in another few weeks.

Love and kisses
Charles

To Marie Syrkin, [May 27, 1939]

May. 27. Al and I are at lunch. I tell him of a new book about Hollywood which maligns, I say, my favorite restaurant. A tells me of a former friend of his with whom he had dinner in that very restaurant when A first came and who went into a long series of comments about social conditions, etc., very violently. When he was through, A merely remarked, "These oysters are very good." A has told the story many times, I suppose, for he told it without enthusiasm. I should have replied, for he has come to dislike this former friend, at least they are no longer such, well, I should have replied, "I bet the oysters were not very good, either," which would be true of oysters here (especially since I know A thinks so). But I am not so adroit and did not say it ... A was in a hurry yesterday and we went into a cheap place to eat—all he wanted was a sandwich. On our way out, A meets a chap and greets him warmly. I can see that the chap is embarrassed. He is dressed like the poorer help around the studio—cheap shirt not particularly fresh, cheap ill-fitting slacks. Clearly, he has not the air of importance which is acquired with position. Yes, he is working. RKO. A does not ask him what he does but shakes his hand warmly and leaves, pleased with himself. Perhaps with his graciousness. Perhaps with his own success, for he tells me that fifteen years ago they were both assistant cutters working side by side. "I thought he was the director," I say, hinting at the reversals of place so common in Hollywood.

To Marie Syrkin, [May 29, 1939]

May 29. A negress on the back seat of the bus—a very fat woman, broad nose, thick lips, halfshut eyes. Coming home from some char work, probably, because she carries a bundle with her—old dress, old shoes. Also in her hand, idly, a spray of flowers, large white flowers with a reddish tinge at the heart, broken off from a bush or bought for a cent in a market; she holds it idly in her hand and looks at it from time to time with dreamy halfshut eyes ... Saturday afternoon I had just settled down to work when the telephone bell rang. Milly. Come to dinner tonight. Certainly. Thank you. Angna Enters is there too.[1] House guest. After dinner, A dozes off. Milly wakes him on the sly. We talk history, dates, why the cross on the bridge at Prague has Hebrew letters—Al has a fantastic story a guide told him, I look up Lowenthal who has another, history of Persia, was Moses an Egyptian, and at ten I leave. When do you have breakfast Sunday morning, I hear Angna ask Milly. We have it in our rooms, says Milly. I want mine at eight-thirty, says Angna, orange juice and three cups of coffee. I must have three cups. I'll tell the boy, says Milly mildly ... Seated in front of me in the street-car coming from the beach is a family of three—mother, son, and daughter. Mother is well on in the thirties, blonde hair—naturally so, worn worried face. The son, twelve years or so, is seated opposite her and the daughter, about nine or ten, beside her. The boy is blonde, too, and a good-looking fellow with quiet, dreamy eyes; the little girl is homely, at least the mouth pulled down at the corners, the sharp angry eyes behind glasses, makes her quite plain. No sooner are they seated than the boy says, Today was one of the most wonderful days I ever had. He speaks softly, gently. The girl says shrilly, I wish we could live in one of those houses—looking at the houses along the shore—then we could go to the beach every morning. The mother does not answer either. The beach they are coming from is cheap, the family is dressed cheaply, but very neat and spotless. Where is the father? Dead? Divorced? After a while the mother says, You know Mr.— I do not catch the name it is spoken so gently. She is talking to the boy. He goes fishing every Wednesday. I think I can get him to take you along. The boy does not answer for a minute or two and then says, in the same gentle tones, I should like it very much. Can I go too? asks the little girl but no one answers her, and she resumes the sour look that she has had all along. The mother and son have eyes only for each other; she takes her pocket handkerchief and wipes his face; he complains of something in his eye

_____

[1] Angna Enters (1907-1989), dancer, mime, painter and author.

which certainly was not enough to make him blink and she opens his eye, raises the upper lid and lowers the lower to look for it. There seems to be a feud in this family, mother and son against the daughter. Perhaps the little girl sees through her mother. Anyway, she stands up at one moment to look out of the window and the boy says to his mother, She stepped on my toes and did not even say excuse me please. And the mother turns to the little girl and says sharply, Why didn't you say excuse me? You should have said excuse me brother. The little girl says nothing and looks out of the window with a bitter face, the corners of her mouth far down, and her eyes bright and dry, looking sharply through her glasses.

To Marie Syrkin, June 1, 1939

Carmel Hotel, Santa Monica

Honey,

I was quite relieved to get your letter and hear that you were reasonably well. However, I did not find your account as funny as it probably is: I feel sad that you should spend your time and energy on these useless trips. These people are all converted, anyway; it is now only a question of diverting them, and I think you have more serious diversions.

As for my plans, everything is still quiet here. I don't know how long this can last: I think every week the last and every week things go on as they have been ever since I got back. Don't think about it or if you do, just think of coming out here: two or three days will be plenty in which to reserve a berth. You will always be able to make last minute arrangements of some sort. Of course, I will let you know just as soon as I know. Why, if you are on your way here and the bottom drops out, we may even go to Mexico or Alaska together (the trip through northern California is beautiful, I know, and as for the trip to Alaska that is not supposed to be dear and is supposed to be quite wonderful.) As for my own work, that goes on, of course.

Love & kisses
Charles

To Marie Syrkin, [June 5, 1939]

June 5. The dinner Saturday night had Walter Conrad Arensberg (whose poems are in the first edition of the Monroe anthology) among the guests.[1] A curious man. Completely German in appearance. Al tells me he is busily engaged in proving Bacon wrote Shakespeare and employs five secretaries for the purpose. Has a three story house full of modern paintings—a very large Rousseau, the original "Nude Descending the Stairs," Brancusi sculpture. Has a mild gleam in his blue eyes somewhat like a madman's and sometimes spoke in a low voice sentences that were uttered like maxims and which I did not understand, although I tried to appear intelligent. Sometimes, what he said was clearly nonsense and understandable as such but seemingly intelligent. For example, the development of the unborn child was being discussed and Doctor Marx, also present, was asked how long after conception it was before the foetus assumed a human appearance. His answer was six weeks. The comment then was that into that brief period all of evolution was compressed. Arensberg found and expressed the appropriate analogy with the six days in which the world was created according to *Genesis*. Then Marx was asked how long it was before a prematurely-born child could live, that is, how old the foetus must be. The answer was six months, and therefore, according to the law of the state or country, a doctor was required to report all premature but dead births where more than six months had elapsed after conception but none where six months had not elapsed. At this Arensberg said that recurrence of the figure six seemed to show there was validity in the Pythagorean doctrine of numbers—which is just nonsense. He had much to say about Christianity which was disparaging, I gathered, but quite incomprehensible to me and I believe fresh and undigested Fraser's *Golden Bough* but one thing he said was striking: it is believed, or he had read of a myth somewhere, that Jesus and Judas were twins—the Persian notion of the constant struggle between good and evil.[2] Doctor Marx was pretty good and told us that the expression "camel" in "camel through the eye of a needle" is a mistranslation of the Greek and that the word should be translated "rope," namely, as "a rope through the eye of a needle so difficult is it for a rich man to enter heaven"—which is really much better. Also "ox-eyed Juno" is a mistaken translation: the true translation should

---

[1] Walter Conrad Arensberg (1878-1954), art collector, poet, and Baconian whose books of poetry included *Poems* (1914) and *Idols* (1916). (DAB).
[2] James George Fraser (1854-1941), *The Golden Bough* (1911-1915).

be Juno appearing like a cow and, likewise, Athena appearing like an owl, instead of owl-eyed; the reference, of course, to the statues by which they were worshipped (before the human figures), the statues like those of Syria and Egypt where the divinities had the shape of animals and birds. This was very satisfactory and I told the story, à propos of painters that were bribed, when Milly asked indignantly why anyone should want to bribe a painter, I told the Chinese story of the princess who was sent beyond the mountains to be the wife of a Hun chief and was a little disconcerted in the middle of it to find everybody listening intently and pleased to hear Angna Enters and Arensberg and his wife express their appreciation of the story and pleasure at hearing it and I caught a glimpse of Al increasing the receptiveness of his hearing instrument to hear the better; and later, when I told of the little boy in the commissary who exclaimed with delight at having a ham sandwich, meaning to illustrate the love of children for simple things, Milly exclaimed, That is a pointless story! Absolutely pointless! But Mrs. Marx, God bless her! said, Anybody who has had a child can see the point of that! Why I wouldn't let my children touch a ham sandwich! And Arensberg told the excellent story of the little girl who saw "sky writing" and rushed in to her mother with the cry that "God is doing his home-work!" ... This morning's *Examiner* has Louella Parson's column headed "Paramount will junk *Knights of Round Table*" and went on to say that since the studio had no star like Gary Cooper or Errol Flynn to act Launcelot and since the picture would have to have a large foreign sale to pay for itself, the studio would not make it, but Al Lewin might make it elsewhere.[1] I was first tempted to call up Al and tell him about it when I read it Sunday night but decided he might not like it since I might have to talk about it to Milly. Besides, it was no whit disparaging. This morning I was glad I hadn't when Miss B told me L. Parsons had called him on the telephone Saturday and had spoken to him before printing the item. On the way to lunch and when we were seated in the restaurant where all the neighboring tables could hear, I said to A, "I know you haven't time to read all the columns carefully. Now in this morning's *Examiner*," and I saw him wince waiting for me to speak of Louella Parsons, I suppose, but I went on to tell him smoothly of Damon Runyon's column and the importance of the Philippines in the east from Franco and his allies. I said nothing about the Parsons column at all but he knew I had seen it and liked my reticence,

---

[1] Gary Cooper (1901–1961), two-time Academy Award-winning best actor for *Sergeant York* (1941) and *High Noon* (1952). Errol Flynn (1909–1959), actor whose films include: *Captain Blood* (1935) and *The Adventures of Robin Hood* (1938) (IDFF).

I think. Anyway, there is no news but this week must see matters cleared up for we have been given no picture as yet.

To Marie Syrkin, [June 6, 1939]

June 6. There is an actor on the lot who is Russian—mujik or Cossack. He usually acts humorous roles and whenever I run into him he is genial and smiling, greeting everybody to right and left, but when he sees me his face freezes—the way a bird dog does when he has "pointed" a bird. His smile is gone and he looks at me out of narrow grey eyes—a face full of hate: white Russian facing Russian Jew. Of course, he greets Al with all friendliness, but that's a possible "boss." ... Miss B came in tonight to tell me that A received an elaborate invitation to the salesmen's convention that P is holding. He glanced at it and without even waiting for Miss B to leave threw it into the waste-paper basket. Last year he was one of their best speakers. She concludes that our stay is limited if that shows his attitude. But I have heard nothing. After lunch, Al asked me to go for a drive. He went downtown to see a sale of furniture. I thought he was going to tell me something of consequence and wanted to be away from the studio where no one could possibly hear him, but if he intended to do so, he changed his mind. We looked at some incredibly shoddy stuff, which I can hardly imagine he really came to see, and came back to the studio.

To Marie Syrkin, [June 7, 1939]

June 7. Yesterday I decided to see Oka, the Japanese who had written to me. I was afraid to telephone for fear I might annoy him at his work (if the address I had was of his job) and his employers should not like it. On the other hand, writing and arranging some meeting-place would be a lengthy matter and I might have to leave this very week-end. I wanted to see him once before I left. So I got on a street-car and transferred and transferred again and at last, as the brief twilight was ending, the car crossed the river and in the night, rather dubiously, I got off near a sign which read "Pay Dump." We had been going through districts of cheap lodging-houses and

---

P = Paramount Studios

drinking-places for some time, factory districts empty at this time, and now had reached the city dumps. I could see Los Angeles across the river, very beautiful in the last red rays of the sun, and walked into a corner shack where a harsh voiced girl was selling drinks over the counter to ask my way. I found the street—a one-way street leading to the top of the bluff overlooking the river and its flats and found the house. The decent looking woman who answered told me go into the yard and ask in the house there. I asked if there were any dogs in the yard and she laughed and said there were cats but no dog. I pushed aside the gate that barred my passage and walked into the yard. Here was another house—a long low building, too small for garage or stable. I knocked at a door—there were several—and another decent-looking woman answered, younger than the other and quite pleasant. I asked for Oka and she smiled and said he was about to take a bath but he would probably interrupt it to see me. I was to go around to another door at the side. I did and in another moment at the screen door a short smiling Japanese in a blue kimono was standing in front of me. He looked rather young and he asked me into his room. It was very small and I could distinguish a cot, an old typewriter, and a map of the Soviets in red on the wall—but whether for sympathy or offense I have no way of telling. We spoke briefly: I apologized for coming without warning; he apologized for the long trip; I explained that something had come up that would prevent me from staying, and we arranged to meet tonight in a cafeteria in the center of that city (Boos's).

Something really had come up. At the last moment Al gave me a ticket to a preview (*Man about Town*).[1] This was held downtown and afterwards I was to meet him if I could. I did, and we all went on to the Stotharts. Here we found Rose Ponselle, the opera-singer,[2] and an assortment of followers: a fat Italian who was her secretary or agent, utterly bored; and her husband, an American polo-player, tall and a rich man's son who was already pretty well in liquor and, his feet resting on a commode, sprawled in the middle of the sitting room, dozing off with a large cognac glass, which he had just replenished, in his hand. After a while, she began to sing as if to sing the walls down—a powerful beautiful voice; dressed in a flame colored gown, very tall, slender, moving her beautiful body about as she sang, sang phony Neapolitan songs ("like paper carnations" Angna Enters

---

[1] *Man About Town*, a 1939 Paramount comedy, directed by Mark Sandrich, ctarred Jack Benny and Dorothy Lamour (HFG).
[2] Rosa Ponselle (1897–1981), a soprano with the New York Metropolitan Opera from 1918 to 1937 (DO).

said), sang arty French songs, sang German, she was very attractive, despite the flat peasant's face. Al thought her like a figure in Gauguin's South Sea pictures—and indeed she looked like one. Herb S has grown thin and he looked radiantly intelligent beside the other faces of her assistants and drink-flushed husband.

To Marie Syrkin, Thursday June 8th [1939]

Hotel Carmel, Santa Monica

Dearest,

I received your brief, unduly delayed, and confessedly sleepy note. In reply:
THE LEASE. The real problem for most people with respect to an apartment is the rent. The rest is comparatively simple. Don't worry. For the rent you pay you can always get another place just as good. But you don't have to—yet. Just tell them you'll know in the summer—like the last time. Anyway, wait.
SUBLEASING. Aside from the perfectly good reasons I have against this feminine and school-teacherish notion of financial enterprise, I may have to spend the summer in the apartment. If I do, I'll pay at least half of the rent, so that your loss will not be staggering. Anyway, wait.
SUMMER VACATION. Seriously, I realize how important this is for you and certainly you ought to spend it in the most enjoyable way. Should it appear best, at the last moment, to go to Europe, I don't think you'll have trouble getting accommodations. People are not crowding the boats the way they used to. Despite the lull, the real danger will come in the middle of the summer when the German harvest is in (August 2nd or so last war). Offhand, the alliance with Russia, which seems likely at the moment in spite of English reluctance, should work for peace by presenting an overwhelming force; on the other hand, I think the Fascist states must continue to expand, by war or threats of war, or demobilize which would be equivalent to a severe defeat.
MY JOB. Matters are now so taut, the situation must snap one way or another any day now. You have almost three weeks before your vacation begins. So hold your horses.

Herb S = Herbert Stothart

Love and kisses, procrastinating correspondent and confounded sleepy-head.

Charles

To Marie Syrkin, [June 9, 1939]

June 9. The motorman keeps peering into the little mirror near his post with a peculiar glint in his eye but I pay no attention to him until he says to me confidentially, "He has spent over a million dollars to have me done away with—tried to poison me twice, tried to run me over—I don't know how many times." We are going along between backyards and lots and there is a narrow path beside the tracks. A girl is walking along this and will not stir for all the motorman's clanging to let the car pass. Finally, she turns off and we go by. "That's one of them now," he turns to tell me. "He wants to get me into trouble; why, he has gone so far as to put little children on the track." I do not ask him who this person is, this Anti-motorman, and smile politely, hoping he will not suddenly decide I am another tool of this arch enemy... The Japanese writer seen in the bright light of the cafeteria looks quite young. He has bad teeth but that does not prevent him from smiling readily; neither does his short height prevent him from bowing stiffly and often. I urge him to help himself and he does—his check is ninety-five cents which is a lot for that place. However, after he has told me that he has a wife and that she has come downtown with him but gone to the library and I suggest we find her and take her with us to a motion-picture and we look for her and do not find her and I decide to buy her a box of candy for her husband to bring her, he is stricken with compunction and urges me gravely not to buy so large a box (two pounds). Doesn't she like candy? He smiles. O, yes, very much. He knows nothing about motion-pictures but has seen them all (cheap theatre for he cannot afford first runs) or almost all and those he has not seen— well, he knows the good ones he has missed; I suspect that he has looked me up, too, for when I tell him how I liked an exhibition of Japanese paintings and had one of my characters in a book ("By the Waters of Manhattan") praise it, he smiles and says, "Yes, go to Tokyo to study art instead of Paris"—which is from the book.[1]

---

[1] *By the Waters of Manhattan* (1930).

To Marie Syrkin, [June 10, 1939]

June 10. I opened the door of A's outer office yesterday to tell Miss B that I was going to the commissary for lunch and caught her listening in on the telephone. I said nothing, of course, and looked as if she were merely listening to see if a connection had been made, and, making a quick motion with my hand towards the commissary, quickly closed the door, and, though I had occasion to go there several times during the afternoon, I said nothing, of course. This morning, when I went in to see the trade papers before A came, she said, NB (A's agent) called Mr. L yesterday and they had a long conversation. It seems (and she named an independent producer) is the most interested. The studio gave Mr. L only two weeks to get another connection, for, of course, if he did, they would settle with him that much cheaper—and much more time than that has now passed. But they were probably waiting for the convention (ending today) to be over, for they have all their conferences among the chiefs then, and next week they will surely talk to Mr. L, if he is not ready to talk to them. She was combing her hair as she spoke and the prospect of being out of a job, which she was looking at in the mirror was not at all inviting. Oh, I said, Mr. L and the studio will probably get together on a picture to make; after all, they must pay him his salary for almost a year and it is to his best interest for his standing to make a good picture or two—and he can." ... I went to lunch with A and he said, among other things, that the studio had sent him an *engraved* invitation to a celebration they were holding tonight at the Ambassador (to round off the salesmen's convention) to which he had sent an *engraved* acceptance. He spoke jestingly and in the same mood I asked if he stressed "engraved" as a pun. Before I went, Miss B told me that I was invited to A's for dinner tonight. There will be company, and it will be a big dinner.

NB = ? (Al Lewin's agent)
Mr. L= Al Lewin

To Marie Syrkin, June 12th [1939]

Carmel Hotel, Santa Monica
Monday

Dearest,

I'd have sent you a wire but there is some uncertainty still about the certainty and so I think a letter would be better.

To begin with, I have received two weeks' notice. This means I am out of the studio by June 24th at the latest. As I thought, they called Al down this morning and incidentally asked him to let me go. He asked for leave to give me two weeks notice and they consented. On the whole, the return trip, carfare and all, was not so bad. This is the certainty.

Now for the uncertainty. They did not call Al down to talk about me. He told me how matters are and, of course, with respect to this you will exercise your best discretion because news travels very fast and any news at all now would not be good. (I will write my folks this Saturday, as usual, and will tell them about myself.) As for Al, they do not intend that he makes any other picture here. They do intend, of course, to pay him. The exact arrangement, however, is still open because this morning's talk was only a preliminary. However, the matter is so far advanced that it may be settled even tomorrow. It may, though, drag on for some time. When Al told me of the notice, he told me that he supposed the studio would pay me at once and I was free to leave right now. I said that as long as his matters were unsettled, certainly as long as he is at the studio and I was paid for being here, I would stay and be of whatever help to him I could. He went on to tell me of two matters with other studios pending. One with a small, but not unimportant producer, is quite warm, and if he makes either connection he may, so he said, be able to take me along. For that reason, he thought I should consider staying on to save the fare. But these matters are not adjusted quickly and neither may jell, for one reason or another, and if they do, they may not include me. In any event, as you see, both for practical and personal reasons, I should stay on for the present. Things may be much clearer by Saturday. In any event, this job has long ago reached a blind alley for me and I cannot regret it. Personally, I do not think either job will prove attractive enough for Al to take and I think I will be free to return to New York in a week or two.

Love & Kisses
Charles

To Albert Lewin, June 28th [1939]

410 West 24th Street, New York City

Dear Al,

Marie has changed her mind about going to Palestine—or even Switzerland. I'll go with her (and my typewriter) to the Adirondacks after school closes. However, I think the dryad will have enough of trees in a week or two.

I suppose and hope—you have daily "sight of Proteus" etc., now that you have forsaken the world.[1] Love to Milly. Marie sends her love to you both. Please remember me to Miss Enters.

Charles

To Albert Lewin, August 12th [1939]

410 West 24th Street, New York City

Dear Al,

Marie left for Switzerland on Wednesday. She should be back September 4th. We went up to the Adirondacks, through the Green Mountains, and another week in Maine (Ogunquit), and came back about the middle of July. The trip did Marie a lot of good and now, rested and brave, she has gone (the darling!), a delegate to the Zionist Convention, to rescue captive Israel.

I have been left with this typewriter and type all the day, merrily, merrily. I hope you have been having as good a time. I send my greetings (very humbly) to the dazzle-women who tread your sands and parquet floors (also rugs) and cry, ha! ha! (This is a French typewriter and is quick to ! and ´ and ` and ^and ç. Also ~.) Love to Zaza!

Seriously, love to Milly.

Charles

---

[1] Referring to Wordsworth's sonnet, "The world is too much with us."

276

To Albert Lewin, August 16, 1939

                                410 West 24th Street, New York City

Dear Al:

> Each day when the sun sets,
> there is no longer any wind,and the surf is
> slow. The colors in the sky change and cannot be named.
> And the years pass
> like smoke in the air.

                              * * *

> On the white sand the waves have left dark stones,
> and in the white sand dark grains may be found:
> these polished stones were once rocks,
> reduced by the sea to a conformity which will not save them
>   from becoming white sand.

                              * * *

That is what I would do. (When you are in New York we can argue about
it.) I thought of a title for the second—"To Fascists Everywhere." Keep it
up!

                                                        CR

To Albert and Mildred Lewin, September 5th [1939]

                                410 West 24th Street, New York City

Dear Al and Milly,

Marie came back on the Queen Mary after a lot of excitement in
Switzerland and France, suspense and all that, but none the worse.[1] We
send our love.

                                                     Charles

---

[1] On September 1st Germany invaded Poland, thus beginning World War II.

To Albert Lewin, October 1, 1939

410 West 24th Street, New York City

Dear Al,

I have just finished (except for re-typing) the book I was working on steadily this summer. About the millinery business and, of course, myself. I put everything else aside to do it. Now I am thinking of a historical book, novel rather than play: it is easier, I suppose, to find a publisher.

I have been hoping to hear from you that you have your hearing back. Have you done anything more about it? I hope you have written much verse and are finding much to keep you pleasantly busy. Marie sends her love and we both send ours to Milly and our other friends.

Charles

To Albert Lewin, October 18, 1939

410 West 24th Street, New York City

Dear Al,

I am sorry Lempert did not come to the Coast. But you can always have the operation, I suppose, and the surgeons will know more about it.

The new book is still being typed. It would take a good stenographer ten days, but I am doing it myself. As for the historical book, it was to be about Jews in the Middle Ages.[1] (Did you know that what the Church condemned as "usury" included much that would be just capitalism today?) However, I put it aside to work out an idea for a prose book—an idea I have had for some time. I intend to show it to you when ready.

If you take the *New York Times*, you saw the review River got last Sunday.[2] Full page and great praise.

---

[1] The first chapter of Reznikoff's "historical book" was published in *The Menorah Journal* with the title "The King's Jews." The entire novel was published in Philadelphia in 1944 as *The Lionhearted* by the Jewish Publication Society of America.

[2] The review of W. L. River's novel, *The Torguts* (NY: Stokes, 1939), which told the story of the migration of the Torgut Mongols into Russia in the 18th century, praised the novel as "a colorful and exotic story and lauded the author for "successfully combin[ing] ... fact and fiction" (*New York Times*. [11 October 1939]: 25).

In a way, I am sorry you are leaving your quiet life for a studio. It takes a long while to get into one's own work. However, I like Dave Loew very much and the two of you ought to get along first rate.[1] If you think I could be of any use, I should like to work for you again. Really work. I don't suppose it possible to work for you two years without becoming a partisan of yours, if one is not a partisan to begin with, as I was. As for salary, that never bothers me. However, if for some reason or other you do not see your way clear to have me around, that will make no difference between us: I have enough respect for myself, perhaps conceit, to think I have my good points, anyway, and certainly enough respect for your judgment to believe your reason, whatever it is, good and sufficient. In any event, I hope you will find in the enterprise pleasure and *mega kudos*.

Marie's love and mine to you and Milly.

Charles

To Albert Lewin, November 29, 1939

410 West 24th Street, New York City

Dear Al,

I have just completed (according to my private schedule) typing the long "novel" I have had on my chest for several years. It runs over a hundred thousand words, which for me is a lot of writing, and I expect to turn it over to an agent, and have it knock about for a time, and then—I'll see. I would send it to you but any suggestion you would make now would, I am afraid, be wasted: I am so sick of the book. I prefer to save your reading and suggestions for some future when I shall be eager to be at the book again. I have another, a better novel if not a better book, on my chest and think I shall write prose, from now on, steadily, as I hope to write verse. As for what I am to do for a living, if anything at present, I am quite uncertain. I have not really tried to find anything and am divided between planning to live very carefully on very little, using up the money I have saved and doing nothing but writing, or—and this I have always thought sensible and no hindrance to doing as much real writing as I have it in me

---

[1] Lewin and David Loew, a former fraternity brother of Lewin's at New York University and founder of the Loew's theater chain, founded Loew-Lewin Productions in 1940 (Felleman 264).

to do—working at a job. Unfortunately, all the publishers of law-books (except the one I worked for) are out-of-town. If I decide to see them, I may take a grand tour which may include San Francisco; if I go there, I will go through Los Angeles and see you. However, I expect that nothing will interfere with my schedule to spend a couple of hours at prose and an hour or so at verse a day and that at the end of the year I shall have another group of verse and another novel. (I need not add that I hope you, too, have some such schedule.)

Marie sent you a copy of *The Menorah Journal*, thinking that you might care to read a little about the illegal immigration of refugee Jews into Palestine.[1] I saw a Yiddish picture, *Mirele Efros*, in which there is a girl who, at times, is a little like Merle Oberon.[2] I also saw a Russian picture, *Shors*, which, in spite of grave faults, is worth seeing. (I find it hard to become as furious at the Russians as you were—and, perhaps, still are—although I wish for the victory of England and France as much as anyone. As you know, I am no friend of communism in this country and dislike Stalin as much as I respect Trotsky, but I do not see how the Soviets could act otherwise: if their present advances are not pro-English, they are certainly anti-German, and the earlier conduct of England and France with respect to Spain and the Czechs has certainly merited nothing better at the hands of Russia.)[3]

I hope you and Milly are well and that you find your new business pleasant. Please give my love and that of Marie to Milly—and yourself—and to our other friends.

Charles

---

[1] *The Menorah Journal* (Autumn 1939) contained Marie Syrkin's article "Aliyah seth" (336–342).

[2] *Mirele Efros*, directed by Josef Berne (1938) was based on the Yiddish play of that name, often called the "Jewish Queen Lear," written by Jacob Gordin (1853–1909). The cast included Berta Gerstein, Michael Rosenberg, Ruth Elbaum, and Albert Lipton.

[3] Referring to the non-aggression pact between the USSR and Germany.

To Henry Hurwitz, December 2, 1938[9?]

364 West 18th Street, New York 11, N. Y.

Mr. Henry Hurwitz, Editor
The Menorah Journal, New York 3, New York

Dear Henry,

I am sorry indeed to be obliged to miss your dinner on the 9th and have no doubt that it will be as enjoyable as your dinners always are. Thank you for asking me. I am still at work at the history of the Jewish community of Charleston—head over heels in it—and must leave for Charleston on the 7th. I should have been there long ago for we have a deadline to meet—the bicentennial celebration.

I told Allen how much I enjoyed "Beds for Bananas." I take my hat off to the writer and editors. As for your article, I feel that any hasty comment on my part would be an impertinence: not the least of its merits is that it stimulates and deserves careful thought.

Cordially yours,
Charles

To Mildred and Albert Lewin, December 27, 1939

410 West 24th Street, New York City

Dear Milly and Al,

We received your handsome gift and Marie undertook to thank you for both of us (I now do so and presume to reproach you for being unnecessarily extravagant). But Marie's boy was operated on for the removal of a cyst on the Friday before Christmas—a minor operation supposedly—and by the next day was running a high fever—almost 104. He is still running a fever but much less and is better. So, although Marie still spends the days and evenings of her Christmas vacation at the hospital, we breathe a little easier.

As I wrote you, I turned my book over to an agent and hoped to forget about it for a while, but he returned it in a week, refusing to show it to any publisher. I have put it aside to look at it again in about a year: I suspect that the agent is mistaken but a good rest will not do the book any harm and I should like to revise it again before showing it anywhere—throw away what I find dull then and clarify all I find obscure. *The Menorah Journal* still promises to use a group of Jewish verse and I have corrected the proofs. Should it appear, I'll have them send you a couple of copies. Please give one to Dimitri Tiomkin for me, since I promised it long ago. But unless *The Menorah* becomes quite prosperous, it will not appear before spring. I am writing another book, really a novel this time, plot, love, and all, and hope to have the first rough draft of it finished in a month, and the research for it completed in another month. Now when I finish the second draft and am ready to revise it, I should really like your opinion of it—but all this is about four months away.

If you have decided upon a picture and would care to send me a script, I should be very glad to make any comments that occur to me and you might find one or two provocative ideas on your part. In the meantime, accept our wishes for a very happy New Year, and we thank you again for all your many kindnesses.

Charles

Many happy birthdays, Milly!

Dear Milly and Al,

Thank you very, very much—and many good wishes for the New Year.

Marie

To Albert Lewin, February 24, 1940

410 West 24th Street, New York City

Dear Al,

I find *Night Music* interesting, since you are interested in it.[1] Otherwise, I would be tempted to say that this is just a play that Odets has put

---

[1] Brooks Atkinson's *New York Times* review of Clifford Odets's play *Night Music*, starring Elia Kazan and Jane Wyatt, begins with the ominous warning, "Now that Odets writes like Saroyan, Doomsday is near" (23 February 1940):18. Atkinson goes on to remark that Odets "who has always clung to the erratic, is now writing entirely without discipline and listening fondly to the sound of his own voice (18). Al Lewin, who is twice made reference to in the play, helped to finance the production (Felleman 264).

together out of his portfolio. He is very generous, to be sure; I think he emptied his portfolio, his card index, his tablets, or whatever he has. The play has more good lines (I liked the two about you, of course) and more odd characters (the cigarstore clerk whose tunes are stolen, the girl in the lobby expecting a telephone call or, rather, hoping for one) than the other plays, I suppose. Perhaps more than all the other plays. And the audience liked it. They kept laughing all through it, more so as the play went on, and applauded at the end for five minutes or so and even cheered—almost the way they would at a political meeting when the candidate steps forward to speak. It was a clever audience, even though it was only the second, not the first, night. In the gallery they quoted the review in *The Times* to each other, knew the reviewer's name, and, passing Alice Hughes downstairs, I heard her say slowly, not for me to hear, I suppose, although she looked straight at me, "I like it better than Saroyan but not as much as Odets." I thought of the play as a French picture with Gabin as the messenger, older, of course, but just as surly, and the girl a prostitute, certainly, and imagined that I might like it very much.

Something is certainly the matter with *Night Music*. It is easy to say that it has no story, as some of the reviewers did, or that the story is incredible because only a detective, dying of cancer, who might be compassionate even to a louse in his hair, as a man about to be guillotined might well be, could stand that hero. I am inclined to think that the trouble is in the play's lack of unity: the hero, as acted and well acted, talks and struts a little as if he came out of Lawson's "Processional," certain incidents, like spending a night on a park bench together, have a little of the fantastic quality of "Liliom"; it should be all "Processional," all "Liliom," or, if Odets's humorous reality, a story with some credibility.[1] But the theme is excellent and could not be better.

I need not tell you how warm and pleasurable, how sad and gay, Marie and I find Freuchen's letters. We thank you very much for sending them. The cracks by Gogarty are good, too, but merely brilliant.

I am still at the new book. The other one is resting quietly in a drawer, except when Marie lets fly at it one of her bolts from the blue. But the dead shall arise; verily I believe in the resurrection and the life. I am glad

---

[1] *Processional: a jazz symphony of American life,* in four acts, by John Howard Lawson (b. 1895) (New York: Seltzer, 1925). *Liliom: a legend in seven scenes and a prologue* by Ferenc Molnar (1878–1952), produced in New York in 1921.

you have Jennings for your first picture.[1] Good luck and love to Millie from both of us.

Charles

Dear Al,

I was so happy to hear that you were making a picture about conditions in Central Europe.[2] It's hard for me to believe that anything but a very moving drama could be the result. God knows there's an overabundance of "material"—some of it seems to have been already staged and directed—like the tales of those ghostly refugee boats in the Mediterranean. I suppose you have read Peter Mendelsohn's *Across the Dark River* which deals with the Jews driven out of the Austrian Burgenland onto a [*illegible*] in the Danube between the frontiers of Austria, Hungary and Czechoslovakia.[3] As a symbol of our time, it's almost too neat, too perfect—and yet it's merely a record of what actually happened.

Please excuse me for getting started in this vein. I had merely wanted to wish you, and the picture, well.

With love to you and Millie,

Marie

To Henry Hurwitz, April 28, 1940

410 West 24th Street, New York City

Dear Henry,

I am very glad, of course, that you like the story and will use it.[4] Particularly because I hope future texts of "The Merchant of Venice" will refer to it and *The Menorah Journal.*

---

[1] Talbot Jennings (1905–1985) wrote the screenplay (adapted from Erich Maria Remarque's novel *Flotsam*) for Loew-Lewin's first production *So Ends Our Night* (1941) directed by John Cromwell and starring Frederic March and Margaret Sullivan (HFG).

[2] *So Ends Our Night* (1941).

[3] Peter De Mendelssohn (b. 1908), *Across the dark river: a novel* (New York: Doubleday, Doran, 1939).

[4] "A Story for a Dramatist (With a Note on *The Merchant of Venice*, and Facsimiles of Three Pages from Leti)." *The Menorah Journal.* 28:3 (Autumn 1940): 269–78.

Your question as to "Jew from Houndsditch" is not at all "over-meticulous." In view of the current notion that there were no Jews in England until Cromwell, it is quite pertinent. My authority is Sir Sidney Lee. In *Elizabethan England and the Jews*, New Shakespeare Society Transactions, Ser. 1, No. 11–13, 1887–92, referred to by Coleman, Sidney Lee says, page 148, "In an anonymous piece, published in 1609 (though probably written earlier), called *Every Woman in her Humour*, a city wife suggests to a neighbor various means of obtaining a dress to enable her to go to court, and concludes the discussion with the words, 'Or if all fail you may hire a good suit at a Jew's or a broker's; it is a common thing, and especially among the common people.'" The play, according to Sidney Lee's note, is to be found in Bullen's *Old Plays*, vol. IV, p. 363. Then, on page 157 of the same article, Sidney Lee goes on to say, "It is curious to note that Stowe, the contemporary historian of London, states that Houndsditch was largely tenanted then, as now, by 'sellers of old apparel'; but he complains that there had lately crept in among the old dwellers a number of pawnbrokers—'a base vermin,' or rather, as St. Bernard thinks it more convenient to term them, 'baptisatos Judaeos,' who take to themselves to be Christians.' When we associate Stowe's words with that practice of hiring court suits at a Jew's mentioned by a dramatist, Elizabethan Houndsditch may fairly be credited with clothiers and pawnbrokers of Jewish origin."

As to "if you prick us, do we not bleed," the slip, as you surmise, is Doctor Lopez's, not mine.

With respect to Leti, my edition (9th) of *The Encyclopedia Brittanica*, says, under the head of Sixtus V, "Leti's well-known biography is full of fables." The signature, "R. G.," indicates, I suppose, Richard Garnett. However, Leti's story is inherently probable, I think, as Shakespeare's version is not.

If you have anything else to question, or find anything questioned, please let me know. I believe I have some authority for everything. Even the invitation by Lopez to have herring. My edition of the *Britannica* says that Greene died of a surfeit of herring and Rhenish wine. We cannot be too meticulous.

Cordially,
Charles

To Albert Lewin, June 25, 1940

410 West 24th St, New York City

Dear Al,

I thought of writing you time and again but the news has been so bad—and daily worse—that everything else seemed too trivial.

I saw the publicity you have been getting—for example that you will be in production by August. At least, the theme will be worth your efforts.

Marie will probably go to Bermuda for three weeks in July. She has a sabbatical leave until February. When she returns from Bermuda, she will go away again. I have been suggesting Alaska.

As for me, I have just finished my second book since my return. Houghton Mifflin have been advertising for Americana and I sent them *Testimony* as "a sample" of a much larger book I might do. They have had it for a couple of months and I have still to hear from them. When I do, I may send them the first book—which I finished last December—although that sort of autobiography seems too unimportant to bother about just now. The second book, which has the historical background I told you about when you were here, seems to be a better book. However, since it is all about Jews, that, too, has its handicap. I turned it over to an agent yesterday.

I tried to enlist last week in an army training camp for civilians, for, truly, I want to learn how to shoot and kill, but, unfortunately, my eyes have gotten worse—although almost perfect with glasses—and are below the army's present minimum (20/100 without glasses). Should this minimum requirement be lowered, I will enlist in anything.

In the meantime, I am going to work at another novel but this will have an American theme and an Irish hero—maybe. (Not Jim Tully.) The next issue of *The Menorah Journal* should have a kind of short story by me—Jews against an Elizabethan background—and, if so, I'll see that you get a copy.

Love to you from Marie and to Millie from both of us.

Charles

To Henry Hurwitz, October 7, 1940

364 West 18th Street, New York City

Dear Henry,

Coleman's note ("The Jew in English Drama, An Annotated Bibliography," by Edward D. Coleman, *Bulletin of The New York Public Library*, volume 42, p. 828) is, in part, as follows: "In the *Connoisseur*, London, May 16, 1754, pp. 122–129, it was first suggested (? by Thomas Percy) that the bond story may have become known to Shakespeare with the contracting parties reversed as to race or religion. Gregorio Leti's Life of Pope Sixtus V, translated from the Italian by Rev. Farnsworth, is cited."

According to the *Encyclopaedia Brittanica* (11th ed.), vol. 25, p. 165, Sixtus V was pope from 1585 to 1590. He was, to quote the *Encyclopaedia*, "impulsive, obstinate, severe, autocratic." He died "execrated by his own subjects; but posterity has recognized in him one of the greatest popes." Of his life by Leti, the same article says, it "is a caricature, full of absurd tales, utterly untrustworthy, wanting even the saving merit of style." (The title of the book from which the photostat was taken is, in part, as follows: *The Life of Pope Sixtus the Fifth*, translated from the Italian of Gregorio Leti by Ellis Farneworth, London, MDCCLIV. The height of the book, according to the library's index card, is thirty-five and a half centimetres, and the photostat reduced the size of the pages. The *Brittanica* gives 1693 as the date of publication of Leti's original book and 1779 as the date of publication of the translation; but neither date seems correct. The *Enciclopedia Italiana*, vol. 20, p. 976, gives the date of publication of the former as 1669. Ellis Farneworth, the translator, died in 1763, according to the library's card.)

Richard Garnett, in his *History of Italian Literature*, pp. 269, 270, is less harsh. "Gregorio Leti," he writes, "was the most representative figure (of numerous penmen of the seventeenth century interesting for their characters or the circumstances of their lives), personifying the spirit of revolt against tyranny spiritual and political. Born at Milan in 1630, he emigrated to Geneva, became a Protestant, and, after a roving life, eventually settled at Amsterdam, where he died historiographer of the city in 1701. He had already constituted himself a historiographer and biographer general, writing the lives of kings, princes, and governors, and depicting the rise and fall of states, as fast as bookseller could commission, or printer put into type. Yet he is not a hack writer, but has an individuality of his own, and although his works are devoid of scientific worth, they served a useful purpose in their day by asserting freedom of speech. Their value is in proportion to the degree in which they subserve this purpose; the most important, therefore, are his lives of Sixtus V and of Innocent the Tenth's rapacious and imperious niece, Olimpia Maldachini. Ranke has clearly shown that the former, which has done more than any other book to determine popular opinion regarding Sixtus, is mainly derived from MS. authorities of little value; which proves that Leti did not invent, but also that he did not discriminate." Of the biography of Sixtus and similar works by Leti, Ranke says (*History of the Popes*, Leopold Ranke, translated by Sarah Austin, London, 1840, p. 115 of the appendix, volume three), "A certain degree of truth cannot be denied to them, nor are they to be wholly disregarded; yet the first glance shows that they are not to be relied upon to any extent, and no general rule can be given as to where the line should be drawn." And again, p. 119, "We have already seen that he compiled without any exercise of judgement or criticism, and transcribed hastily."

Sidney Lee (1859–1926), writing of the sources of *The Merchant of Venice* in his *Life of William Shakespeare* (1915 ed.), says, p. 131, among much else, "The plot is a child of mingled parentage. For the main thread Shakespeare had direct recourse to a book in a foreign tongue—to '*Il Pecorone*,' a fourteenth-century collection of Italian novels by Ser Giovanni Fiorentino, of which there was no English translation. ("The Italian collection was not published till 1558." Note by S. L.) There a Jewish creditor demands a pound of flesh of a defaulting Christian debtor, and the latter is rescued through the advocacy of 'the lady of Belmont,' who is wife of the debtor's friend. The management of the plot in the Italian novel is closely followed by Shakespeare. A similar story of a Jew and his debtor's friend is very barely outlined in a popular mediaeval collection of anecdotes called '*Gesta Romanorum*' ..." Likewise, in an early article in *The Gentleman's Magazine*, 1880, vol. 248, Sidney Lee, then Sidney L. Lee, wrote (*The Original of Shylock*, p. 197, note): "*Il Pecorone* of Ser Giovanni Fiorentino (Milano, 1558), which Shakespeare certainly consulted in his treatment of the bond-episode." Earlier, J. Payne Collier printed the stories to which Sidney Lee refers. Collier (*Shakespeare's Library*, vol. 2) merely asserts that "they may have served as the foundation" of *The Merchant of Venice*. In his introduction, he adds, "The story of *The Merchant of Venice*, as regards the penalty of flesh for the non-payment of money as a stipulated time, is unquestionably of oriental origin. It was, however, written in Italian by Giovanni Fiorentino, as early as 1378, although not printed until nearly two centuries afterwards. Whether it had previously found a place in *Gesta Romanorum* may be a question of difficult solution, but we certainly trace it there at a very early date. It has recently been printed by Mr. Wright, in his 'Latin Stories of the Thirteenth and Fourteenth Centuries'…but the merchant is not represented as a Jew."

I used Sir Sidney Lee's essays (to which Coleman refers) for his studies of the Jews in Elizabethan England. I found nothing in any of his writings about Leti's story. Lee may have thought it unworthy of comment. However that may be, I think we may conclude that the story of Sixtus and the merchants may have been current in Shakespeare's time and that Shakespeare, as well as Leti afterwards, may have heard or read it. (That the story appeared much earlier in fiction does not matter even with respect to its truth, for life, as has been said, imitates art.) Certainly, Leti's story is more plausible (at least to Jews) than Shakespeare's and is sufficient, I think, to support my fiction—if no scholar's thesis.

Very truly yours,
Charles

To Henry Hurwitz, October 22, 1940

364 West 18th Street, New York City

Dear Henry,

I agree that it would be a good thing to put the note after the story. I have taken out all reference to Collier because I have since discovered—I vaguely remembered *something* about him—that he was a forger of Shakespeariana. Whatever he stands for in the note is probably so but I have thought it better to go to one of his sources—Douce. I hope this will not cause you much additional expense.

Cordially,
Charles

I suppose you are using the photostats. I am not at all sure now that they are reduced in size and would not say so without actual measurement.

To Albert Lewin, October 27th [1940]

364 West 15th Street, New York City
Sunday

Dear Al,

I have not written you for some time, I know. But there has really been little to write about—or rather little to say: we moved, as you see by the above—a rather nice flat, a little nicer than where we had lived and a little cheaper; Marie has been to Mexico and come back, written an article for her paper which *World Digest* wants to reprint on Jewish Indians in Mexico; I am revising the book I began to write in Hollywood which both Marie and my agent (rather ex-agent) thought dreadful—all about the millinery business, my father, mother, and myself; I turned my brief novel about the Jews in early England over to the *The Menorah* to sink or swim there—and I don't know whether or not it will be published; I have been made a contributing editor of *The Menorah Journal* (no salary); I read the newspapers and listen to the radio as eagerly as I suppose you do and have, I imagine, the same hopes and despair about France and England and this country and all countries; I saw the *Hollywood Reporter* a week or so ago for old times' sake and see that you are almost through production with "Flotsam"; but in all this there was nothing to write you about.[1] However, now I have a piece of news: read *To the Finland Station* by Edmund Wilson.[2] It is a long time since I read something so exhilarating; I think you will like the chapter on Anatole France—I have only read the first one hundred and fifty pages of the book. But this is exciting, stimulating—the kind of book that makes one glad to be alive. I send you this brief and badly-typed note by air mail. I have just put the book down, and I want you to know about it and I hope you will like it. Other than that, I have no news. I hope you are well and happy, and that Milly is, too, and all our friends.

Charles

---

[1] "Flotsam" was released with the title *So Ends Our Night* (1941).
[2] Edmund Wilson (1895–1972), *To the Finland Station* (1940).

To Henry Hurwitz, [Received November 6, 1940]

Dear Henry,

I found nothing wrong. As for your query about "Farnsworth" (in Coleman's note): that is the way it is printed in the *Bulletin*. It is wrong but I did not wish to make a point of it by using *sic* nor did I think I ought to change it. If you are changing the page that precedes the photostats, may I suggest that you omit my name and include the name of the translator, which is Farneworth; again, I wonder if "photostats" is not too colloquial— if correct—for a titlepage. I know I used it but, though it may be all right for a note, "photostat copy" may be better. According to the *Oxford Dictionary*, which is all I have here (at home), "Photostat" refers to the machine but it may be used attributively, which would make "photostat copy" correct but no authority for "photostats" as the page has it and I used it, although I have heard it used like that right along. But perhaps the title-page should be somewhat more formal.

C.

To Albert Lewin, November 9, 1940

364 West 18th Street, New York City
Saturday

Dear Al,

I have just finished reading *To the Finland Station*. The last third is not as good as the first, written hurriedly, I think, and unfair to Trotsky, but still it is the most exciting book I have read in a long time. I am not at all sorry that I urged you to read it.

I have been offered a job here working for a Jewish encyclopedia (published in England): the pay is the least I ever worked for ($30 a week); the people are friendly but that means you work a little longer at night and sometimes Saturdays and holidays always. However, I took it partly for the discipline since I have been having it pretty easy for some time.

The newspapers here are falling all over themselves praising Preston Sturgis' new picture.[1] I haven't seen it yet but I saw *The Great McGinty*. I

---

[1] Preston Sturgis's follow-up to *The Great McGinty* was 1940's *Christmas in July* starring Dick Powell and Ellen Drew (HPG).

liked some of it very much but it is a confused and essentially O. Henryish picture: it might have been made into something of more scope. I am looking forward to seeing your picture.

Marie saw your name among a list of those for Roosevelt. We were glad to see it. Our acquaintances among the Communists tell us that the party was for Wilkie. This, no doubt, is part of that great strategy that turned Germany over to Hitler and France to Laval. Marie sends her love to you and Millie—and I do, too.

Charles

To Henry Hurwitz, November 13, 1940

364 West 18th Street, New York City

Dear Henry,

I am glad you liked the novel. Of course, you may have as much of it as you want. I, too, was somewhat bothered by a story of English persecution just now (and was very glad to have my English lady who wished to give the Jews land—she is a fact).

I look forward to your gathering at 7.

Cordially,
Charles

To Henry Hurwitz, December 3, 1940

364 West 18th Street, New York City

Dear Henry,

May I ask you to send a copy of this issue to Albert Lewin, 514 Ocean Front, Santa Monica, California?

May I also ask you to let me see the manuscript of "The King's Jews" before sending any of it to the printer—to make changes, if necessary? I'll call for it whenever you say.

Cordially,
Charles

To Albert Lewin, December 17, 1940

364 West 18th Street, New York City

Dear Al,

I spoke to Paul this evening: he received your letter and has answered it by airmail. I hope Bob succeeds in getting into whatever will be best for him, and I am sure Paul will help him all he can.

Here's to seeing you in January!

Marie and I wish you and Milly and all our friends a merry Christmas and a happy New Year.

Charles

To Henry Hurwitz, January 11, 1941

Dear Henry,

Many thanks for sending me Mr. Nelson's letter.

It seems to me that the trouble with Mr. Nelson is that he does not distinguish between the truth of a story as symbol and its truth as history. Historical fiction must be symbolically true but by the very term "fiction" it is not history. Now I think my story is justified because it symbolizes the betrayal of the Jew—the way his gifts have been accepted again and again and turned against him. This I believe historically true and to justify a story such as mine.

The note was not an exhibition of scholarship and did not pretend to exhaust the subject of the sources of "The Merchant of Venice." It was merely to show the source of my story and, more than that, all the doubt I could find as to its historical truth. If we had not published the note, Mr. Nelson, as a scholar, might have had some justification for objection.

As a critic of historical fiction, he can only object to my story—apart from the fundamental question of its symbolic truth—on the ground of plausibility. For historical fiction, like all fiction, must be plausible. Well, I think my story is. I think it is plausible that Jews should be found in Elizabethan England. (In an earlier letter I mentioned, I believe, the evidence for it). I think it plausible, too, that Shakespeare, the successful playwright and theatre manager, great though he was, should be more

293

concerned with writing a popular play than defending an unpopular and alien cause.

I have no objection to your showing this to Mr. Nelson, particularly since he has gone to considerable trouble in writing his letter.

Cordially,
Charles

I might add, for Mr. Nelson's benefit, that "at least to a Jew" was a Nordic understatement. I meant to anybody.

To Henry Hurwitz, January 23, 1941

364 West 18th Street, New York City

Dear Henry,

This is, I suppose, a synopsis or outline of the writer's life. But it is so artlessly told I am afraid only a sympathetic person would find it interesting. My advice would be not to waste such rich lives as those of Abraham and his son on this brief narrative. I think she should try to write a novel, putting down as much detail as she can remember. She may have a good book in time, even if it may have to be rewritten by one who could keep its simplicity. But I do not see this story for *The Menorah Journal* even if rewritten now. As for propaganda as the letter suggests, it can hardly be that since the farming ended in failure—for whatever reason. But the writer has an important story and should tell it: the story of a noble experiment that did not succeed in spite of hard work, strength, and courage.

Charles

To Albert Lewin, March 2, 1941

364 West 18th Street, New York City

Dear Al,

I saw *So Ends Our Night* Saturday.[1] Today I wrote you a long letter about it. I said pleasant things about the picture and unpleasant things. Then I reread the letter and thought, "Hell, he's probably thoroughly sick of any discussion of the picture by this time. Besides, it's made; it's released." So I whittled the letter. I whittled away and whittled away and then I had just about one sentence. Marie came home just then and read the letter. "Can't you just say something pleasant?" she said, and added in the way wives have, "Besides, Al doesn't give a damn about your opinion." "Maybe not," I said, "But this is all I have to say that I think important." Unfortunately, she had a cold yesterday and could not go with me to the picture and so did not know what I was talking about. Now this is what the letter had boiled down to: "Some scenes and episodes—such as that of the spy and his sisters—could not be better; but I wish you had made the picture only about the hard-boiled refugee who went back, keeping, of course, such bits as his attempts to make the young fellow hard."

"Why," Marie said, "this is not only unpleasant but casual and hoity-toity." "Look," I said, "I am not casual just because I am brief. I want it to be so exciting that the audience will sit on the edge of their seats, clench their fists, bite their lips, and groan. And if we threw away a lot of the young love and just concentrated on a hard-boiled refugee who is gentle to his fellow refugees and wants to make the kid hard, preaching hardness all the time, and yet goes back to see his wife before she dies, put in all the narrow escapes he has until he succeeds—don't you see, don't you see?" Marie looked at me coldly. I suppose she is right. The picture is made and out and means a lot not only to you but to Jews and refugees everywhere and, of course, I would hardly mention that angle and what is the use of saying anything at all but the pleasant things of which I could say plenty. Well, perhaps this is the use: Idwal Jones said to me, when you were making *Spawn of the North*, "Jules Furthman has structure but he can't write dialogue; Talbot Jennings is the man for that."[2] Of course, you know

---

[1] *So Ends Our Night* was a 1941 David L. Loew and Albert Lewin production directed by John Cromwell, written by Talbot Jennings (based on Erich Maria Remarque's *Flotsam*), and starring Frederic March and Margaret Sullavan (MPG).

[2] *Spawn of the North*, a 1938 film produced by Lewin, directed by Henry Hathaway, starring George Raft, Henry Fonda, and Dorothy Lamour, was written by Jules

that as well as Jones. I suppose Jennings is safe enough if the book he is working on has the structure which Jones thought he lacked. And maybe Jones never said that at all. Maybe I should have sent you a pithy telegram of praise.

Well, I am going to send you my book of verse as soon as I get it from the printer. And if you tear into it I won't like what you say but I will like very much the man who says it and think, pleased, he respects me enough to tell me the truth. As he sees it, of course. And, secretly, I will probably think you are all wrong. As of course you do of me.

All this aside, I hope you make a lot of money on the picture. And receive much praise. I saw Cecelia Ager's review in *PM* and like her for it. Marie sends her love to you and Milly. So do I. She will probably write you after she has seen the picture. Don't pay attention to what she says.

Charles

To Henry Hurwitz, March 17, 1941

364 West 18th Street, New York City

Dear Henry,

I have sent you a copy of my new book *Going To and Fro and Walking Up and Down*. You will, of course, recognize the title as Lowenthal's quotation from *Job*.

I owe you an explanation about my failure to acknowledge previous publication of some of these poems in *The Menorah Journal*. As you know, I have always been careful to do so in every book that had the imprint of a publisher—and intend to do so in such a case and wherever it might do the *Journal* any good. But in this case of completely private publication I cannot see that it will do the *Journal* any good and might only seem, on my part, pretentious.

Yours, Charles

Furthman, Talbot Jennings and an uncredited Dale Van Every (MPG). Jules Furthman's (1888–1966) other credits include: *Shanghai Express* (1932), *To Have and Have Not* (1944) and *The Big Sleep* (1946) (IDFF).

To Albert Lewin, April 20, 1941

364 West 18th Street, New York City

Dear Al,

I was very glad to get your letter praising much in the book. I never expect much to be really good in this sort of thing and—no doubt I have said this time and again—look at this kind of writing as a way of making a living rather than an end of life. As a way it may be fairly successful; as an end seldom. (Parenthetically, I wasn't thinking of you among the witty and wrong—nor of anybody, and am sorry that the "witty," which would certainly apply to you, made you suspect that the "wrong" did, too.[1] I had in mind the compulsion of human society upon all and each of us.)

Some time has passed now since I saw *So Ends Our Night* and much of it is still vivid in my mind: all the episodes revolving about Steiner and where Kern is trying to sell to the German agent and his sisters are asking about his father at the bureau. Marie couldn't see the picture at the Music Hall but will now that the Loew theatres are beginning to show it.

Love from both of us to you and Millie.

Charles

---

[1] The passage in question appears in the "Autobiography: Hollywood" section of Reznikoff's *Going To and Fro and Walking Up and Down* (1941):

IV

I like this walk in the morning
among the flowers and trees.
Only the birds are noisy.
But if they talk to me,
no matter how witty or wrong,
I do not have to answer;
and if they order me about,
I do not have to obey.

297

To Albert Lewin, May 5, 1941

364 West 18th Street, New York City

Dear Al,

The Woman in White, in a prologue and four acts, was published by Wilkie Collins in 1871 and produced at the Olympic Theatre in London that year. It was considered "altogether admirable" by some critics, although others felt that the last act was not as good as the others. It was not quite an adaptation of the novel, according to the author, but rather the same characters and the same plot used afresh as a play. I am inclined to think that the play was far from "terrible" and decidedly worth getting hold of.

But it is not in The New York Public Library nor in the Library of Congress (according to the index in the New York Public Library) nor at Columbia. It may be in the Harvard Library or in the Folger Library at Washington (both have important collections of plays), but their catalogues are not available in New York.

I suppose private publication by Collins—he published a dramatization of *The Moonstone* in the same way—was to comply with a legal technicality of the time and the edition could not have been large and never have been on sale. I suppose, too, that the library of the British Museum has a copy, but that may not be available now. I note also that a motion picture was released by Pathé in 1917 (Lloyd Lonergan made the adaptation for *Tannhäuser* and Ernest C. Warde directed); accordingly, there may be a copy of the play on the Coast.

However, should you be unable to find a copy of the play or should you want a condensation of the novel, nevertheless, and should you think that I could be of any use to you that way—of course, I think "condensation" right up my alley—I'd be glad to pitch into it. It just so happens that the Encyclopedia I was working for ran out of money last week. They expect to get a new grant next month but, in the meantime, I am free. In any event, you know I am very glad to do what I can and if you have other suggestions as to how I can be of any help in this matter—or any other—call on me.

My edition of *The Encyclopedia Brittanica* (1910) has this interesting sentence: "Count Fosco in *The Woman in White* is perhaps his masterpiece; the character has been imitated again and again, but no imitation has ever attained to the subtlety and humour of the original."

Charles

To Albert Lewin, May 11, 1941

364 West 18th Street, New York City

Dear Al,

The New York Library does not have the play version of *The Moon-stone*. The card in the index reads: "The Moonstone: a dramatic story, in three acts. Altered from the novel for performance on the stage. By Wilkie Collins. This play is not published. It is privately printed for the convenience of the author. London. C. Dickens and Evans, 1877."

The Los Angeles Public Library, or the Santa Monica Library for that matter, may be able to get the book for you, because the Library of Congress will send books if the reader pays the expressage. They may not do this if they think the book rare. If so, you ought to be able to get a copy by photostat at the cost of about thirty cents for every two pages. However, no library will do this if any copyright question may be raised. But I don't think there should be any question here at this date.

Love from Marie and me to you and Millie.

Charles

To Henry Hurwitz, June 7, 1941

364 West 18th Street, New York City

Dear Henry,

I am enclosing a copy of the letter I am sending Dr. Grayzel. If you approve of the changes indicated, I hope it is not too late to make them.

Thanking you very much for your interest, I am,

Cordially yours,
Charles

To Solomon Grayzel, June 7, 1941

364 West 18th Street, New York City

The Jewish Publication Society of America

Dear Doctor Grayzel:

Mr. Henry Hurwitz, editor of *The Menorah Journal*, very kindly sent me a copy of the letter addressed to him with reference to the historical novel of which *The Menorah Journal* is printing the beginning.

I am much obliged to you for the questions you raise. With respect to the first, as to David's' "square beard of a good Jew" (page 2), I had in mind the picture of Suesskind of Trimberg and meant merely a square beard such as a good Jew might well have, and not that all good Jews must have square beards. But I can see that your interpretation of my phrase is the more likely one. Accordingly, I think it would be better for the line to read "and the full beard of a good Jew (the corners of which must not be." By "the second and lesser night" (page 6) of Passover, I meant merely that it was the lesser night, not from a religious standpoint, but psychologically. And socially. That I think true. Here I do not think that your interpretation, although certainly possible, is the likelier for the casual reader.

As for the objection to the statement that the evening service was not among those prescribed (page 10), I confess that I imagined that the doubt of its requirement lasted a good deal longer than it did. For the purpose of publication again it might be sufficient to end the sentence as "bad grace" and strike out the rest of the sentence from "now that he was there" until and including "sticklers for whatever they knew." But this may not be best for *The Menorah Journal*, since the matter is already set up in pages. Accordingly, I am going to suggest to Mr. Hurwitz that if it is not too late and he thinks the change one for the better, he has the sentence read as follows: "David could scarcely leave without a bad grace, now that he was there, although this service was at first not prescribed, since it took no temple offering, unlike the services for the morning and afternoon; but by now, for perhaps a thousand years, it had been observed by Jews everywhere." I hope this is not objectionable.

I am sending you the rest of the novel under separate cover. Mr. Hurwitz used the first 36 pages and there are 220 pages in all. I now feel that another hundred pages might be added and that certain relationships, the love of Alan for Jessica, for example, might well be amplified. (I changed Alan to Roger for *The Menorah Journal*.) When Mr. Hurwitz first read the novel, he pointed out—and I agreed—that the casual reader might fail to distinguish between the English of today and those of seven hundred years ago. The remedy lies, I think, in amplifying the part of Margaret de Quincy, who was Simon de Montfort's aunt, and who actually had the project for settling Jews on her lands. I should also like to enlarge the part of the admirable Hugh of Avalon, Bishop of Lincoln. But before setting about this revision and amplification—I expect to do so, anyway, sooner or later—I should like to know if you are interested in the book, for your present interest will give the matter urgency.

Sincerely,
Charles Reznikoff

To Albert Lewin, July 27, 1941

364 West 18th Street, New York City

Dear Al,

As an old specialist in Mark Twain, you read, no doubt, "The Mysterious Stranger." I just did—for the first time. Reread it now and I think you will find parts very good.

I hope your pictures are getting on. The Encyclopedia I worked for came to life (after an injection of cash) and sent for me about the middle of June. I've been working since, learning a lot, and doing some of my own work, too.

Marie went to England for a brief vacation. She had been working hard on an answer to Jay Nock's slimy articles in *The Atlantic* and had it accepted by a magazine of some standing—non-Jewish.[1] But she had to be mild.

Love to Milly.

Charles

---

[1] Marie Syrkin's response, "How Not to Solve the Jewish Crisis," to the two Albert Jay Nock articles entitled "The Jewish Problem in America" (*The Atlantic* [June and July 1941]), was published in *Common Ground* 2:1 (1941): 73–78.

To Henry Hurwitz, July 27, 1941

364 West 18th Street, New York City

Dear Henry,

I have just heard from Doctor Grayzel. He is sending the manuscript on to the publication committee for their decision. He agrees with us that the story ought to be expanded and generously makes a number of suggestions for which I am very grateful. Of his detailed comments, only the first three concern *The Menorah* right now and are as follows:

"The beard could be fixed up if you said, '... the beard of a good Jew, the corner of which, the *peot*, must not be ...'

"The second night of Passover may be a social and psychological let-down, and if you indicate it as such, you will be within your rights. But if you hint that a medieval Jew considered it less important, you are wrong.

"Your change in the matter of the evening service is all right, though it pre-supposes more knowledge of Talmudic argumentation on the part of David than his character justifies."

I am sorry to have changes at this late date but am glad to have Doctor Grayzel's comments *before* printing. I am ready to run into the office whenever you say to fix the proofs.

Cordially,
Charles

To Albert Lewin, [August 1941]

364 West 18th Street, New York City
Saturday afternoon

Dear Al,

The news from Russia which you called "less hopeful" when you wrote on August 5th is worse today, but I am encouraged by the fact that Doctor Marx was optimistic. I remember that he was quite right about the extent of the damage at Munich, particularly with respect to the Balkans, when many, myself among them, were not so gloomy. I like his reasoning based on the training of the reserves.

We have *The Bible of the World* but I went for the Hindus and the Chinese. Besides, they come first. I, too, have always found the *Koran* disappointing as literature and that is true of all Arab poetry I have read;

but, like you, I am ready to blame the translations. Your illustrations of god as Opponent—the Trees of Knowledge and of Life and the Tower of Babel—remind one at once of Prometheus; certainly, the notion of God as Father is quite late and, of course, the questioning of that notion, as in Job, later still. The thing to bear in mind in reading the Old Testament is that it is really an anthology covering at least a thousand years and, most likely, including the unwritten traditions, much more than that. And, unlike other anthologies where each contribution is arranged according to the date of composition, early and late material and material from various districts and countries are more or less interwoven and much early material has been revised again and again. Accordingly, there are very primitive notions, including that of God as merely a local deity, just one among others. It is quite possible that Moses thought of Him as merely the God of the district around Sinai.

Talking of Moses, I see you are back to your old friend Akhnaton. But I have never found that very convincing. The pure monotheistic doctrine does not appear among the Jews until much later than the Exodus (the books of the Bible that describe the Exodus were probably not written until almost a thousand years afterwards). The Bible itself was put in final form about 200 B.C. The Exodus was about 1500 B.C. Besides, one might argue that Akhnaton, whose ideas were so contrary to the stock Egyptian notions, got his idea of a single abstract deity from the early religious belief of the Semites—or a misunderstanding of them. I like this notion best: it involves an error by Akhnaton and a degeneration of the early Semitic belief which took a thousand years to complete the circle.

Nor am I convinced that Moses was not a Jew—among other reasons—because the Jews did not describe his descent from Abraham. No more than I am that Jesus was the Messiah, according to Jewish standards, because the New Testament so meticulously details his descent from David. (By the way, Moses is not mentioned, except once I think, and if so in a very minor way, in the *Haggudah* which the Jews read at the Passover celebration of the Exodus—at the *Seder*. The reason given is to discourage hero worship.) According to the narrative, the Jews had been slaves for quite a while and slaves, I suppose, are not as proud, nor as careful, of their descent as noblemen. However, Moses might have been an Egyptian. By analogy to the great leaders of the proletariat, Marx, Engels, Lenin, and Trotsky, none of whom was a member of that class. It should not be hard for Jews to believe that race, per se, means nothing. King David was partly Moabite.

You are a little hard on the early Jewish heroes. Cain would hardly be considered a Jew and, as for Jacob, he is one of three patriarchs. Nor are the stories of misdeeds taught to children as exemplary. Perhaps that's the trouble with reading a Bible in an anthology; the moralizing is dull and left out. Jacob really had an awful time for his deceit and it's all there; that he himself was deceived was only part of it. He was deceived because he had run away from home and he ran away because he had to. However, this is true: in early stories, the trickster ranks among the heroes and generally is better off than the real heroes; Ulysses alone survives when Achilles and Hector have long been among the powerless dead. And German folktales are full of successful cheating. Trickery was the primitive weapon of the weak and unprotected before, as you point out, they learnt about the high-class weapons that Christianity found in the arsenal of Judaism.

Charles

To Albert Lewin, January 31, 1942

364 West 18th Street, New York City

Dear Al,

I am very glad that you are working at the script of *The Moon and Sixpence*.[1] I am certain that it is a good script and I do not like to think that it will be a commercial flop. I remember that you told me once that Thalberg sent the Marx Brothers on tour until they had tested their jokes on hundreds of audiences. Is there no way of testing a play based on your script before shooting? If you'd like me to, I'd like to read the script.

I like the first stanza of your poem very much. I am not sure about the second—except "untabulated breath" which I like. I think the second stanza will bear thinking about. But I am glad that you are writing verse again. I still find it a great pleasure, although like all pleasures it has its alloys. One of them is trying to make a second stanza as good as the first.

Millie's activity does not surprise me. Rudolph Marx's present optimism does. I cannot imagine on what basis he believes the Germans will collapse by May. Or even November.

---

[1] Lewin wrote and directed the 1942 film *The Moon and Sixpence* starring George Sanders and Herbert Marshall (Felleman 275).

Of course, I'm pleased that you like "The King's Jews."[1] There's a lot the matter with it, including the title. *The Menorah* was afraid to publish more than the mere beginning for fear that the story might now be construed as anti-English. And it might, too. So I've put it aside. At least a publisher has it and has had it for seven months—I will not stir him up. The first book I did after my return to New York is in a drawer and I do not even show it. It's altogether out of tune with the times. However, I'm working at a third. And the encyclopedia job is holding up. They gave me a small increase to show their good will and, when the experts fall down, they throw me a good article to do besides the usual Americana—Josephus, Justinian, Rodrigo Lopez.

Love to Millie and from Marie to you both.

Here's hoping Rudolph Marx is right again!

Charles

To Albert Lewin, March 8, 1942

364 West 18th Street, New York City

Dear Al,

Let me congratulate you on Maugham's magnificent letter. I hope you can use it in the ads.

As for the script itself, I express my opinion with some diffidence. My experience, as you know, has taught me that what reads very well may not sound like much and, on the other hand, that which reads like a very dull scene may be very effective when properly acted. Accordingly, I speak quietly. I like the script very much and I think it ought to be an effective picture. I think the method you have chosen excellent and, now that you have written it as you have, it seems the only way in which the novel could have been turned into a script.

I have a few suggestions: one or two that are slight and one or two that I consider more important. To begin with, I do not find the valet business interesting. I am inclined to think that Sasha Guitry in his *Story of a Cheat* would not allow all that business to interrupt his introduction.[2] However,

---

[1] Reznikoff's "The King's Jews: A Historical Novel" appeared in *The Menorah Journal* 29:3 (Autumn 1941): 312–328.

[2] Sacha Guitry wrote, directed and starred in the 1936 French comedy *Le Roman d'un Tricheur* (*The Story of a Cheat*) (MPG).

this is a slight matter. To go on to a somewhat more important matter, I thought Maugham's way of getting the author into Mrs. Strickland's home after Strickland ran away excellent—the meeting with the lady novelist bursting with the news, the author's embarrassment at finding himself with a date for tea; on the other hand, I am not at all convinced that Mrs. Strickland would send for the author (who is practically a stranger) as she does in the script. But I am sure that once he is in the house she would turn to him as she does in the novel. I am certain, of course, that you have excellent reasons for making the change you did. Perhaps suspense is one of them.

Again, I like the way Maugham handled the incident with the prostitute; I do not think that Strickland would ever have bought the girl a drink (scene 111). You may be building up to the regeneration scene, but I am not convinced. I am also not convinced that Mrs. Strickland would instantly decide to get a divorce—even if she were convinced that Geoffrey had reported the facts. I do think that Strickland ought to be married to Ata (to satisfy the censorship if nothing else) but he would not stop at committing bigamy. But that may be in the censor's list of prohibitions, too.

I did not think the Stroeve part particularly effective in the novel—the story of an attachment to an unworthy person had been told by Maugham much more effectively in *Of Human Bondage*—but I do think it should be very effective on the stage or screen and I think you have done very well by it. As a very minor suggestion, I do not think Strickland should merely light a cigarette as he does (scene 293); I think he would begin arranging his easel, brushes, palette, to resume his painting. Another slight suggestion is that I do not see Blanche (scene 297) just sitting with her hands in her lap at the chess game; she would be knitting or sewing, darning Strickland's socks or mending something of his. I like your incident (scene 381) of the roach or whatever it is that they fish out of the soup and watch running away.

I now come to a more important matter. I am not at all convinced of Strickland's regeneration at the end. I almost shuddered when he said, "Love." I see Strickland as a gangster—without a gang; callousness for art's sake. He is not regenerated by his art—to show you how mean he is he burns his best work. If that's not pure cussedness, it's insanity. In the Middle Ages a gangster like Robin Hood was all right if he robbed only the rich (as if the poor had anything), and in the Bohemia of the 1890s a gangster is all right if he does what he does for art's sake. Well, that fits in with the popular conception of an artist and so Strickland has plenty of plausibility. Logically, he ought to stick to his character as Maugham has written him—unreconciled to society and any unit of it, for good reasons or bad, to the miserable end. I do not even see him taking time away from his painting to wipe the blood from Ata's brow.

I am returning the script under separate cover. I had great pleasure reading it, and thank you very much for sending it.

As for the direction of the picture, certainly you ought to be good at it. I congratulate you and the picture at the opportunity.

Marie and I send our best wishes and love to you and Millie.

Charles

To Henry Hurwitz, November 17, 1942

364 West 18th Street, New York City

Dear Henry,

Here they are—the first of the historical short stories about Jewish pioneers in the United States and the fragment from the book (if you use it no reference need be made to the book).[1] I hope you like them.

Cordially,
Charles

To Henry Hurwitz, Nov 25th [1942?]

364 West 18th St, New York City

Dear Henry,

Freehof's *The Small Sanctuary* came today.[2] It is handsome and, running through it, I think I shall find the book very useful.

I thank you for it—and no less for the inscription.

Cordially
Charles

---

[1] "Jews Enter Georgia." *The Menorah Journal*. 31:2 (Summer 1943) 125–36 "Pharisee: From a Historical Novel." *The Menorah Journal*. 32:2 (Autumn 1944): 203–15.

[2] Solomon Bennett Freehof (1892–1990), *The Small Sanctuary: Judaism in the Prayer-book* (1942).

To Henry Hurwitz, November 26, 1942

364 West 18th Street, New York City

Dear Henry,

According to the records of the trustees of the colony of Georgia, commissions to take subscriptions and collect money for the charter were granted to Mr. Anthony da Costa, Francis Salvador, and Alvaro Lopez Suaso. Leon Hühner ("The Jews of Georgia in Colonial Times," *American Jewish Historical Society Publications*, No. 10, pp. 68, 69) says, "Francis Salvador was at this time one of the directors of the Dutch East India Company, and was one of the wealthiest merchants in England. He made frequent loans to the British government and his charities annually went into considerable sums." The original name of his family, according to Hühner in an article on another Francis Salvador ("Francis Salvador, A Prominent Patriot of the Revolutionary War'" *American Jewish Historical Society Publications*, No. 9, p. 108), was "Jessurum Rodriguez"; according to Cecil Roth (*History of the Jews in England*, p. 214), "Jessurum Rodrigues." "Francis" might very well be inserted the first time Salvador is mentioned (p. 2).

I called "Jews in Georgia" a "historical short story" because dialogue and descriptions, more or less, are imaginary; it does not deviate from, but it certainly is not, the record. Accordingly, it is not history nor, if you like, fiction; but I don't really care what it is called. I am glad you like it and I hope others will.

I should like a general title for the series very much. But I don't like the title suggested. Besides, *The Jews Come to America* is already the title of a book by Masserman and Baker. I want a title that will cover Jewish pioneering in the Middle West and on the Coast, in the territories of the United States as well as in the original colonies. Do you like *American Chronicles:* or *Chronicles of Early America:* to be followed by the specific title?

Cordially,
Charles

To Albert and Mildred Lewin, December 25th 1942

364 West 18th Street, New York City

Dear Al and Milly,

We were very pleased to get your greetings and your beautiful gift—which is now added to the many we have received from you and which brighten our apartment. We wish you both a very happy New Year.

Al, I tried to see the artist whose water-colors we found interesting in the Metropolitan. In fact, I made three trips to see him—not for your sake alone or his—but partly to catch glimpses of the boarding-house in which he lived (a dreadful place). I could not find him in. He was leaving in a day or two—perhaps for the army—and so I finally left word with his landlady that you had seen his work at the Met and liked it and that, if he cared to, he might get in touch with you at MGM. I hope he did.

I saw *The Moon and Sixpence* the day it opened at The Rivoli, but nothing I had to say about it seemed worth saying again. I was not at all conscious of the "static" effect which *Time*, I think, complained, but then I noted that they carried the picture in their list of "current and choice."[1] I had already written you that I thought your method of adaption the best possible for that particular book. I did not think you would care for my praise of your directing—knowing how little I know about that. I still did not like the ending but I realized that your hand in this matter was forced. The real censorship motion-pictures has is, of course, that of the audience. Just as, for example, it would be a great disappointment to a child if the eldest brother in a fairy story were to win the princess, so a code has been formulated for, and adopted by, the audiences that watch motion-pictures, and I well realize it is a rule of that code that the hero must not only be punished for his wickedness but must, in the end, change for the better. However, you can enlarge on this topic much better than I. I hope the picture is doing as well financially as was to be expected.

I have been trying to get into some kind of war work. In the meantime, I am beginning a new book.

A happy New Year to you and Milly and to all our friends and allies.

Charles

---

[1] 1 A review of Lewin's film *The Moon and Sixpence* appeared in *Time* 40:16 (19 October 1942): 96f. Despite the reviewer's comment that the film "is more like a still life than a moving picture," the film was, as Reznikoff mentions, noted as "Current & Choice" in *Time*'s October 26, November 2, 9, 16, 30, and December 14, 1942 issues (96).

To Henry Hurwitz, [Rec. Feb., 23, 1943]

364 West 18th Street, New York City

Dear Henry,

Other titles are: *Jew in Boston* (1762); *Gold Rush Days* (San Francisco, 1849); *Jew in Kansas* (1856); *Jew Among the Indians* (Nebraska, 1869). More titles later—but not until I get the book about Maccabeans out of the way or at least on the way.

Yours,
Charles

To Albert Lewin, February 26th 1943

364 West 18th Street, New York City

Dear Al,

I think I told you that when you were working on *Mutiny* for MGM I was writing *Admiralty* for the American Law Book Company, when you were working on *The Good Earth* I was writing *Agriculture*, and when you left MGM I left (by request) the American Law Book Company. Now you are back at MGM and I am back at the American Law Book company. If I were a California seer I would see some significance in this parallelism, but since I am just a New Yorker I must let the facts stand alone. Anyway, I'm back at *Corpus Juris*.

I went most unwillingly. I remember telling you that I had been asked to resign and that this had been unfair, for I never did a better piece of work at the law than my last. Of course, nobody believed this—except my immediate chief. Well, he's the head of the department now. And he asked me to come back. I remember telling you that if I were not married I would not work at all but just do my writing. I could carry myself for another year at my present scale of living but then I'd be flat broke. This is generally supposed to be uncomfortable. If I were not married, I think I could make my money last two, three, or even four years, and that would give me more chance to get a book over. But I am married and of the two books I have finished since I came back from the Coast, the Jewish Publication Society's editor says that they will probably publish one next year but won't promise anything and the other book can't be read at all by the rockets' red glare.

310

However, I've just begun work at a third book and hope to finish it this year. The subject is Jewish, of course, but I will not have to show it to the Jewish Publication Society and won't—unless they publish the book they have. And the work at the law book company is a lot easier than it used to be. At least I find it so now. Of course, I can't do all the work at my own book that I'd like to but I expect to manage. So much for that.

I am very glad that you are working at *Madame Curie*.[1] I cannot imagine a subject that you'd like better. Whenever I think of how stupid the Poles have been—and are—about the Jews, it restores my faith in humanity to think that Madame Curie was Polish.

I put off answering you until I saw how things were shaping up at the law book company and in my own work. I have been working for the company for five weeks now and I think I can hold the job and do my own work, too. However, I am pretty tired at night—as you can see by all the mistakes in this letter.

Please give my love to Millie and all our friends. Marie sends her love to Millie and you.

Charles

To Henry Hurwitz, May 23, 1943

364 West 18th Street, New York City

Dear Henry,

I hope the corrections are clear and, where the changes are mine, that they meet with your approval.

As for the next two in the series (to use singly or together as you wish), I would appreciate the latest date.

Cordially,
Charles

I hope you have received much praise for the story of the Jewish seaman: it is excellent and the sincerity of the writer shines through the words. I liked the Humbert Wolfe article, too. It is excellent of its kind—but they are not in the same class.

---

[1] *Madame Curie* was to be Lewin's first directorial assignment for MGM when he returned there in 1942, but as Felleman notes, he "lasted only 10 days before being removed from the production by [the film's producer] Sidney Franklin ... and replaced with Mervyn LeRoy" (280–81).

To Albert Lewin, October 11, 1943

364 West 18th St, New York City

Dear Al,

I hope you like your job but I've just left mine. I managed to do almost no work of my own this year. When the Jewish Publication Society a few weeks ago offered me a thousand dollars outright for the short novel (of which you saw the beginning in *The Menorah Journal*)—or $750 against royalties—I chose the latter and with what I have ought to have enough to carry me for a couple of years. I have two books I want to do. I left the law book company with much friendship on both sides—at least expressions of it—which was better than last time.

Where is the Wilde script?[1]

Marie sends her love to you and Millie. Remember me to Millie—busy and beautiful at her noble tasks. And a happy New Year to you all!

Charles

To Albert Lewin, November 19, 1943

364 West 18th Street, New York City

Dear Al,

It seems to me that you have done an excellent job with *Dorian Gray*. But the experts have already told you that.

I found the novel tiresome. I was somewhat surprised at that. After all, it was the first title (I think) that the Bonis took for "The Modern Library" and it was a book every intelligent high-school boy had to read. And now I found the book as disagreeable as a perfumed man, as unexciting as an exhibition of fireworks, and the best of the wisecracks, which are the best of the book, have lost their savor. If I may change your script (p. 168) a little, I can hear the voice of Oscar Wilde (in a gown of purple plush) crying in his wilderness of orchids, "Absolve me, *Walter* Pater, quia peccavi!"

---

[1] Lewin wrote the screenplay and directed the film version of Wilde's novel *The Picture of Dorian Gray* for MGM. The film was released in 1945 and starred George Sanders, Hurd Hatfield, Donna Reed, and Angela Lansbury (Felleman 275–76).

I was very curious, then, to see what you did with the book and how you managed to clean this homosexual stable. I think you did, Hercules; you improved the story immensely by the use of the painter's niece; you kept all the good episodes, like that of the sailor letting Dorian go because he looks so young and Dorian's fright at Selby at the approach of Gladys (the gardener, I think, in the book); and, most important, you kept enough of Wilde's wit to give the story his distinctive flavor—the wit still has flavor as you use it, and you use it to salt the script and do not serve it up in chunks as he does.

Your first hurdle, of course, was Dorian's wish not to lose his beauty—a very feminine thought. You switched that nicely to a wish not to grow old—which a man might very well have. By the way, the wish not to lose his beauty (to stay young like the figures on Keats' vase) is the root from which the novel springs. Now, you can lose your beauty (according to Wilde) by thinking—Hardy has the same thought somewhere, I think—by being wicked, and by becoming old. Wilde discarded the first because he would have to make his hero a philosopher or a Fabian Socialist or something like that and then, reversing the proposition in the usual Wilde manner, his proposition becomes: if you keep your beauty you are good. Accordingly, Dorian's beauty becomes a mask that enables him to be wicked, practically without recognition except for a stray lord or two. In other words, the visible face has become the famous cap of German fairy stories that makes the wearer invisible. However, all this is by the way.

Your next hurdle was the Sybil Vane affair. Now in Wilde that is pure homosexuality: Dorian loves Sybil as an actress and not as a woman and when she becomes a bad actress he can't stand her. I am not at all convinced by Wilde's explanation of why a great actress becomes a bad one and I can well see that an actress reciting Shakespeare, good or bad, may be equally tiresome to a motion-picture audience. They might find Dorian absolutely justified. Yes, I think your singer is better and so is the seduction. At least that's masculine. I am inclined to wish that less stress were put on the failure to be "a good woman" (although this may be sound Victorian) and maybe it would be enough to indicate that Dorian is just tired of her—at least for the time being. However, I don't consider this important and, as you well realize, it is very important that the audience at this point does not become fed up with Dorian and can be kept, holding their thumbs, until he writes his letter proposing marriage and redeems himself.

As for the murder of the painter, Wilde does not motivate that adequately though he does his best to. And, though it is much more wicked to

313

kill for no good reason—I am thinking here of Coleridge's *Ancient Mariner*—a motion-picture audience might more readily understand the wish to conceal the unpleasant fact of the aging and ugly picture from Gladys. I agree with you then in this and think you might even emphasize it. By the way, I see—and admire—how you do much more than Wilde with Dorian having to face the fact of the murder in casual conversation and investigation. I have forgotten what Aristotle calls it—if he mentions it—but it is certainly dramatic.

You certainly tightened up the end of the story and gave it the accelerated speed which the novel lacks. I don't see what you can cut. Indeed, I don't know what you can spare and I hope you won't have to drop any of it. That's all I can say, Al. I am sorry to sound the stooge and that all I can say is yes. O yes, I don't like the unexpected reformation or repentance of Dorian—I didn't like it in *Moon and Sixpence*, either—but it doesn't seem very important in this script. Just a necessary sop, I suppose, to the thousand-headed Cerberus in the seats.

Thank you very much for letting me see the script. I am returning it by registered mail. I wish you the best of luck shooting it. Give my love to Millie and remember me to your friends who were friendly to me. Marie sends her love to you and Millie.

Charles

To Albert and Mildred Lewin, December 26, 1943

364 West 18th Street, New York City

Dear Al and Milly,

This is a grey winter afternoon. The weather forecast this morning was rain turning to snow—or snow turning to rain. I am trying out a new mop—on the kitchen floor—which I bought at Macy's. The maid who used to come in twice a week is utterly gone. I have alas been washing the windows with something else that I bought at Macy's. But they look as streaked as ever. Marie in a bathrobe, left forefinger in her mouth, is writing one of her lugubrious compositions. Suddenly the doorbell rings. My God, who is that? What is that?

I go into the hall. The light of the automatic elevator flickers, descends, ascends, stops at our floor. Out comes an expressman holding a package in his hand. "Oh, it's the proofs from Philadelphia," she says gloomily.

But it isn't the proofs from Philadelphia. It's a basket of fruit, bright and sweet, from you with a beautiful Chinese card and a wise saying and your good wishes for the coming year. "What a delightful interlude!" says Marie. Truly enough. Thank you both very much—and we both wish a very happy new year to you all!

Charles

To Albert and Mildred Lewin, December 28, 1943

364 West 18th Street, New York City

Dear Al and Milly,

Now the book came. I am in the embarrassing position of a publicity man who, having hailed two previous productions, finds that he has a third on his hands which it is in his heart to praise and be thankful for—but he has already used his adjectives.

It is the kind of a book that I think of as "an annual": that is, if I taste the pleasure of it daily, say two or three pages a day and study a plate or two a day, why at the end of a year of this epicurean existence I may be learned as well. For this prospect, a mere thank you seems a mild expression, indeed, but (and not for the first time, I am afraid) words fail.

Charles

Since I intend to study the book too—I can't guarantee to make it an annual devotion, but it's certainly something to find on the table after art in Textile—I'd like to thank you also. What a pin! What fruits! What a book! What a Santa Claus!

Marie

To Albert Lewin, [January 30, 1944]

364 West 18th Street, New York City
Sunday

Dear Al,

The script came this week and I read it with great interest. Incidentally, Page 53 had been left out. I was sorry, too, that the discarded pages had not been sent along, for I was thrown back upon my memory—and it is not as good as yours. I remembered, however, an axiom of motion-pictures —was it yours?—that, although the source of the picture may be a novel, the picture itself, as an art form, is closer to the dance. Now from this I take a practical sub-axiom: much is plausible and will be taken for granted in a motion-picture that would be unacceptable in a novel or story, where the reader can stop to turn back the pages and weigh an incident he is called upon to accept. Accordingly, I am willing to grant the murder of Basil (which is necessary to your story), not merely because he was the innocent instrument of Dorian's downfall or because of Dorian's irritation at his preaching (all this helps, of course, to weave the web of reality), but simply and principally because Dorian is wicked. Any incidental reason will do to light the fuse. But the incident is much less acceptable in the novel—in fact, improbable.

On the other hand, I do not find David's tale as you have it (page 162, top of page) acceptable. I do not find it plausible—at a glance—that he would act the way he did for any reason that he gives nor can I believe, as I listen to it, that any servant applying for a job would think he can get it by gossip about a previous employer. But I do not find this explanation by David necessary for his presence. I know he moves in Dorian's circle and he might well be going to Selby because Gladys is there and she would return with him to London because Dorian had looked ill and had been distracted and had left mysteriously. In other words, I think the plausibilities are with the action you want and the explanations are merely distracting. Besides, David's explanation throws a shadow upon him and we all want him to marry Gladys. I suppose you have excellent reasons for this change but I can't see them at a glance. And, after all, I have no more time—as a spectator.

So much for the change with which I quarrel most. As for the reformation of Dorian which I did not like at first, I am now prepared to accept it. Not only because the spectators would want it, but because there is now more preparation for it. Besides, I will admit that it helps make Dorian more of a figure in the round: he is not merely the aesthete in search of beauty and sickened only by ugliness; he is also the sensualist in search of sensation—any sensation (Wilde has that contradiction, too, of course); but he is also a man of some good intentions who is in search of an inner peace by way of morality. I think all this blurs the outline of Dorian's character but it makes him more human and, after all, you have the essential story. Your new reason for Dorian's destruction of the picture—that it was the instrument of his own destruction and would remove the temptation to live as he had been doing—is ingenious and

316

characteristic of you; still, though it should stay in the script, this is not what makes the destruction plausible. Essentially, the ugliness of the picture is the excuse for that.

Now for slight matters—some merely typographical.

Page 6, last speech of Lord Henry: no question mark.

Page 10, Lord Henry's second speech: add "own" to read "To realize one's own Nature."

Page 31, before we are shown The Two Turtles's stage: we should see the interior after closing time, empty except for the proprietor, bartender, porter, etc., cleaning up.

Page 35. I think you have built up what James Vane sees and this is good because it gives us much more reason for his unusual worry and manner.

Page 35: change "youth" to "life" in Dorian's speech, "Perhaps because he felt," etc. I don't think Dorian would use "youth." And the rest of the dialogue would be just as true.

Page 47, Lord Henry's last speech: I think it should read "infatuated with."

Page 81: I see you now have Victor and another servant remove the portrait. I liked the bit about the dealer in picture-frames called in to do it. That showed the trouble Dorian went to to keep his secret from the servants.

Page 82: when Dorian sets the rocking-horse swaying, he might say "Sir Tristan," as if it reminds him how he, as well as Sybil, once thought of himself as a knight and how far away that knighthood has become.

Page 110, Dorian's second speech: change "everything" to "something" in "because I know everything about his."

Page 110, Basil's speech directly following: change "will" to "would" in "what gentleman will be seen."

Page 130: I don't think a character such as Lord Gerald Chapman is described to be would affirm "that the inherited stupidity of the race," etc. This is certainly an idea and unlikely to be said by one who has an entire lack of them. All this is trifling enough.

The best of luck in this production, Al.

Please give Milly my love. Marie sends hers to you both.

Charles

I am returning the script by registered mail.

To Albert Lewin, [January 31, 1944]

Monday evening

Dear Al,

Just a word. I remember writing that Dorian's repentance did not seem to matter much in the script, and yet, if the destruction of the picture turns on this, it *must* matter much. It seems to me—I haven't the book at hand—that in the novel the destruction, or rather the attempted destruction, was only aesthetic: Dorian was so disgusted at its ugliness. And that would be logically in line with the book—sin is to be condemned, not because it is immoral, but simply because it is ugly. On the other hand, if Dorian repents of his wickedness because it was immoral, he should not attempt to destroy the picture at all but would keep it to gaze upon and remind him of his sin. He might even expose it to the world as a confession. That would be a true repentance.

Charles

To Henry Hurwitz, February 29, 1944

364 West 18th Street, New York City

Dear Henry:

I appreciate the invitation to be your guest at the next *Menorah* dinner. However, I can't go to this one. Many thanks, and I hope it will come off as well as the last.

Of course, there is no urgency whatever about the changes, etc. If you'll let me know when you have the time, I'll be in to see you.

I must tell you how much I relished the review by Hannah Arendt in the last issue.[1] If she can do others as well, I hope to read her often in *The Menorah*.

Cordially yours,
Charles

---

[1] "Portrait of a Period," Hannah Arendt's review of Stefan Zweig's *The World of Yesterday: An Autobiography*, appeared in *The Menorah Journal*. 31:3 (Autumn 1943) 307–15.

318

To Henry Hurwitz, June 23, 1944

364 West 18th Street, New York City 11

Mr. Henry Hurwitz,Editor,
The Menorah Journal, 63 Fifth Avenue, New York City.

Dear Henry:

I like your comments on both "Pharisee" and "Gold Rush Days" very much—praise, of course, but also the other kind.[1] This sort of writing, which is essentially communal, is like the production of a play: to be changed and changed again as a preview shows this point not clear or that point (most desirable) not made. All I ask of criticism is that it aims as I do, and when I get that, as in your letter, I must be most thankful.

I'll be glad to come to your house any evening after the Fourth.

Cordially,
Charles

To Henry Hurwitz, September 8, 1944

364 West 18th Street, New York City

Dear Henry,

In re "Pharisee": suppose we change Alexander's name to Jason. This simple Greek name was common among the Jews. In fact, it was the name of a high priest.

As for the "argument" of the story, of course the reader must know what the extract is about. But I don't want to strip the book, and the extract itself, of whatever suspense these have. I am attaching a tentative introductory note, assuming that the extract you select begins on Page 32. It seems to me that all names are sufficiently explained in the text itself. However, I may be wrong.

Cordially,
Charles

---

[1] "Pharisee: From a Historical Novel." *The Menorah Journal.* 32:2 (Autumn 1944): 203–15. "Gold-Rush Days (1849)." *The Menorah Journal.* 33:2 (Autumn 1945): 153–61.

To Albert Lewin, March 5, 1945

                    364 West 18th Street, New York 11, New York

Dear Al,

Just a note about the audience at the Capital. I came at the end of the picture. The audience was what the Bible might call "a mixed multitude"—many Egyptians among the Israelites. They had come, I supposed, to see Lena Horne and Robert Walker as well as the picture and hear the band.[1] A very young fellow, obviously an intellectual, seemed lost in thought as the last of the picture faded out, and then murmured, "Excellent!" I am not as good a judge of an audience's reactions as Mr. Le Baron, for example, but its interest, I thought, was definitely held: they laughed at the right places, were properly silent, and gasped and shrieked at the colored picture and the dummy on the floor. A woman behind me—after the murder of the painter—kept saying, "Uh, uh!", at each twist in the plot. After a while, I became part of the audience myself and followed the picture with interest. I still think it very good. When I left there was a riot to get into the theatre.

Be well and give our love to Milly.

                                        Charles

To Henry Hurwitz, May 1, 1945

                    364 West 18th Street, New York 11, New York

Dear Henry,

Many thanks for letting me know about the stories for the Zionist Organization. However, I feel I ought not to undertake anything like this as long as I am engrossed in the novel I am working at. It will take me all of two or three months to finish the first draft. After that, I might be glad to forget about it for a while—to do a better job revising it later.

---

[1] Lena Horne (1917–), actress and singer whose films include: *Cabin in the Sky* (1943) and *Broadway Rhythm* (1944). Robert Walker (1918–1951), actor best known for his role in Alfred Hitchcock's *Stranger on a Train* (1951) (IDFF).

If the official of the Organization asked for me—and it was not your kindness that suggested my name—please thank him for me.

Cordially,
Charles

To Albert Lewin, May 31, 1945

364 West 18th Street, New York 11, New York

Dear Al:

I sent you yesterday, parcel post insured, Paul McPharlin's *A Repertory of Marionette Plays*.[1] It has several from the French and I bought it for this reason. It hasn't many illustrations and is not in the best of condition (nevertheless, I had to pay Gotham Book Mart the publication price—$6). I have seen an excellent book by Duranty in the 42nd Street Library, *Théâtre des Marionnettes du Jardin des Tuileries*, Paris 1863, and another collection, *Théâtre Lyonnais de Guignol*, Lyon 1890. These books run over three hundred pages and the Duranty book has excellent illustrations. If you want the originals of the plays McPharlin has—I think he has a play from each collection—that won't be expensive in photostat. If you have access to a machine that enlarges microfilm (slow reading and hard on the eyes), both books can be photographed on microfilm for a cent or two a page—depending on the size of the page. Volume three of the Simond book can be done that way, too.

I am having the chapter entitled, "Code of Duelling Established in France," in J. G. Milligen's *The History of Dwelling*, London 1841, copied in photostat, as well as an article in *Chambers' Journal* for May 18, 1867, on this "code." Both should be ready in two or three days. The following is from a little book called *The Art of Dwelling* by "A Traveler", London 1836, for the information of "young continental tourists":

"TO BE IN POSITION, a person should stand with right and left shoulder in a line with the object he wishes to hit; his head bent to the right, and his eyes fixed on the object. His feet should be almost close together; his left arm hanging down, and his right holding the pistol, with the muzzle pointing to the ground close to his feet: he should keep his

---

[1] Paul McPharlin (1903–1948), *A Repertory of Marionette Plays*.

shoulders well back, and his stomach rather drawn in: then, stamping his feet twice or thrice on the ground to feel that he stands firmly, let him raise his right arm steadily, bending it at the elbow, and drawing the pistol into a line with the object, bring that part of the arm between the shoulder and the elbow close to the side—throw out the muscles strongly and let it cover the breast as much as possible. During this time the eyes should be fixed upon the object he fires at; and he must carefully single out, if possible, some small particle upon it. If aiming at a man, for instance, mark well one of the ... gilt buttons upon his coat. A person can never fire with accuracy unless he aims at some small object. Were he to endeavor to hit a man, he would very probably miss him ... I should recommend my friends to wear a black coat upon these occasions ... The arm being closed well in to the side, and the pistol raised to the proper level, bring the head straight, keeping the eyes turned as much to the right as possible, and the pistol directed steadily towards the small object that has been noticed: to be cool, collected, and firm and think of nothing but placing the ball on the proper spot; when the word is given, pull the trigger carefully, and endeavor to avoid moving a muscle in the arm or hand—move only the forefinger, and that with just sufficient force to discharge the pistol ..."

THE CHALLENGE. "A man should conduct himself (however grievous the offence he has received) during the whole affair, with the greatest possible politeness. His cartel should be written carefully ... simply stating, first, the cause of the offence; secondly, the reason why he considers it his duty to notice the affair; thirdly, the name of his friend; and lastly, requesting a time and place may be appointed. Upon arriving at the releager (place of meeting), he should make a point of saluting his antagonist; again also when taking his station; and if his ball takes effect, a third salute and an expression of regret should always precede his quitting the field ..."

THE SECOND should measure out the ground, load the pistols, and be attentive in stationing the parties. In choosing the ground two things are to be observed,—first to avoid the sun in the face; and then, if possible, to choose a spot with a hedge, or wall, or some other dark object in the background; for this is a material assistance in firing, it being much more easy to find an object when there is something dark behind it ...

"About six in the morning is the best time for meeting in the summer, seven in the spring and autumn, and eight in the winter.... Arrived at the releager, where it is always advisable to get the start of his adversary, he should walk about, cooly puffing his cigar, leaving his second to forward the arrangement, and mark out the ground, observing himself, however, that all is correctly done. Having taken his station ... the seconds should now retire about eight yards from the line of fire equidistant from the antagonist's [sic]; the two surgeons should be about two yards behind them. This ought to be the position previous to the signal for firing.

THE SIGNAL is a matter of importance; frequently there is none given, and the parties draw lots for firing. Formerly, the challenger has the privilege of firing first. The plan I prefer ... is to fire on a given signal, and I think none better than dropping a handkerchief; but even giving the word fire is sufficient. The period most trying to a duellist is from the time the word "ready" is given until the handkerchief drops ... He should give the word to the second "all's ready." On the reply "all's ready" he should turn his eyes slightly towards the left, and pull the trigger as the handkerchief falls. His surgeon ... should close round him, with his second, the moment the discharge has taken place.

"A pace in duelling is about three feet. Duels are generally fought at ten, twelve, and fourteen paces. If a man has a good shot for an opponent, and is but an indifferent shot himself, it is decidedly to his advantage to fight at the shortest distance ..."

Bel Ami's duelling friends might tell him some of the above by way of advice.[1]

C.

To Henry Hurwitz, March 28, 1946

364 West 18th Street, New York 11, New York

Dear Henry,

I have read the draft of the memorandum with the care it merits, and think it would profit by condensation. I don't think anyone would question the value and necessity of what—speaking so generally—you are contending for. But perhaps many do; otherwise you would not go into so much argument and exposition. I am inclined to think there is too much.

Cordially
Charles

---

[2] *The Private Affairs of Bel Ami* was Lewin's third film as writer/director. The 1947 release, adapted from Guy de Mauppasant's novel *Bel-Ami*, starred George Sanders, Angela Lansbury, and Ann Dvorak (Felleman 276).

To Henry Hurwitz, July 12, 1947

364 West 18th Street, New York 11, New York

Dear Henry:

I have gone through the story again and left out a sentence here and a paragraph there and made other changes. I still like it.

I thought about the criticism in the note carefully. The point of my story is that a Jew who is readily supposed to be a coward turns out to be a hero, and I must tell that story through the eyes and words of the research worker and the commanding officer. Were I to tell the story from the point of view of the Jew, I might have a good story but I should not have the twist I want. However, should you and Mr. Lesser still think the story weak, I am old enough to allow for valid differences of taste and opinion and will send you another in the series which I hope will please you. I have left the canceled sheets with the story so that the changes may be seen at a glance.

Cordially yours,
Charles Reznikoff

To Henry Hurwitz, October 25, 1947

364 West 18th Street, New York 11, New York

Dear Henry:

With respect to the page proofs of "Thorns and Roses" to appear in the Autumn issue, the expression "editors of *The Menorah Journal*" (p. 359)—since Mr. Lesser is with you—does not necessarily include, it seems to me, the contributing editors. I did not think they were supposed by anybody to determine editorial policy in particulars but merely to be sympathetic to the general purpose of the magazine and to write for it more or less regularly.

But I haven't changed my mind since I argued in your home one evening against using the article in question. Quite ineffectually, it seems.

Faithfully yours,
Charles

To Henry Hurwitz, March 30, 1951

364 West 18th Street, New York 11, New York

Dear Henry:

I will be delighted to be your guest at the dinner on the 10th. In the Middle Ages I would be expected to recite at least an ode. But I see I won't have to say a word (of which I'm very glad). Nevertheless, I will send you a group of verse one of these days for the *Journal*—to use or return as you please.

Yours,
Charles

To Albert Lewin, December 8, 1951

364 West 18th Street, New York 11, New York

Dear Al:

I tried to see your picture the opening night but though I came early the theatre was sold out.[1] However, I got in last night. Your uncle Mindlin came in and sat down next to me. I would have greeted him but was not sure it was he until I left and saw his wife. Then it was too late. If he writes you and says he was riveted to his seat while your picture was on the screen, believe him: he was.

To pick out the parts that pleased me very much and that I could see over and over again: the Spanish singing and dancing in the café; the visit of the toreador to Pandora when she is trying on her wedding gown; the knifing of the Dutchman, particularly the swinging light when overturned and the final thrust; and the bull fighting. I am glad you gave Mme. D'Alverez a bit because she is good. It is a pity that Ava Gardner's voice is not as good as her very good looks—but I suppose by this time you are heartily tired of hearing about the picture.[2] There it is, and I hope it crowds the theatres.

---

[1] Lewin's 1951 film, *Pandora and the Flying Dutchman* starred James Mason and Ava Gardner (Felleman 276–77).

[2] Ava Gardner (1922–1990), actress whose other credits include: *The Killers* (1946) and *Bandwagon* (1953) (IDFF).

I have a sort of a theory, which, no doubt, others have, too: that speech as *speech* is not as effective from the screen as on the stage. When I heard a stanza as good as that from the *Rubaiyat*, or Webster's magnificent lines, they seemed to me not sufficiently effective—through no fault of yours or the actor's. Just as Barrymore on the stage, as I remember him now, was better than Olivier on the screen, although not a better actor. I suppose speech is most effective when there is no changing scenery and no violent action to distract the auditor. Our eyes are simply more attentive than our ears. I might cite the Greeks who kept their violence off-stage, perhaps for a theatrical reason as well as the one generally given, and the present performance of Shaw's interlude; also Al Lewin's production of Oscar Wilde where the good lines were most effective when thrown away. However, I am not going to write an essay on a subject about which you know much more than I.

Good luck on the picture and love to Milly.

Charles

To Albert and Mildred Lewin, December 28, 1951

364 West 18th Street, New York 11

Dear Al and Millie:

Your beautiful gifts came last night just as Marie was about to return to Brandeis. Their beauty and your generosity touched us deeply. (Marie will thank you herself from Waltham.) We hope the New Year will bring you much happiness.

Charles

326

To Albert Lewin, October 20, 1953

The American Jewish Archives, Hebrew Union College
Clifton Avenue, Cincinnati 20, Ohio

Dear Al:

I expect to be in Cincinnati for two or three months working at the Louis Marshall papers.[1]

I hope the picture turned out as well as we hoped.[2]

Charles

Love to Millie.

To Albert Lewin, July 15, 1955

Dear Al:

I have just sent you, air mail first class (but not insured, as you suggested), the pictures you ordered. I also found a copy of the edition of the Flaubert book that was mutilated and have included the artist's conception of Moloch.

Love to you and Millie from Marie and
Good luck!

Charles

---

[1] Reznikoff was the editor of *Louis Marshall: Champion of Liberty; Selected Papers and Addresses* (1957).

[2] Lewin's *Saadia*, a 1954 film adaptation of Francis d'Autheville's novel *Échec au Destin*, starred Cornel Wilde and Mel Ferrer (Felleman 277).

To Albert Lewin, September 11, 1955

364 West 18th Street, New York 11, N.Y.

Sr. Albert Lewin
Estudios Churubusco-Azteca, S.A.
Calzada de Tlalpan y Rio Churubusco, Mexico, D.F.

Dear Al:

The Metropolitan Museum photostats were reposing at 880 Fifth Avenue. I picked them up and sent them to you last Wednesday (air mail, first class, insured). I hope you have them.

The half-time job at the magazine turned into a time-and-a-half job in the way these jobs do. But I hope to get it organized. As soon as I succeed, I hope to be free to find other illustrations for the lecture sequence. But I am always free to do what you or Millie want right away.

Love to you and Millie from both of us.

Charles

To Albert Lewin, May 25, 1958

364 West 18th St., New York 11, N.Y.

Dear Al

I am sorry that sneezing has complicated life in Florence and hope that when you receive this it will be gone. As for my own disabilities, the present one is leaving, I guess; anyway, I am working. I am reminded of a story Paul liked to tell—and I suppose I told you. When he was an intern one of his patients was an old Negro, "I don't know why I should be sick," he complained to Paul. "I never let a germ into the house." I asked Paul what he was sick of. Diabetes and syphilis. I may have the first but I don't think I have the second—which puts me out of the class of the best writers according to the Baroness Blixen.[1]

My love to Millie. Marie sends hers to both of you.

Charles

---

[1] Isak Dinesen (1885–1962), Danish writer.

To Marie Syrkin, April 8, 1961

Dear Marie:

Since there is now the possibility that I may actually have some money to leave in case I die, until I have the opportunity of making a formal will, I wish you to know—and everybody else concerned—that I want you to have everything I have, tangible and intangible.

Incidentally, although I do not think the occasion will arise in the immediate future—and I certainly hope not—I want you to know that I want the simplest possible Orthodox Jewish funeral—burial in a plain wooden box and no speeches.

Your husband,
Charles Reznikoff

To Marie Syrkin Reznikoff
24 Concord Avenue
Cambridge, Mass.

To George Oppen, Feb. 7,'62

Dear George:[1]

I can't tell you what is good or bad in this book of verse. The only one who can decide that is you yourself in answer to the question what do you really want to say. I can only tell you what I like and why I like it. But you must not let yourself be misled by that—and you won't be.

As for the technique of saying what you want to say, you know as much about it as I do. You have sufficient interest in the meaning and sound of words and sentences and you know that the sound and rhythm is part of the meaning: that is why we write in verse—when we do.

C.

---

[1] George Oppen (1908-1984), American "objectivist" poet. His books include: *Discrete Series* (1934), *The Materials* (1962) and *The Collected Poems of George Oppen, 1929-1975* (1975).

To Albert and Mildred Lewin, March 7, 1963

364 West 18th Street, New York 11, N.Y.

Dear Millie and Al,

Marie and I were very glad to hear from you and to suppose that so far your trip was instructive and delightful. We hope it will continue to be—at least—delightful.

I had a fine trip. I hope my listeners enjoyed it as much as I did. (You see I am still reliving it.) However, at one of the parties a most beautiful graduate student got drunk and told me that she had wasted three-quarters of an hour listening to me. One of the other guests tried to console me by telling me—in a whisper—that she was a leader in the local Birch society.

Love to you both from Marie and

Charles

To Albert Lewin, March 16, 1963

364 West 18th Street, New York 11, N.Y.

Dear Al,

We were glad to receive your card from India and to know that you are continuing on the path of illumination and, we hope, pleasure.

Nothing much new here. I have just received an excellent review in a periodical that seems to be devoted to the use of coarse words in refined society: imagine, they print a play entitled, "The Toilet," instead of using "bathroom."[1] Marie is still busy cleaning up the house, an occupation she refers to bitterly as "archaeology."

She sends her love to you and Milly* and so do I.

Charles

*Millie

---

[1] Leroi Jones's (Amiri Baraka's) play *The Toilet* was first published in *Kulchur 9*, the issue which contained Gilbert Sorrentino's review of *By the Waters of Manhattan*: "As a craftsman, Reznikoff is, in a word, superb. His poems seem casual, and easy, but they are constructed with rigid discipline ..." (75).

To Albert Lewin, May 11, 1963

364 West 18th Street, New York 11, N.Y.

Dear Al,

I hope this note finds you still in Japan.

Thursday night I heard Robert Graves read some of his verse at Hunter College—or rather tried to for, though I sat in the tenth aisle, I could only catch a word or two. But the hall was jammed and he received an ovation when he was through. Marie and I expect to meet him tomorrow at a cocktail party for him at Forest Hills.

I suppose you will be back in New York any day now with all the wealth of information you have acquired—for those who have not seen and experienced what you did.

Marie and I send our love to you and Millie.

Charles

To Celia and Louis Zukofsky, August 2, 1970

180 West End Avenue, New York, N.Y. 10023, Apt. 24 H

Dear Celia and Louis,

We received the "Autobiography" and the "Catullus" with their inscriptions and Marie and I are very grateful to you both. I need not tell you that the books are beautifully printed and no doubt both of you put a lot of thought and work into *t h a t*. However, an evaluation of the contents is more difficult for me since, as you know, I have little Latin and know even less about music. Besides, the "Catullus" obviously is nothing I would comment on casually: it represents much thought and work and is an impressive and unique achievement. I can only say now that we both hope that the comments of reviewers and the sales will prove most gratifying.

Sincerely,
[Charles]

We hope Paul is feeling and doing well.

To Carl Rakosi, September 21, 1970

180 West End Avenue, New York, N.Y. 10023
Tel: 212-874-0178

Dear Carl,[1]

I liked your poems very much and so did Marie. She brought them to Shlomo Katz, editor of *Midstream*, and he accepted them for publication. I suppose you will hear from him—if you have not already.

As for my own verse for use by the local temple in their High Holiday services, I have no objection, of course. In fact, I am pleased and honored. This is something like being called up to the Torah in an Orthodox service.

We look forward to seeing you in October. In the meantime, Marie and I wish you and yours—and everybody—a very happy New Year.

[Charles]

To Sylvia Burke, May 21, 1973

180 West End Avenue, Apt. 22 F, New York, N.Y. 10023

Miss Sylvia Burke, University of Judaism
6525 Sunset Boulevard, Los Angeles, California 90028

Dear Miss Burke,

As I said when you telephoned about a poem with which to surprise Marie at the luncheon in her honor, I am not particularly good at writing to order—much as I should like to in this case. However, as I also said, if nothing good enough occurs to me, I would send what I wrote almost forty years ago: it is "By the Waters of Manhattan," published by New Directions a few years ago and, strangely enough, the poem seems much more appropriate now than when written.

With best wishes for the luncheon and all you and your associates plan,

[Charles Reznikoff]

---

[1] Carl Rakosi (1903–), American poet whose volumes include: *Two Poems* (1933), *Selected Poems* (1941), *Ere-Voice* (1971) and *Collected Poems* (1986).

To Eliot Weinberger, November 22, 1974

180 West End Avenue, Apartment 22 F, New York, N.Y. 10023

Dear Eliot Weinberger,[1]

Thank you for your kind letter of October 28th. I would be glad to send you—as a gift, of course—copies of the continuation of *Testimony* and *By the Well of Living and Seeing* which Harvey Shapiro told you about. But I revised *Testimony 1891-1900* and combined it with my manuscript of *Testimony 1901-1910*. The Ferry Press is to publish this in England (with the American rights) early next year. As for *By the Well of Living and Seeing*, I suggested this title to the Black Sparrow Press for the selection of my verse which they have just published and I promised not to distribute any more copies of the different book of verse I had printed—at least until next year—not to cause any confusion. Incidentally, John Martin of Black Sparrow Press is planning to get out all I have written, verse and prose. However, I certainly appreciate your interest and will have it in mind and wish you and those working with you success.

Sincerely,
Charles Reznikoff

To Eliot Weinberger, February 17, 1975

180 West End Avenue, Apartment 22 F, New York, N.Y. 10023

Dear Eliot Weinberger,

Thank you for your letter of the 4th. I would certainly like to become a contributor to the magazine you are planning. I am working at a group of verse which you may find interesting but I will not have it ready for a month or so and when I have I'll send it to you.

With best wishes for the success of all you plan,

Sincerely,
Charles Reznikoff

---

[1] Eliot Weinberger, editor of *Montemora* magazine.

To Eliot Weinberger, May 24, 1975

180 West End Avenue, Apartment 22 F, New York, N.Y. 10023

Dear Eliot Weinberger,

Thank you for your letter of the 18th. Last year (November 22nd) I wrote you that I had revised *Testimony (1891–1900)*, which I had privately printed, and combined it with my manuscript of *Testimony (1901–1910)* and that the Ferry Press of England was to publish this in England, with the American rights, early this year. However, I have recently received a letter from England in which I am told that it would not be published because the cost of printing in England has gone up beyond expectation. The Black Sparrow Press intends to publish it later in its collection of all my verse (the first volume in November) but I do not think there is any objection by John Martin of the Black Sparrow Press to any magazine publication beforehand and so I am sending you a group from *Testimony (1891–1910)* for your consideration. You are free, of course, to use what you like, all of the group or none.

Incidentally, other groups under the major heading "The South" include: "Social Life," "Neighbors," "Domestic Difficulties," "Machine Age," "Children at Work," "Streetcars and Railroads," "Shipping," "Property," "Thefts—and Thieves." and "Persons and Places." Similar headings are in the groups under the general titles, "The North" and "The West."

Charles Reznikoff

To Eliot Weinberger, January 10, 1976

180 West End Avenue, Apt. 22 F, New York, N. Y. 10023

Dear Eliot Weinberger,

In reply to your letter of the 6th, I received my copy of *Montemora*—and your check. Thank you for both. I must also thank Burton Watson for the praise you quote in your letter and Geoffrey O'Brien for his review. I found much else in the issue that I liked and respect—to use words that are merely tepid. I should add that I noted a kind of harmony in subject matter and rhythm with *Testimony* in Burton Watson's translations from the Chinese.

I expect to send you a group of verse as soon as I have ready what I think may be of interest and wish you and all who are working with you a happy New Year and, if you will forgive me for the pun, many editions.

Charles Reznikoff

Charles Reznikoff died on January 22, 1976.

Index

European Caravan, 184–85
Evening in Greenwich Village, 79, 101, 117
Evreinov, Nikolai Nikolaevich, 53

Fadiman, Clifton, 113, 117
Family Chronicle, 8, 15, 60n, 240, 243,
    256–59, 286
Faure, Elie, 30, 251
Five Groups of Verse, 10, 57
Fletcher, John Gould, 191
Flynn, Errol, 269
Fontanne, Lynn, 173, 182
Ford, Ford Madox, 25
Frank, Waldo, 46
Freeman, Joseph, 14, 162–63, 168–69,
    171, 175, 184, 208
From Morn Till Midnight, 26
Front Page, The, 161
Futility, 19–21

Gieseking, Walter, 53
Gladstone, W. E., 68
Gobineau, Joseph Arthur, 37
Goethe, Johann Wolfgang von, 74
Gogol, Nikolai Vasilievich, 73
Going To and Fro and Walking Up and
    Down, 296–97
Golden Bough, The, 268
Gold Rush Days, 310, 319
Goldsmith, Oliver, 51
Goldwyn, Samuel, 255
Gomperz, Theodor, 56
Good Earth, The, 6, 310
Grass, 47
Graves, Robert, 11
Greed, 43–44
Greeley, Horace, 10
Growth of the Soil, 25

Hale, Louise, 31
Halper, Albert, 192, 195–96
Harlow, Jean, 211–12
H.D., 25
Hemingway, Ernest, 59
Herzl, Theodor, 76
Hindemith, Paul, 53
Hirschbein, Peretz, 169

Hitler, Adolf, 5, 194, 203, 221–22, 225,
    247, 254, 292
Holocaust, 5–6, 9
Homer, 68, 83
Hospitality, 31
Hoyt, Helen, 23
Hudson, W. H., 54
Hurwitz, Henry. See Menorah Journal.
Huxley, Aldous, 46

Ibsen, Henrik, 38
In Memoriam: 1933, 202, 205–08
In the Country, 153

James, Henry, 110
James, William, 134n
Jennings, Talbot, 226–28, 239, 244, 284,
    295–96
Jeremiah in the Stocks, 69, 79, 153, 187, 190
Jerusalem the Golden, 139n, 208n
Jews Enter Georgia, 307–08
Jews of Charleston, The, 8, 281
Johan Kreisler, 35
Journey's End, 66, 116
Joyce, James, 7, 25, 27, 248
Juno and the Paycock, 53

Kallen, Horace, 134–35
Keats, John, 7
Keyserling, Count, 51
Kittredge, George Lyman, 6, 35

Lardner, Ring, 43
Lewin, Albert, 6, 8–11, 13–14, 20–61, 63,
    66, 68, 91–92, 149, 151-53, 155–56,
    180–88, 197, 200–04, 206–15, 276–84,
    286, 290–93, 295–99, 301, 302–07,
    309–18, 320–23, 325–38, 330–31
Lewisohn, Ludwig, 30
Libbey, Laura Jean, 51
Lindsay, Vachel, 6
Lionhearted, The, 15, 221–22, 229, 240,
    257–59, 278–79, 281, 286, 292,
    300–02, 305, 307
Loew, David, 279
Louis Marshall: Champion of Liberty, 8, 327
Lunt, Alfred, 173, 182

338

Printed October 1997 in Santa Barbara
& Ann Arbor for the Black Sparrow Press by
Mackintosh Typography & Edwards Brothers Inc.
Text set in ITC-New Baskerville by Words Worth.
Design by Barbara Martin.
This first edition is published in paper wrappers;
there are 250 hardcover trade copies;
100 numbered deluxe copies; & 20 copies
lettered A to T have been handbound in
boards by Earle Gray.

MILTON HINDUS was born in New York City in 1916 and entered CCNY at age 15. He received B.A. and M.S. degrees there and did further graduate work at Columbia University and the University of Chicago. In 1986 he was awarded an Honorary Doctorate of Humane Letters (DHL) by Brandeis University. In 1948, while serving as Assistant Professor in the College of the University of Chicago, he was recruited to become a member of the founding faculty of Brandeis University. He is the author/editor of 15 books, one of which was the first book in English on Louis Ferdinand Céline and which has subsequently been translated into French and Japanese; a second edition has appeared in English and a third is scheduled for 1997 by *transaction's* Library of Conservative Thought. Two of his other books were devoted to Proust, two to Walt Whitman, and one to Scott Fitzgerald. A book of his poems, *The Broken Music Box* was published by the Menard Press in London.

Milton Hindus is also the author of *Charles Reznikoff: A Critical Essay* (Black Sparrow, 1977) and another book on Reznikoff commissioned by the National Poetry Foundation, *Charles Reznikoff: Man and Poet*. He was a contributor to the Charles Reznikoff issue of *Sagetrieb*, published in 1994 to mark the centenary of Reznikoff's birth.

In 1971 CHARLES REZNIKOFF wrote the following about his own life:

"I was born in Brooklyn in 1894. I spent a year at the University of Missouri's School of Journalism when I was sixteen and found out that journalism is more concerned with news than with writing and that I—to use the old adage—was much more concerned with dog bites man than with man bites dog. I then wanted just to stay at home and write but my parents insisted that some education might be helpful. So I went to New York University's law school chiefly because the curriculum called for only two or three hours of classes daily. However, I became so involved in the study of law that I had little time or mental energy for any writing. I was graduated in 1915 and admitted to the bar of the State of New York in 1916. But, after a few months of practice and legal responsibility, few as my clients were, it seemed to me that I would have more time and mental energy if I became a traveling salesman. That was true. But, when the Great Depression began after the First World War, I went to work as one of the editors for an encyclopedia of law for lawyers and did other editing as well as writing.

"I had always been—and am still—more interested in verse than in prose and it seemed to me that it would be best to print, whatever I managed to write, privately just to get it off my chest rather than to keep hunting for a hospitable magazine or publisher. After a while, some of my privately printed books were published by The Objectivist Press which Louis Zukofsky, George Oppen and I had formed to print our own books—though the first of our publications was a book of verse by William Carlos Williams."